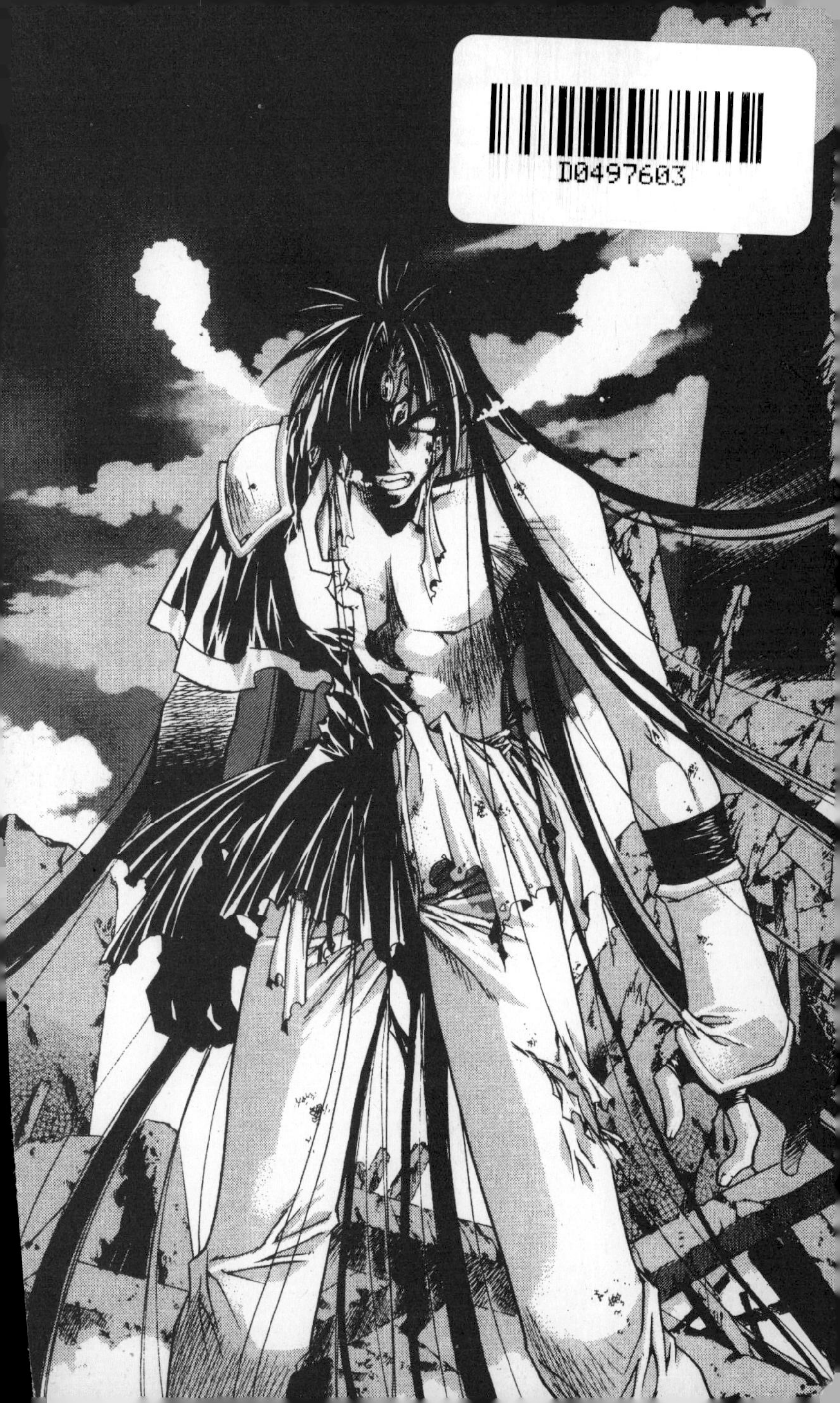

ALSO AVAILABLE FROM ☺TOKYOPOP®

MANGA

.HACK//LEGEND OF THE TWILIGHT
@LARGE (October 2003)
ANGELIC LAYER*
BABY BIRTH*
BATTLE ROYALE*
BRAIN POWERED*
BRIGADOON*
CARDCAPTOR SAKURA
CARDCAPTOR SAKURA: MASTER OF THE CLOW*
CHOBITS*
CHRONICLES OF THE CURSED SWORD
CLAMP SCHOOL DETECTIVES*
CLOVER
CONFIDENTIAL CONFESSIONS*
CORRECTOR YUI
COWBOY BEBOP*
COWBOY BEBOP: SHOOTING STAR*
CYBORG 009*
DEMON DIARY
DIGIMON*
DRAGON HUNTER
DRAGON KNIGHTS*
DUKLYON: CLAMP SCHOOL DEFENDERS*
ERICA SAKURAZAWA*
FAKE*
FLCL*
FORBIDDEN DANCE*
GATE KEEPERS*
G GUNDAM*
GRAVITATION*
GTO*
GUNDAM WING
GUNDAM WING: BATTLEFIELD OF PACIFISTS
GUNDAM WING: ENDLESS WALTZ*
GUNDAM WING: THE LAST OUTPOST*
HAPPY MANIA*
HARLEM BEAT
I.N.V.U.
INITIAL D*
ISLAND
JING: KING OF BANDITS*
JULINE
KARE KANO*
KINDAICHI CASE FILES, THE*
KING OF HELL
KODOCHA: SANA'S STAGE*
LOVE HINA*
LUPIN III*
MAGIC KNIGHT RAYEARTH* (August 2003)

MAGIC KNIGHT RAYEARTH II* (COMING SOON)
MAN OF MANY FACES*
MARMALADE BOY*
MARS*
MIRACLE GIRLS
MIYUKI-CHAN IN WONDERLAND* (October 2003)
MONSTERS, INC.
PARADISE KISS*
PARASYTE
PEACH GIRL
PEACH GIRL: CHANGE OF HEART*
PET SHOP OF HORRORS*
PLANET LADDER*
PLANETES* (October 2003)
PRIEST
RAGNAROK
RAVE MASTER*
REALITY CHECK
REBIRTH
REBOUND*
RISING STARS OF MANGA
SABER MARIONETTE J*
SAILOR MOON
SAINT TAIL
SAMURAI DEEPER KYO*
SAMURAI GIRL: REAL BOUT HIGH SCHOOL*
SCRYED*
SHAOLIN SISTERS*
SHIRAHIME-SYO: SNOW GODDESS TALES* (Dec. 2003)
SHUTTERBOX (November 2003)
SORCERER HUNTERS
THE SKULL MAN*
THE VISION OF ESCAFLOWNE
TOKYO MEW MEW*
UNDER THE GLASS MOON
VAMPIRE GAME*
WILD ACT*
WISH*
WORLD OF HARTZ (COMING SOON)
X-DAY*
ZODIAC P.I. *

For more information visit www.TOKYOPOP.com

*INDICATES 100% AUTHENTIC MANGA (RIGHT-TO-LEFT FORMAT)

CINE-MANGA™

CARDCAPTORS
JACKIE CHAN ADVENTURES (November 2003)
JIMMY NEUTRON
KIM POSSIBLE
LIZZIE MCGUIRE
POWER RANGERS: NINJA STORM
SPONGEBOB SQUAREPANTS
SPY KIDS 2

NOVELS

KARMA CLUB (April 2004)
SAILOR MOON

TOKYOPOP KIDS

STRAY SHEEP

ART BOOKS

CARDCAPTOR SAKURA*
MAGIC KNIGHT RAYEARTH*

ANIME GUIDES

COWBOY BEBOP ANIME GUIDES
GUNDAM TECHNICAL MANUALS
SAILOR MOON SCOUT GUIDES

CHRONICLES OF THE
CURSED SWORD

Volume 2

Story by
YEO BEOP-RYONG
Art by
PARK HUI-JIN

Los Angeles • Tokyo • London

Translation - Yongju Ryu
English Adaptation - Matt Varosky
Associate Editor - Jason Fogelson
Graphic Designer - Tomas Montalvo-Lagos
Copy Editor - Tim Beedle
Retouch & Lettering - Stacy Hyun Choi
Cover Design - Gary Shum
Editor - Jake Forbes

Managing Editor - Jill Freshney
Production Coordinator - Antonio DePietro
Production Manager - Jennifer Miller
Art Director - Matt Alford
Director of Editorial - Jeremy Ross
VP of Production - Ron Klamert
President & C.O.O. - John Parker
Publisher & C.E.O. - Stuart Levy

Email: editor@TOKYOPOP.com
Come visit us online at www.TOKYOPOP.com

A  Manga

TOKYOPOP Inc.
5900 Wilshire Blvd. Suite 2000
Los Angeles, CA 90036

ISBN: 1-59182-255-6

First TOKYOPOP printing: September 2003

10 9 8 7 6 5 4 3

Printed in the USA

Chronicles

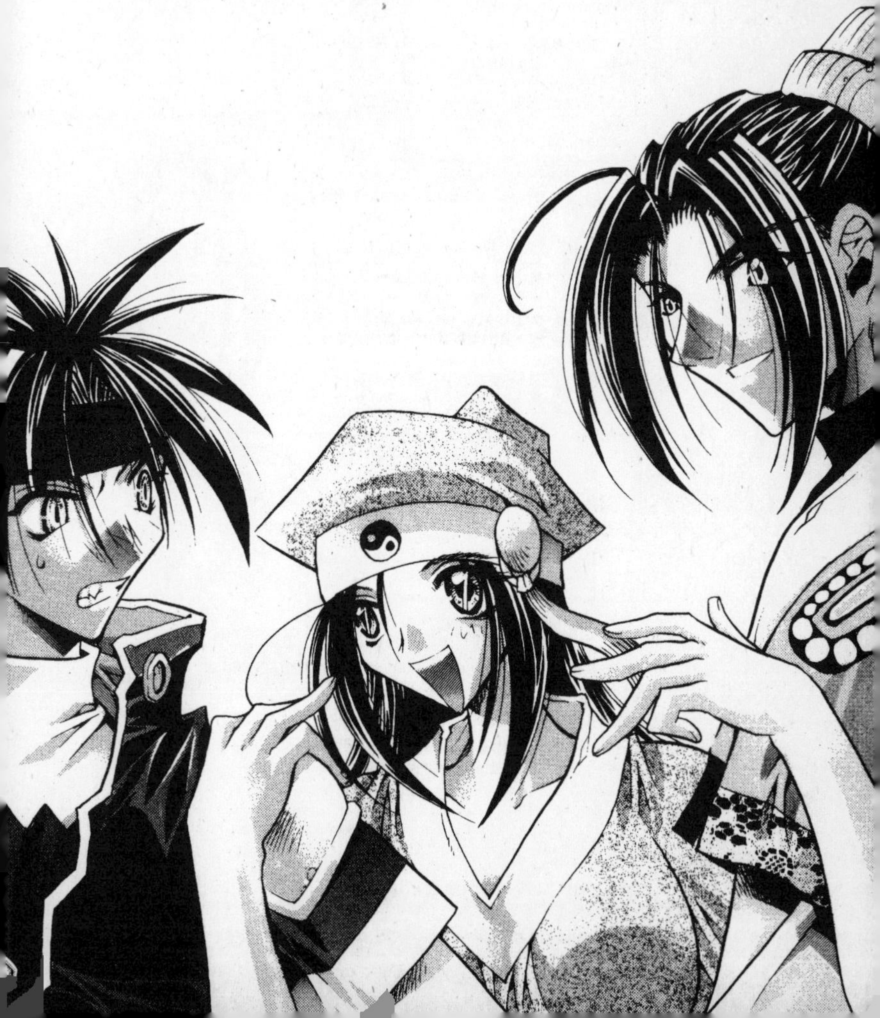

CHRONICLES OF THE CURSED SWORD

the cast of characters

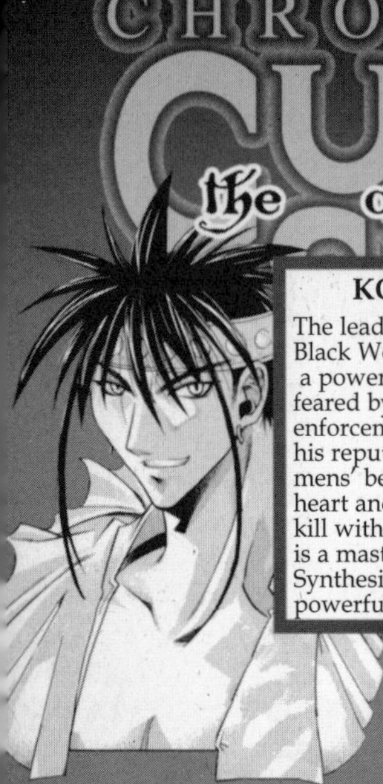

KOUCHIEN

The leader of the Black Wolf Bandits, he's a powerful fighter feared by local law enforcement. Despite his reputation, he has his mens' best interests at heart and does not like to kill without reason. He is a master of the Four Synthesis technique, a powerful ki attack.

THE PASA SWORD

A living sword that hungers for demon blood. It grants its user incredible power, but at a great cost—it can take over the user's body, and in time his soul.

JARYOON, KING OF HAHYUN

Noble and charismatic, Jaryoon is the stuff of which great kings are made. His brother, the emperor, has been acting strangely and apparently has ordered Jaryoon to be executed, so the young king now travels to the capital to get to the heart of the matter. A great warrior in his own right, he does not have magical abilities and is unaccustomed to battling demons.

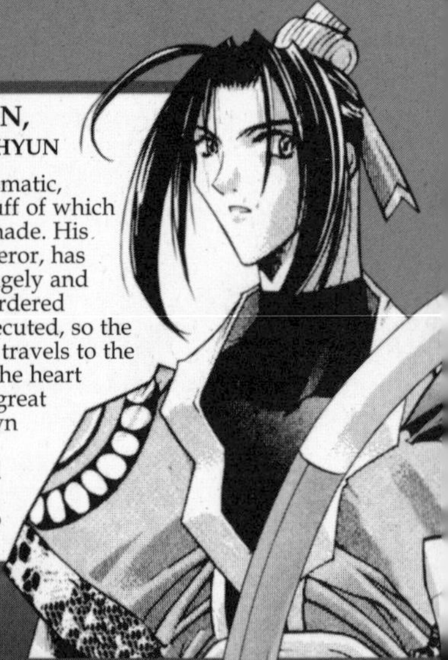

SHYAO LIN

A sorceress, and Rey Yan's traveling companion. Shyao grew fond of Rey during their five years of study together with their master, and thinks of him as her little brother. She's Rey's conscience— his sole tie to humanity. She also seems quite enamored with the handsome Jaryoon.

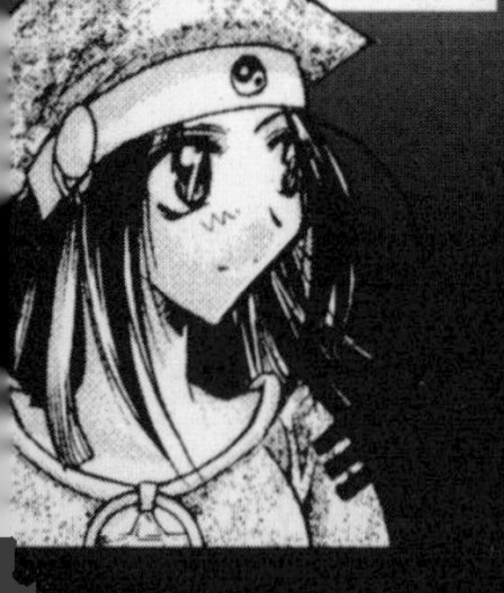

REY YAN

Rey's origins remain unknown. An orphan, he and Shyao were raised by a wise old man who trained them in the ways of combat and magic. After the demon White Tiger slaughtered their master, Rey and Shyao became wanderers. Rey wields the PaSa sword, a weapon of awesome power that threatens to take over his very soul. Under the right circumstances, he could be a hero.

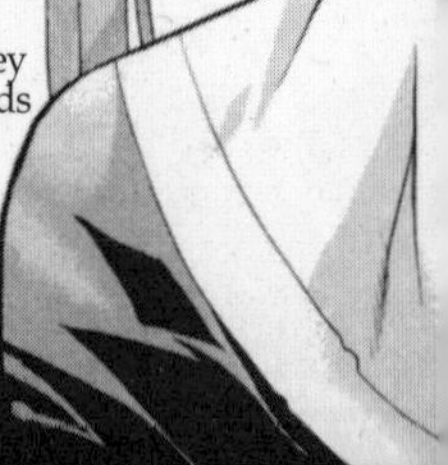

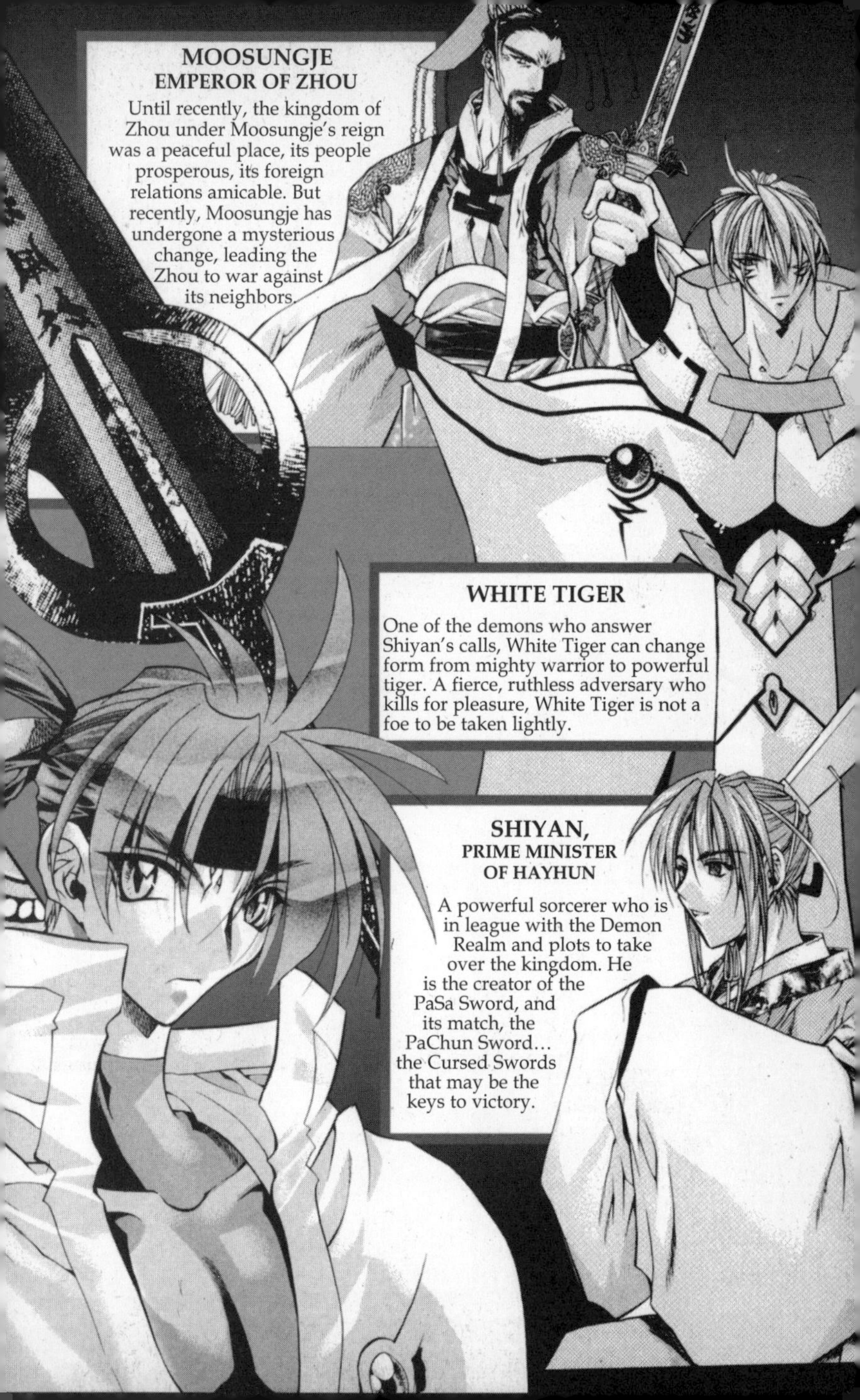
MOOSUNGJE
EMPEROR OF ZHOU
Until recently, the kingdom of Zhou under Moosungje's reign was a peaceful place, its people prosperous, its foreign relations amicable. But recently, Moosungje has undergone a mysterious change, leading the Zhou to war against its neighbors.
WHITE TIGER
One of the demons who answer Shiyan's calls, White Tiger can change form from mighty warrior to powerful tiger. A fierce, ruthless adversary who kills for pleasure, White Tiger is not a foe to be taken lightly.
SHIYAN,
PRIME MINISTER
OF HAYHUN
A powerful sorcerer who is in league with the Demon Realm and plots to take over the kingdom. He is the creator of the PaSa Sword, and its match, the PaChun Sword… the Cursed Swords that may be the keys to victory.

The story so far...

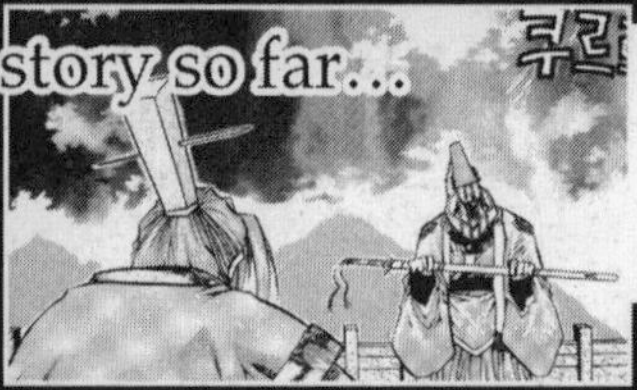

Prime Minister Shiyan presented the Emperor Moosungje with the magical Pachun sword, after which the formerly peaceful Moosungje attacked his neighboring kingdoms.

The Emperor's brother, Jaryoon, King of Hahyun, was attacked by a demon assassin, apparently under orders from the Emperor himself.

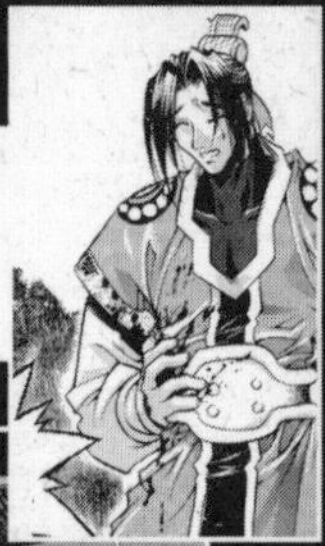

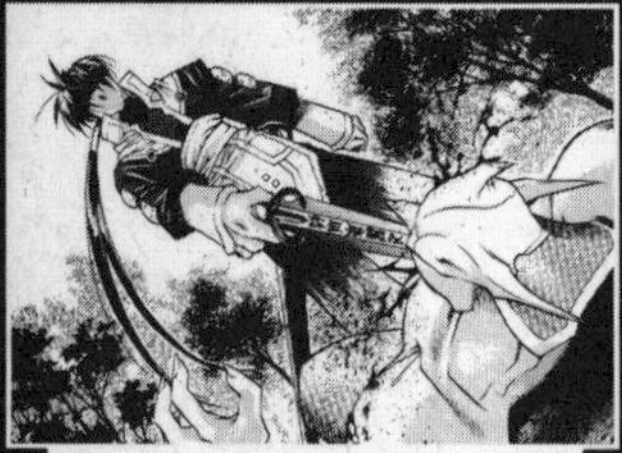

Rey Yan and Shyao Lin rescued Jaryoon using Rey's cursed sword. In thanks, Jaryoon let his rescuers stay in his palace.

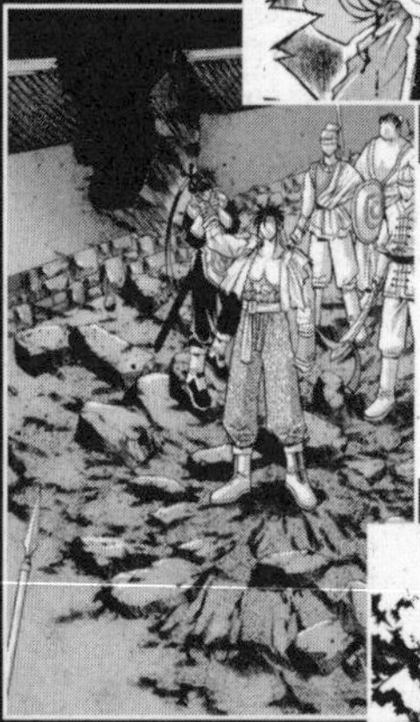

Kouchien, the bandit leader, led a raid on the palace the night Rey and Shyao were staying...

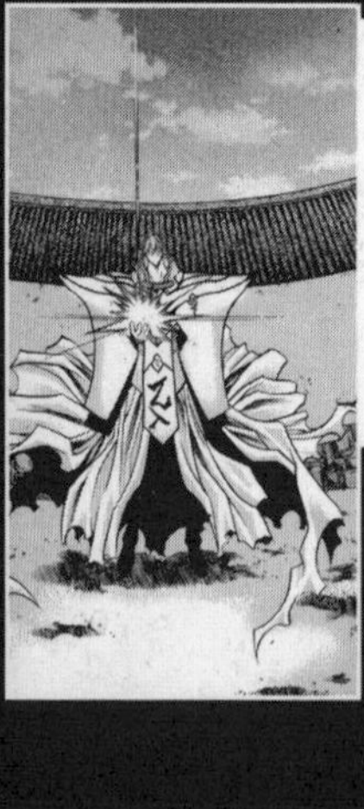

...but when the demon White Tiger appears, Jaryoon and Kouchien realize that they have a mutual enemy.

Rey ignores Shyao's warning and uses the PaSa sword to battle White Tiger. But the more of the demon's blood that the PaSa tastes, the more Rey loses control.

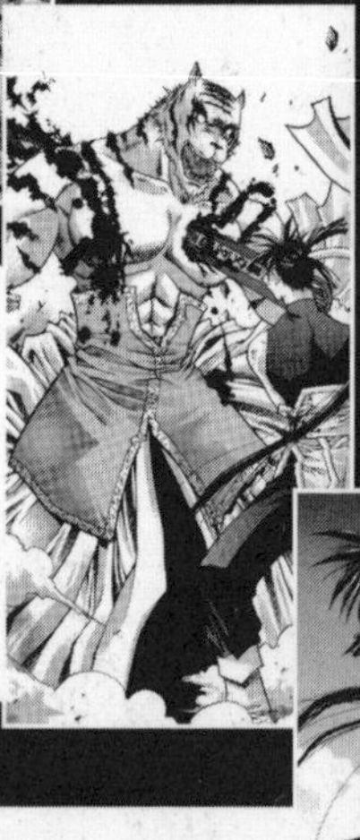

White Tiger's mortal form has been defeated, but now Rey is under the control of the PaSa sword.

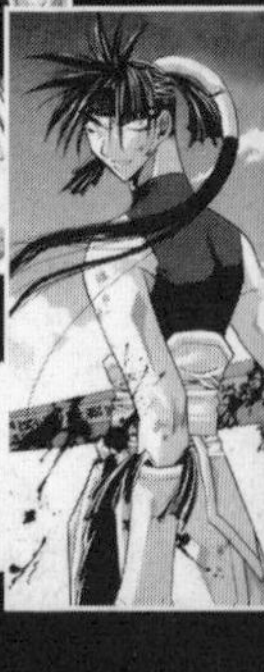

Chronicle 6
Rey's Madness

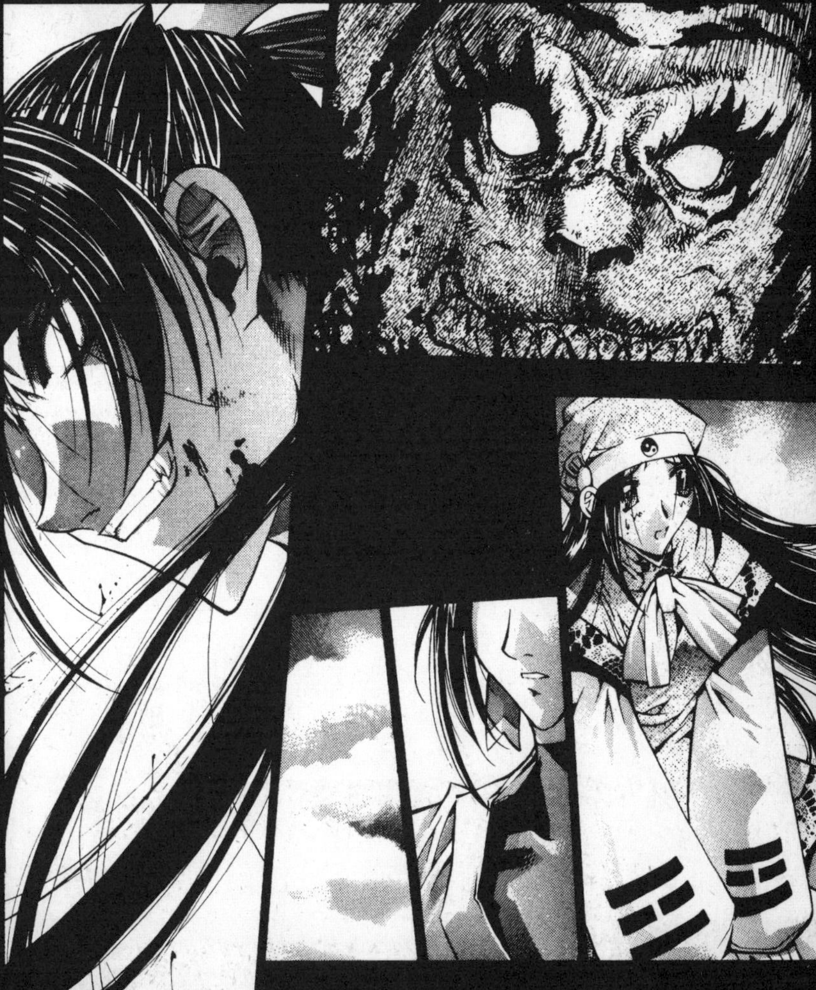

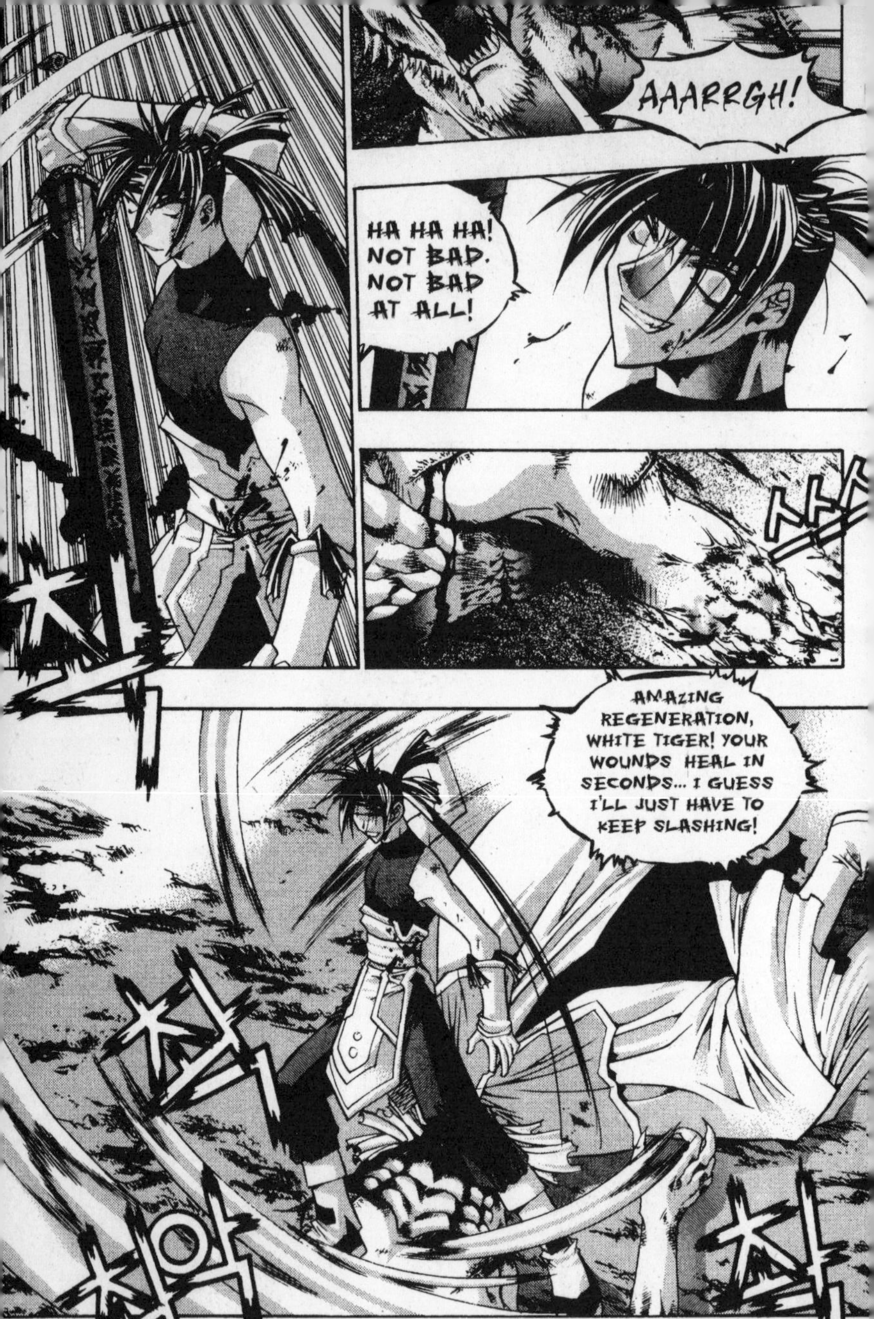
AAARRGH!
HA HA HA! NOT BAD. NOT BAD AT ALL!
AMAZING REGENERATION, WHITE TIGER! YOUR WOUNDS HEAL IN SECONDS... I GUESS I'LL JUST HAVE TO KEEP SLASHING!

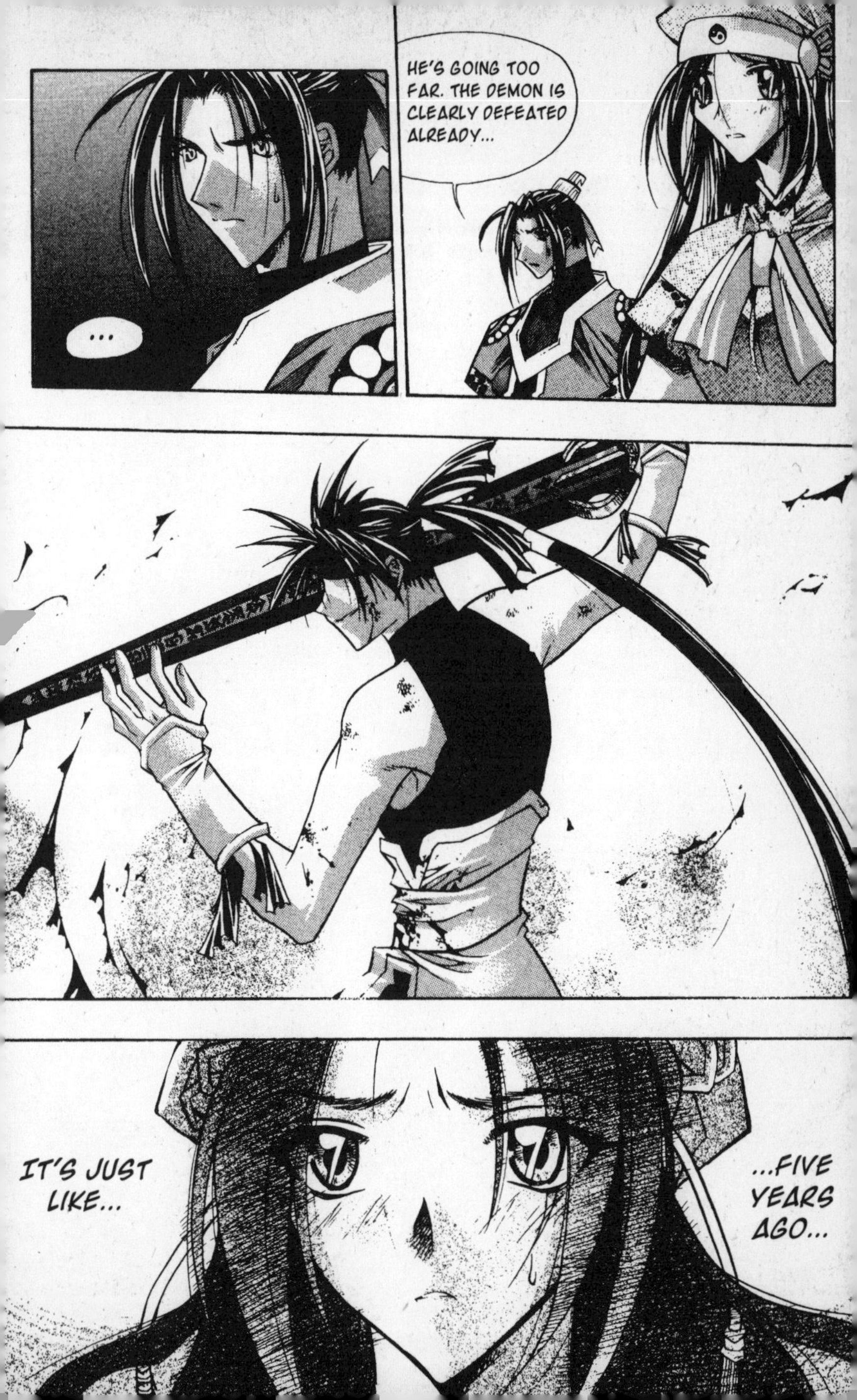
...
HE'S GOING TOO FAR. THE DEMON IS CLEARLY DEFEATED ALREADY...
IT'S JUST LIKE...
...FIVE YEARS AGO...

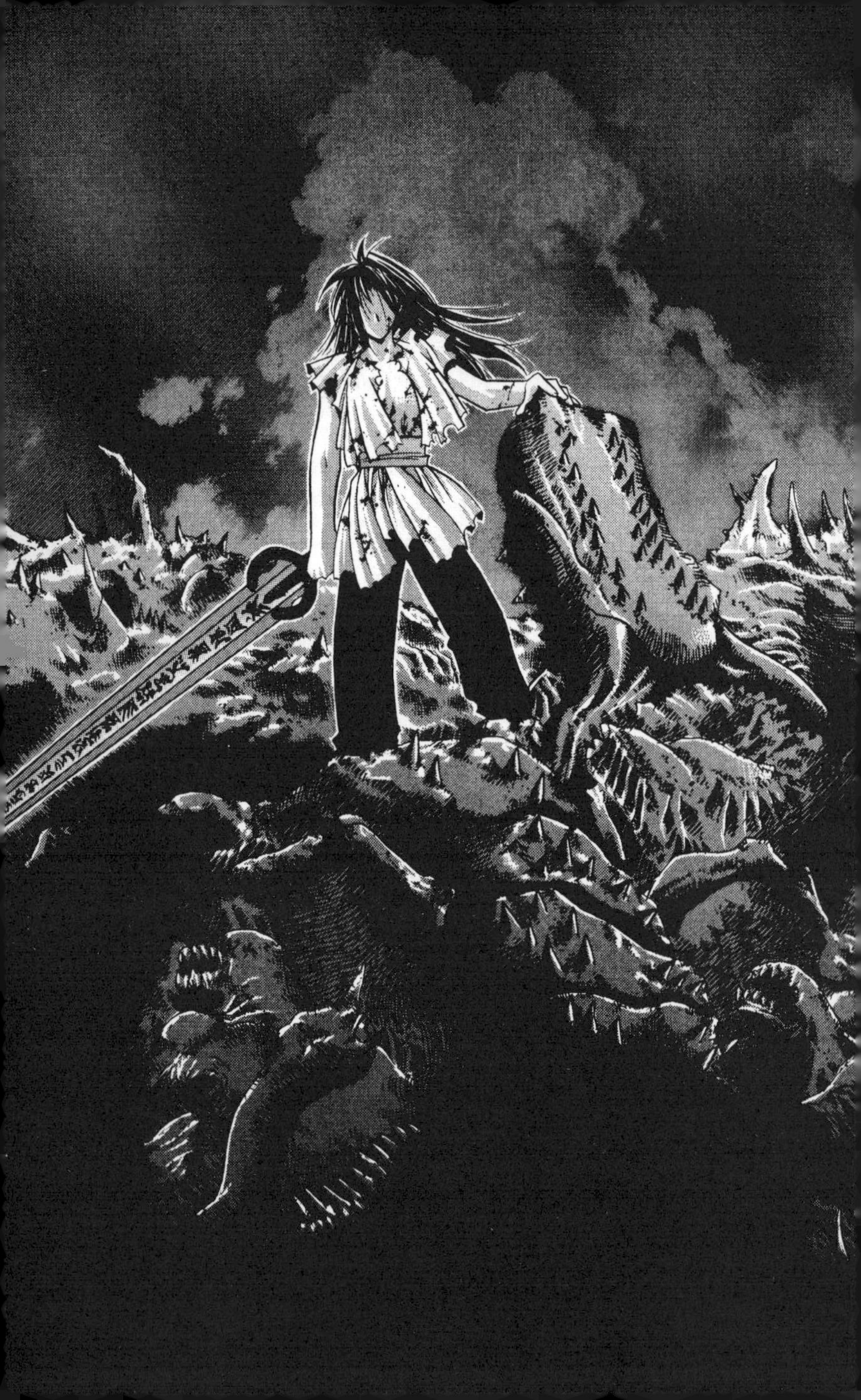

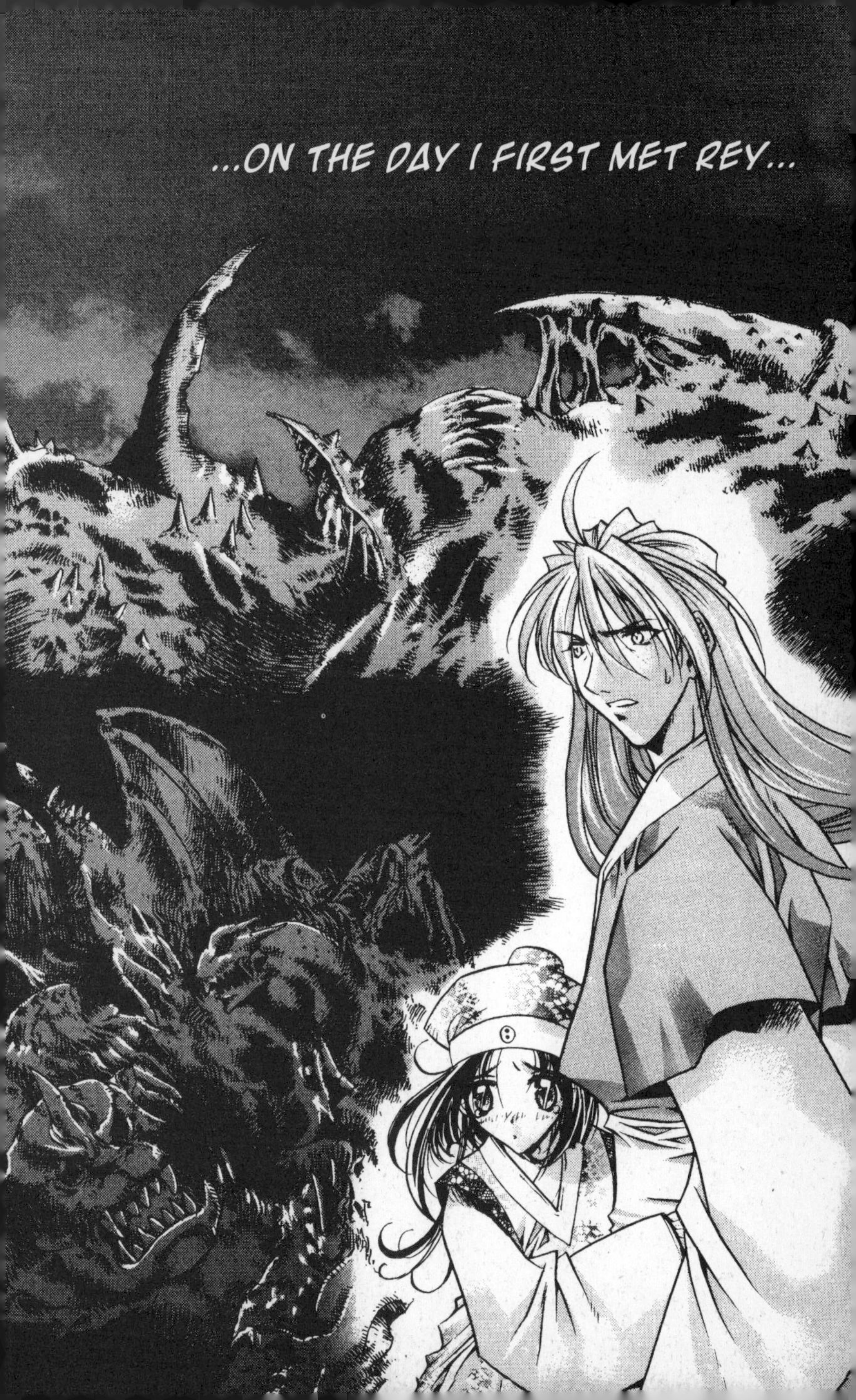
...ON THE DAY I FIRST MET REY...

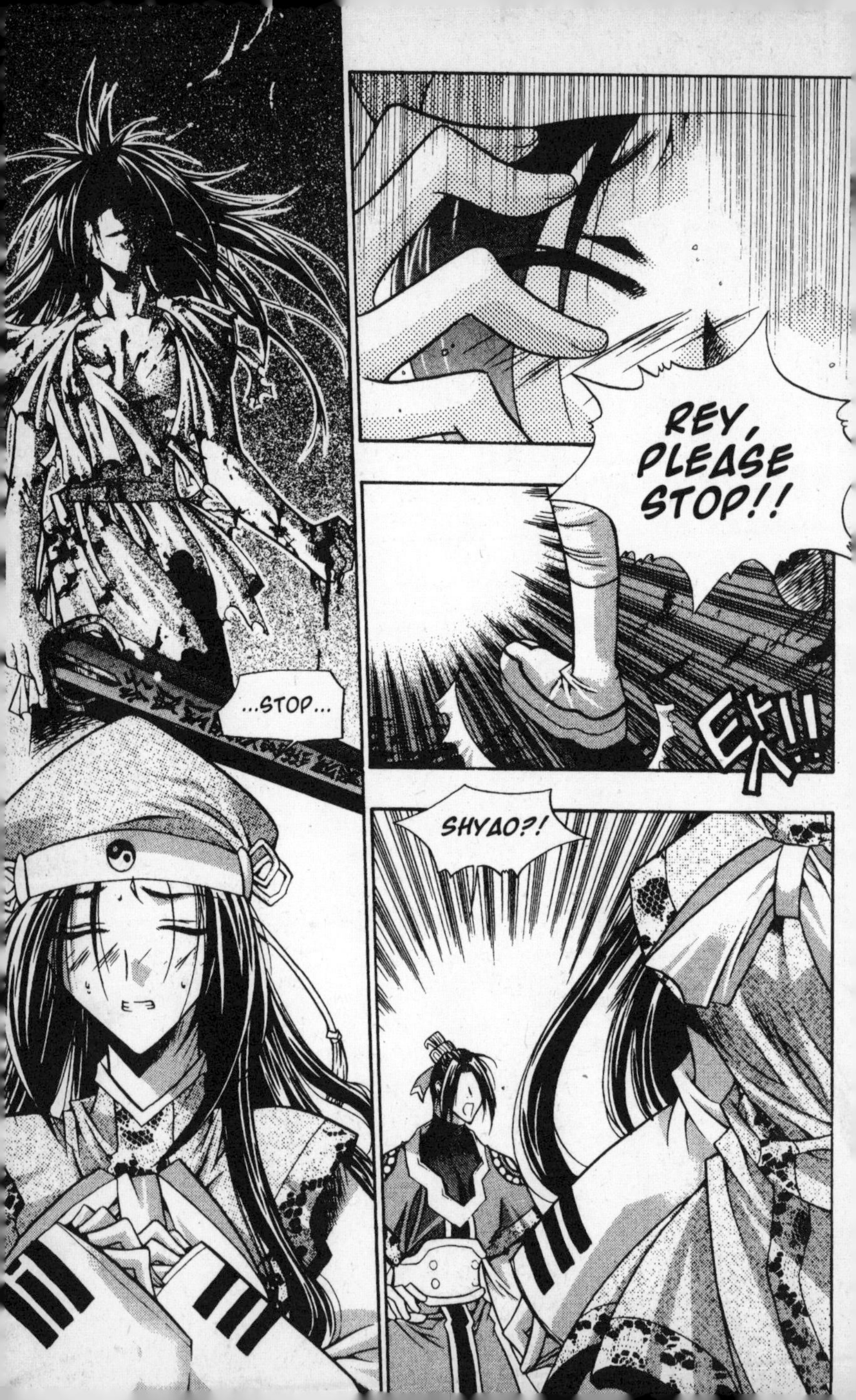

...STOP...
REY, PLEASE STOP!!
EK!!
SHYAO?!

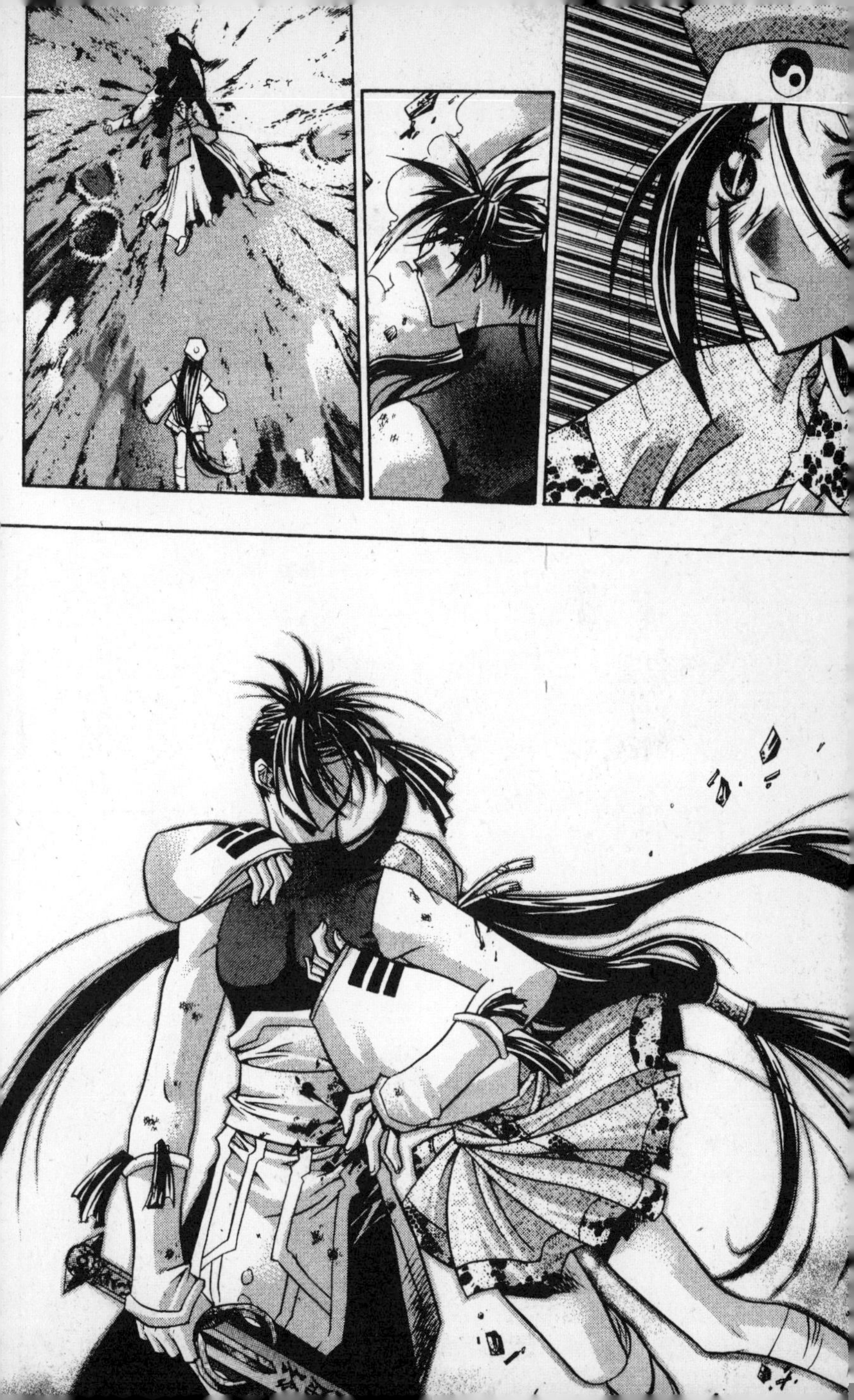

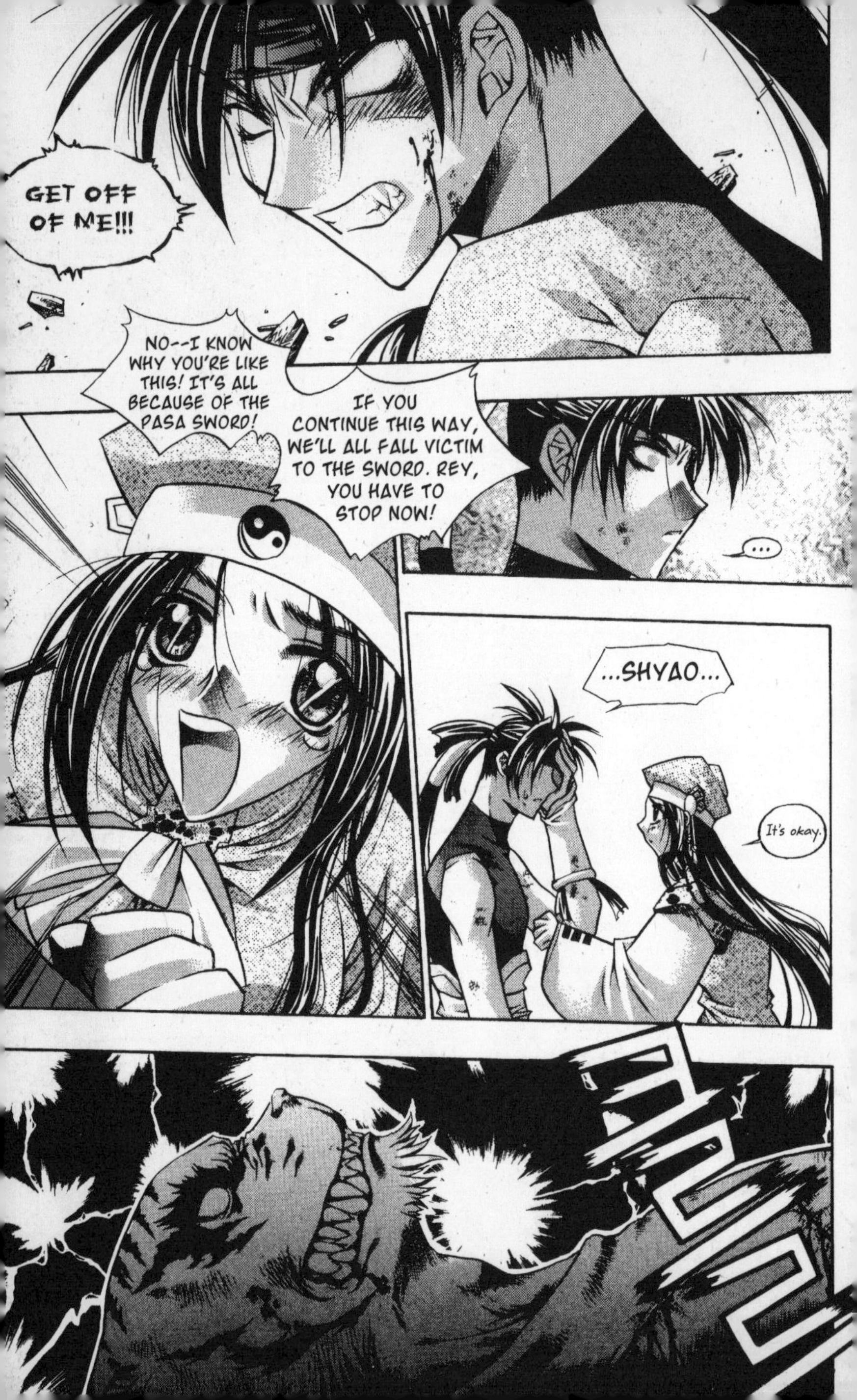
GET OFF OF ME!!!
NO--I KNOW WHY YOU'RE LIKE THIS! IT'S ALL BECAUSE OF THE PASA SWORD!
IF YOU CONTINUE THIS WAY, WE'LL ALL FALL VICTIM TO THE SWORD. REY, YOU HAVE TO STOP NOW!
...
...SHYAO...
It's okay.

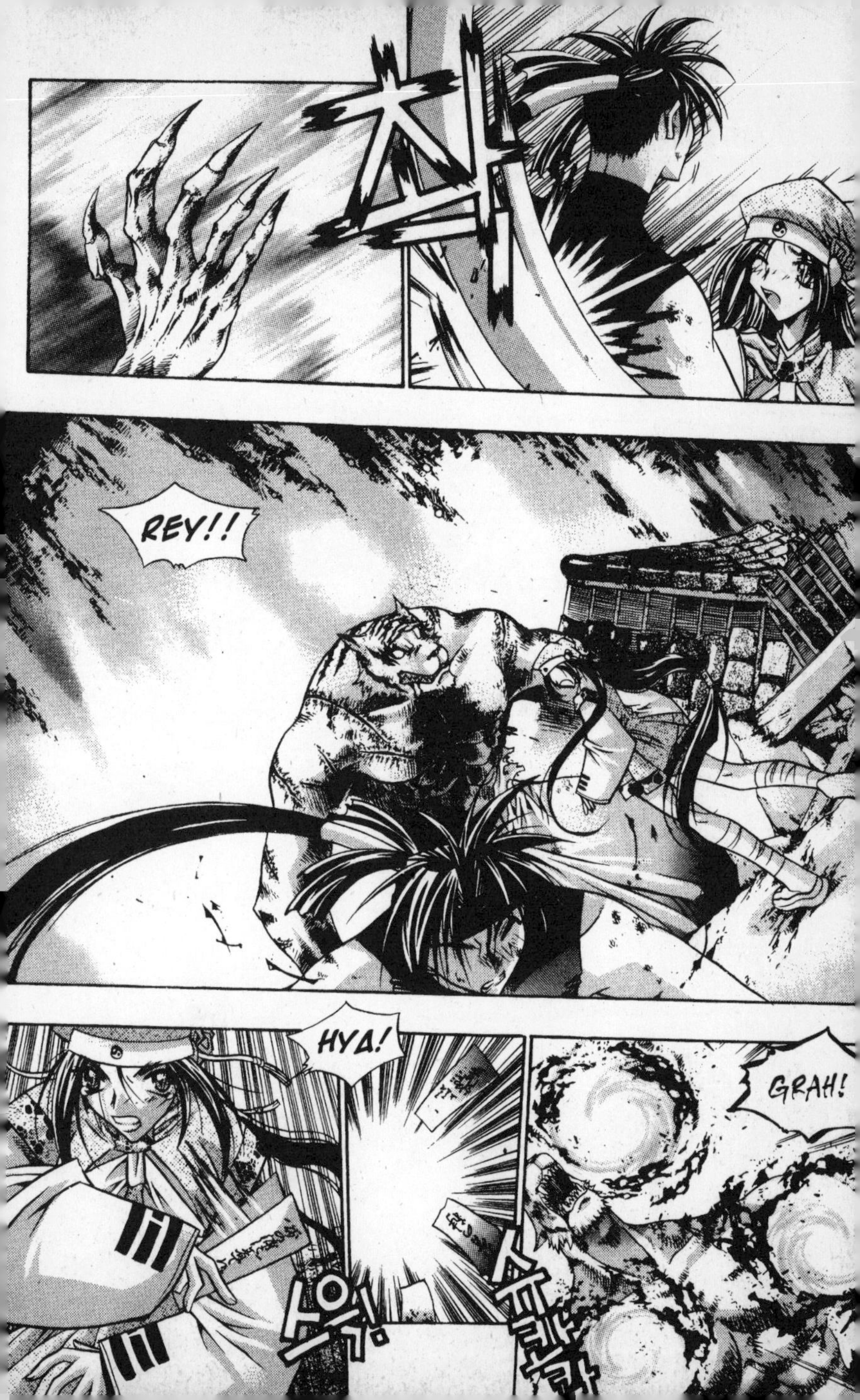
REY!!
HYA!
GRAH!

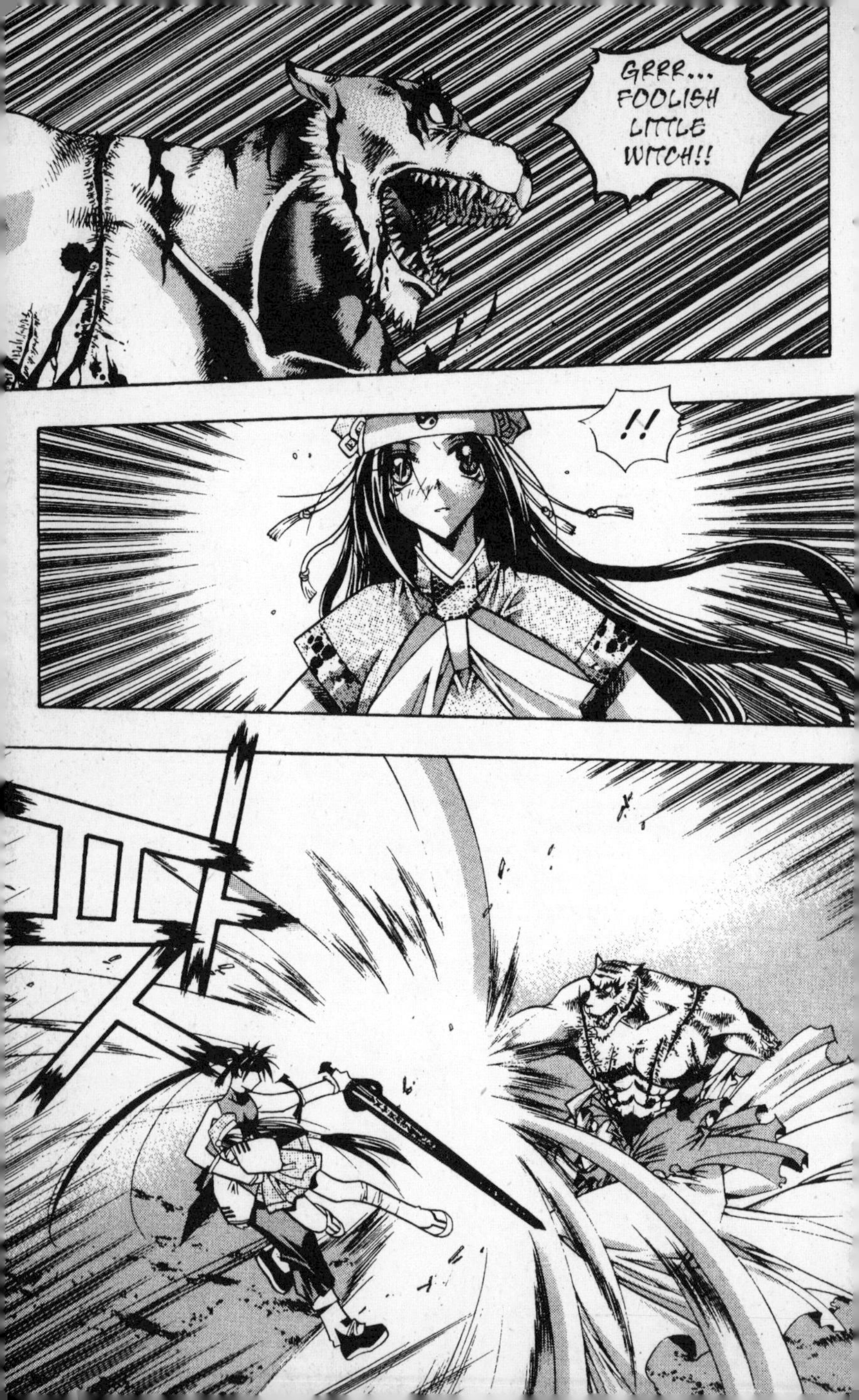
GRRR... FOOLISH LITTLE WITCH!!
!!

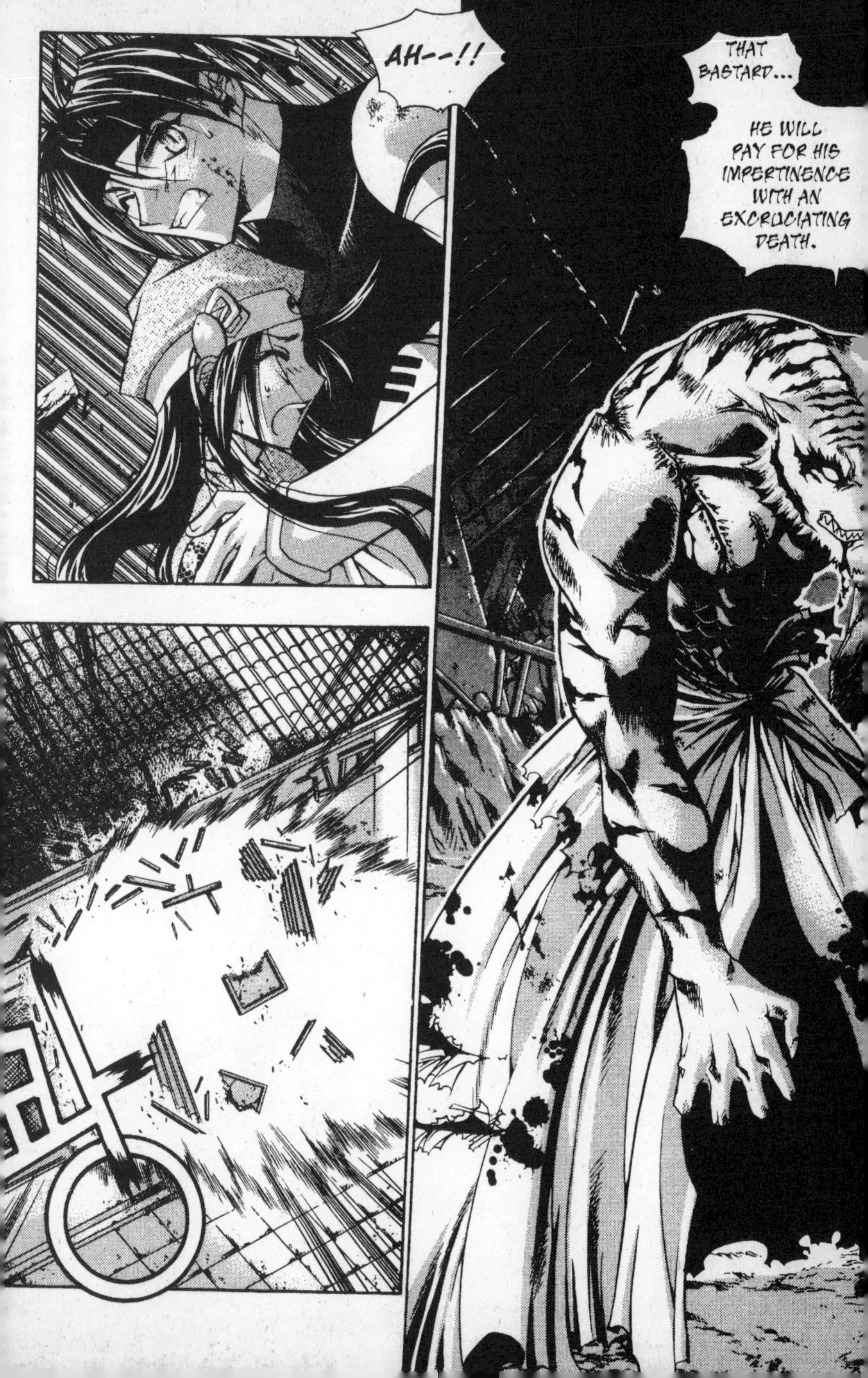
AH--!!
THAT BASTARD...
HE WILL PAY FOR HIS IMPERTINENCE WITH AN EXCRUCIATING DEATH.

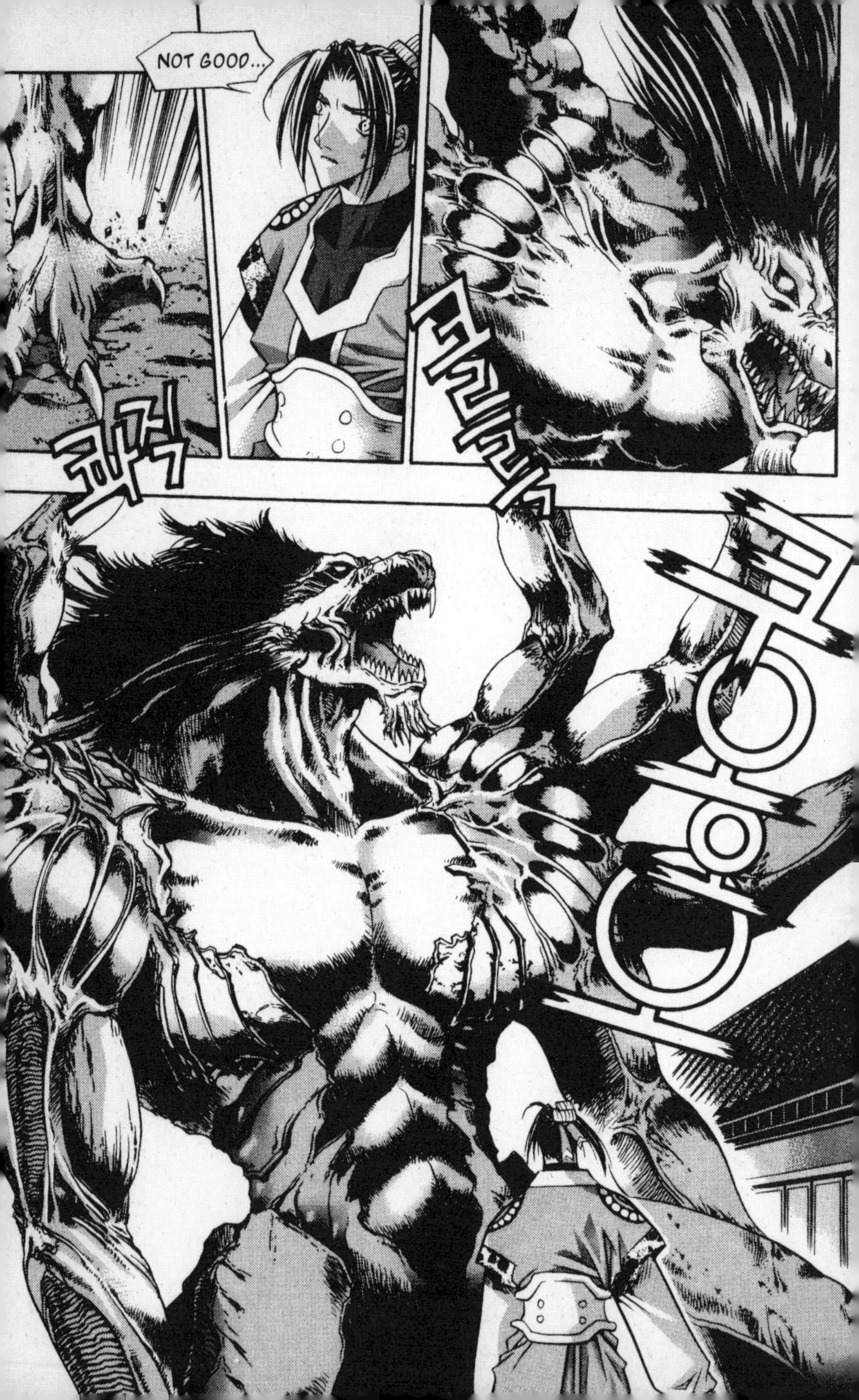
NOT GOOD...
콰직

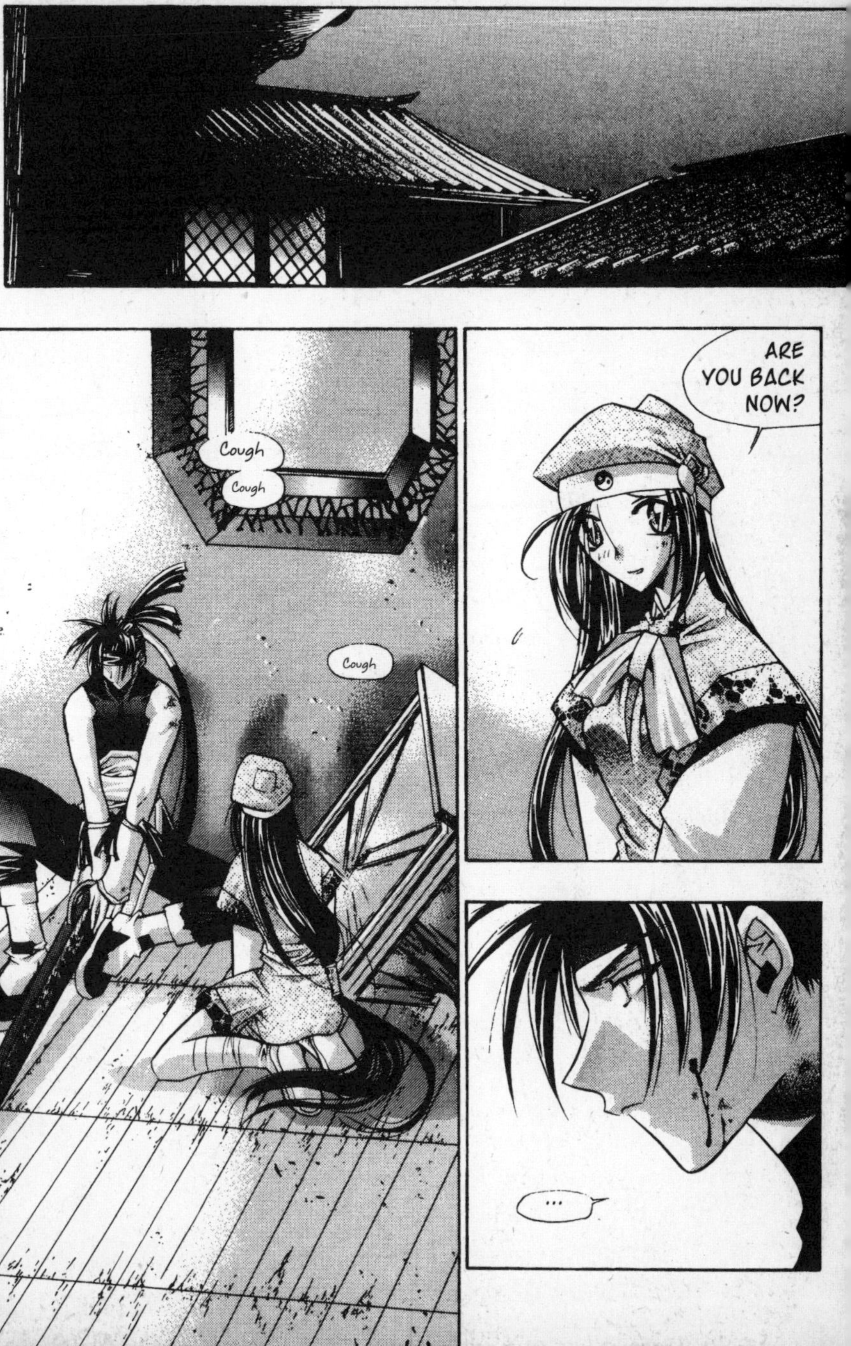
Cough
Cough
Cough
ARE YOU BACK NOW?
...

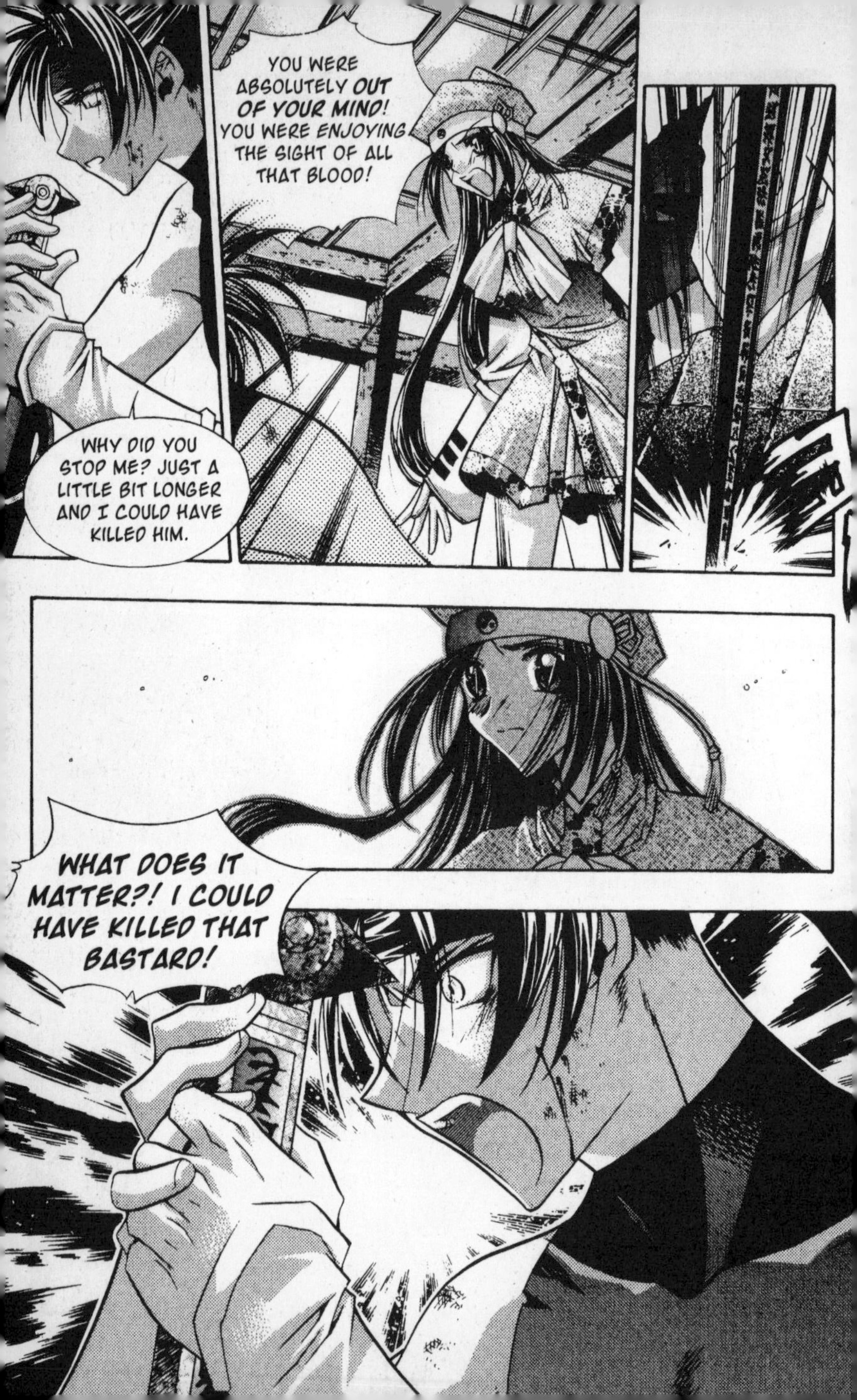
YOU WERE ABSOLUTELY OUT OF YOUR MIND! YOU WERE ENJOYING THE SIGHT OF ALL THAT BLOOD!
WHY DID YOU STOP ME? JUST A LITTLE BIT LONGER AND I COULD HAVE KILLED HIM.
WHAT DOES IT MATTER?! I COULD HAVE KILLED THAT BASTARD!

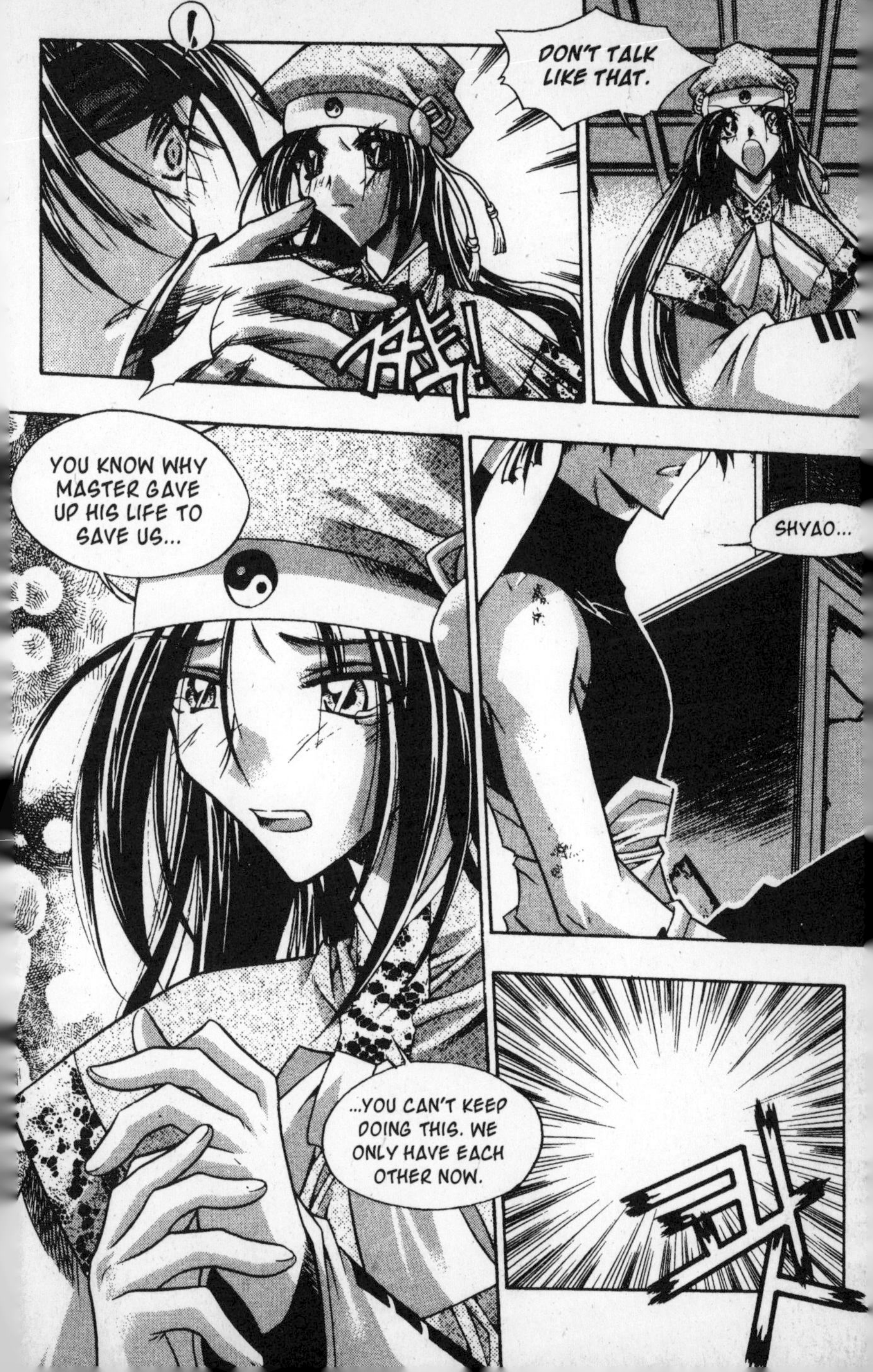
!
DON'T TALK LIKE THAT.
YOU KNOW WHY MASTER GAVE UP HIS LIFE TO SAVE US...
...YOU CAN'T KEEP DOING THIS. WE ONLY HAVE EACH OTHER NOW.
SHYAO...

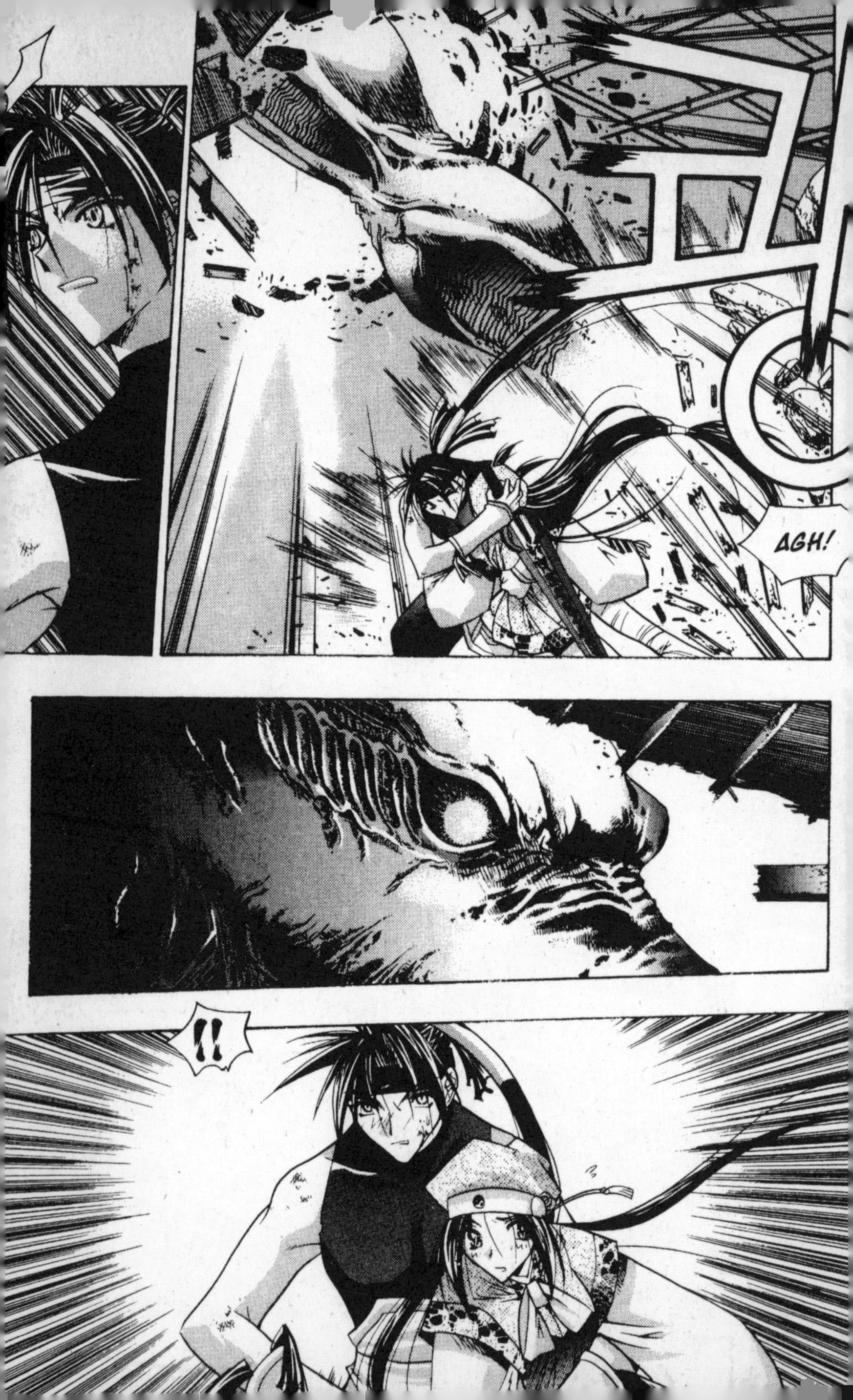
AGH!
!!

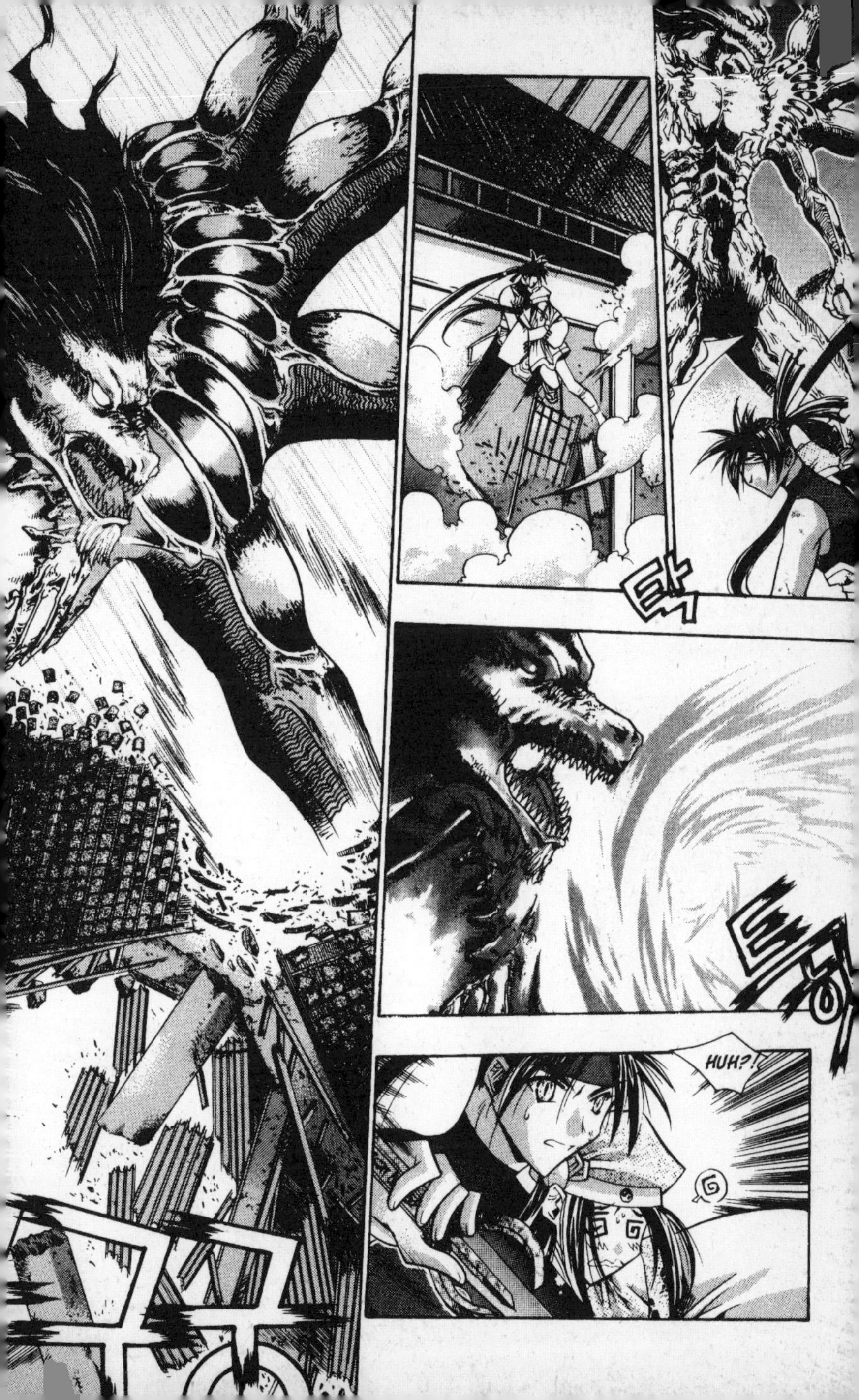
탁
HUH?!

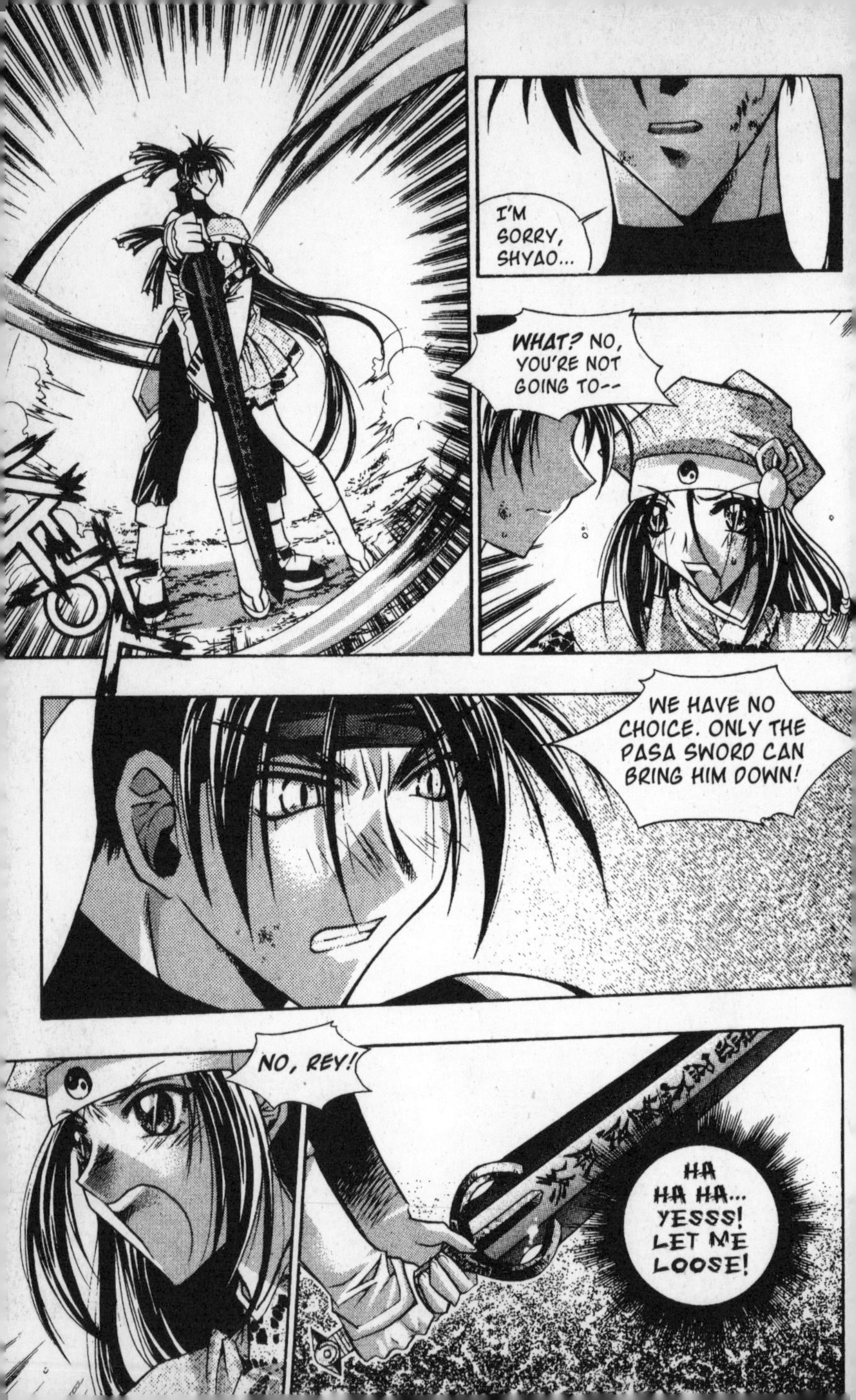
I'M SORRY, SHYAO...
WHAT? NO, YOU'RE NOT GOING TO--
WE HAVE NO CHOICE. ONLY THE PASA SWORD CAN BRING HIM DOWN!
NO, REY!
HA HA HA... YESSS! LET ME LOOSE!

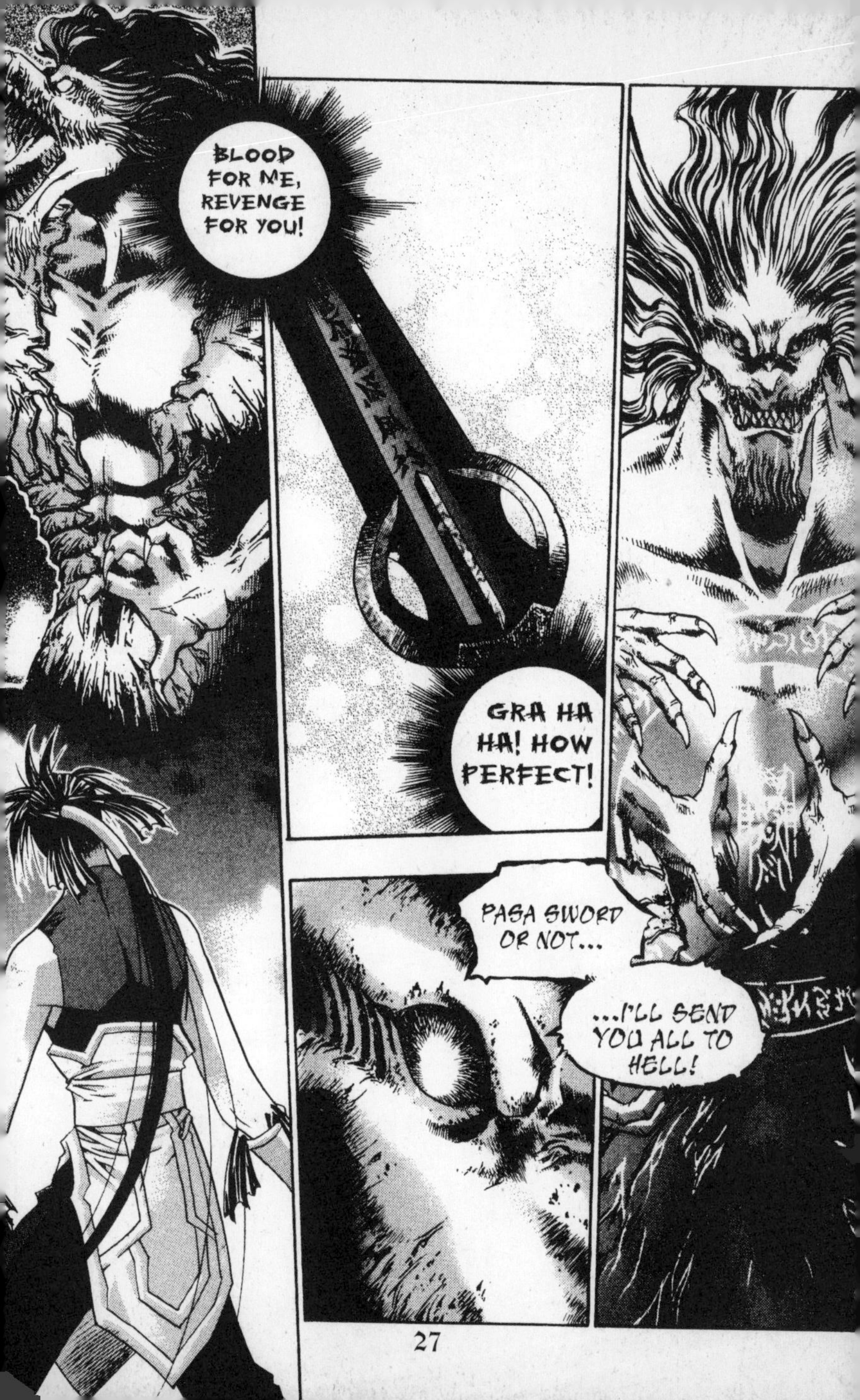
BLOOD FOR ME, REVENGE FOR YOU!
GRA HA HA! HOW PERFECT!
PASA SWORD OR NOT...
...I'LL SEND YOU ALL TO HELL!

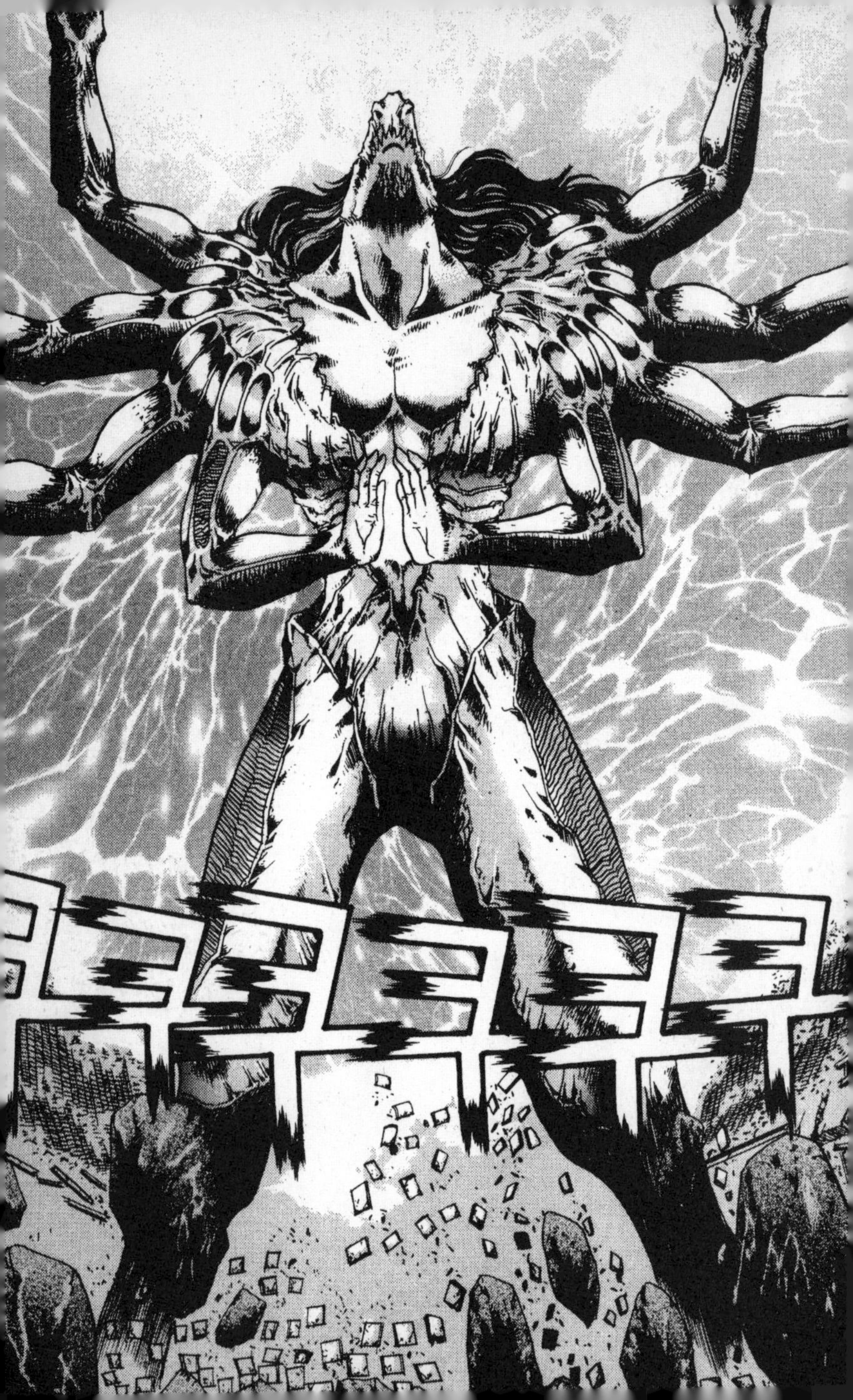

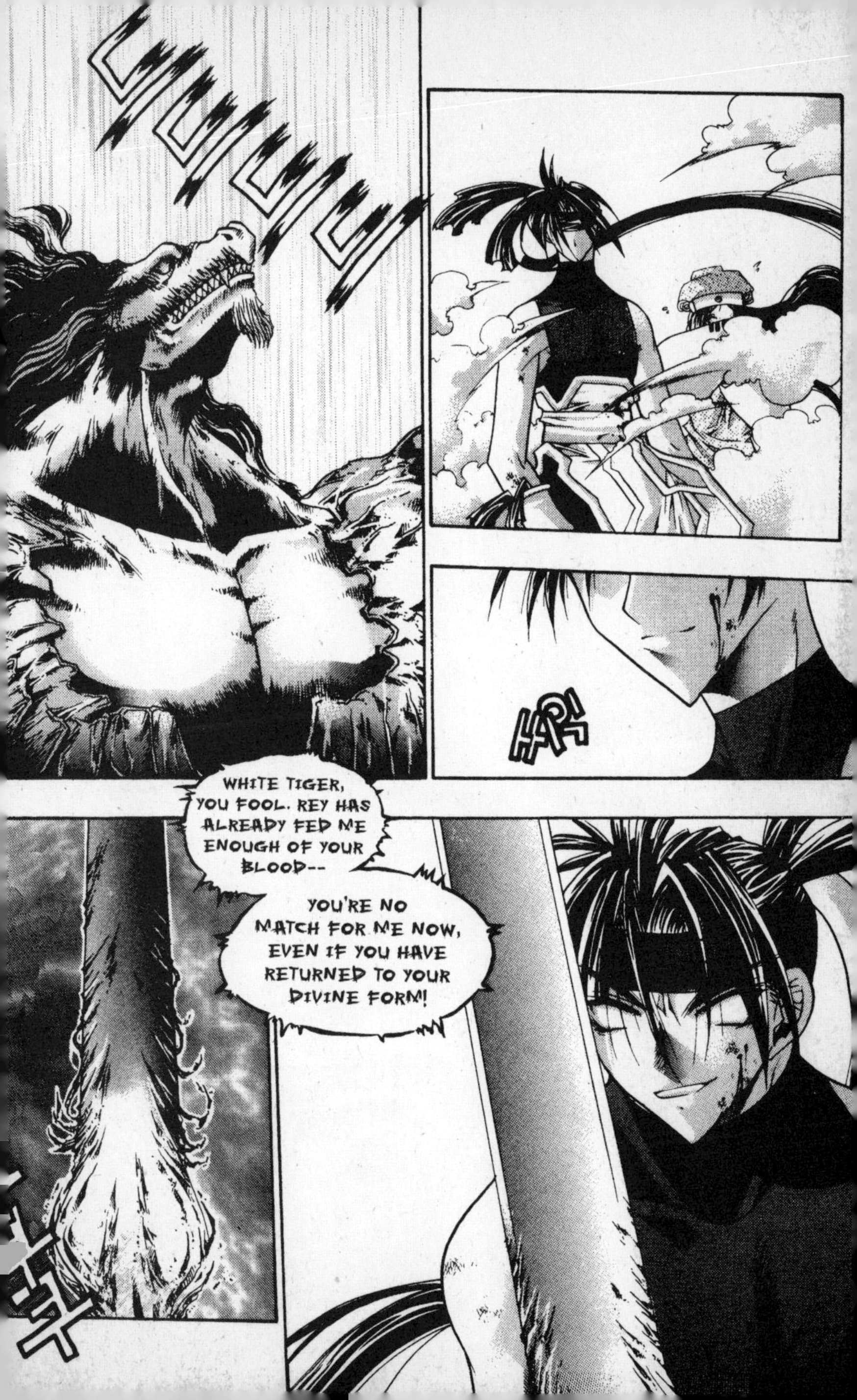
WHITE TIGER, YOU FOOL. REY HAS ALREADY FED ME ENOUGH OF YOUR BLOOD--
YOU'RE NO MATCH FOR ME NOW, EVEN IF YOU HAVE RETURNED TO YOUR DIVINE FORM!

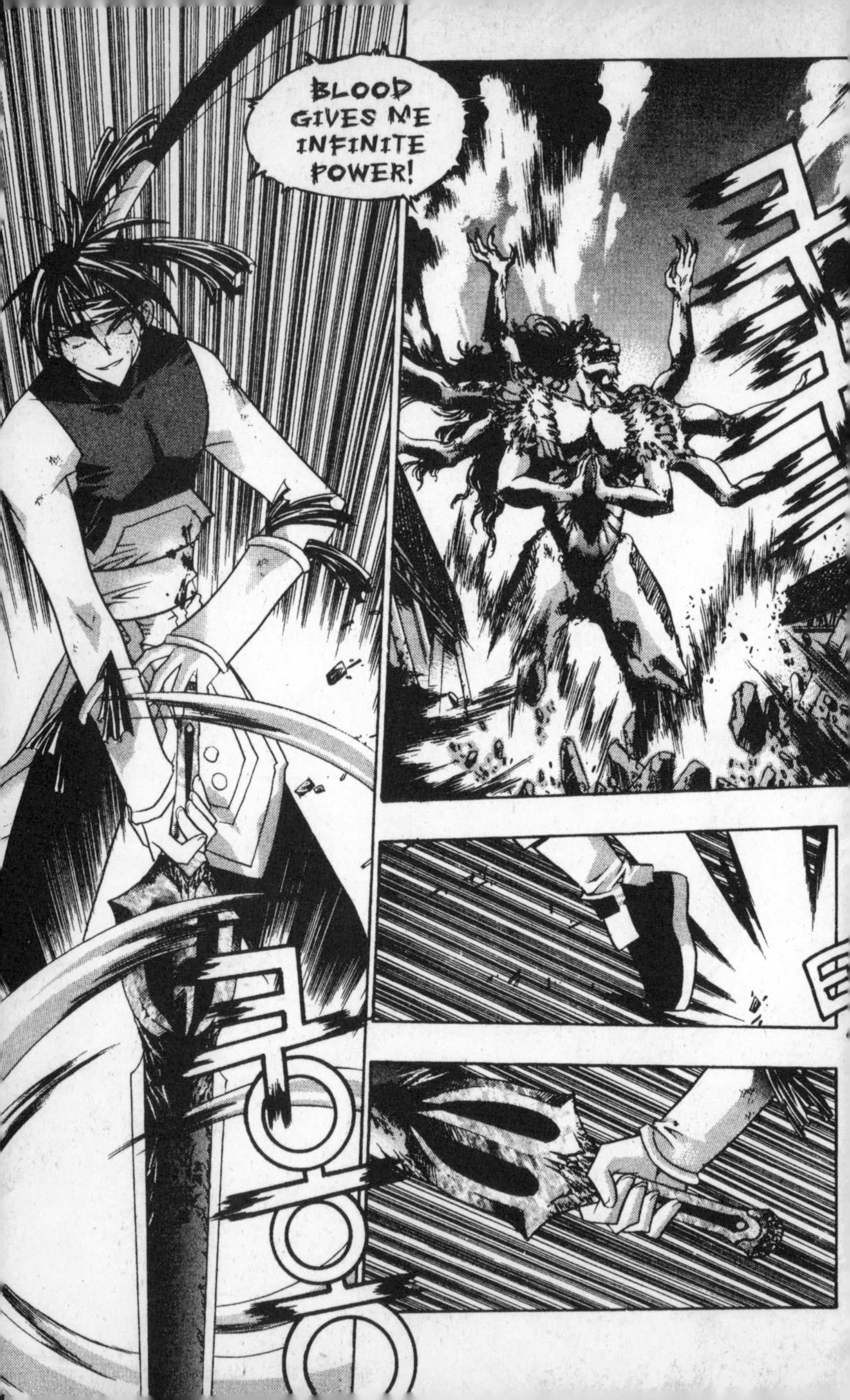
BLOOD GIVES ME INFINITE POWER!

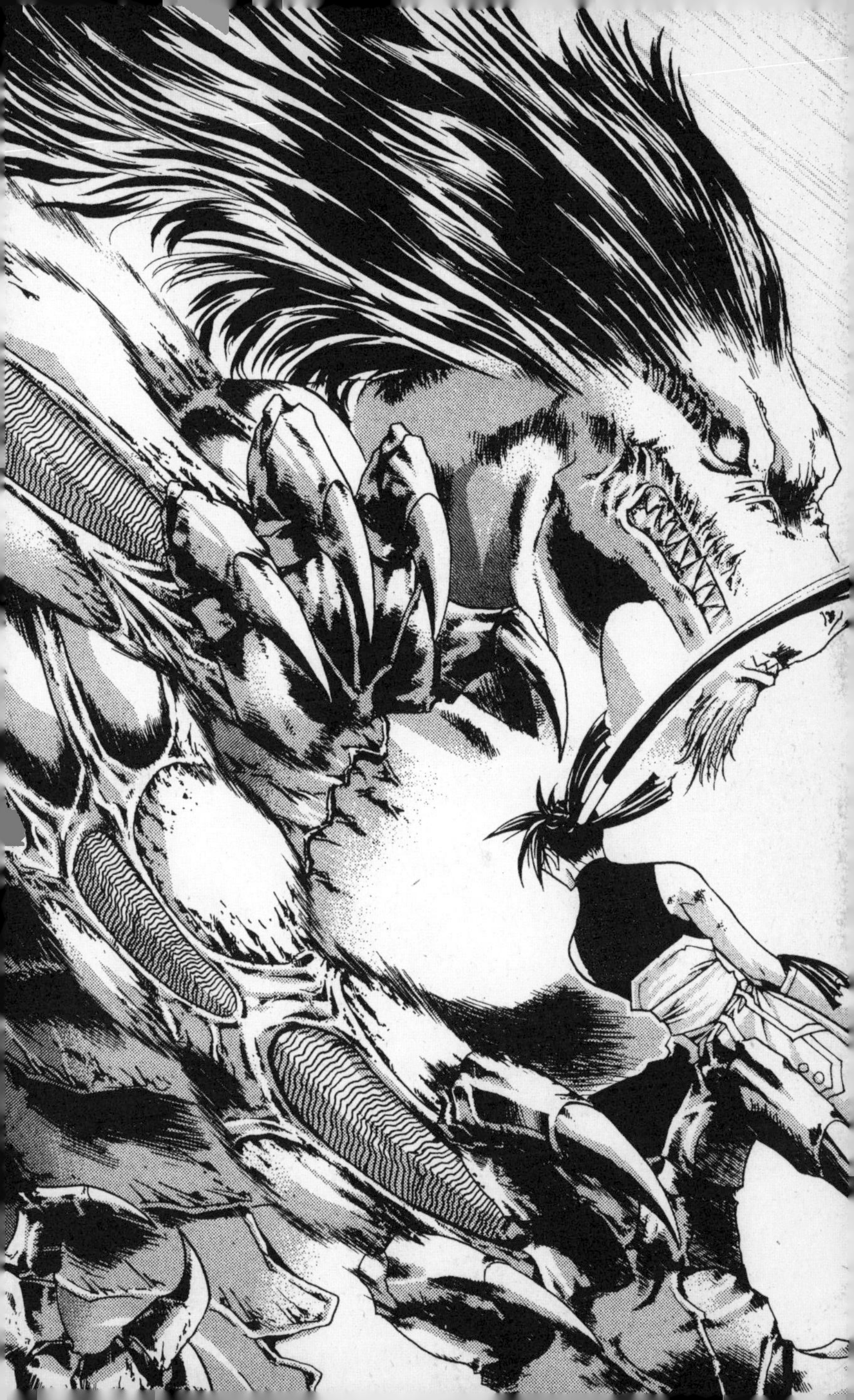

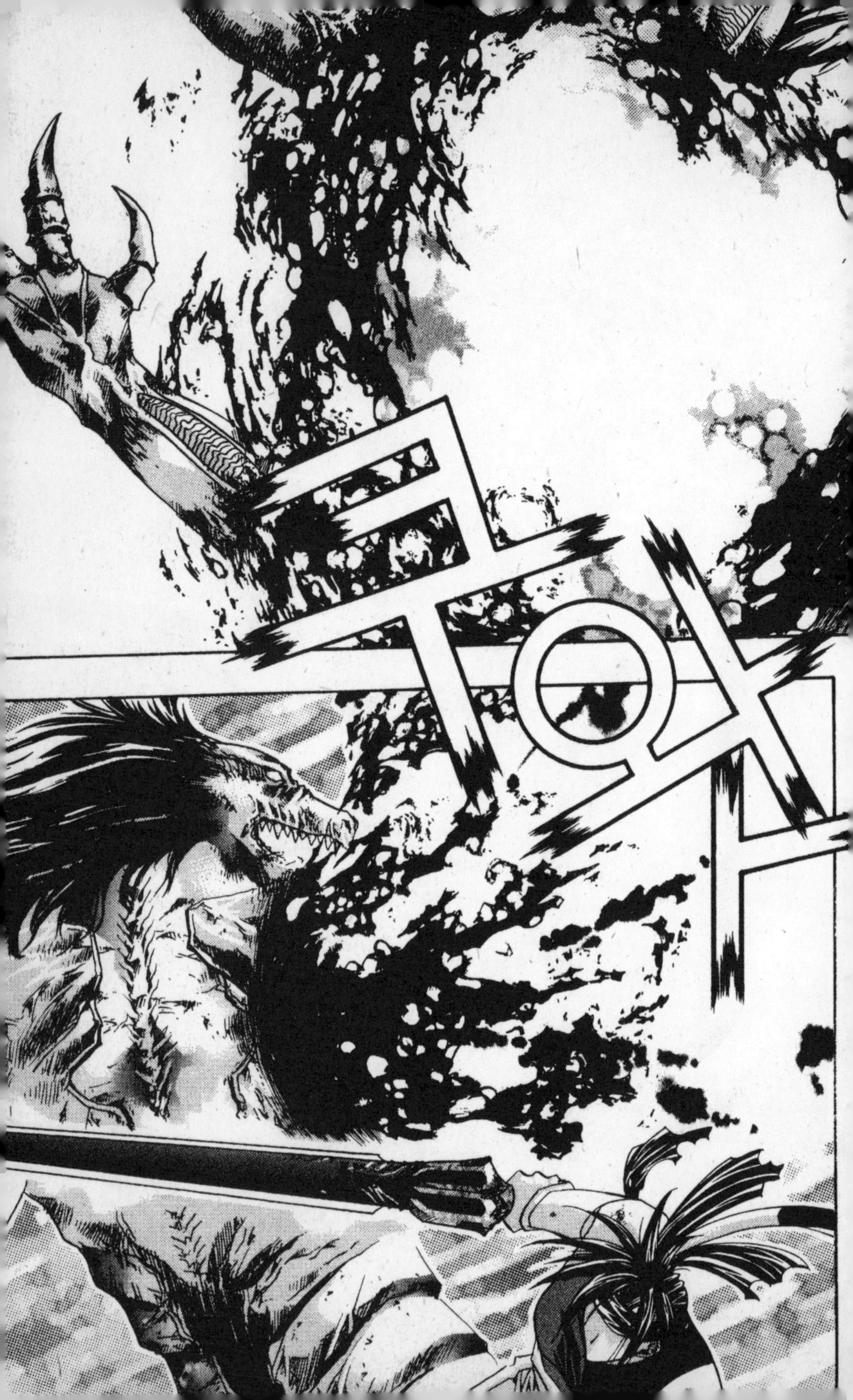

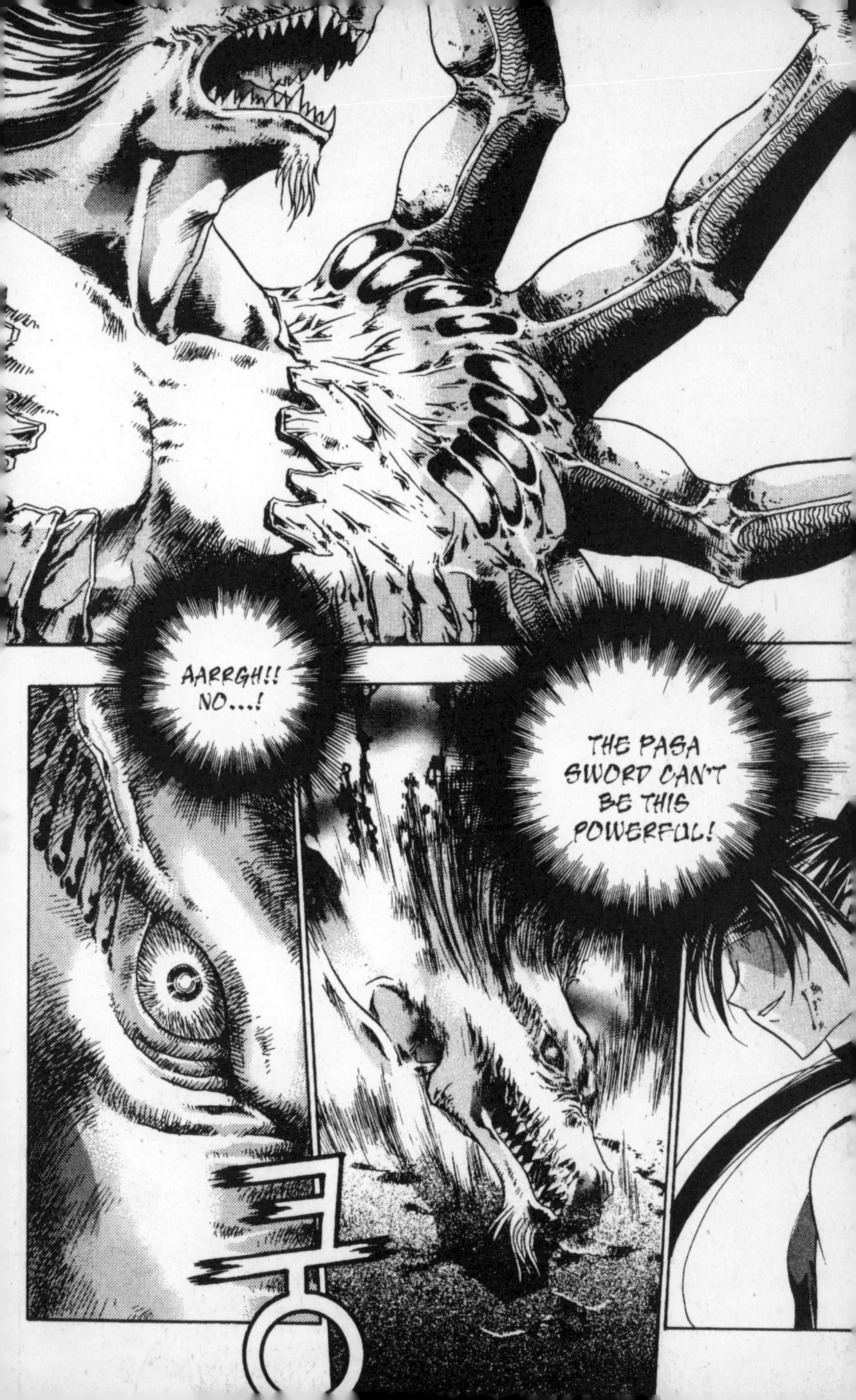
AARRGH!! NO...!
THE PASA SWORD CAN'T BE THIS POWERFUL!

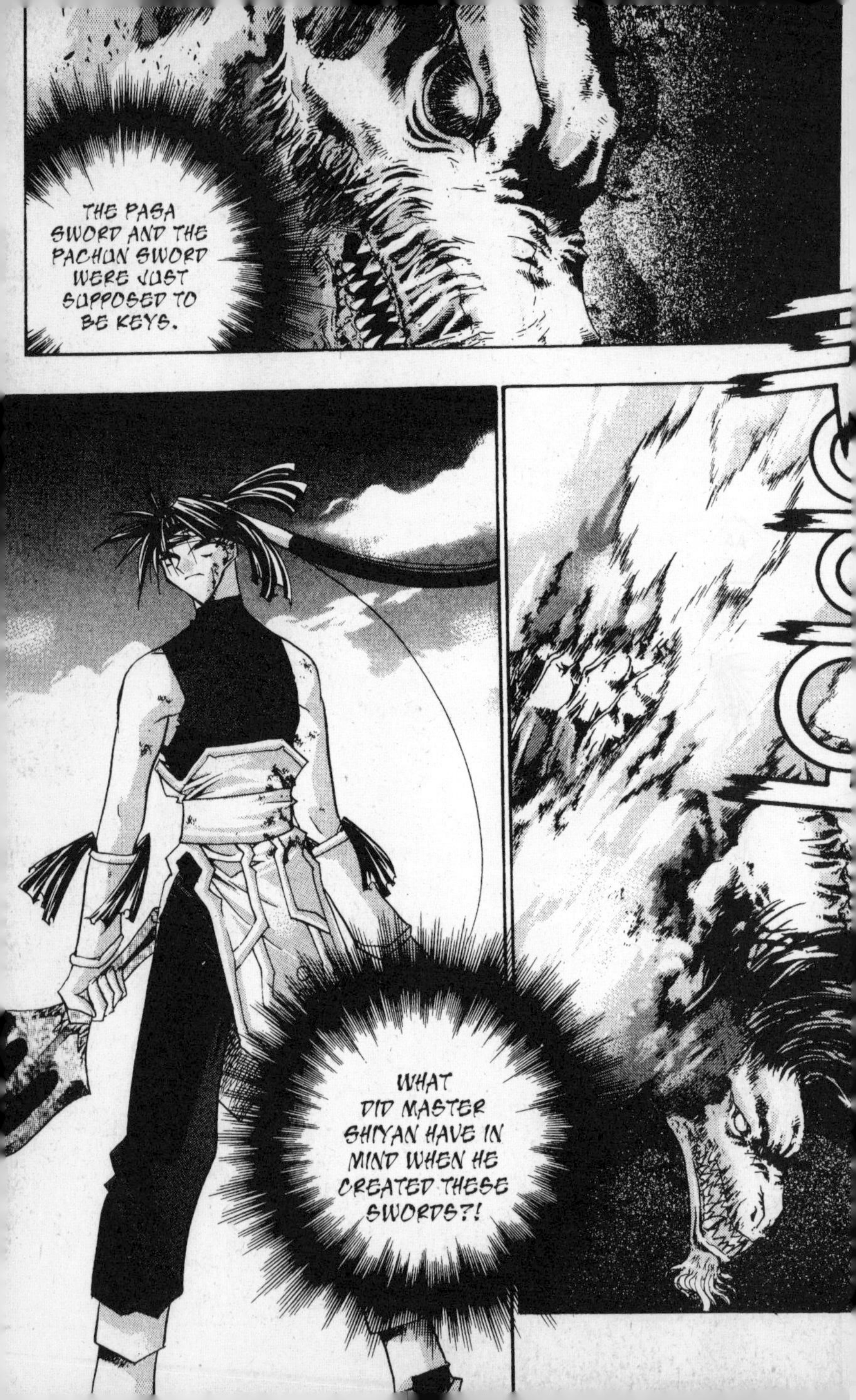
THE PASA SWORD AND THE PACHUN SWORD WERE JUST SUPPOSED TO BE KEYS.
WHAT DID MASTER SHIYAN HAVE IN MIND WHEN HE CREATED THESE SWORDS?!

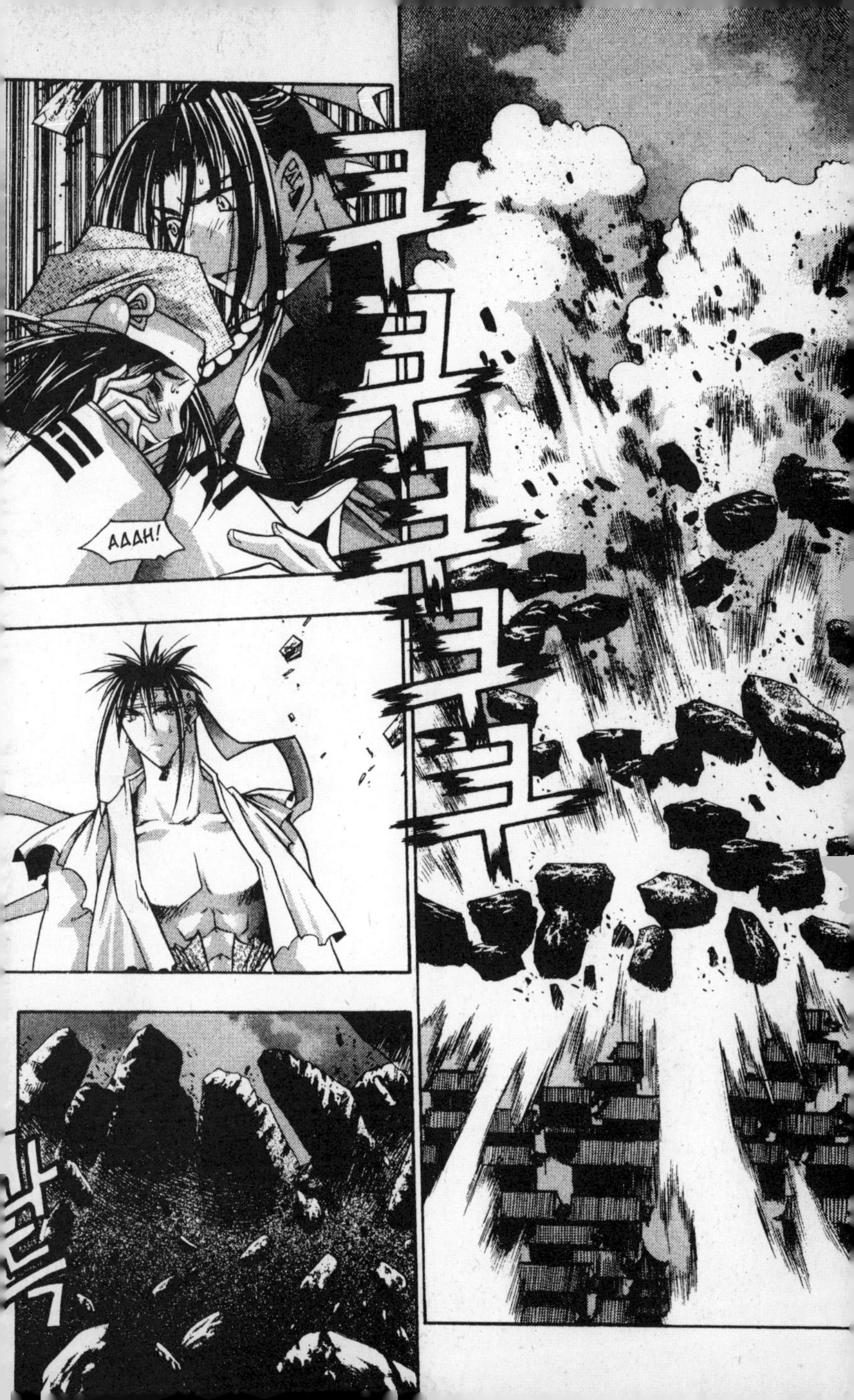
AAAH!

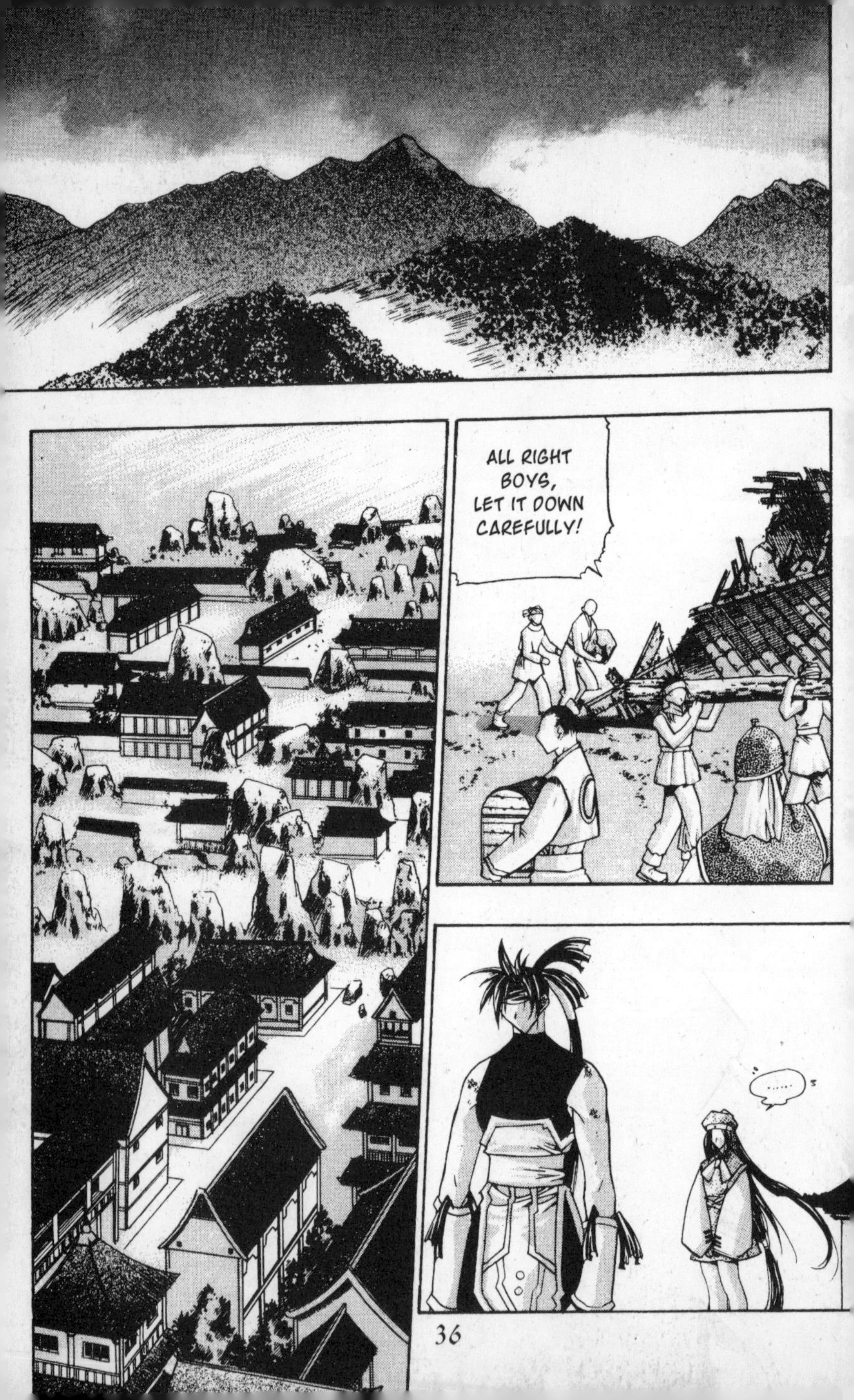
ALL RIGHT BOYS, LET IT DOWN CAREFULLY!
......

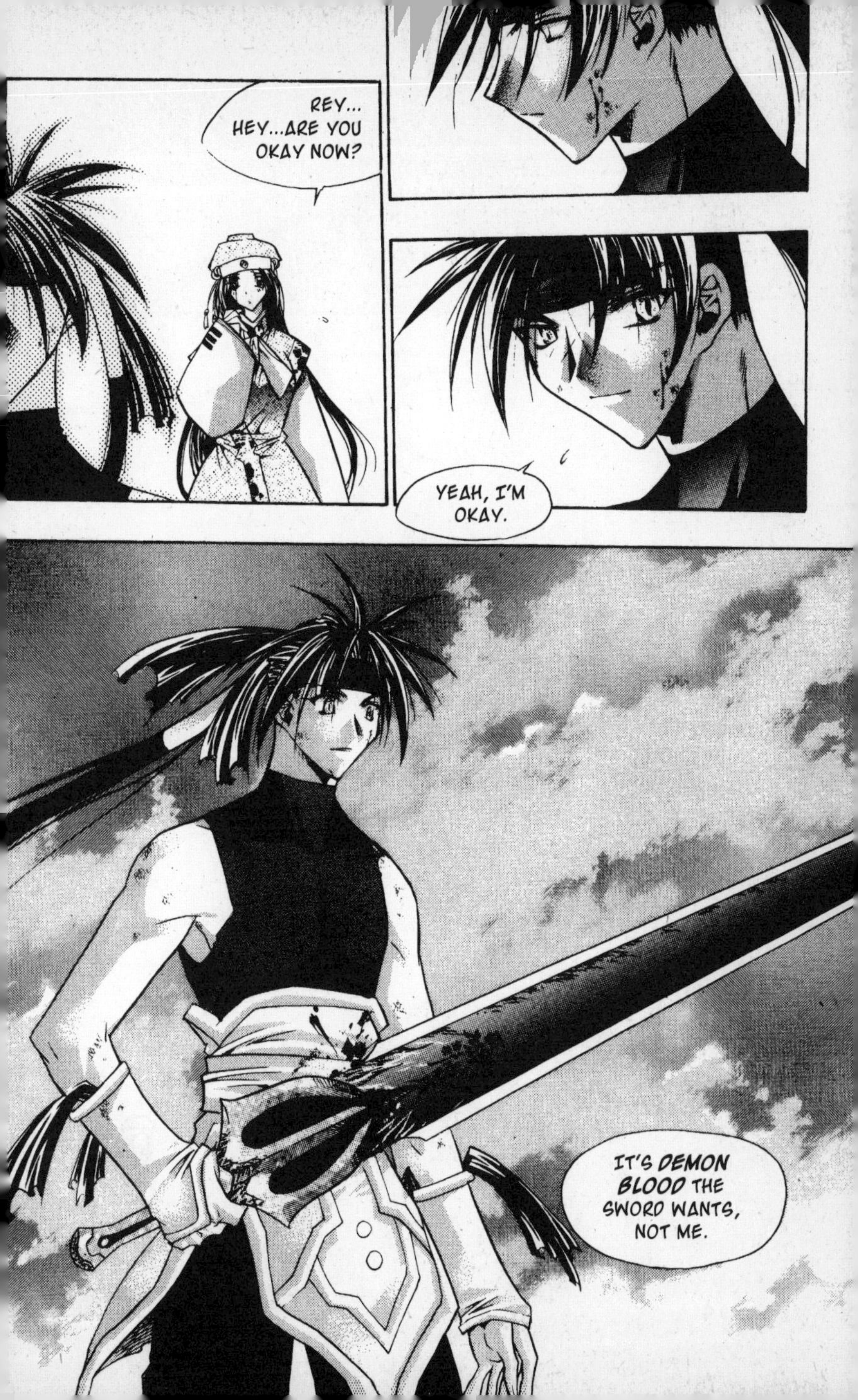
REY... HEY...ARE YOU OKAY NOW?
YEAH, I'M OKAY.
IT'S DEMON BLOOD THE SWORD WANTS, NOT ME.

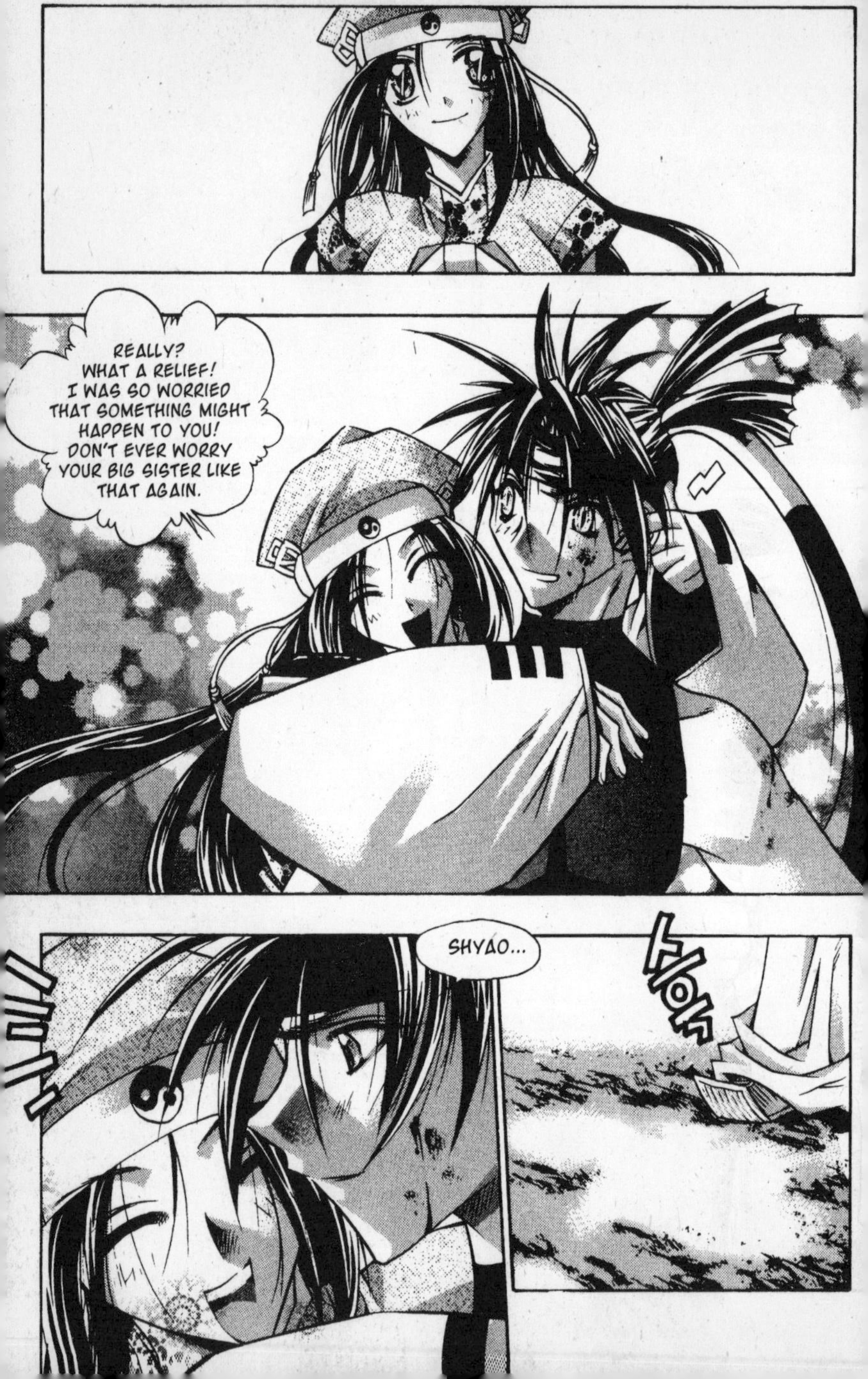
REALLY? WHAT A RELIEF! I WAS SO WORRIED THAT SOMETHING MIGHT HAPPEN TO YOU! DON'T EVER WORRY YOUR BIG SISTER LIKE THAT AGAIN.
SHYAO...

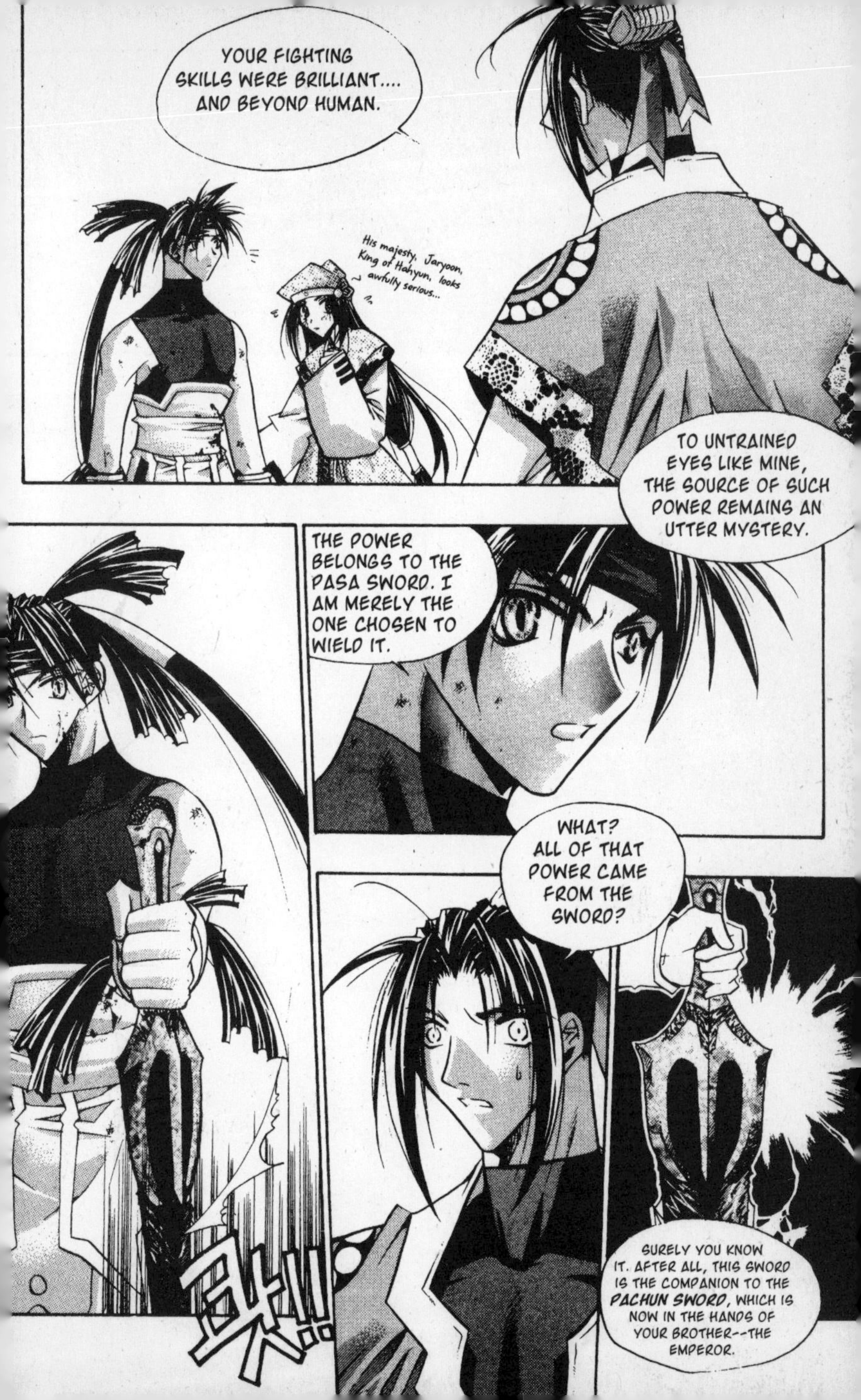
YOUR FIGHTING SKILLS WERE BRILLIANT.... AND BEYOND HUMAN.
His majesty, Jaryoon, King of Hahyun, looks awfully serious...
TO UNTRAINED EYES LIKE MINE, THE SOURCE OF SUCH POWER REMAINS AN UTTER MYSTERY.
THE POWER BELONGS TO THE PASA SWORD. I AM MERELY THE ONE CHOSEN TO WIELD IT.
WHAT? ALL OF THAT POWER CAME FROM THE SWORD?
SURELY YOU KNOW IT. AFTER ALL, THIS SWORD IS THE COMPANION TO THE PACHUN SWORD, WHICH IS NOW IN THE HANDS OF YOUR BROTHER--THE EMPEROR.

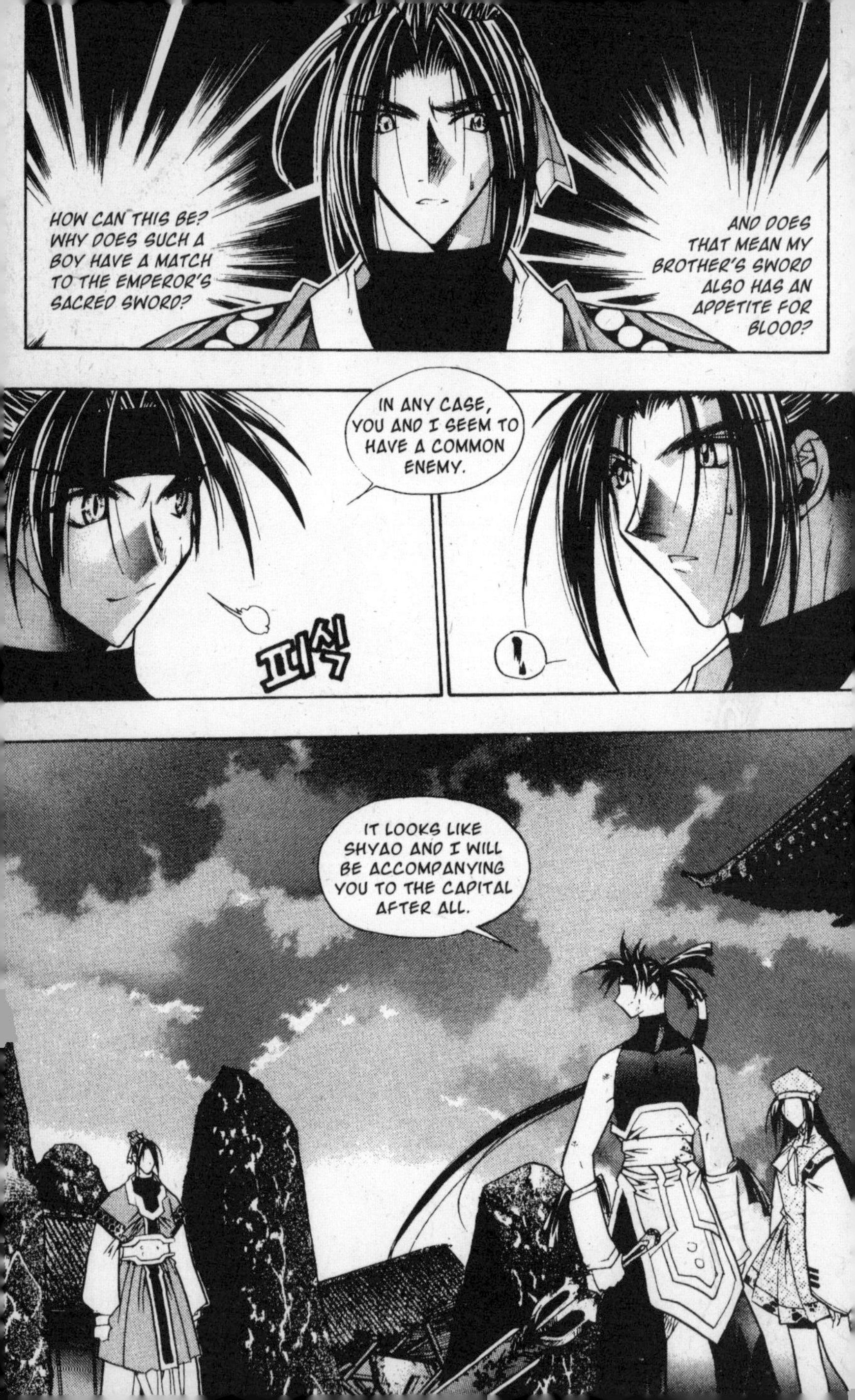
HOW CAN THIS BE? WHY DOES SUCH A BOY HAVE A MATCH TO THE EMPEROR'S SACRED SWORD?
AND DOES THAT MEAN MY BROTHER'S SWORD ALSO HAS AN APPETITE FOR BLOOD?
IN ANY CASE, YOU AND I SEEM TO HAVE A COMMON ENEMY.
피식
!
IT LOOKS LIKE SHYAO AND I WILL BE ACCOMPANYING YOU TO THE CAPITAL AFTER ALL.

Chronicle 7

The Demon Tree

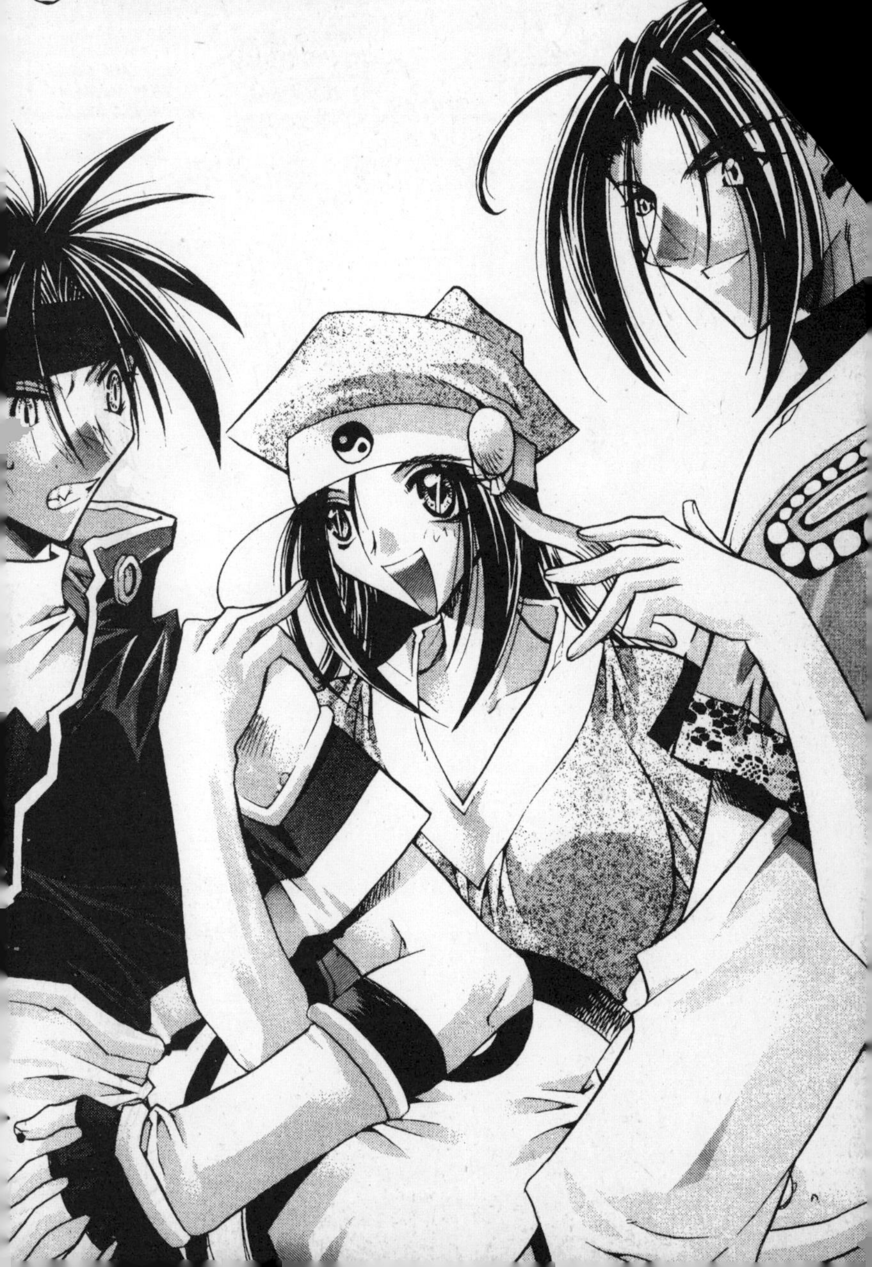

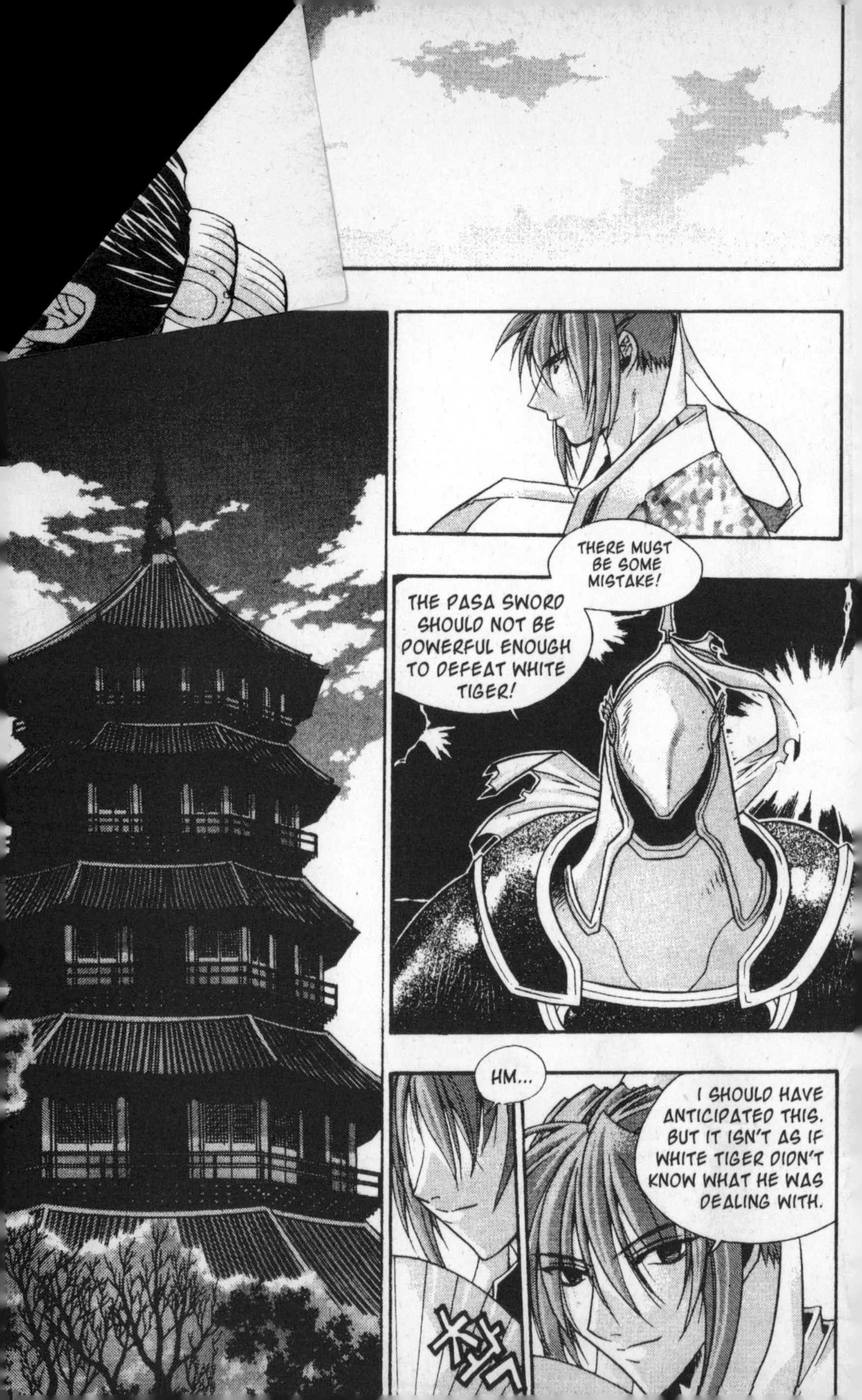
THERE MUST BE SOME MISTAKE!
THE PASA SWORD SHOULD NOT BE POWERFUL ENOUGH TO DEFEAT WHITE TIGER!
HM...
I SHOULD HAVE ANTICIPATED THIS. BUT IT ISN'T AS IF WHITE TIGER DIDN'T KNOW WHAT HE WAS DEALING WITH.

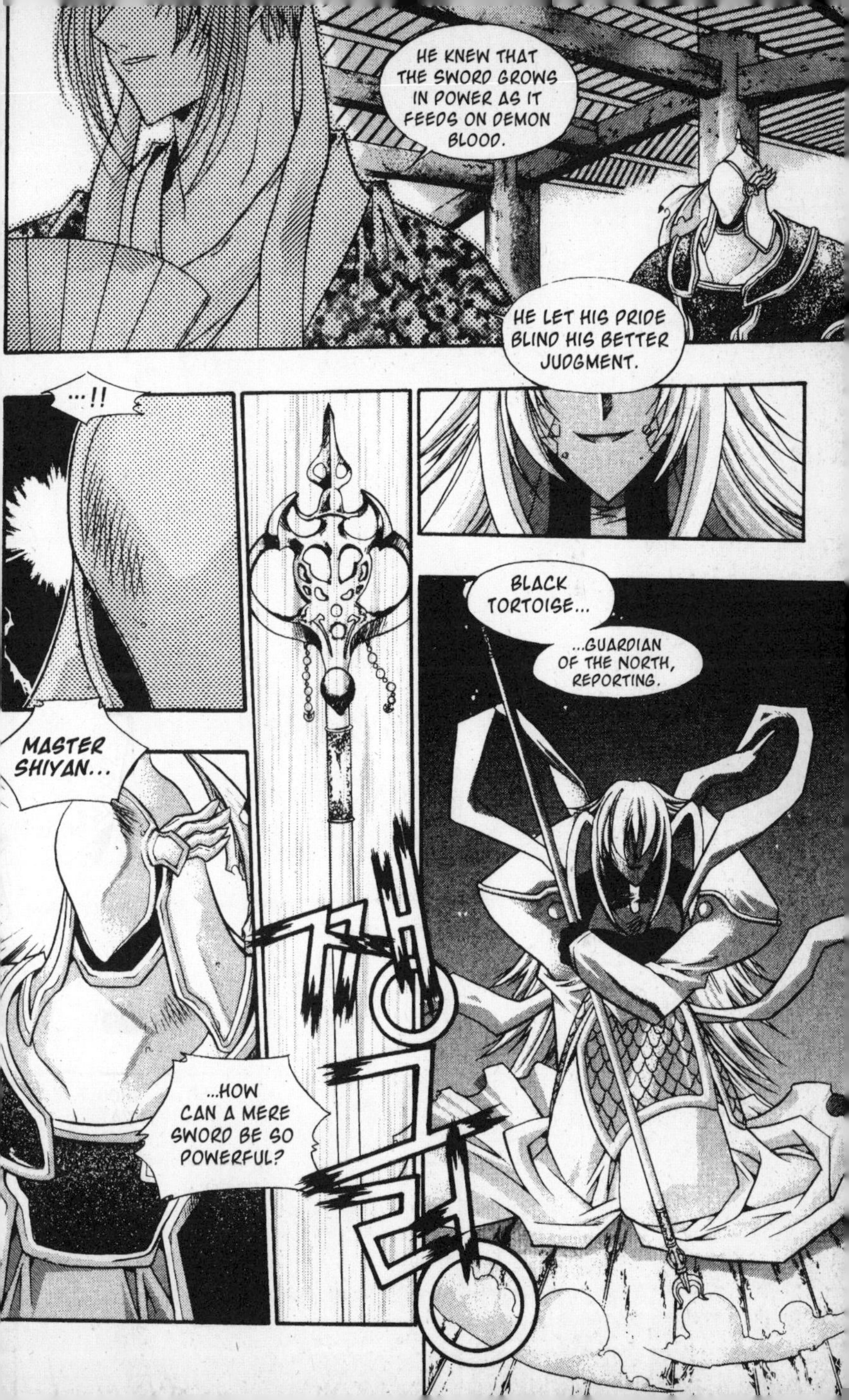
HE KNEW THAT THE SWORD GROWS IN POWER AS IT FEEDS ON DEMON BLOOD.
HE LET HIS PRIDE BLIND HIS BETTER JUDGMENT.
...!!
MASTER SHIYAN...
...HOW CAN A MERE SWORD BE SO POWERFUL?
BLACK TORTOISE...
...GUARDIAN OF THE NORTH, REPORTING.

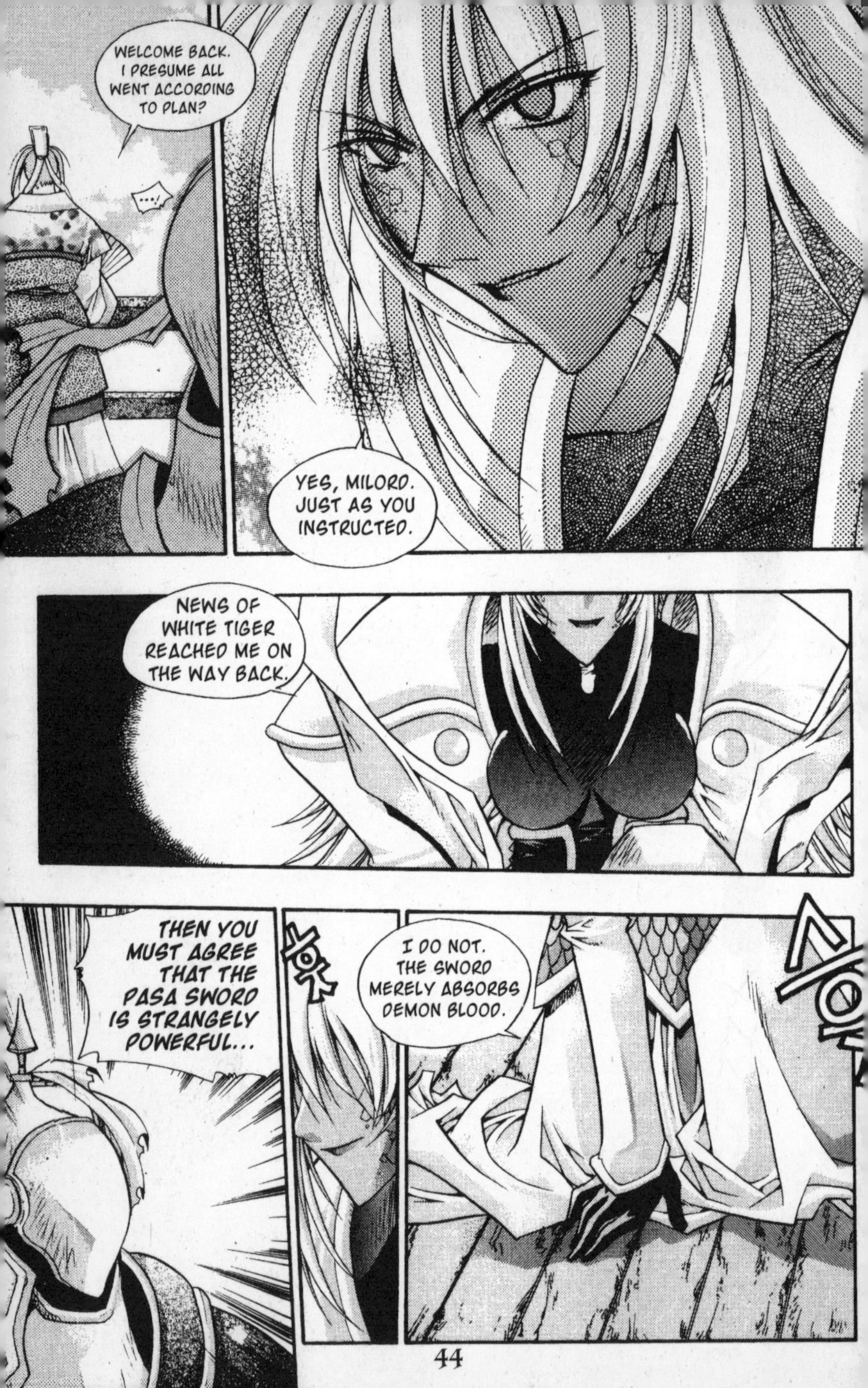
WELCOME BACK. I PRESUME ALL WENT ACCORDING TO PLAN?
...!
YES, MILORD. JUST AS YOU INSTRUCTED.
NEWS OF WHITE TIGER REACHED ME ON THE WAY BACK.
THEN YOU MUST AGREE THAT THE PASA SWORD IS STRANGELY POWERFUL...
I DO NOT. THE SWORD MERELY ABSORBS DEMON BLOOD.

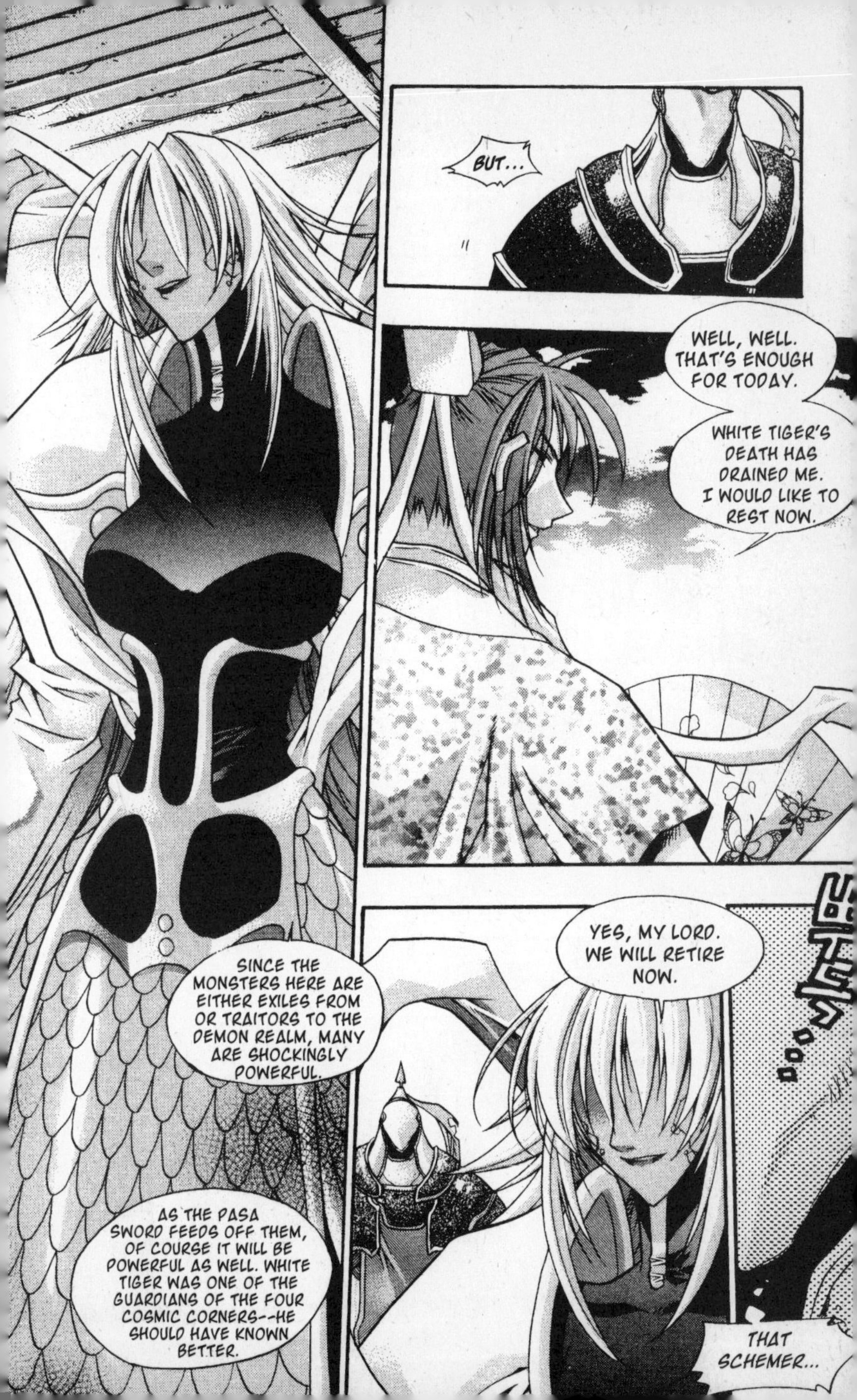
SINCE THE MONSTERS HERE ARE EITHER EXILES FROM OR TRAITORS TO THE DEMON REALM, MANY ARE SHOCKINGLY POWERFUL.
AS THE PASA SWORD FEEDS OFF THEM, OF COURSE IT WILL BE POWERFUL AS WELL. WHITE TIGER WAS ONE OF THE GUARDIANS OF THE FOUR COSMIC CORNERS--HE SHOULD HAVE KNOWN BETTER.
BUT...
WELL, WELL. THAT'S ENOUGH FOR TODAY.
WHITE TIGER'S DEATH HAS DRAINED ME. I WOULD LIKE TO REST NOW.
YES, MY LORD. WE WILL RETIRE NOW.
THAT SCHEMER...

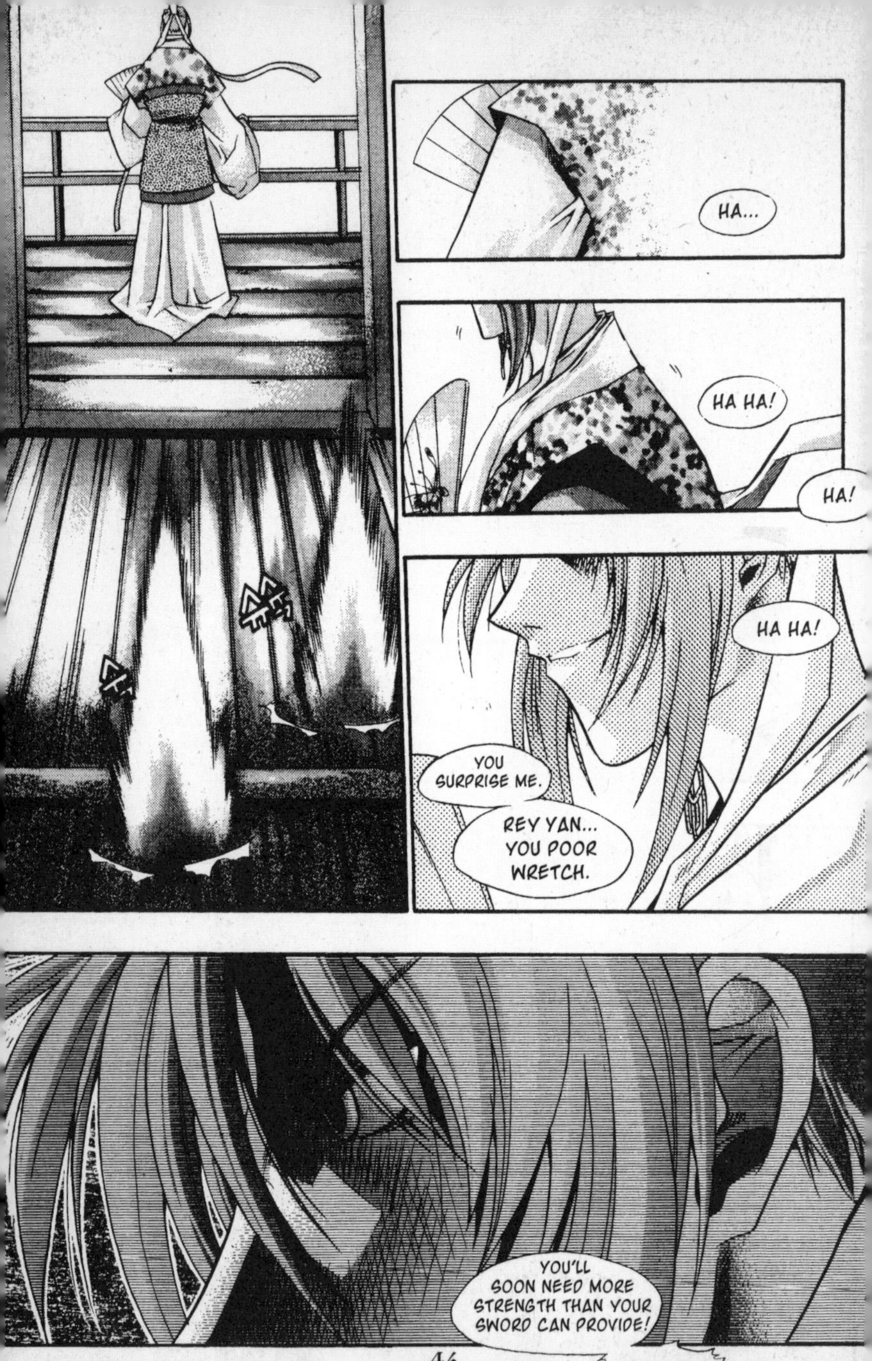
HA...
HA HA!
HA!
HA HA!
YOU SURPRISE ME.
REY YAN... YOU POOR WRETCH.
YOU'LL SOON NEED MORE STRENGTH THAN YOUR SWORD CAN PROVIDE!

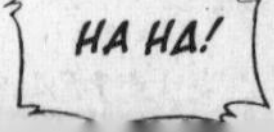
HA HA!

HA HA HA
HA HA!

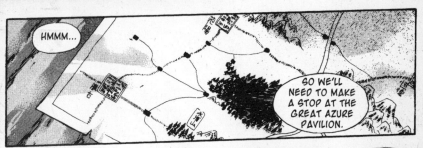

HMMM...

SO WE'LL NEED TO MAKE A STOP AT THE GREAT AZURE PAVILION.

YES--IT WAS MY MASTER'S FINAL WISH.

WELL THEN, LET'S TAKE THIS ROUTE.

YOUR MAJESTY, THAT ROUTE IS VERY DANGEROUS!

WHAT DO YOU MEAN?

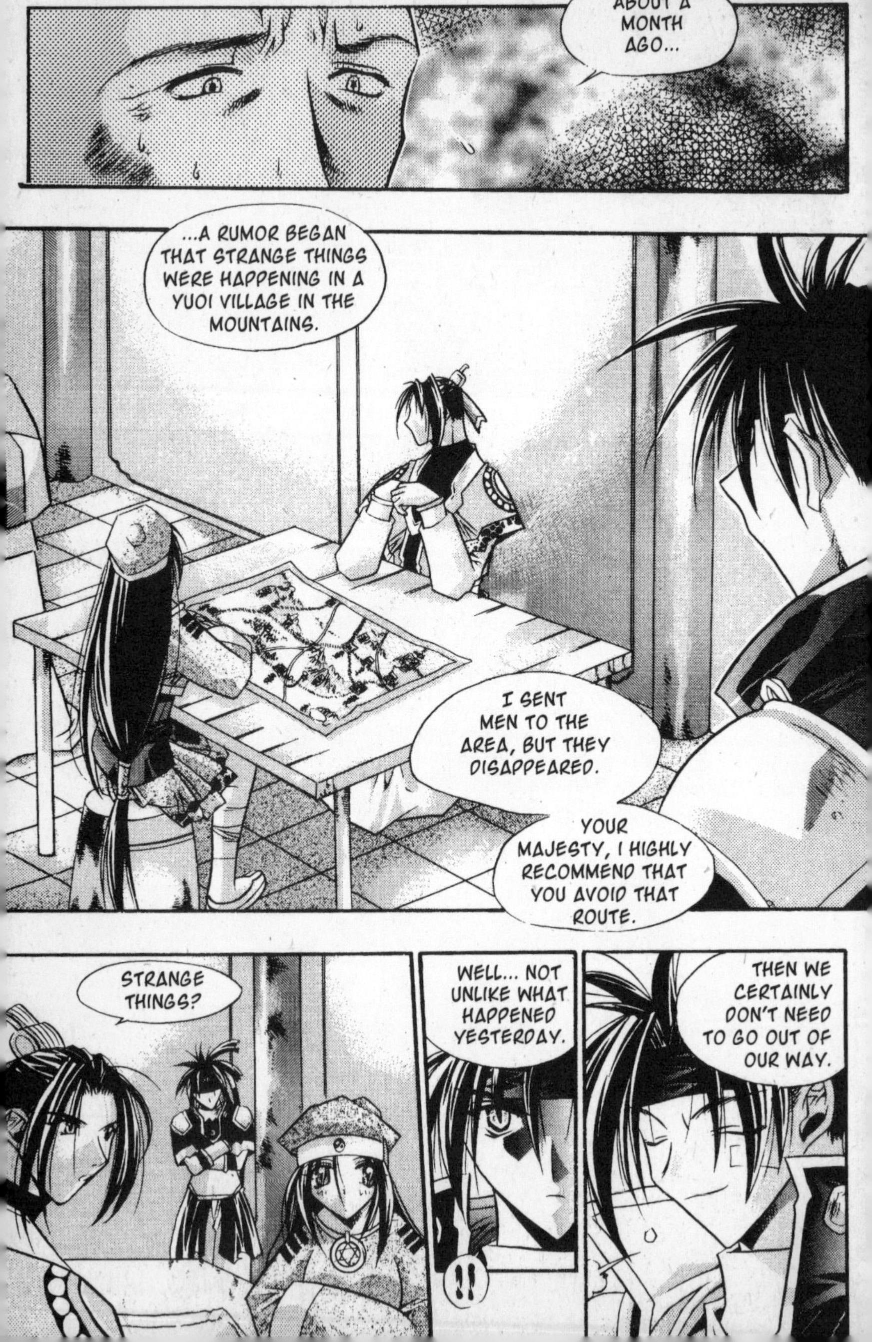
ABOUT A MONTH AGO...
...A RUMOR BEGAN THAT STRANGE THINGS WERE HAPPENING IN A YUOI VILLAGE IN THE MOUNTAINS.
I SENT MEN TO THE AREA, BUT THEY DISAPPEARED.
YOUR MAJESTY, I HIGHLY RECOMMEND THAT YOU AVOID THAT ROUTE.
STRANGE THINGS?
WELL... NOT UNLIKE WHAT HAPPENED YESTERDAY.
!!
THEN WE CERTAINLY DON'T NEED TO GO OUT OF OUR WAY.

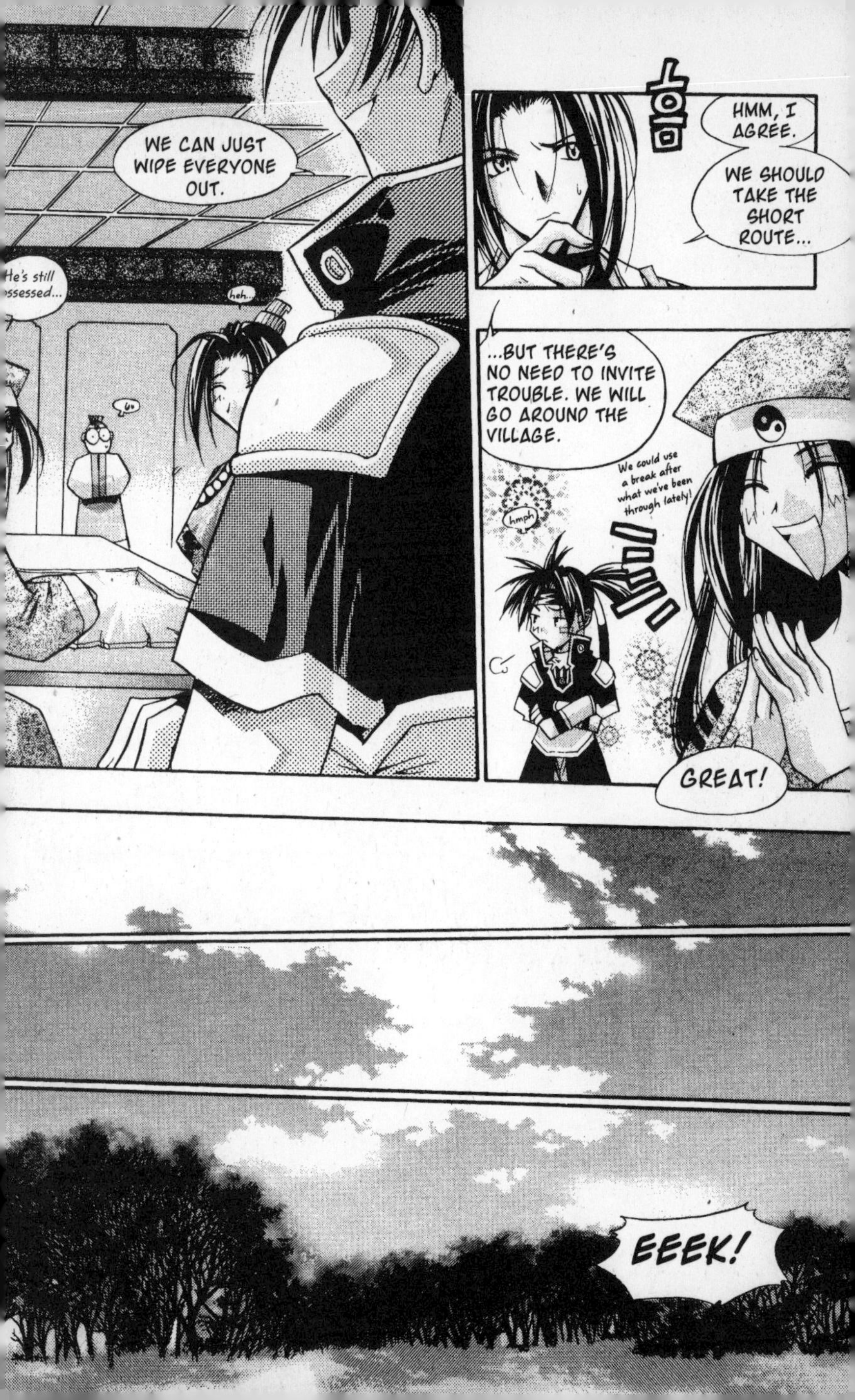
WE CAN JUST WIPE EVERYONE OUT.
He's still
ossessed...
heh...
흠
HMM, I AGREE.
WE SHOULD TAKE THE SHORT ROUTE...
...BUT THERE'S NO NEED TO INVITE TROUBLE. WE WILL GO AROUND THE VILLAGE.
We could use a break after what we've been through lately!
hmph
GREAT!
EEEK!

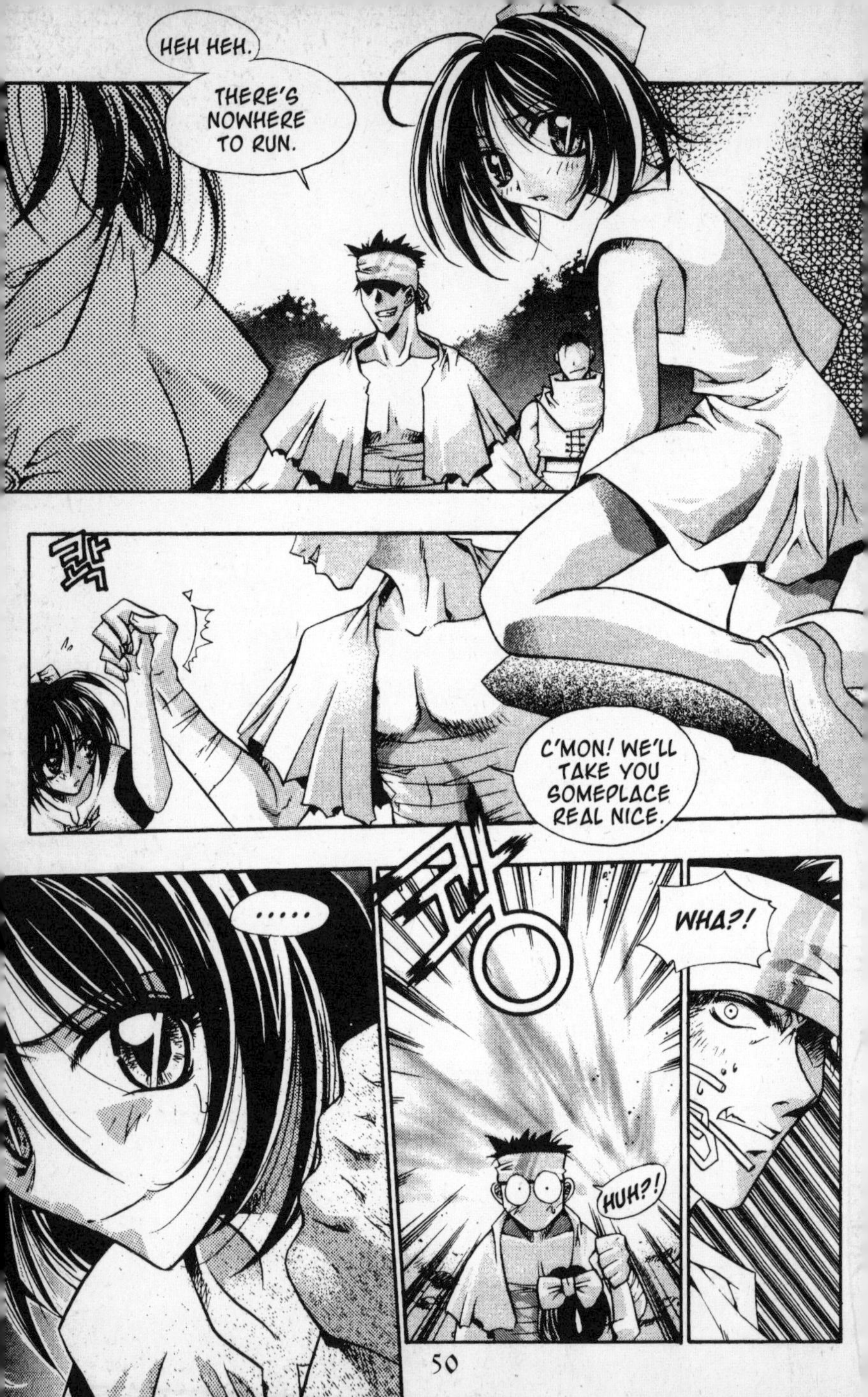
HEH HEH.
THERE'S NOWHERE TO RUN.
C'MON! WE'LL TAKE YOU SOMEPLACE REAL NICE.
.....
HUH?!
WHA?!

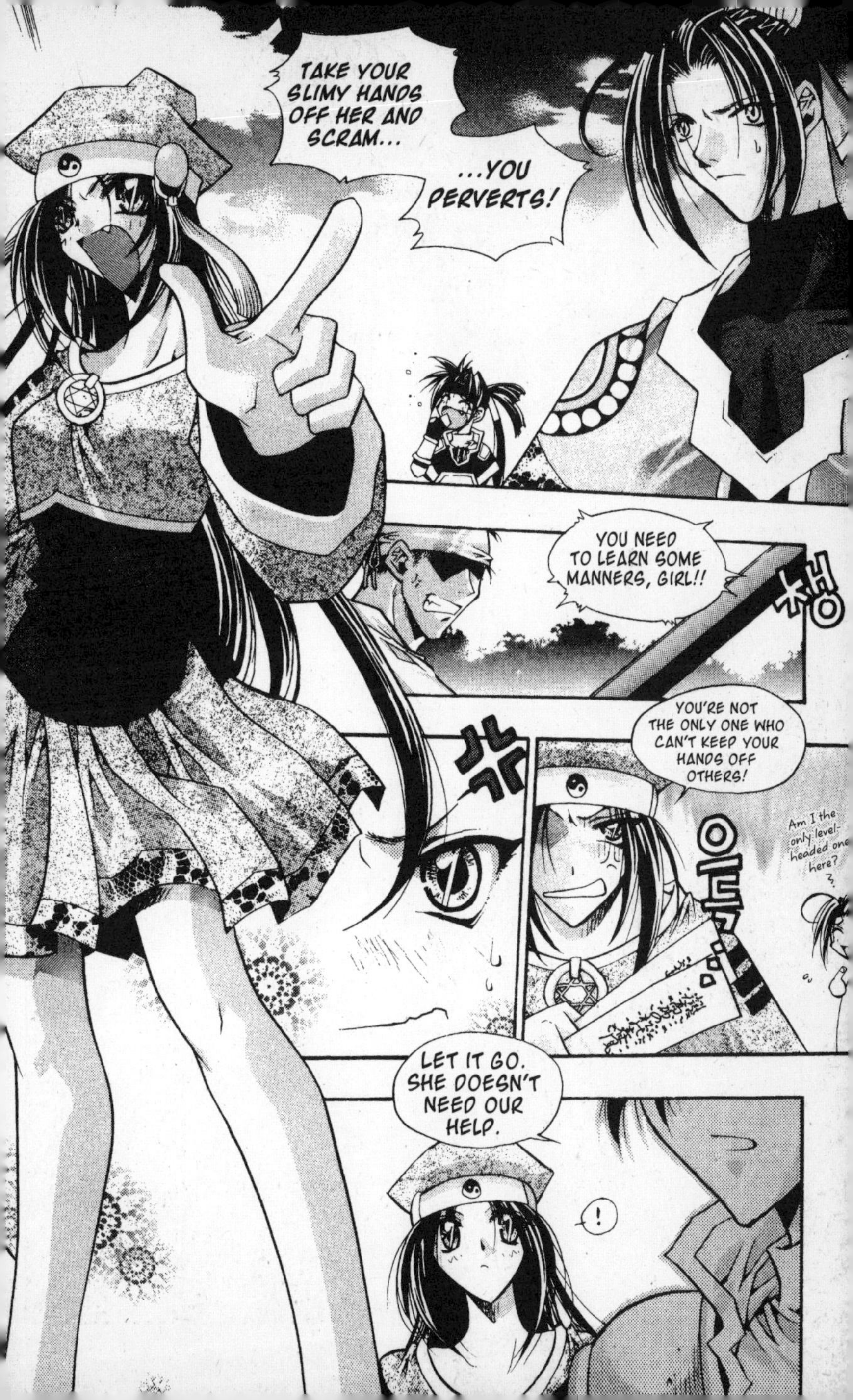
TAKE YOUR SLIMY HANDS OFF HER AND SCRAM...
...YOU PERVERTS!
YOU NEED TO LEARN SOME MANNERS, GIRL!!
YOU'RE NOT THE ONLY ONE WHO CAN'T KEEP YOUR HANDS OFF OTHERS!
Am I the only level-headed one here?
LET IT GO. SHE DOESN'T NEED OUR HELP.
!

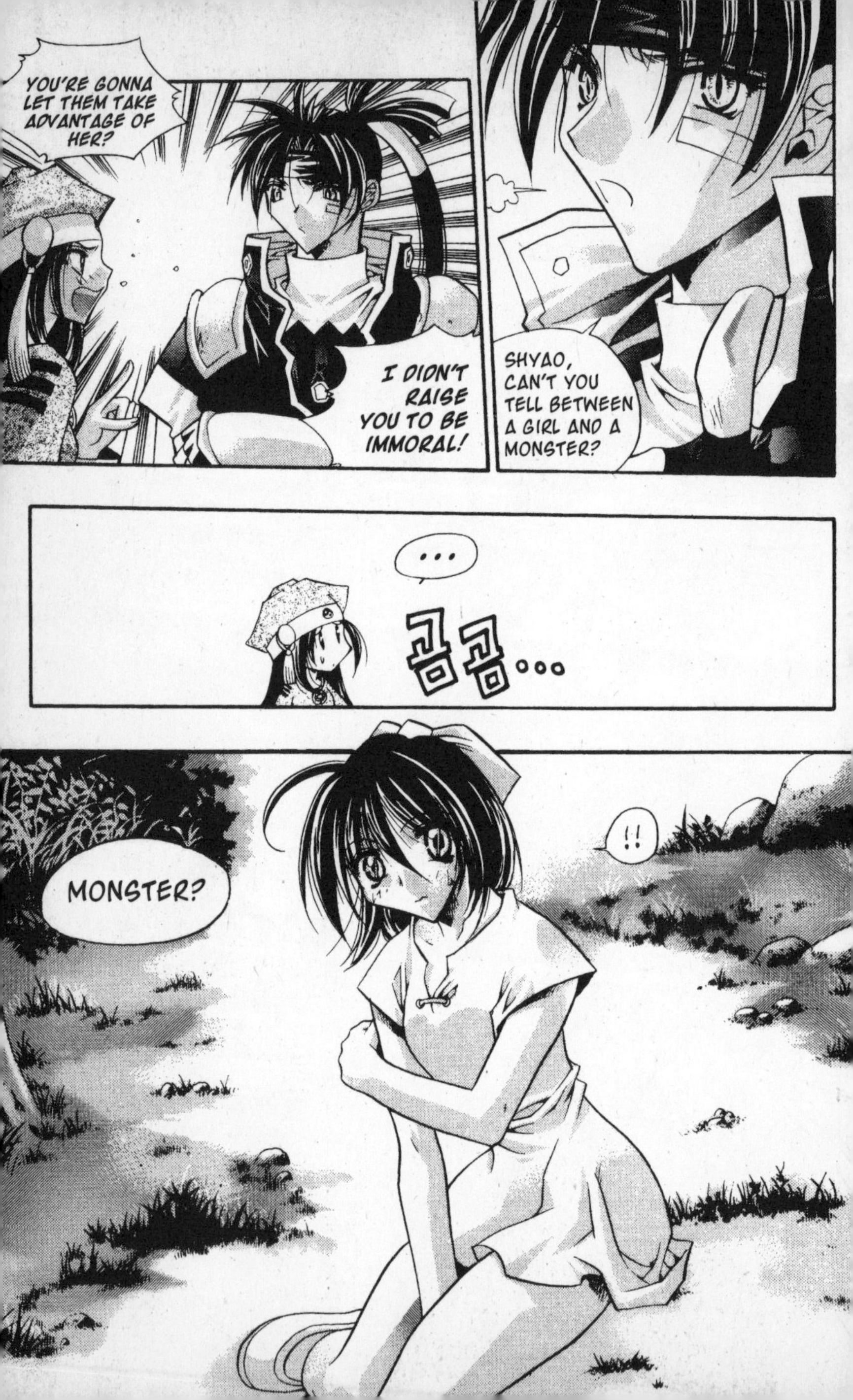
YOU'RE GONNA LET THEM TAKE ADVANTAGE OF HER?
I DIDN'T RAISE YOU TO BE IMMORAL!
SHYAO, CAN'T YOU TELL BETWEEN A GIRL AND A MONSTER?
...
곰곰...
MONSTER?
!!

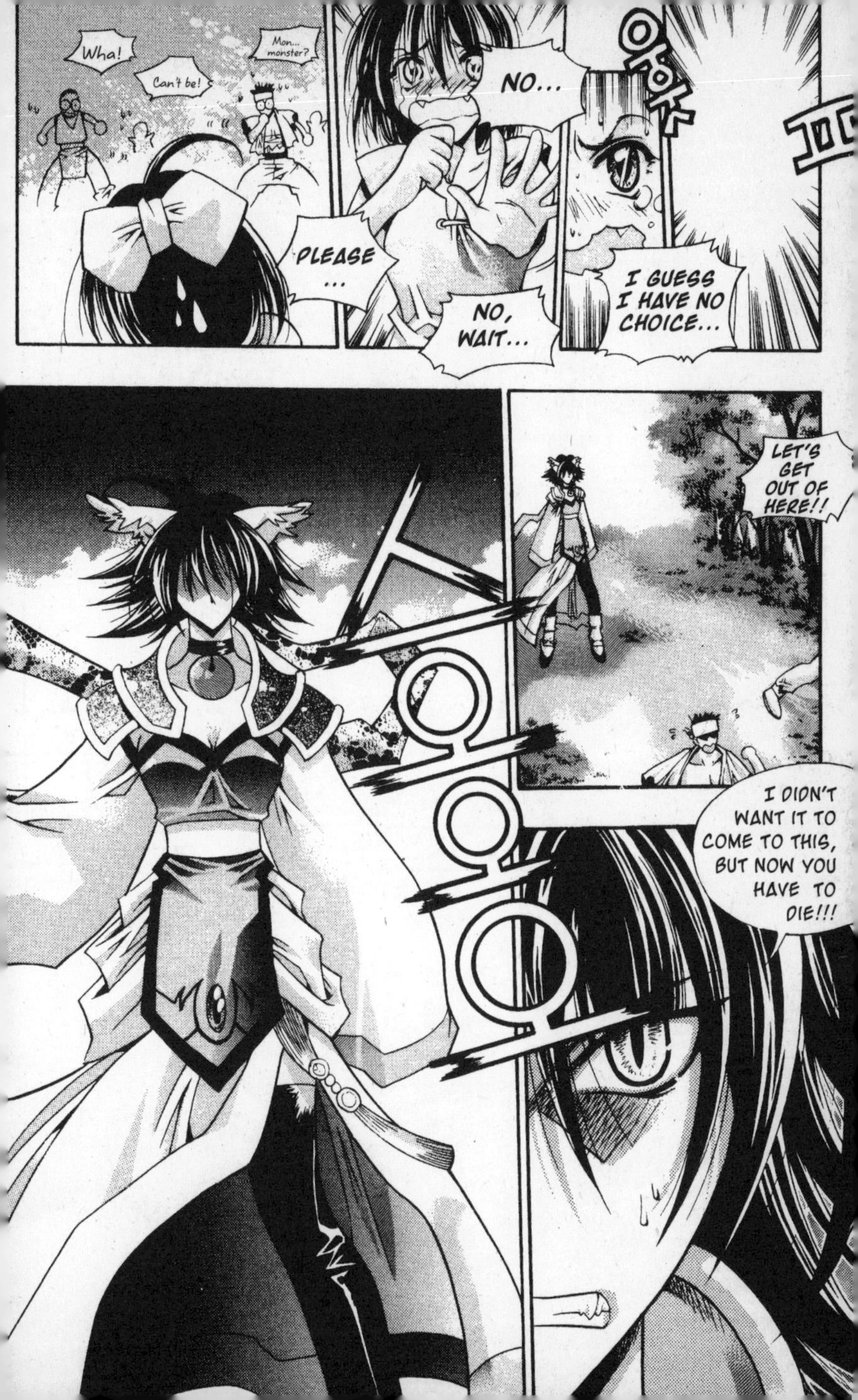
Wha!
Can't be!
Mon... monster?
PLEASE ...
NO...
NO, WAIT...
I GUESS I HAVE NO CHOICE...
LET'S GET OUT OF HERE!!
I DIDN'T WANT IT TO COME TO THIS, BUT NOW YOU HAVE TO DIE!!!

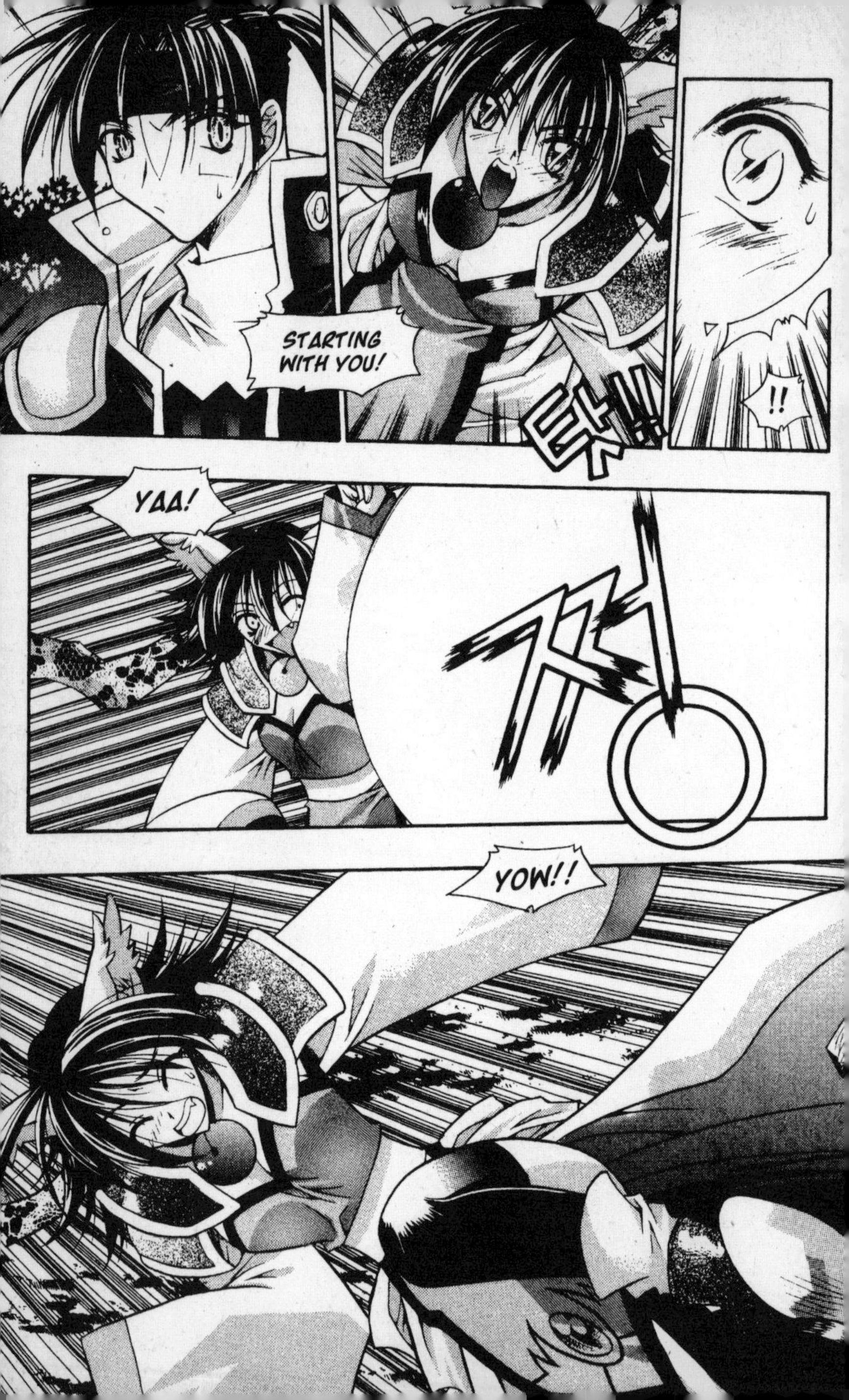
STARTING WITH YOU!
EH!!
!!
YAA!
YOW!!

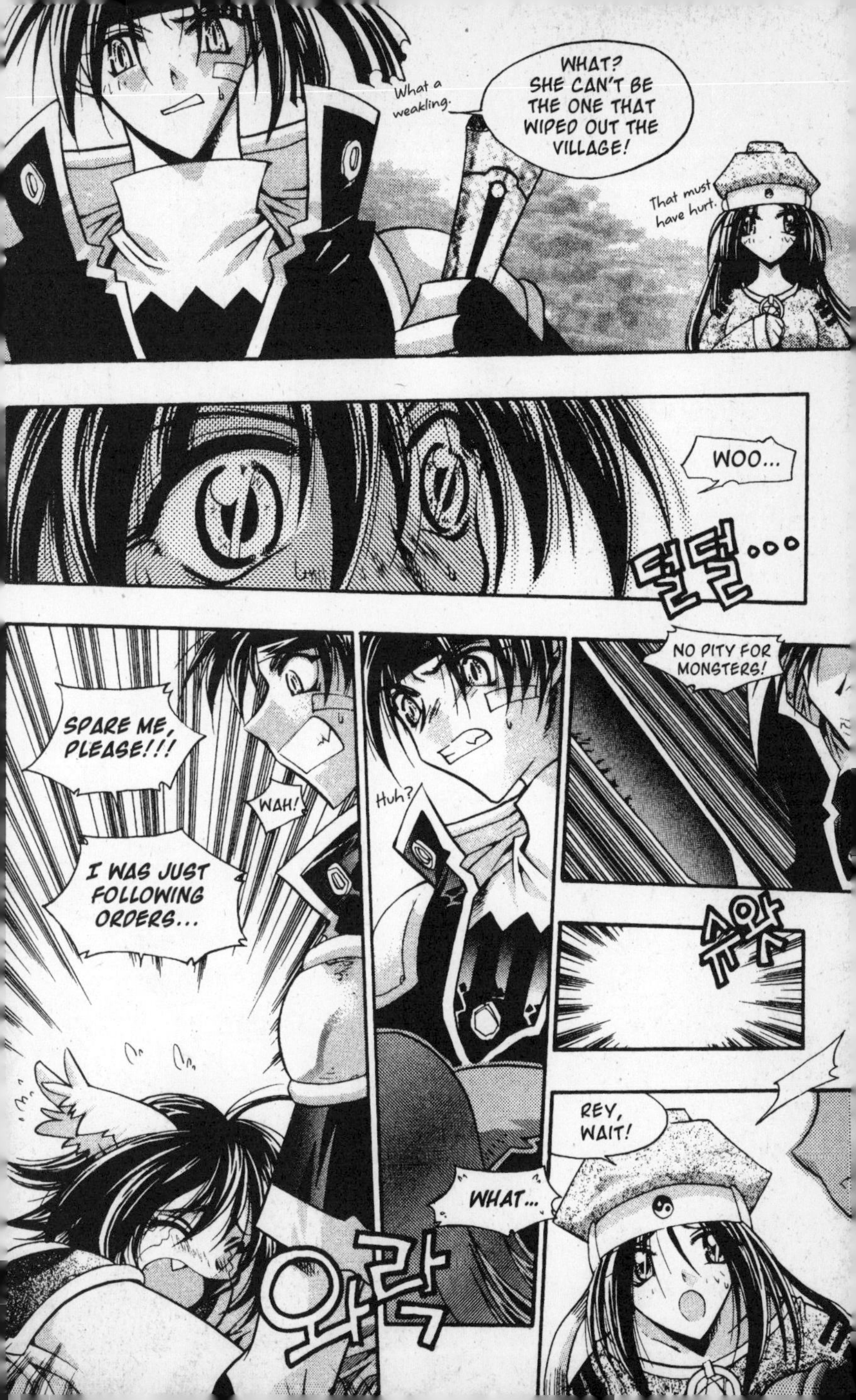
What a weakling.
WHAT? SHE CAN'T BE THE ONE THAT WIPED OUT THE VILLAGE!
That must have hurt.
WOO...
덜덜...
SPARE ME, PLEASE!!!
WAH!
I WAS JUST FOLLOWING ORDERS...
와락
Huh?
WHAT...
NO PITY FOR MONSTERS!
REY, WAIT!

OH! THANK YOU! THANK YOU! THANK YOU!

LET'S HEAR HER OUT FIRST, OKAY?

I THOUGHT HE'D **KILL** ME!

Thank you!

It's okay...

Shyao, she's a monster!

But kind of cute, like a kitten...

HE WON'T HURT YOU.

WILL YOU TELL US WHAT HAPPENED IN THE VILLAGE?

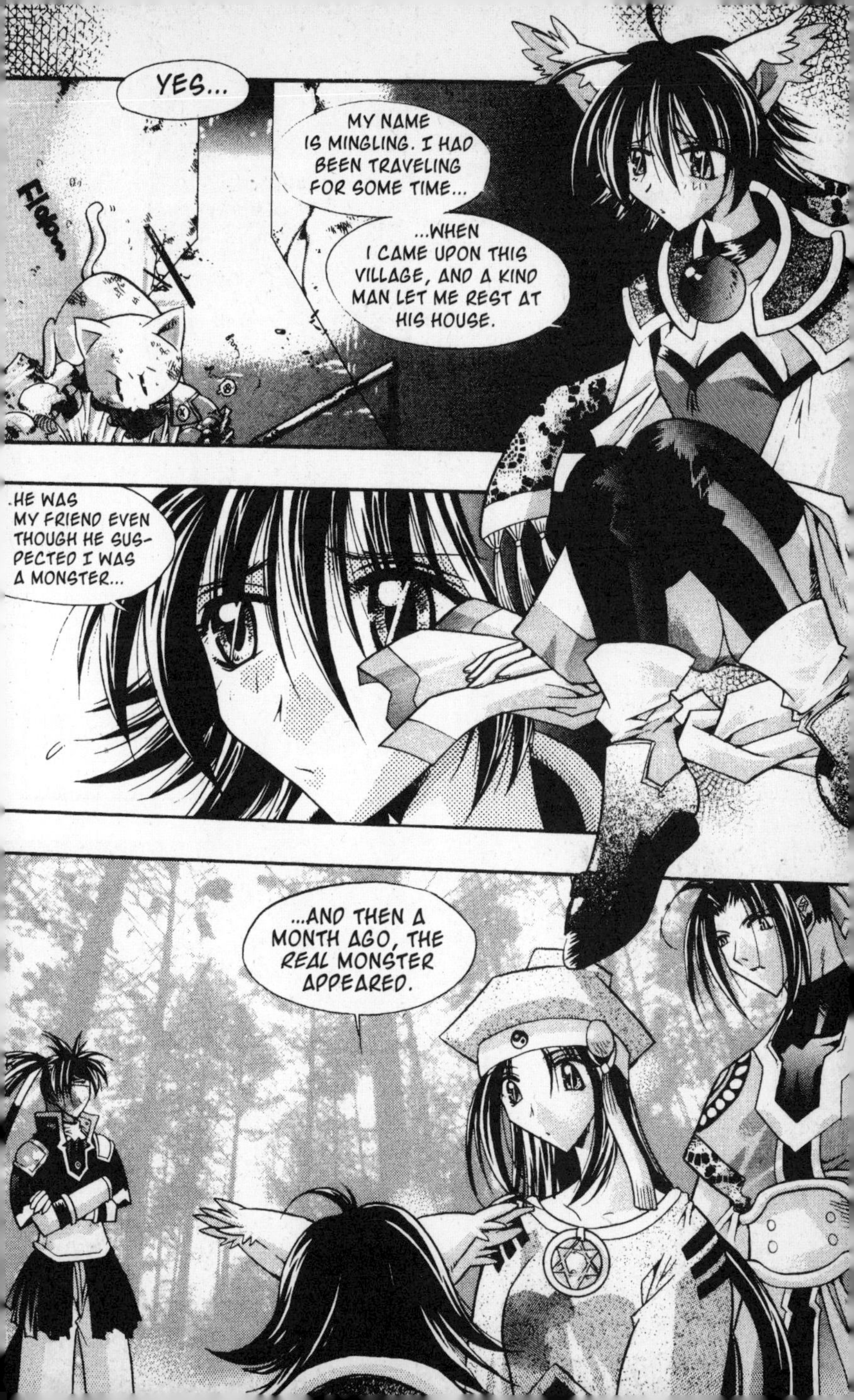
YES...
Flop
MY NAME IS MINGLING. I HAD BEEN TRAVELING FOR SOME TIME...
...WHEN I CAME UPON THIS VILLAGE, AND A KIND MAN LET ME REST AT HIS HOUSE.
...HE WAS MY FRIEND EVEN THOUGH HE SUS-PECTED I WAS A MONSTER...
...AND THEN A MONTH AGO, THE REAL MONSTER APPEARED.

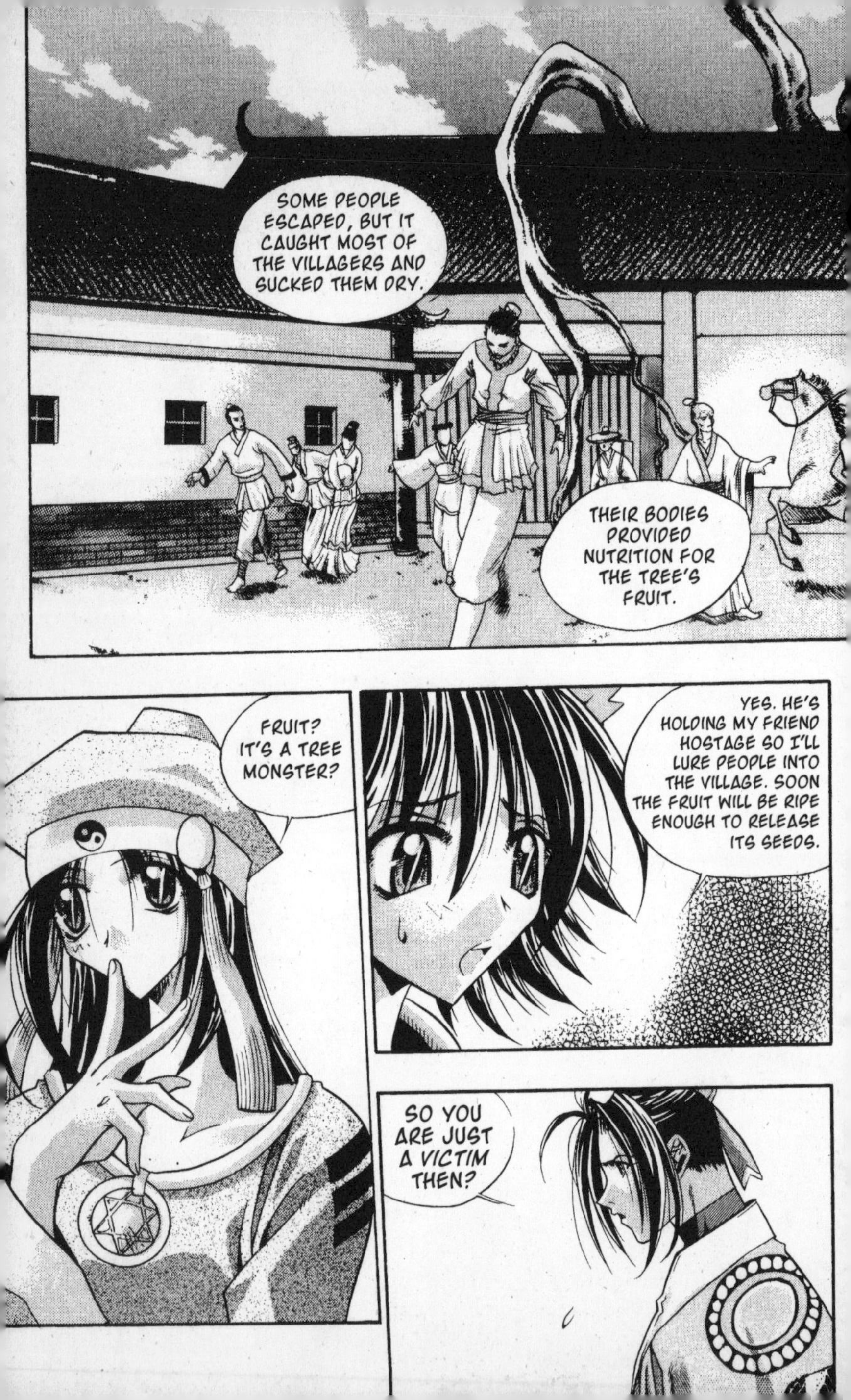
SOME PEOPLE ESCAPED, BUT IT CAUGHT MOST OF THE VILLAGERS AND SUCKED THEM DRY.
THEIR BODIES PROVIDED NUTRITION FOR THE TREE'S FRUIT.
FRUIT? IT'S A TREE MONSTER?
YES. HE'S HOLDING MY FRIEND HOSTAGE SO I'LL LURE PEOPLE INTO THE VILLAGE. SOON THE FRUIT WILL BE RIPE ENOUGH TO RELEASE ITS SEEDS.
SO YOU ARE JUST A VICTIM THEN?

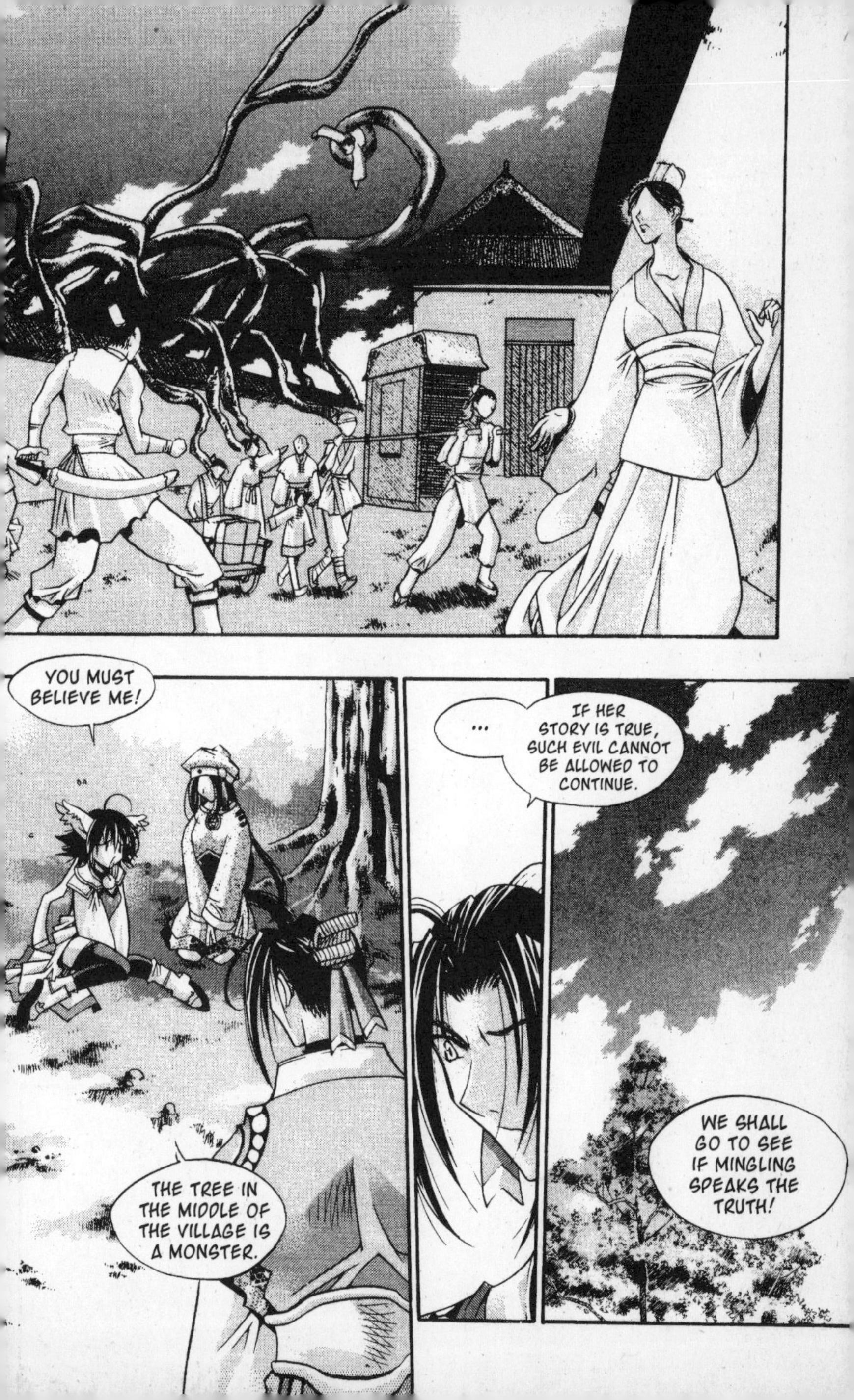
YOU MUST BELIEVE ME!
THE TREE IN THE MIDDLE OF THE VILLAGE IS A MONSTER.
...
IF HER STORY IS TRUE, SUCH EVIL CANNOT BE ALLOWED TO CONTINUE.
WE SHALL GO TO SEE IF MINGLING SPEAKS THE TRUTH!

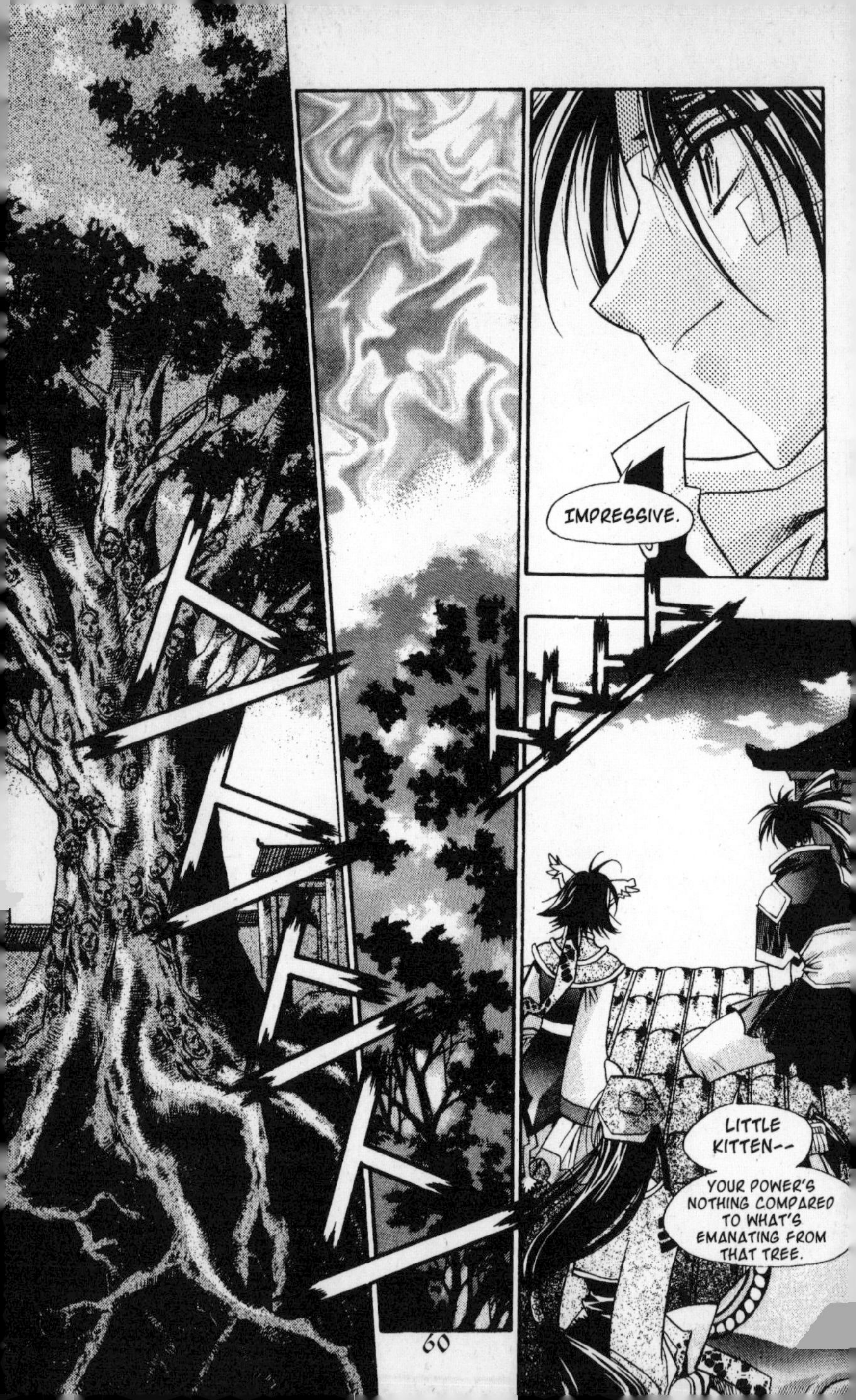
IMPRESSIVE.
LITTLE KITTEN--
YOUR POWER'S NOTHING COMPARED TO WHAT'S EMANATING FROM THAT TREE.

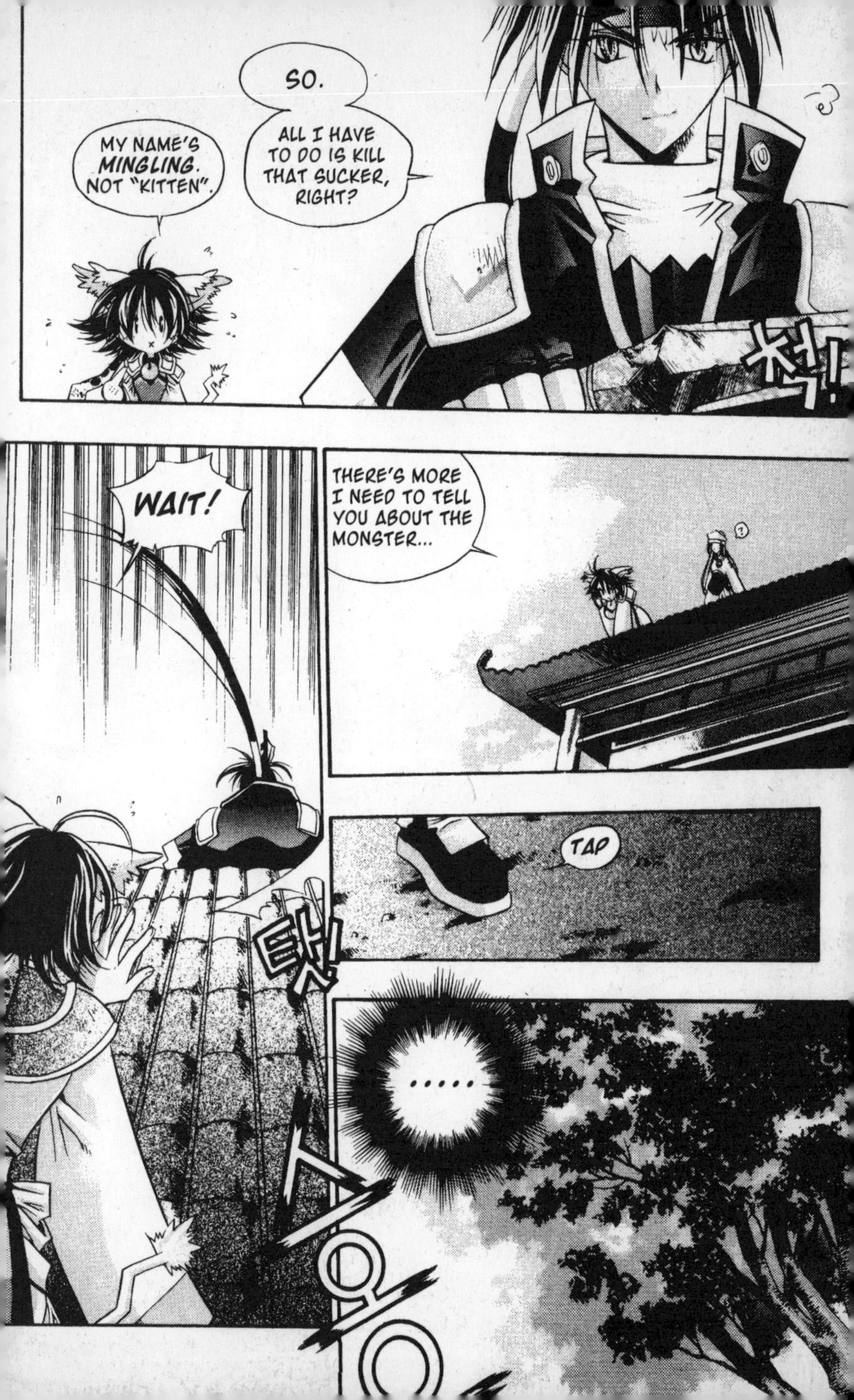
MY NAME'S **MINGLING**. NOT "KITTEN".
SO.
ALL I HAVE TO DO IS KILL THAT SUCKER, RIGHT?
척!
WAIT!
탓!
THERE'S MORE I NEED TO TELL YOU ABOUT THE MONSTER...
TAP
.....

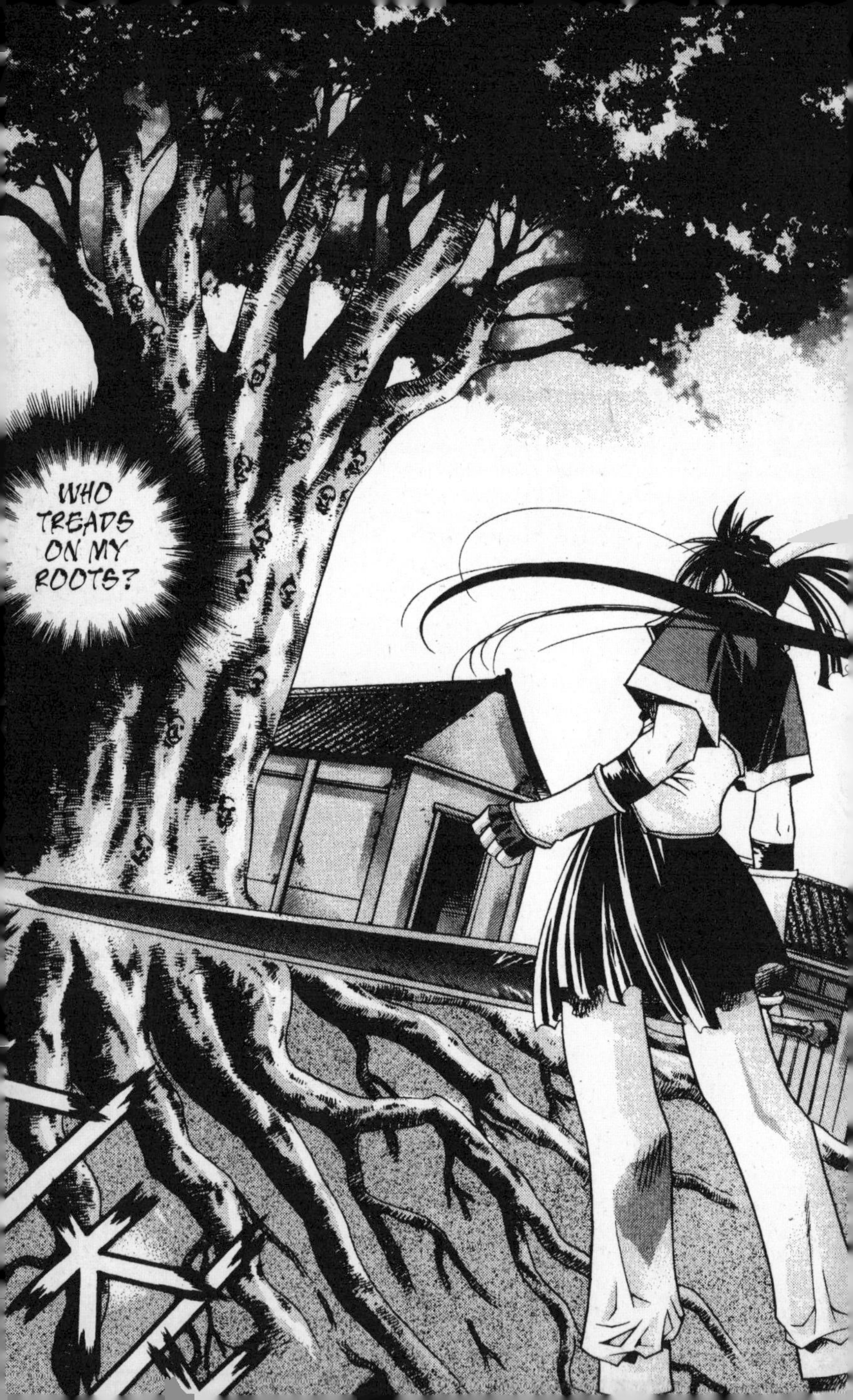
WHO TREADS ON MY ROOTS?

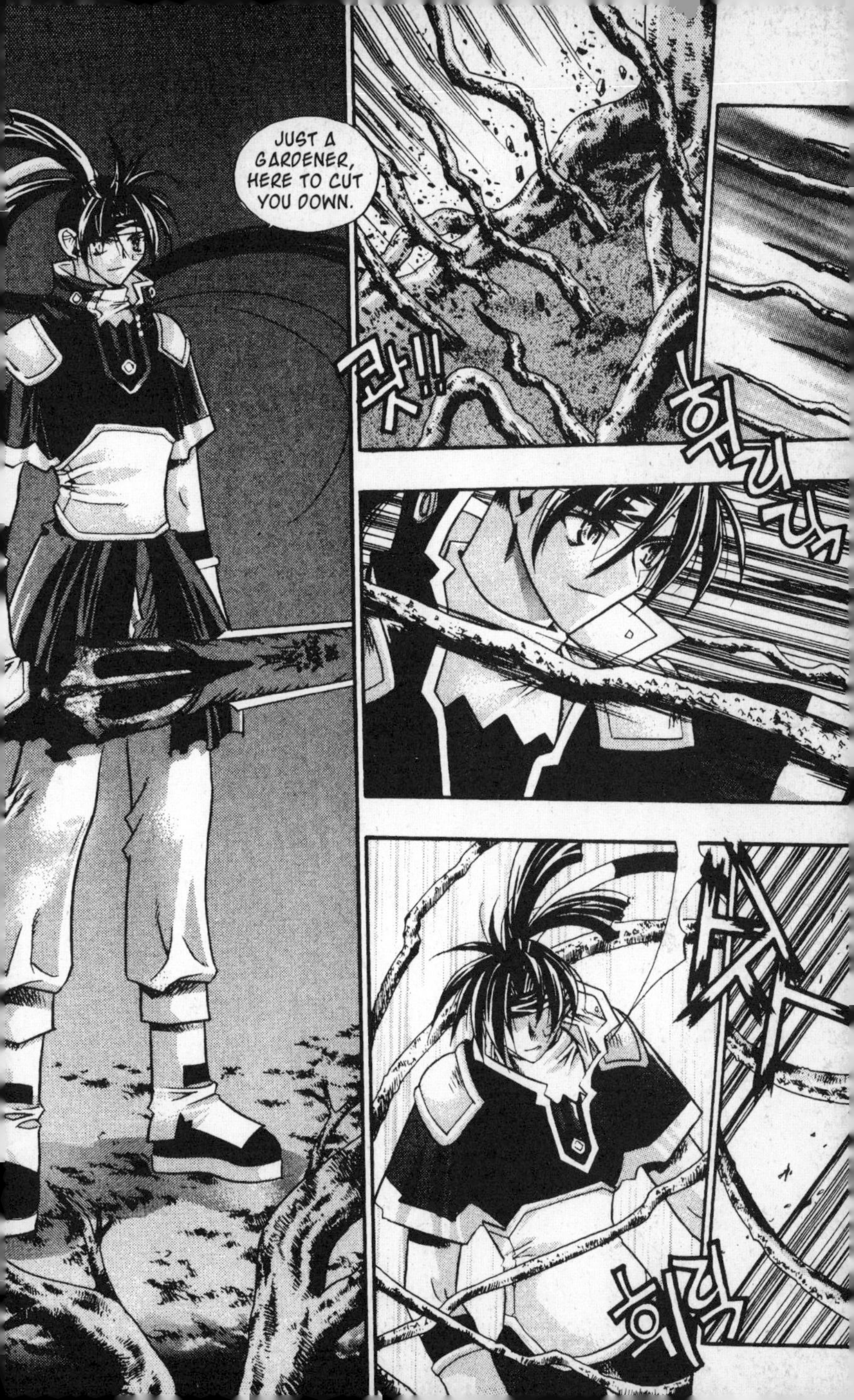
JUST A GARDENER, HERE TO CUT YOU DOWN.

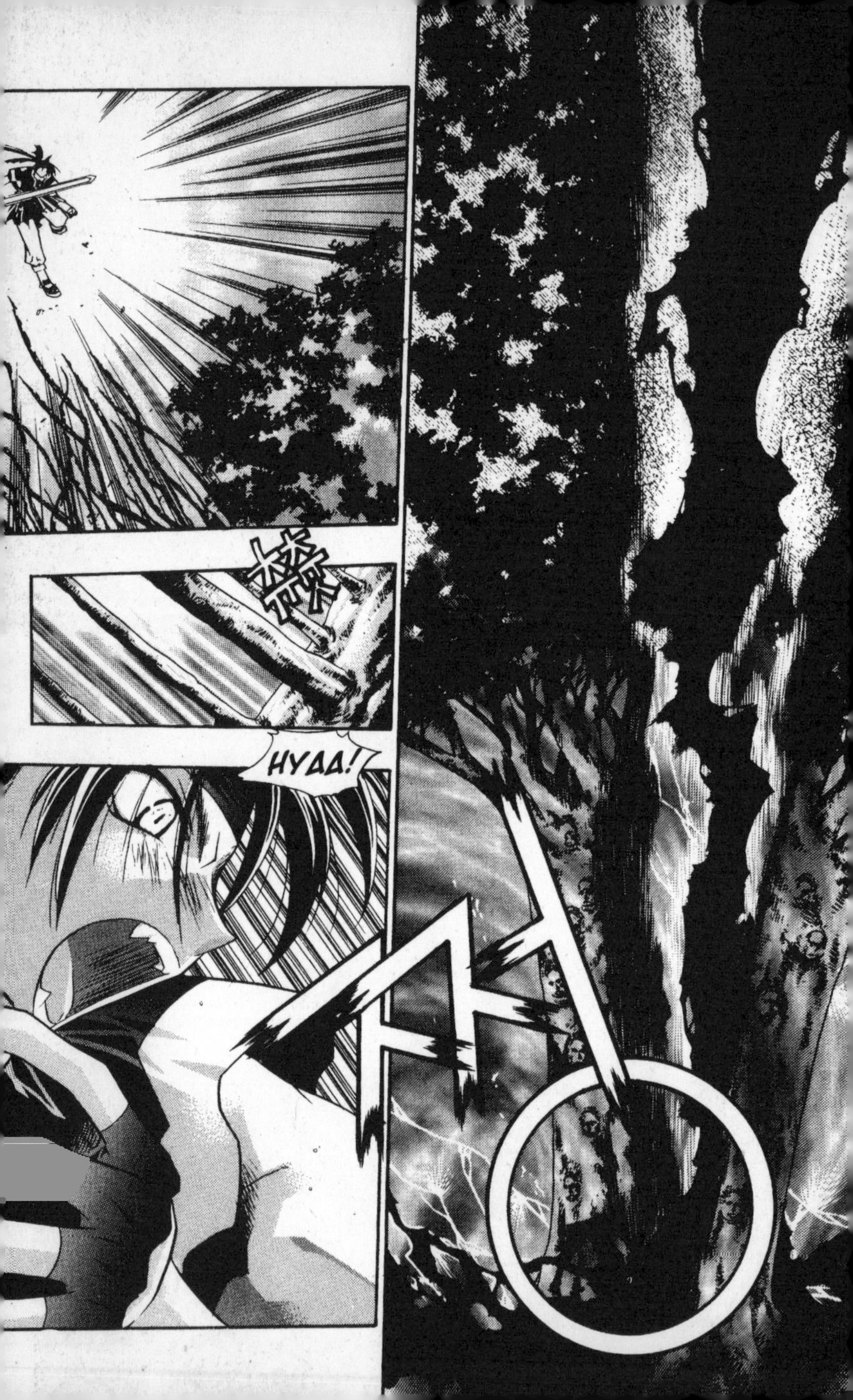
HYAA!

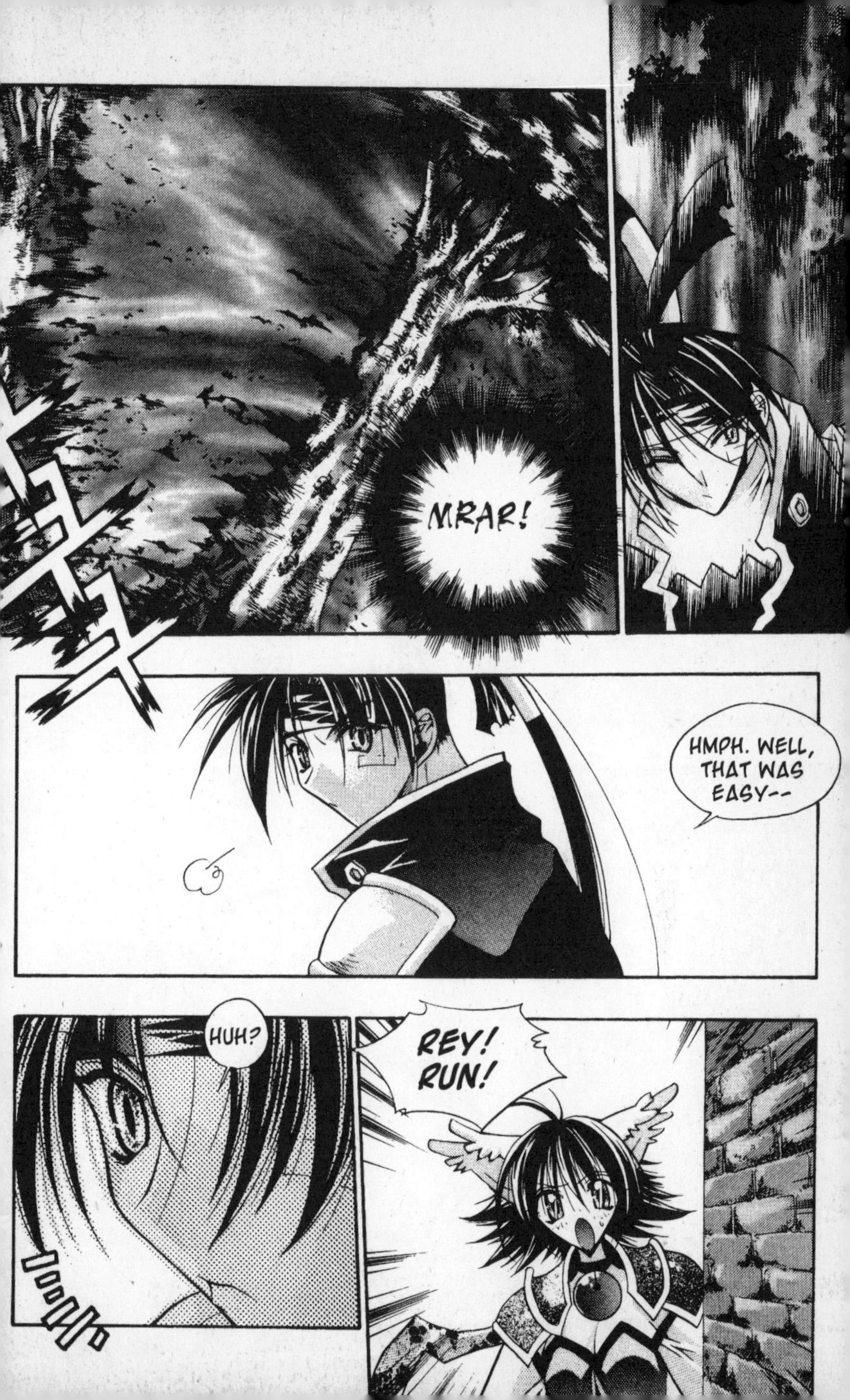
MRAR!
HMPH. WELL, THAT WAS EASY--
HUH?
REY! RUN!

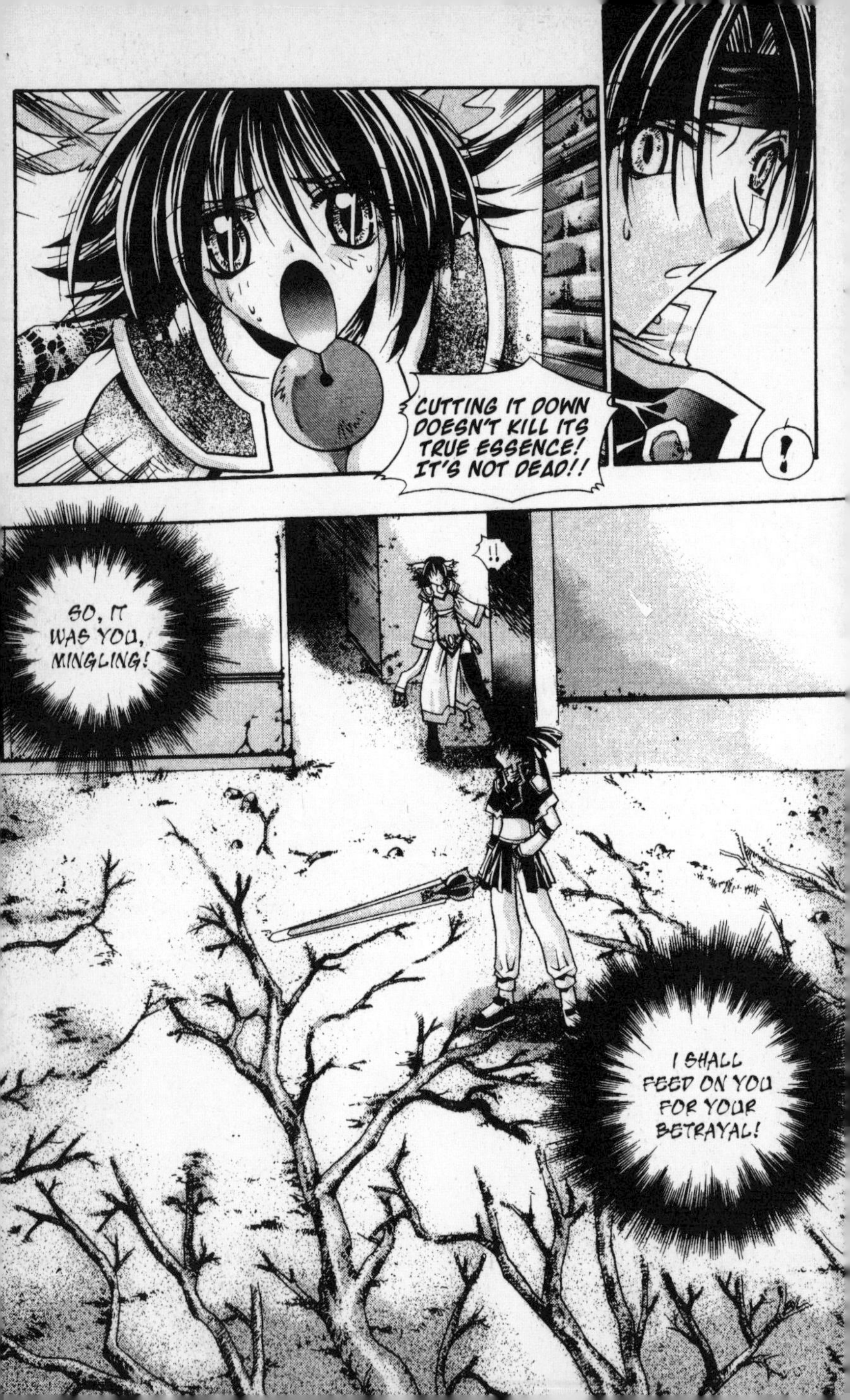
CUTTING IT DOWN DOESN'T KILL ITS TRUE ESSENCE! IT'S NOT DEAD!!
!
SO, IT WAS YOU, MINGLING!
!!
I SHALL FEED ON YOU FOR YOUR BETRAYAL!

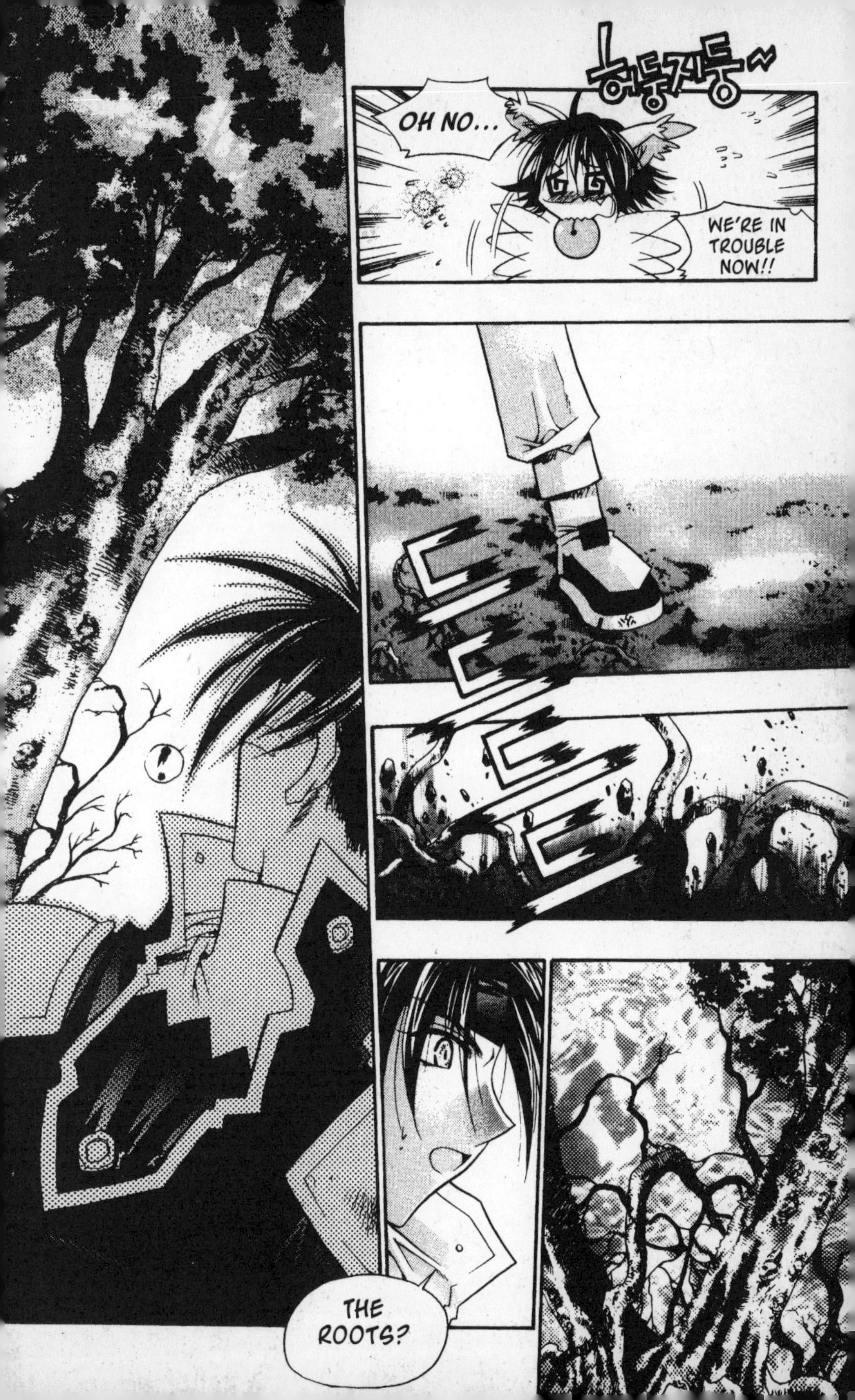

허둥지둥~
OH NO...
WE'RE IN TROUBLE NOW!!
THE ROOTS?

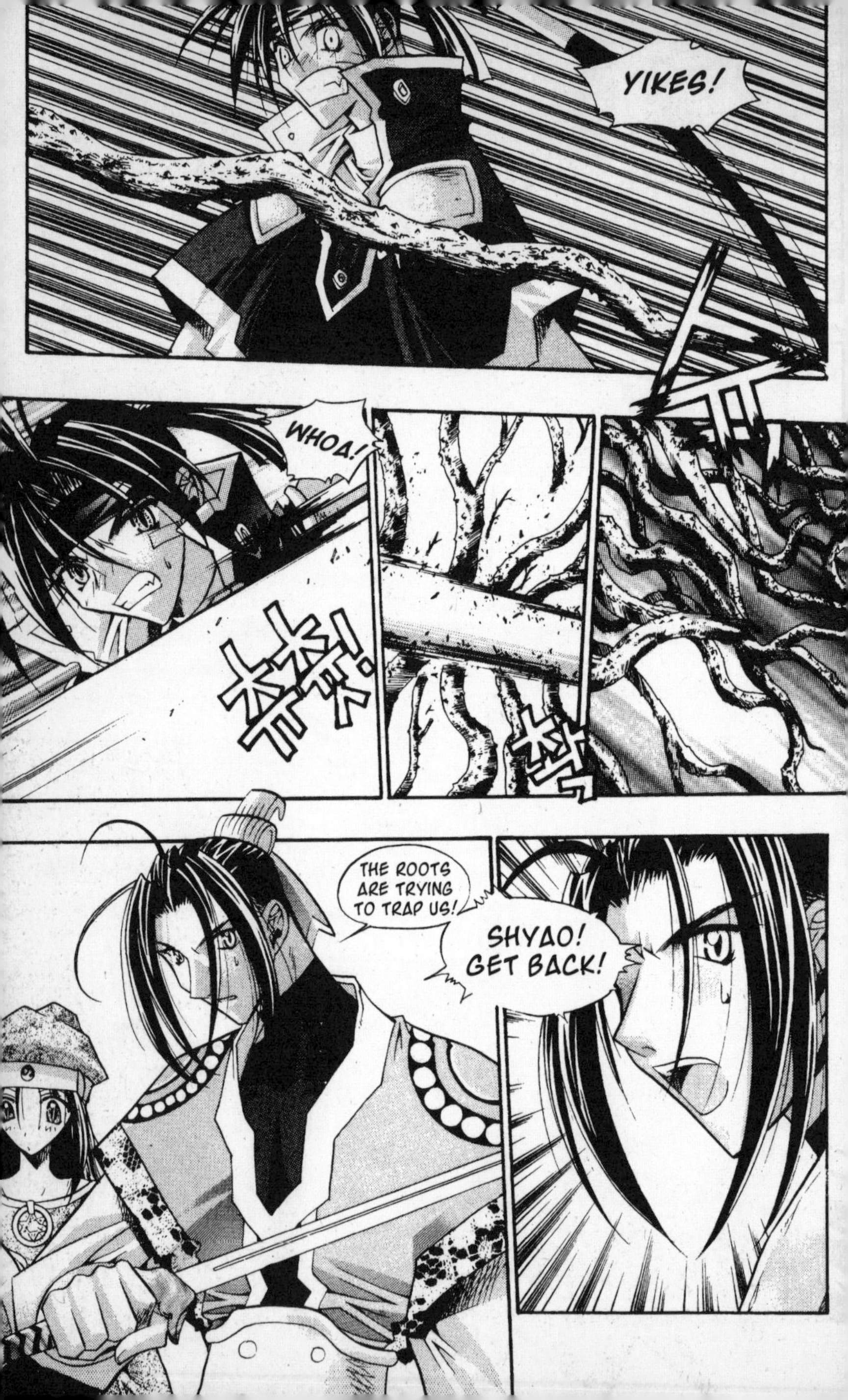
YIKES!
WHOA!
THE ROOTS ARE TRYING TO TRAP US!
SHYAO! GET BACK!

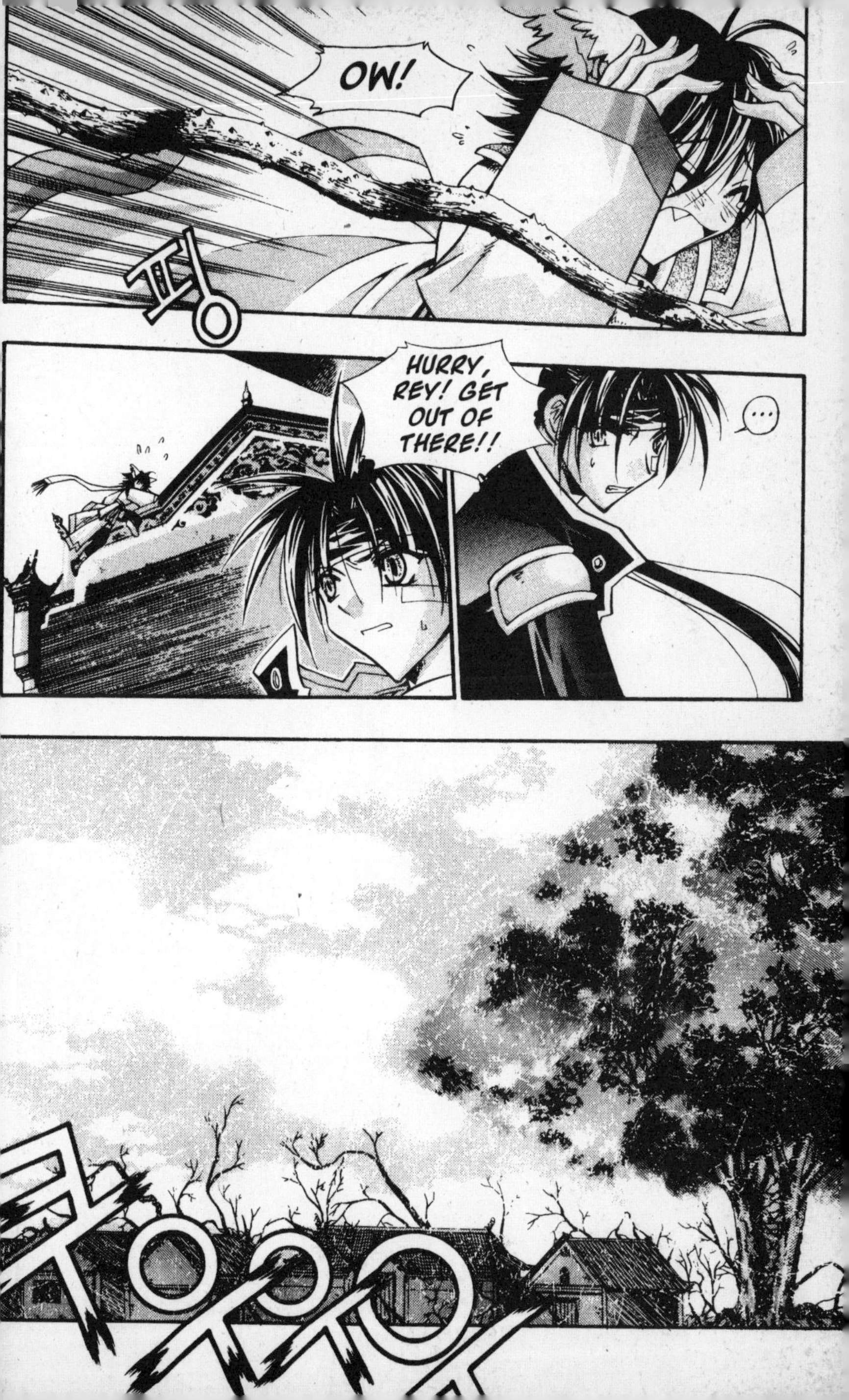
OW!
HURRY, REY! GET OUT OF THERE!!
...

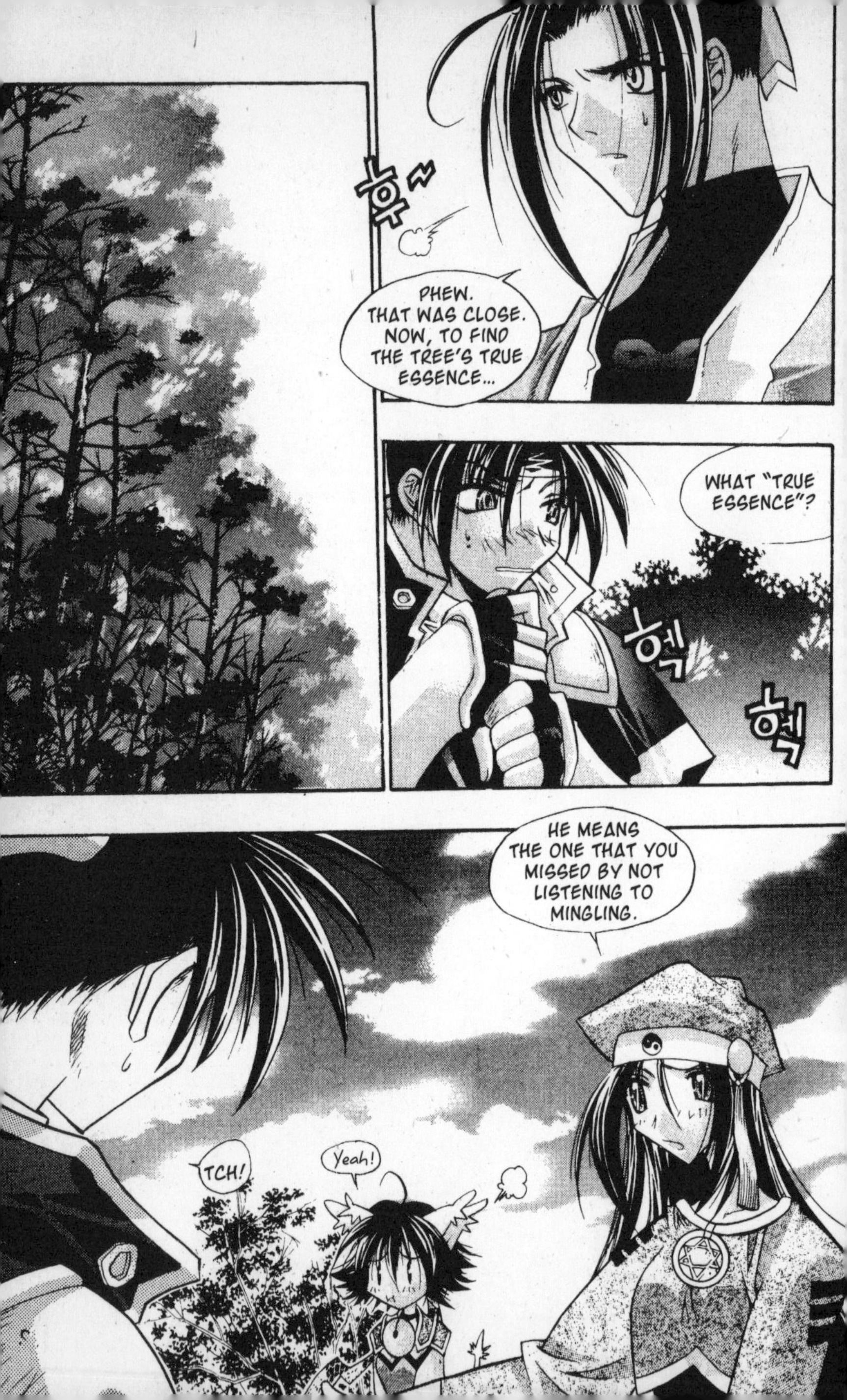
후~
PHEW. THAT WAS CLOSE. NOW, TO FIND THE TREE'S TRUE ESSENCE...
WHAT "TRUE ESSENCE"?
헥
헥
HE MEANS THE ONE THAT YOU MISSED BY NOT LISTENING TO MINGLING.
TCH!
Yeah!

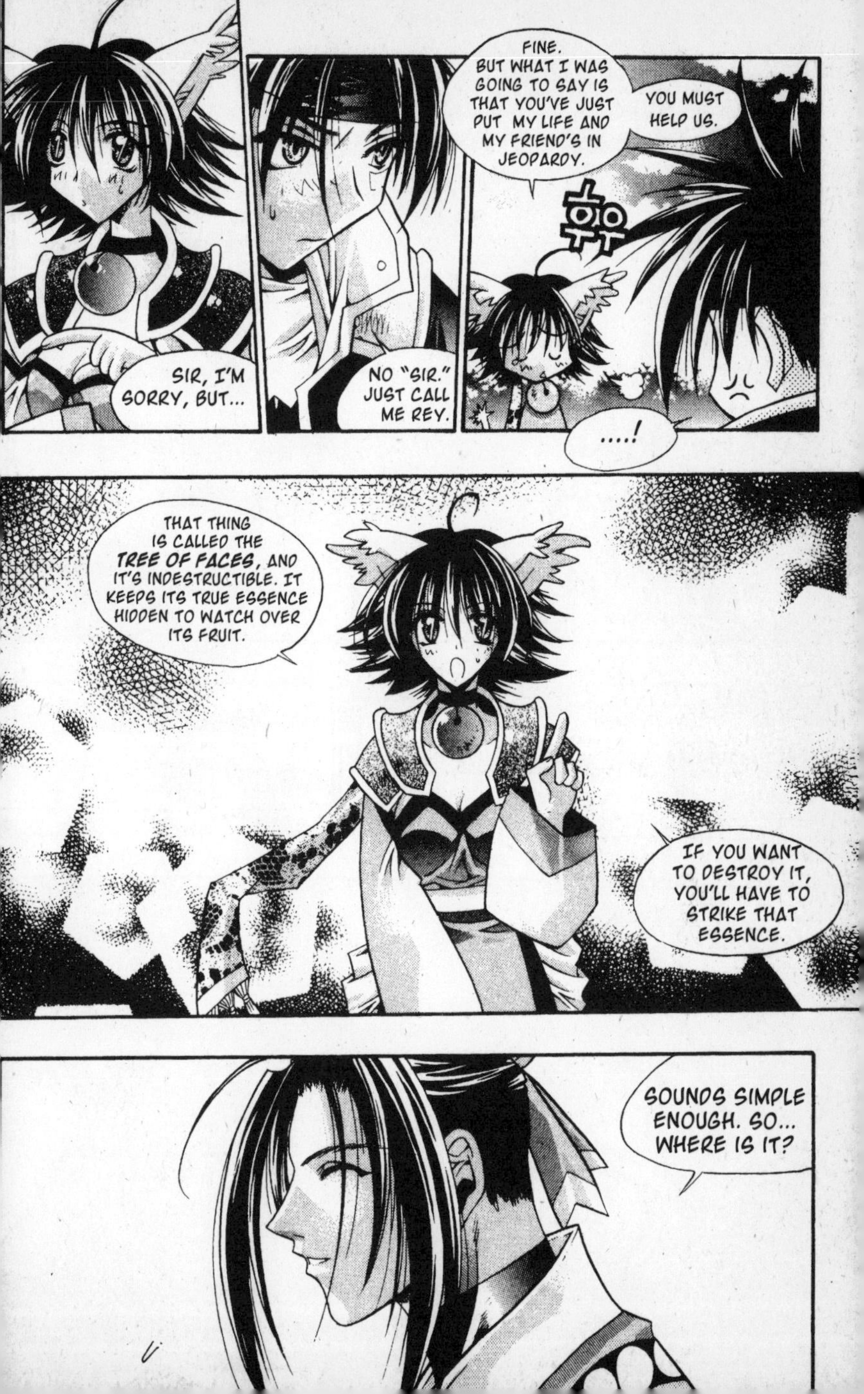
SIR, I'M SORRY, BUT...
NO "SIR." JUST CALL ME REY.
FINE. BUT WHAT I WAS GOING TO SAY IS THAT YOU'VE JUST PUT MY LIFE AND MY FRIEND'S IN JEOPARDY.
YOU MUST HELP US.
....!
THAT THING IS CALLED THE **TREE OF FACES**, AND IT'S INDESTRUCTIBLE. IT KEEPS ITS TRUE ESSENCE HIDDEN TO WATCH OVER ITS FRUIT.
IF YOU WANT TO DESTROY IT, YOU'LL HAVE TO STRIKE THAT ESSENCE.
SOUNDS SIMPLE ENOUGH. SO... WHERE IS IT?

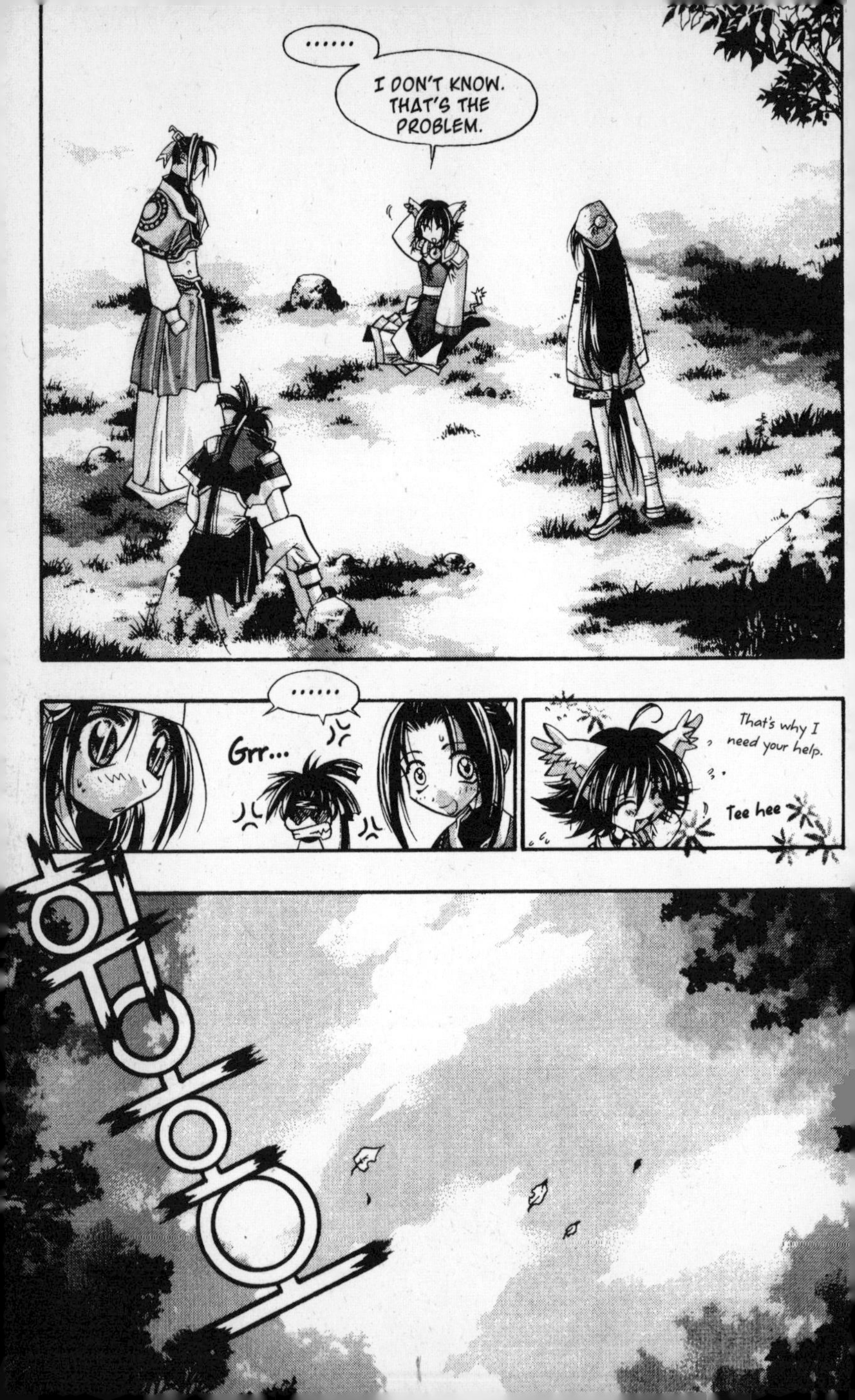
......
I DON'T KNOW. THAT'S THE PROBLEM.
......
Grr...
That's why I need your help.
Tee hee

Chronicle 8
A Decoy

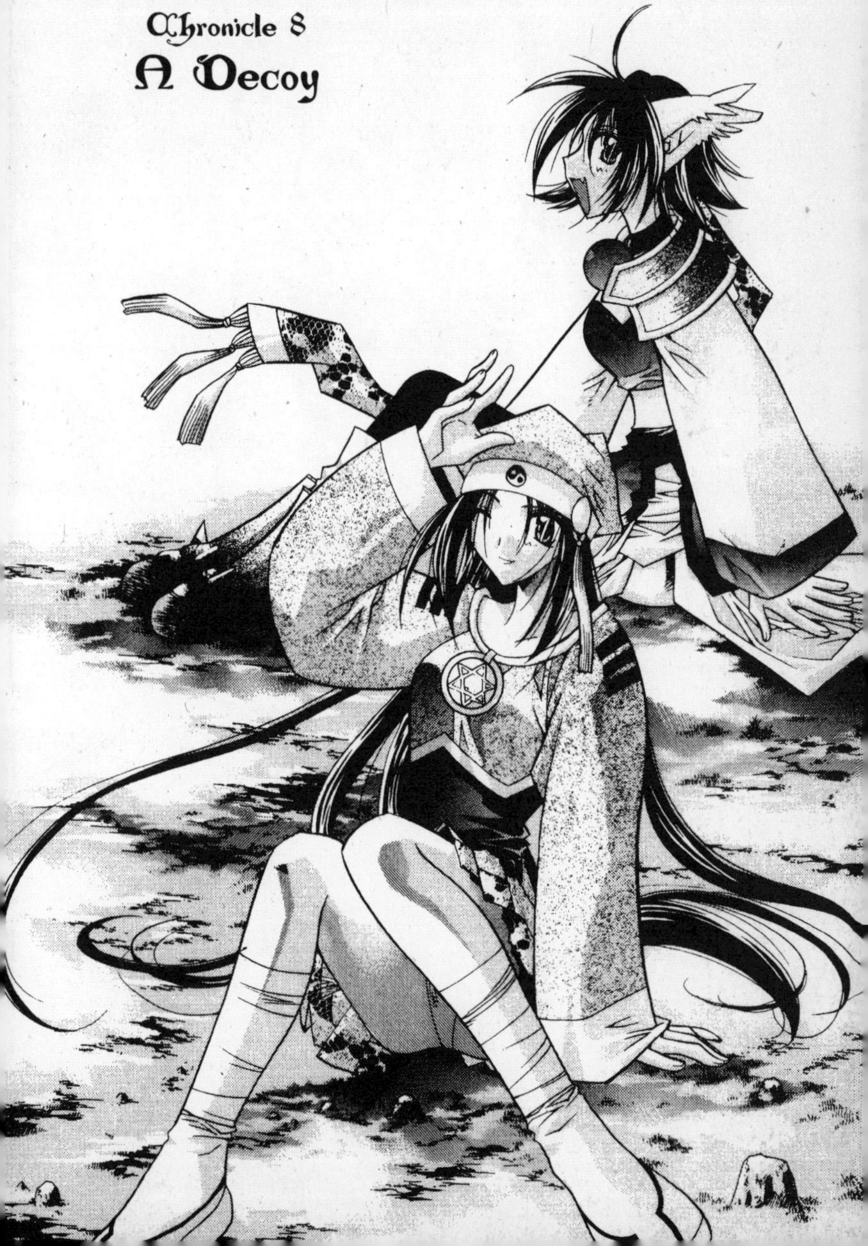

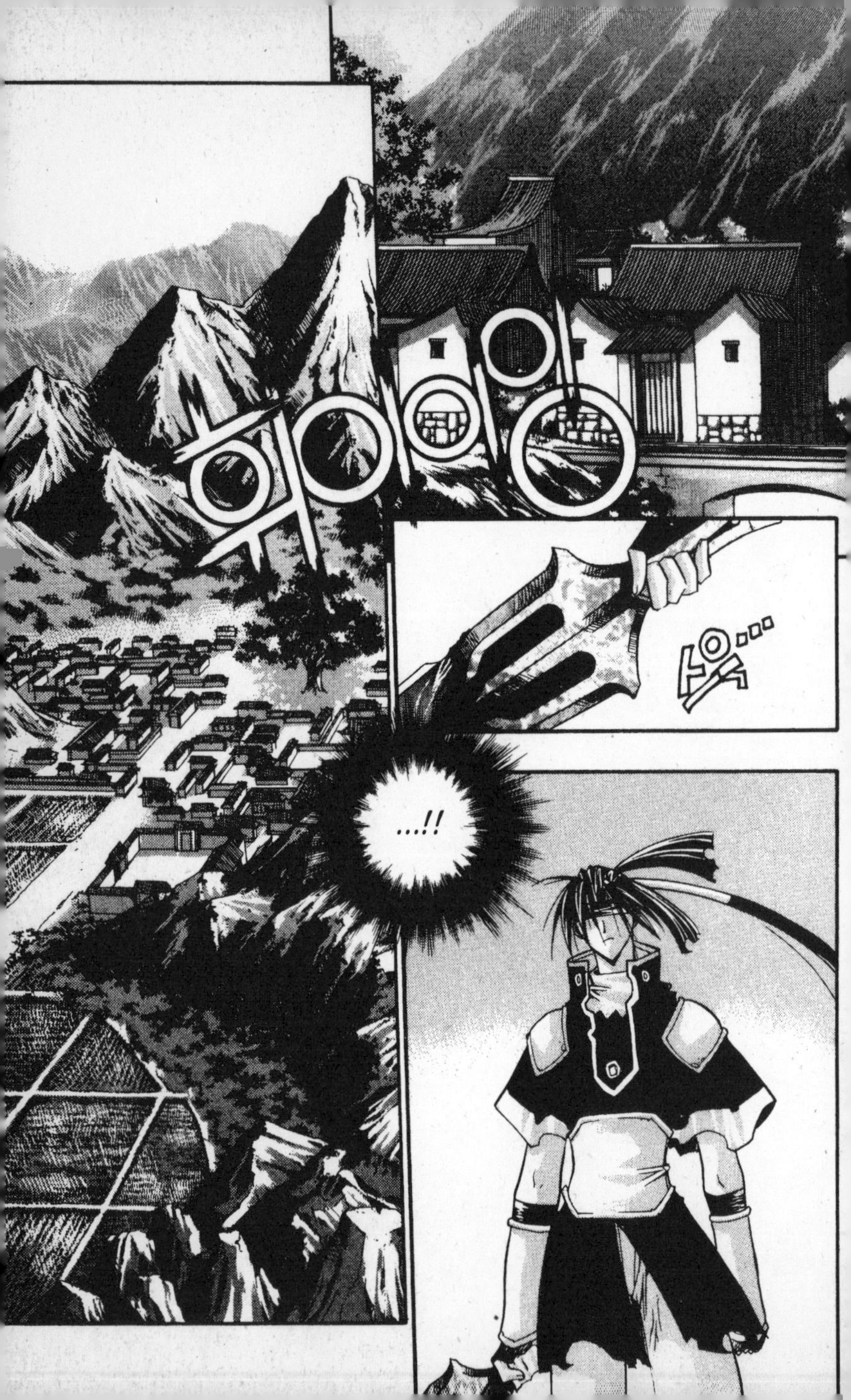
...!!

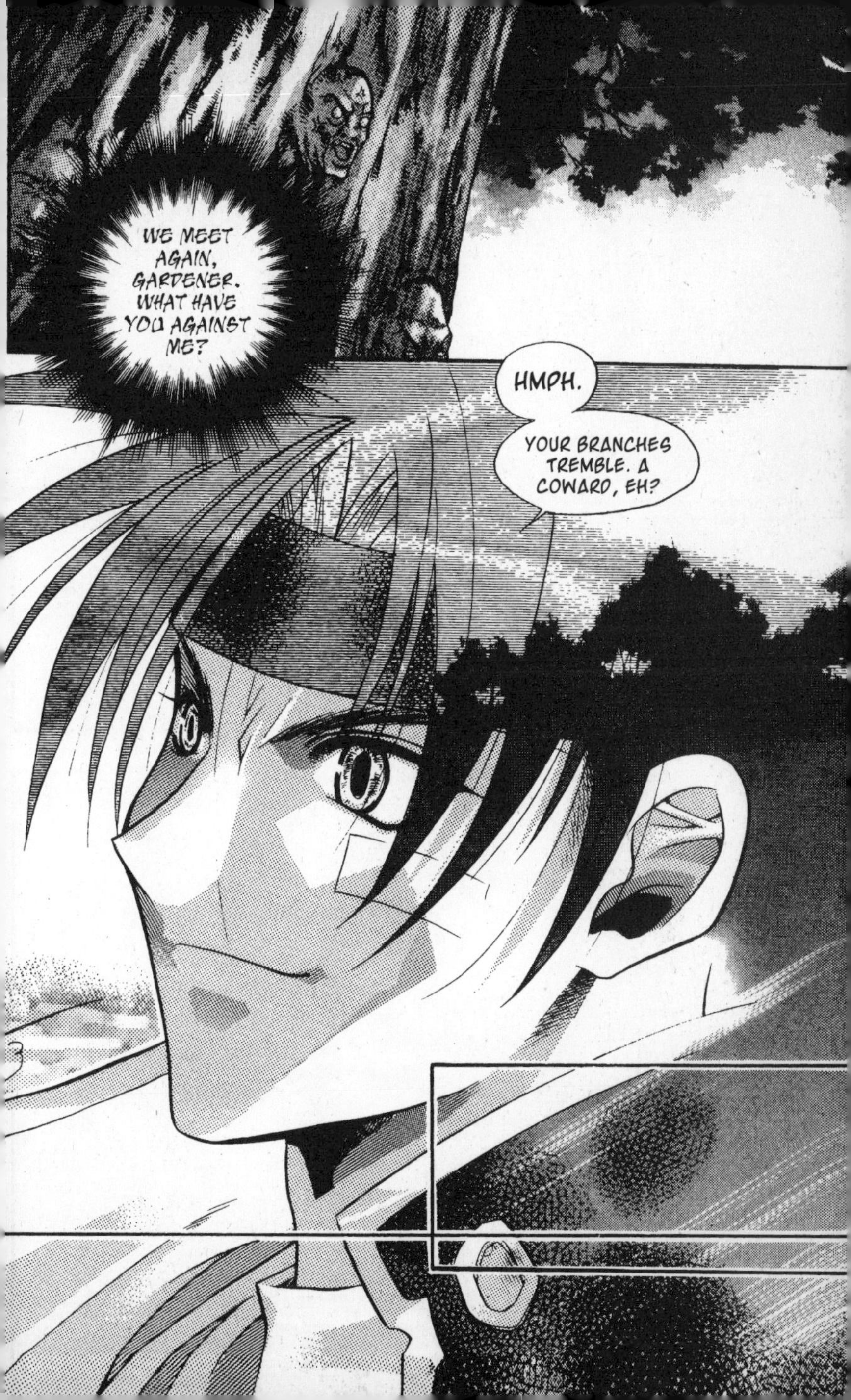
WE MEET AGAIN, GARDENER. WHAT HAVE YOU AGAINST ME?
HMPH.
YOUR BRANCHES TREMBLE. A COWARD, EH?

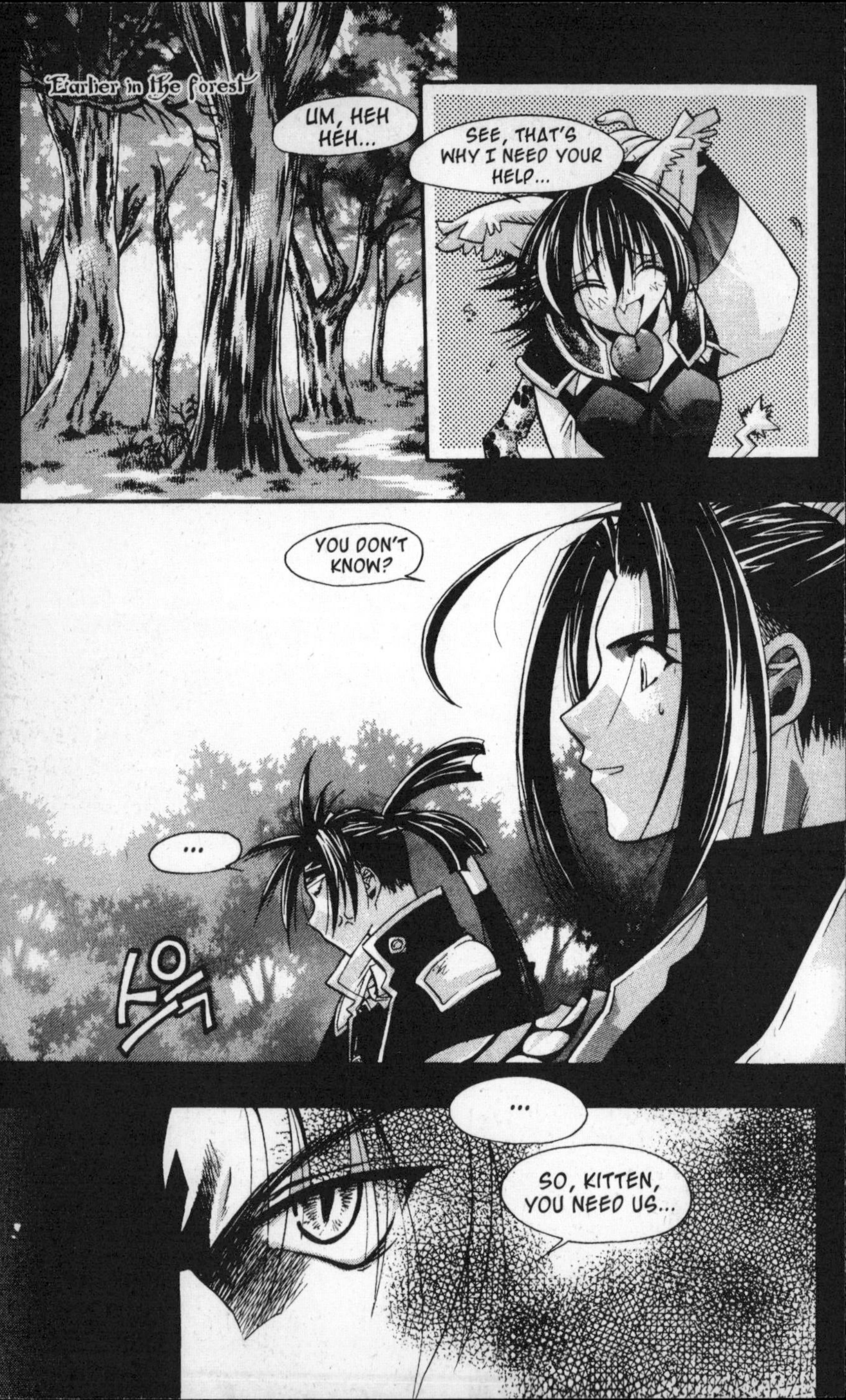
Earlier in the forest
UM, HEH HEH...
SEE, THAT'S WHY I NEED YOUR HELP...
YOU DON'T KNOW?
...
...
SO, KITTEN, YOU NEED US...

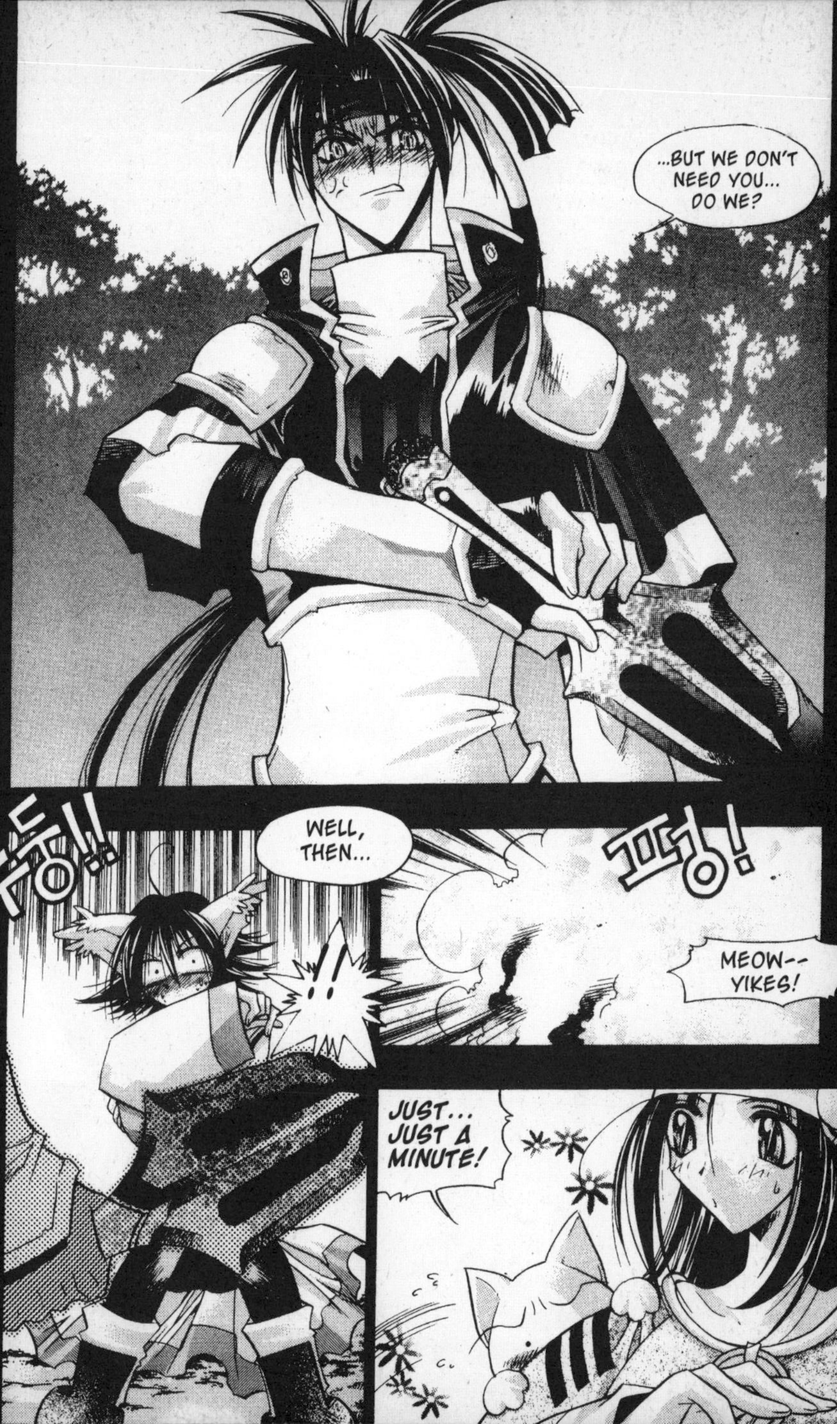
...BUT WE DON'T NEED YOU... DO WE?
둥!!
WELL, THEN...
펑!
MEOW-- YIKES!
JUST... JUST A MINUTE!

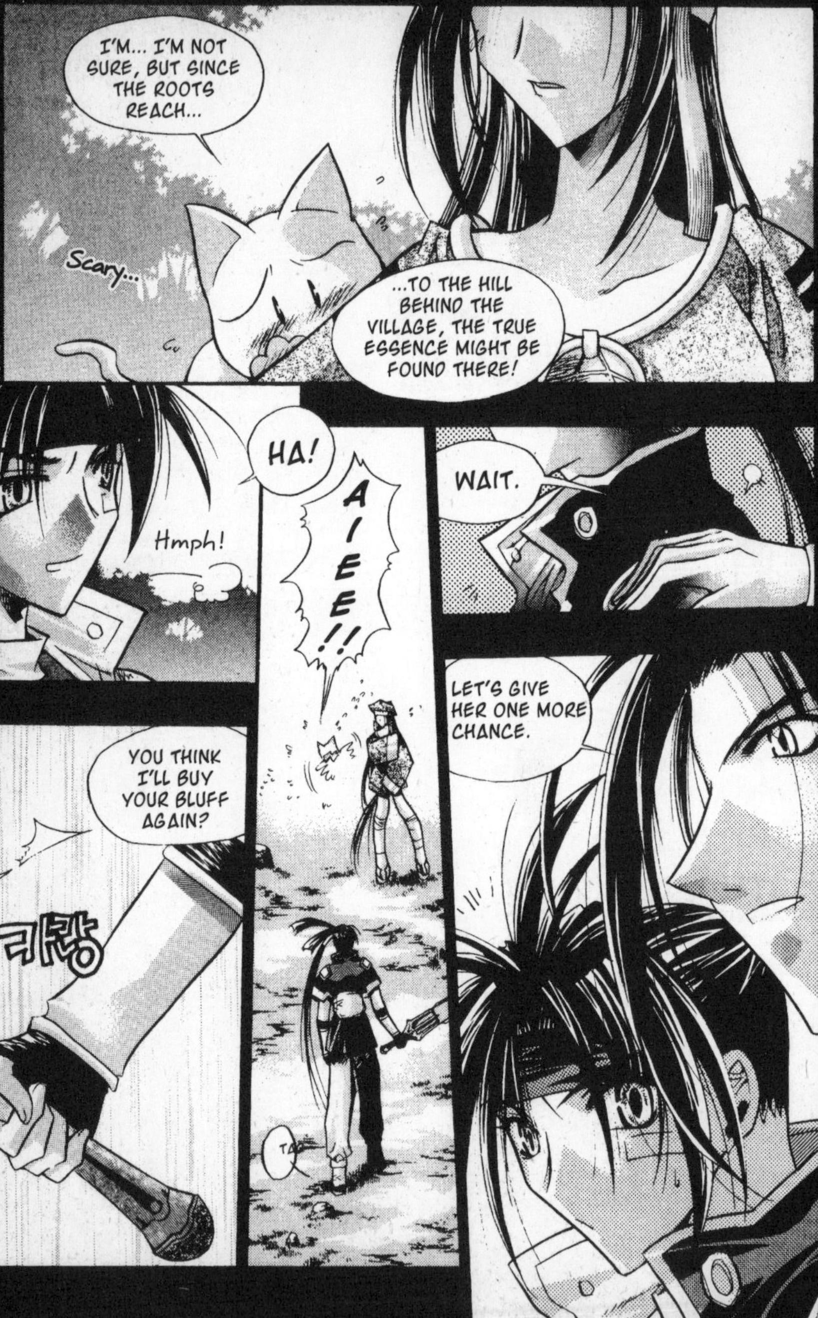
I'M... I'M NOT SURE, BUT SINCE THE ROOTS REACH...
Scary...
...TO THE HILL BEHIND THE VILLAGE, THE TRUE ESSENCE MIGHT BE FOUND THERE!
Hmph!
YOU THINK I'LL BUY YOUR BLUFF AGAIN?
HA!
AIEE!!
TA
WAIT.
LET'S GIVE HER ONE MORE CHANCE.

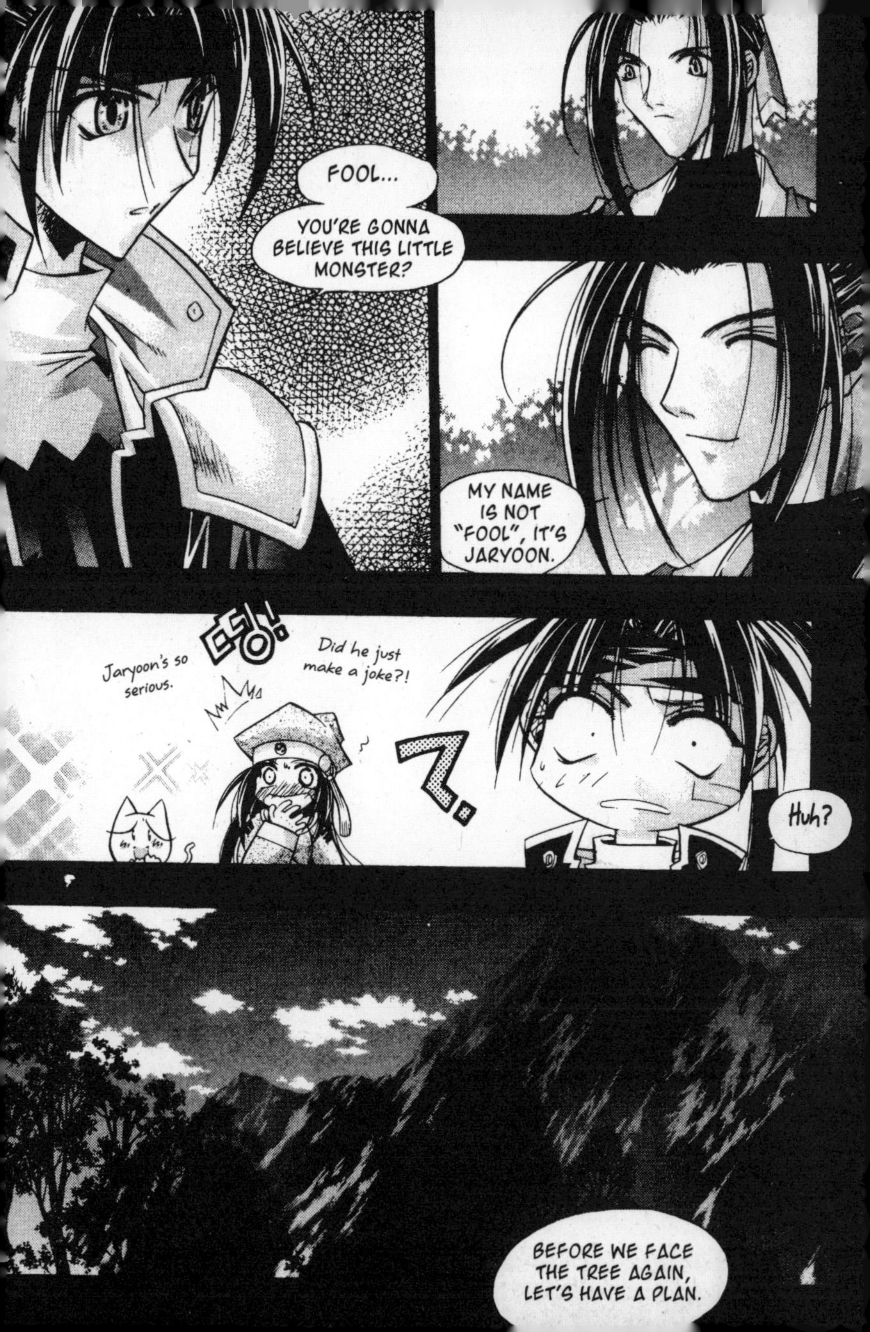
FOOL...
YOU'RE GONNA BELIEVE THIS LITTLE MONSTER?
MY NAME IS NOT "FOOL", IT'S JARYOON.
Jaryoon's so serious.
Did he just make a joke?!
?
Huh?
BEFORE WE FACE THE TREE AGAIN, LET'S HAVE A PLAN.

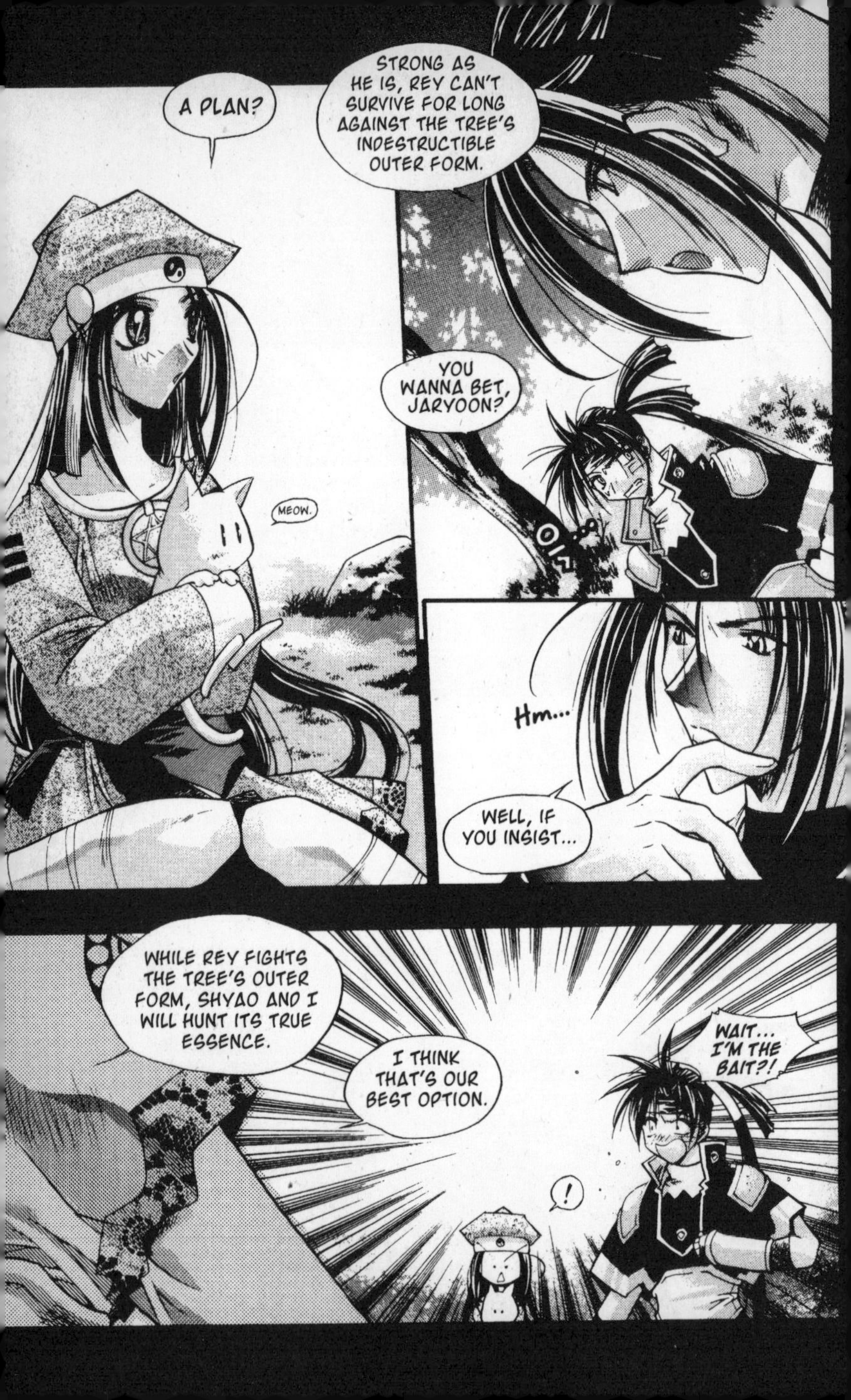
A PLAN?
MEOW.
STRONG AS HE IS, REY CAN'T SURVIVE FOR LONG AGAINST THE TREE'S INDESTRUCTIBLE OUTER FORM.
YOU WANNA BET, JARYOON?
Hm...
WELL, IF YOU INSIST...
WHILE REY FIGHTS THE TREE'S OUTER FORM, SHYAO AND I WILL HUNT ITS TRUE ESSENCE.
I THINK THAT'S OUR BEST OPTION.
WAIT... I'M THE BAIT?!
!

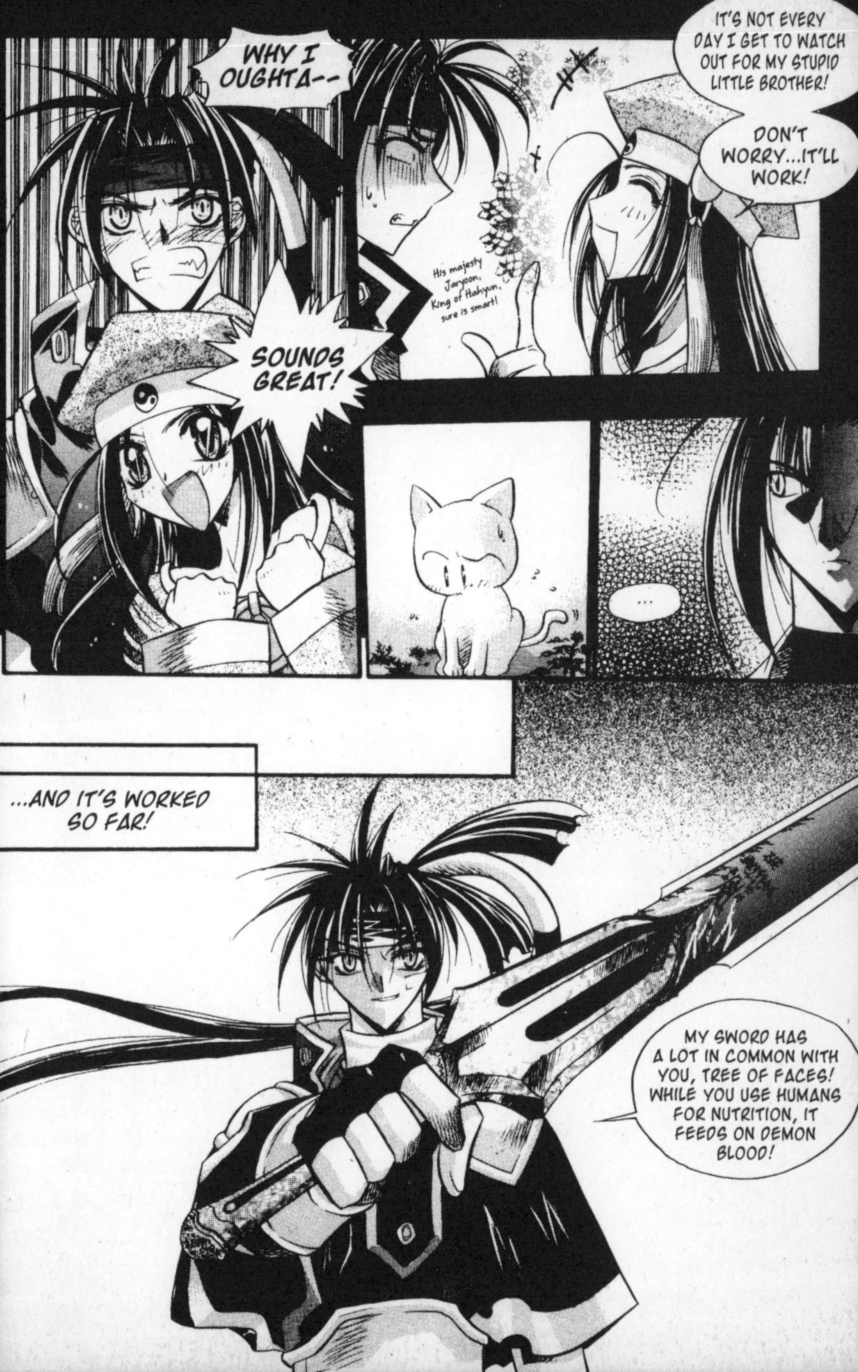
WHY I OUGHTA--
SOUNDS GREAT!
IT'S NOT EVERY DAY I GET TO WATCH OUT FOR MY STUPID LITTLE BROTHER!
DON'T WORRY...IT'LL WORK!
His majesty Jaryoon, King of Hahyun, sure is smart!
...
...AND IT'S WORKED SO FAR!
MY SWORD HAS A LOT IN COMMON WITH YOU, TREE OF FACES! WHILE YOU USE HUMANS FOR NUTRITION, IT FEEDS ON DEMON BLOOD!

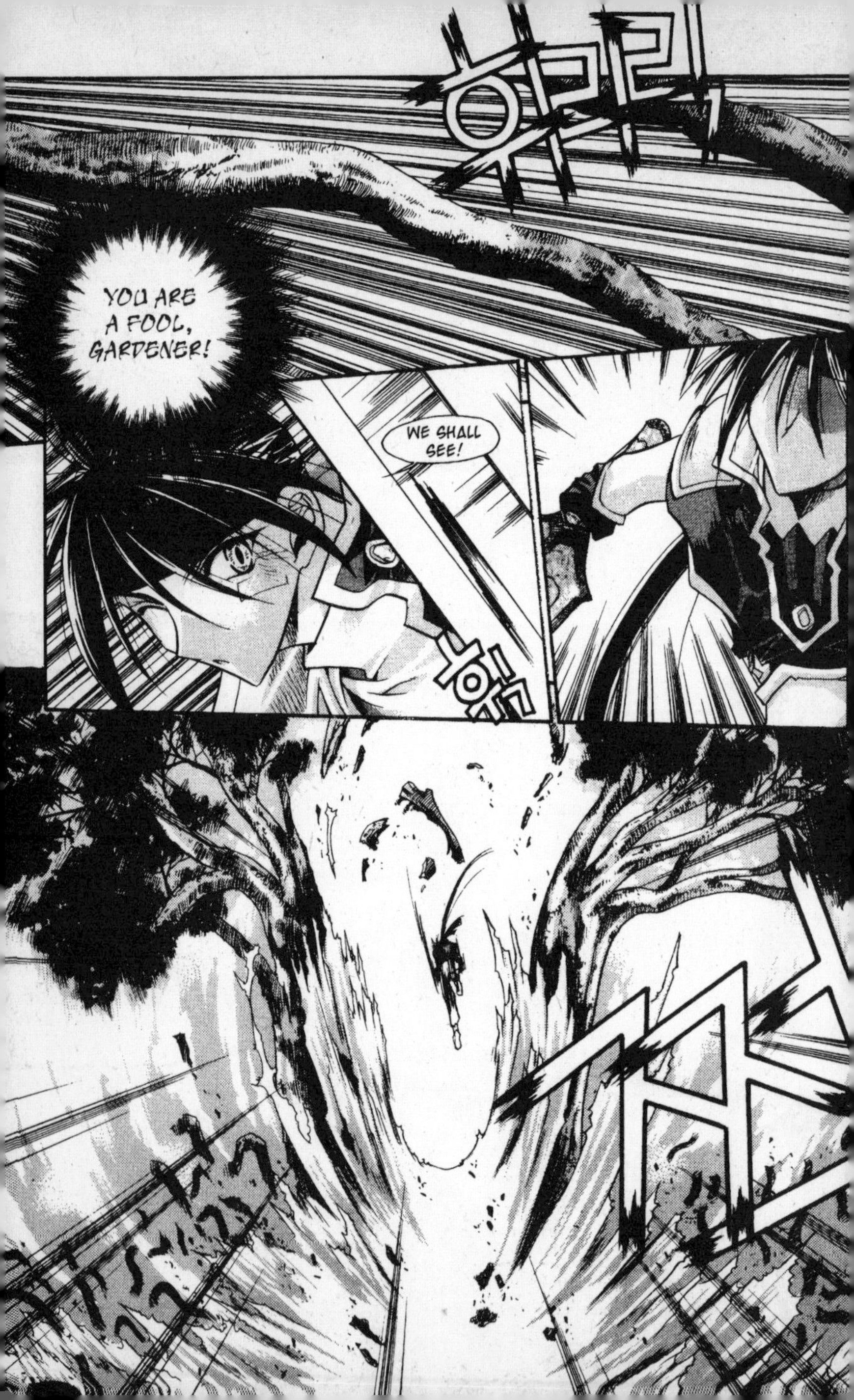
YOU ARE A FOOL, GARDENER!
WE SHALL SEE!

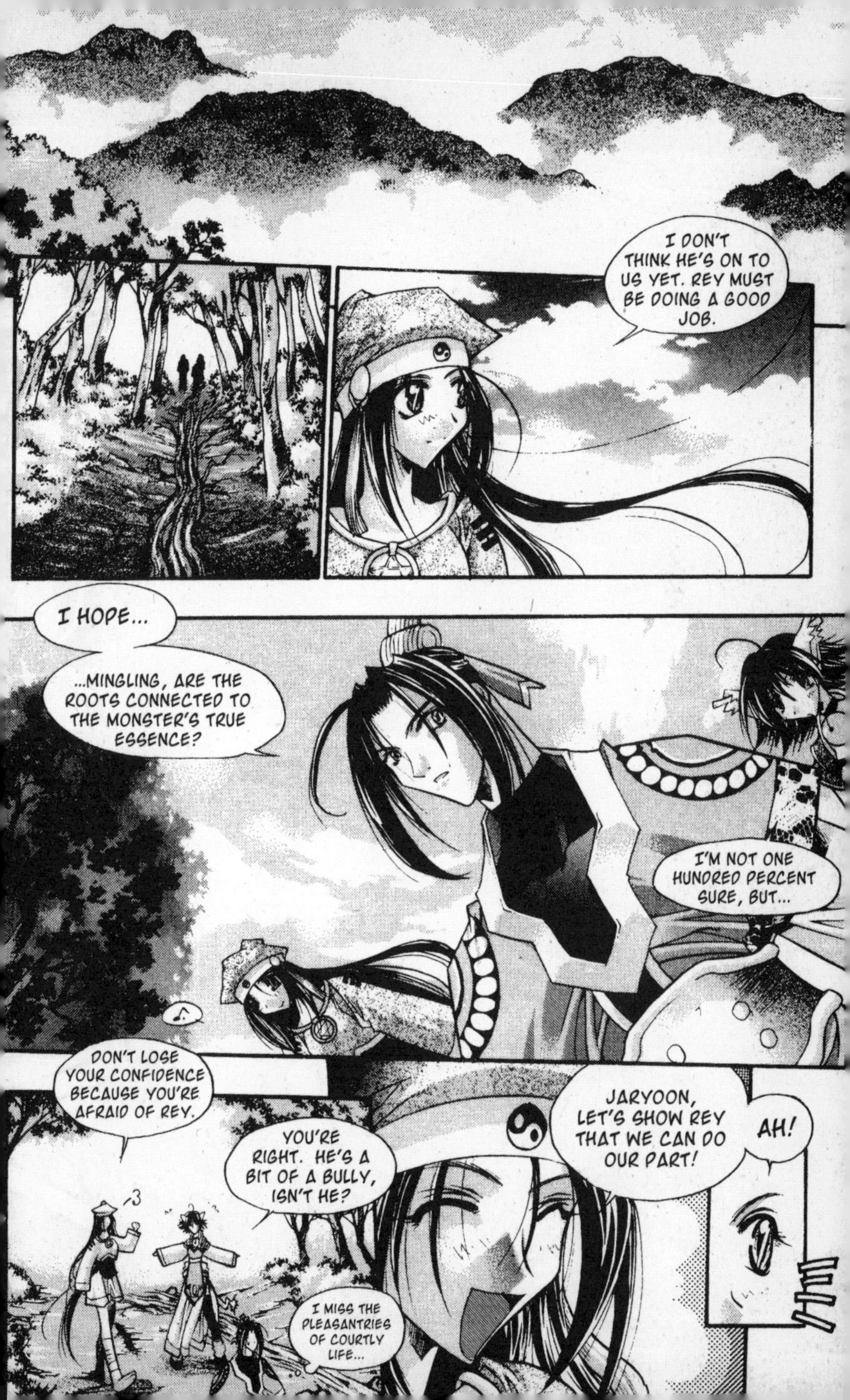
I DON'T THINK HE'S ON TO US YET. REY MUST BE DOING A GOOD JOB.
I HOPE...
...MINGLING, ARE THE ROOTS CONNECTED TO THE MONSTER'S TRUE ESSENCE?
I'M NOT ONE HUNDRED PERCENT SURE, BUT...
DON'T LOSE YOUR CONFIDENCE BECAUSE YOU'RE AFRAID OF REY.
YOU'RE RIGHT. HE'S A BIT OF A BULLY, ISN'T HE?
I MISS THE PLEASANTRIES OF COURTLY LIFE...
JARYOON, LET'S SHOW REY THAT WE CAN DO OUR PART!
AH!

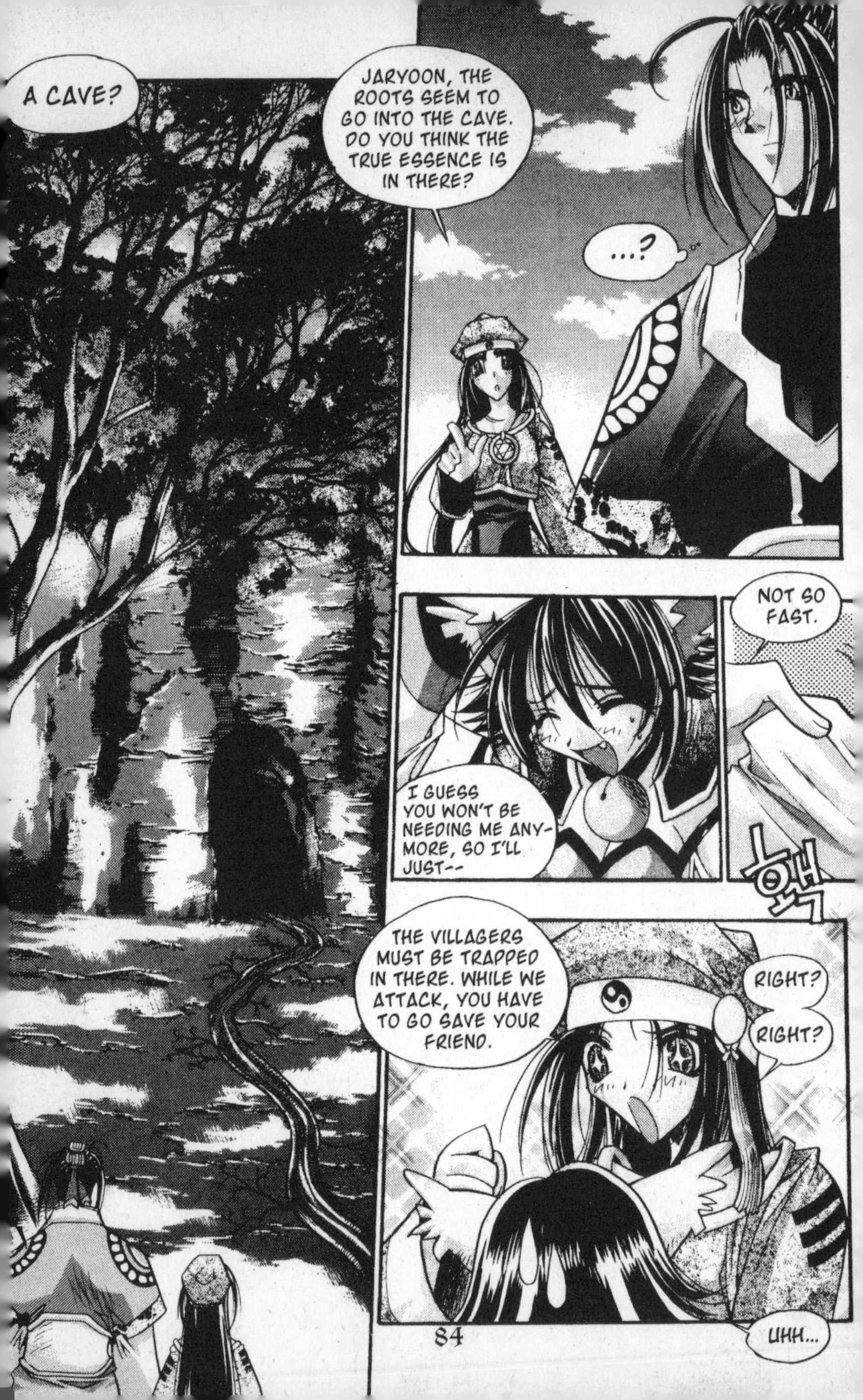
A CAVE?
JARYOON, THE ROOTS SEEM TO GO INTO THE CAVE. DO YOU THINK THE TRUE ESSENCE IS IN THERE?
...?
I GUESS YOU WON'T BE NEEDING ME ANY-MORE, SO I'LL JUST--
NOT SO FAST.
헉
THE VILLAGERS MUST BE TRAPPED IN THERE. WHILE WE ATTACK, YOU HAVE TO GO SAVE YOUR FRIEND.
RIGHT?
RIGHT?
UHH...

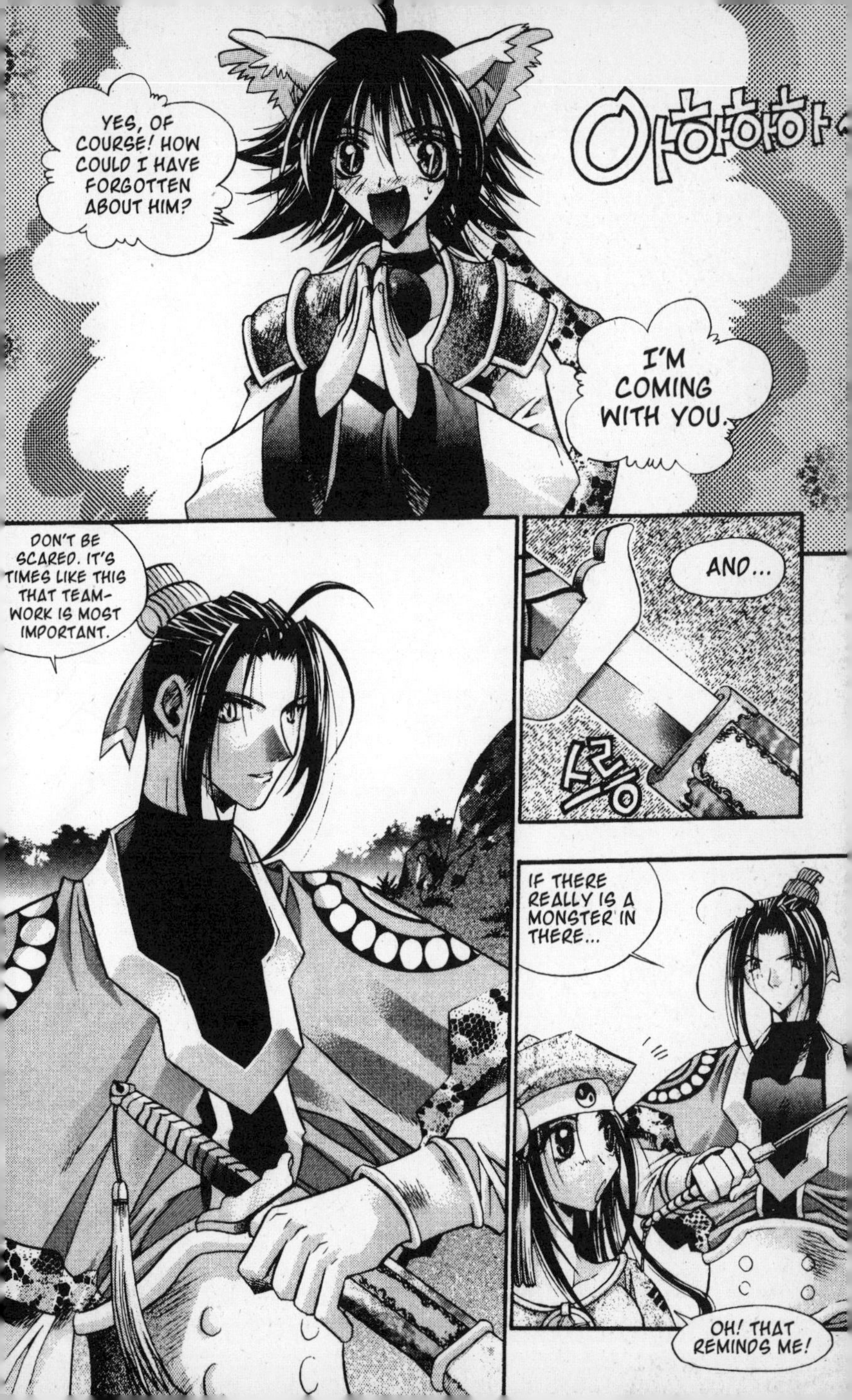
YES, OF COURSE! HOW COULD I HAVE FORGOTTEN ABOUT HIM?
아하하하
I'M COMING WITH YOU.
DON'T BE SCARED. IT'S TIMES LIKE THIS THAT TEAM-WORK IS MOST IMPORTANT.
AND...
스릉
IF THERE REALLY IS A MONSTER IN THERE...
OH! THAT REMINDS ME!

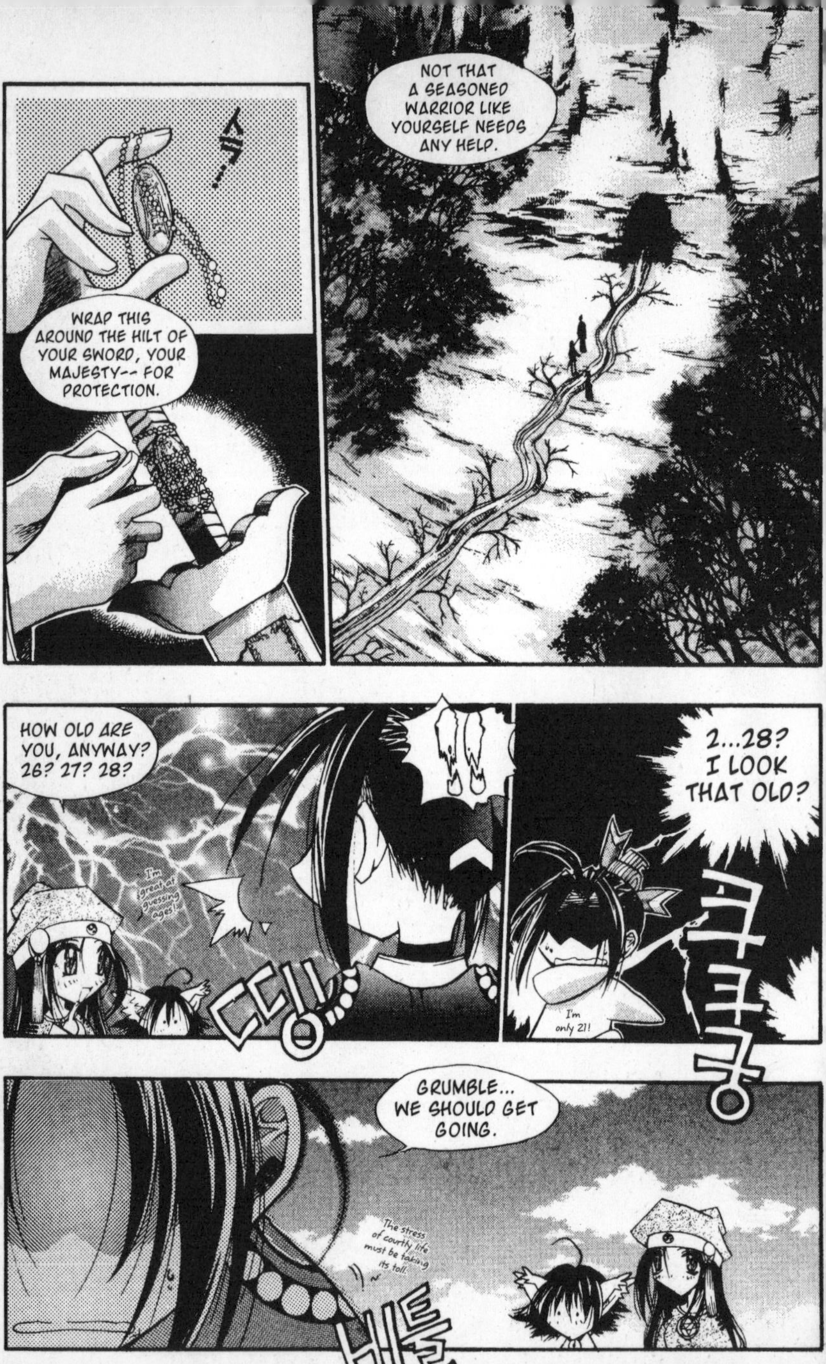
WRAP THIS AROUND THE HILT OF YOUR SWORD, YOUR MAJESTY-- FOR PROTECTION.
NOT THAT A SEASONED WARRIOR LIKE YOURSELF NEEDS ANY HELP.
HOW OLD ARE YOU, ANYWAY? 26? 27? 28?
I'm great at guessing ages!
2...28? I LOOK THAT OLD?
I'm only 21!
GRUMBLE... WE SHOULD GET GOING.
The stress of courtly life must be taking its toll.

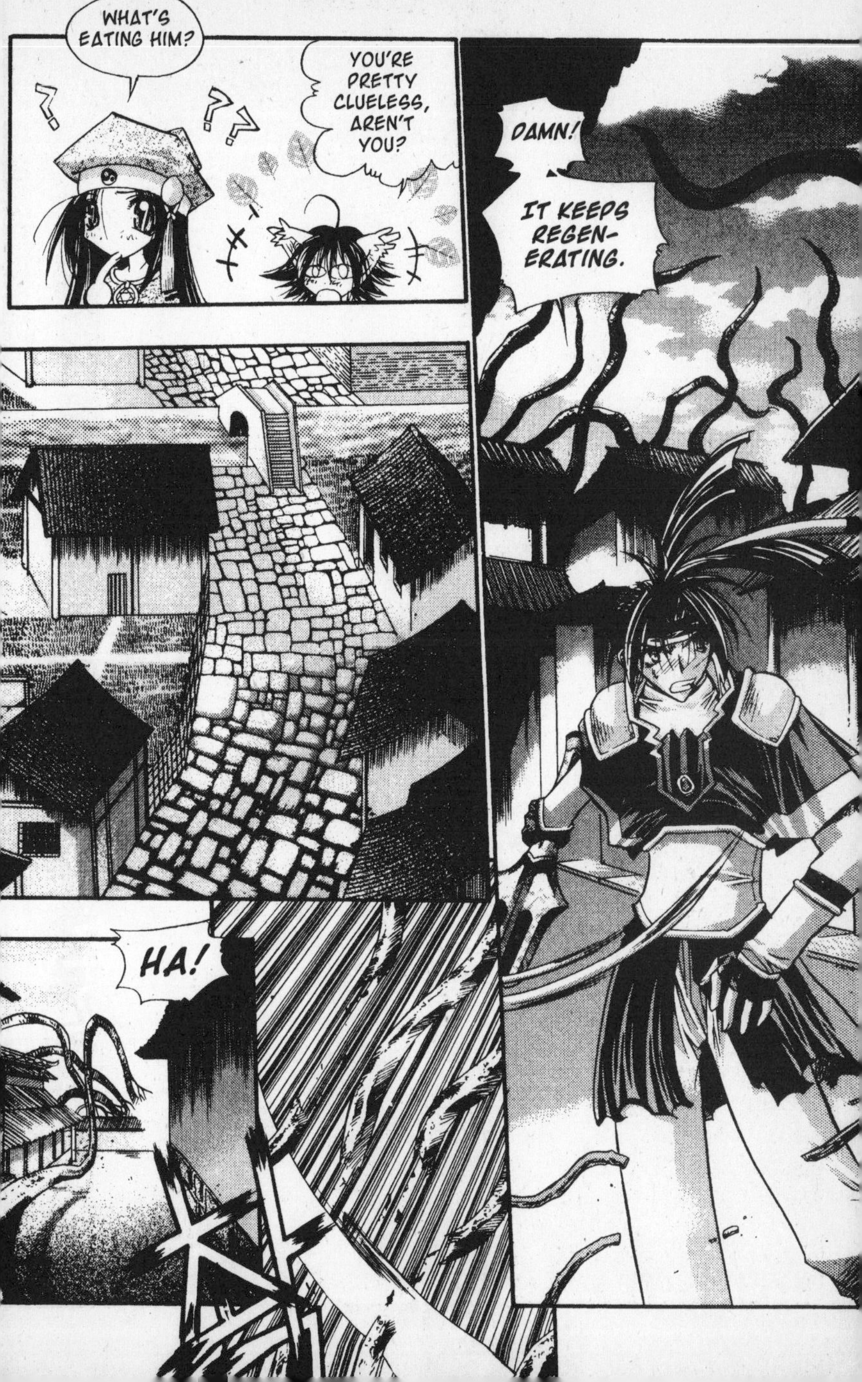
WHAT'S EATING HIM?
YOU'RE PRETTY CLUELESS, AREN'T YOU?
HA!
DAMN!
IT KEEPS REGEN-ERATING.

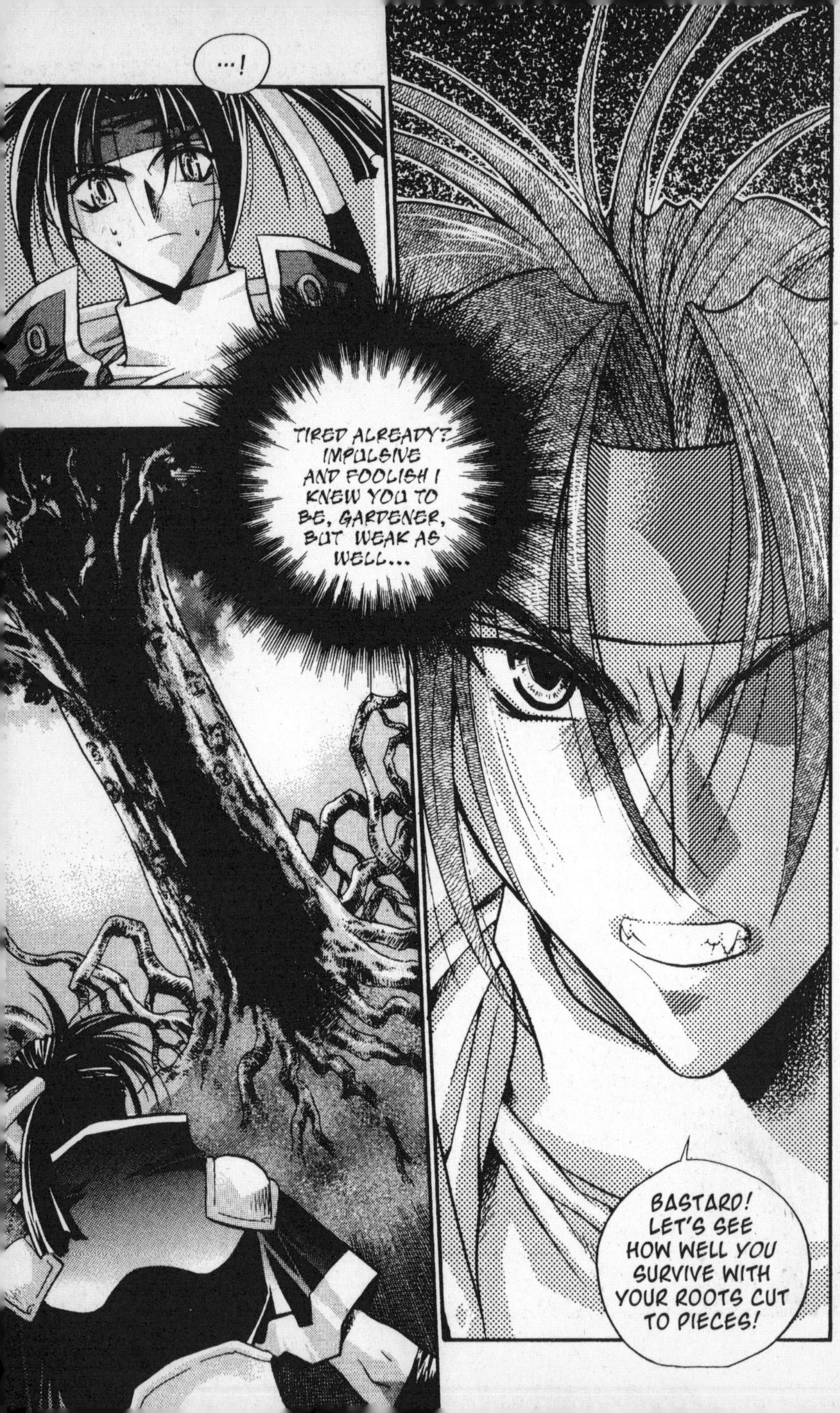
...!
TIRED ALREADY? IMPULSIVE AND FOOLISH I KNEW YOU TO BE, GARDENER, BUT WEAK AS WELL...
BASTARD! LET'S SEE HOW WELL YOU SURVIVE WITH YOUR ROOTS CUT TO PIECES!

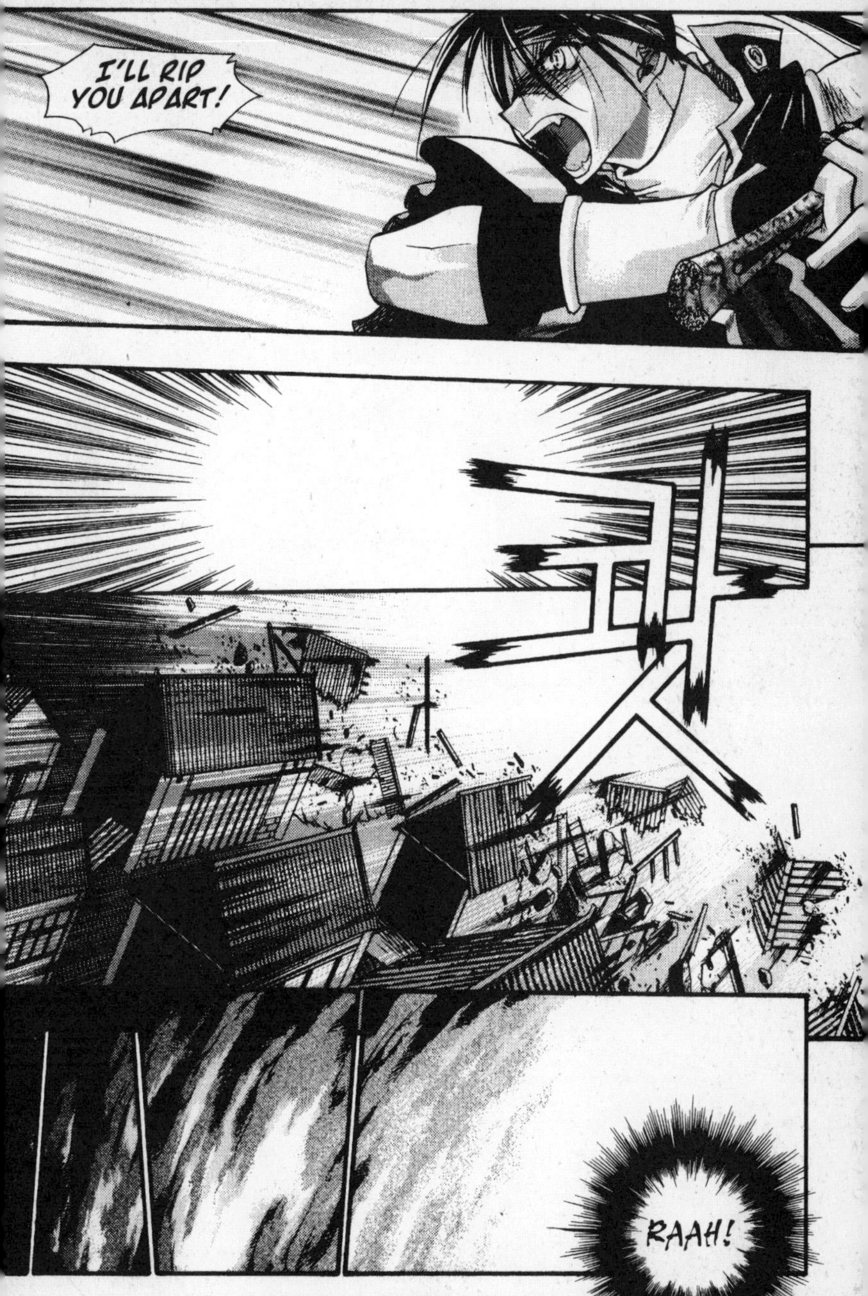
I'LL RIP YOU APART!
RAAH!

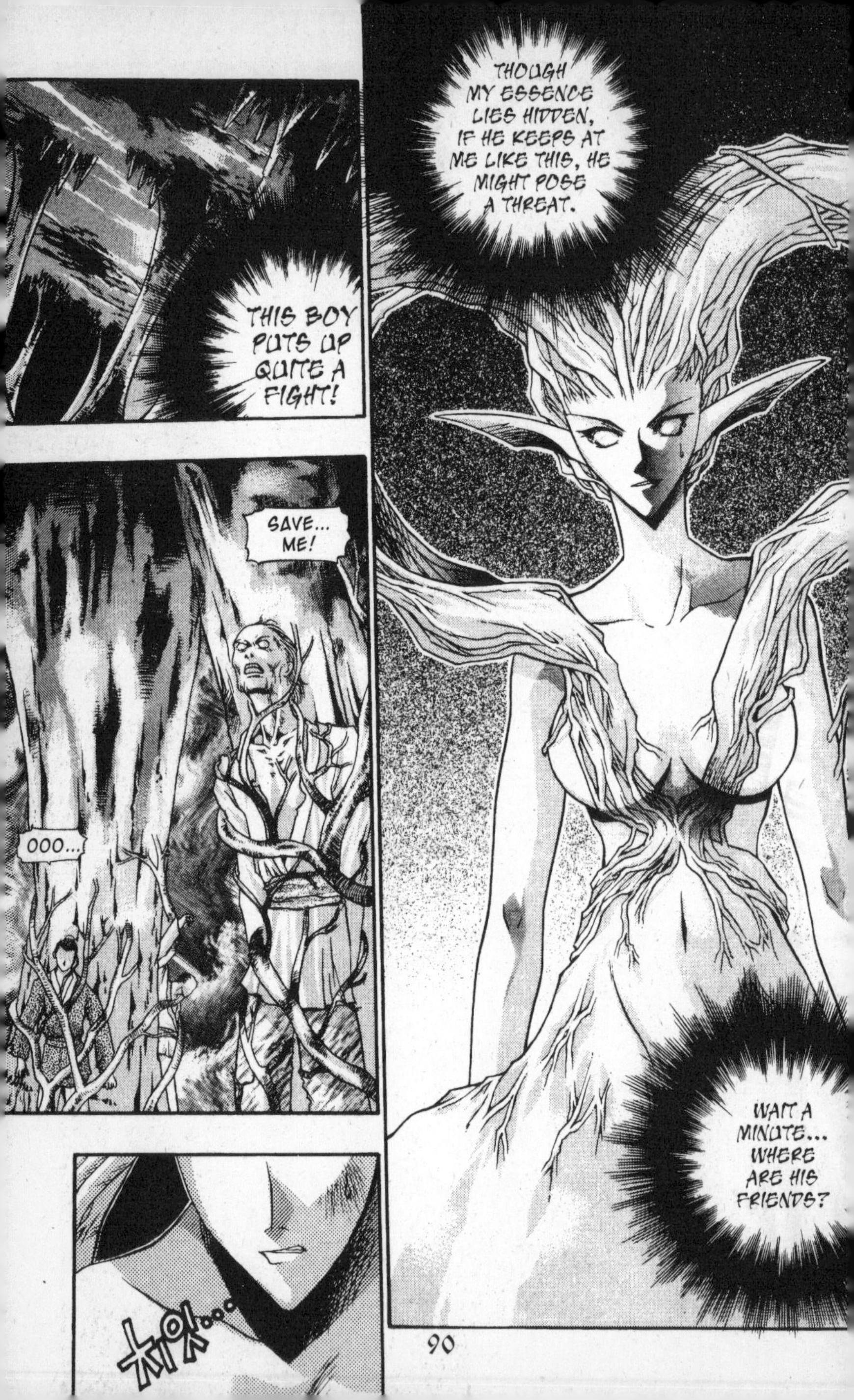
THIS BOY PUTS UP QUITE A FIGHT!
SAVE... ME!
OOO...
THOUGH MY ESSENCE LIES HIDDEN, IF HE KEEPS AT ME LIKE THIS, HE MIGHT POSE A THREAT.
WAIT A MINUTE... WHERE ARE HIS FRIENDS?

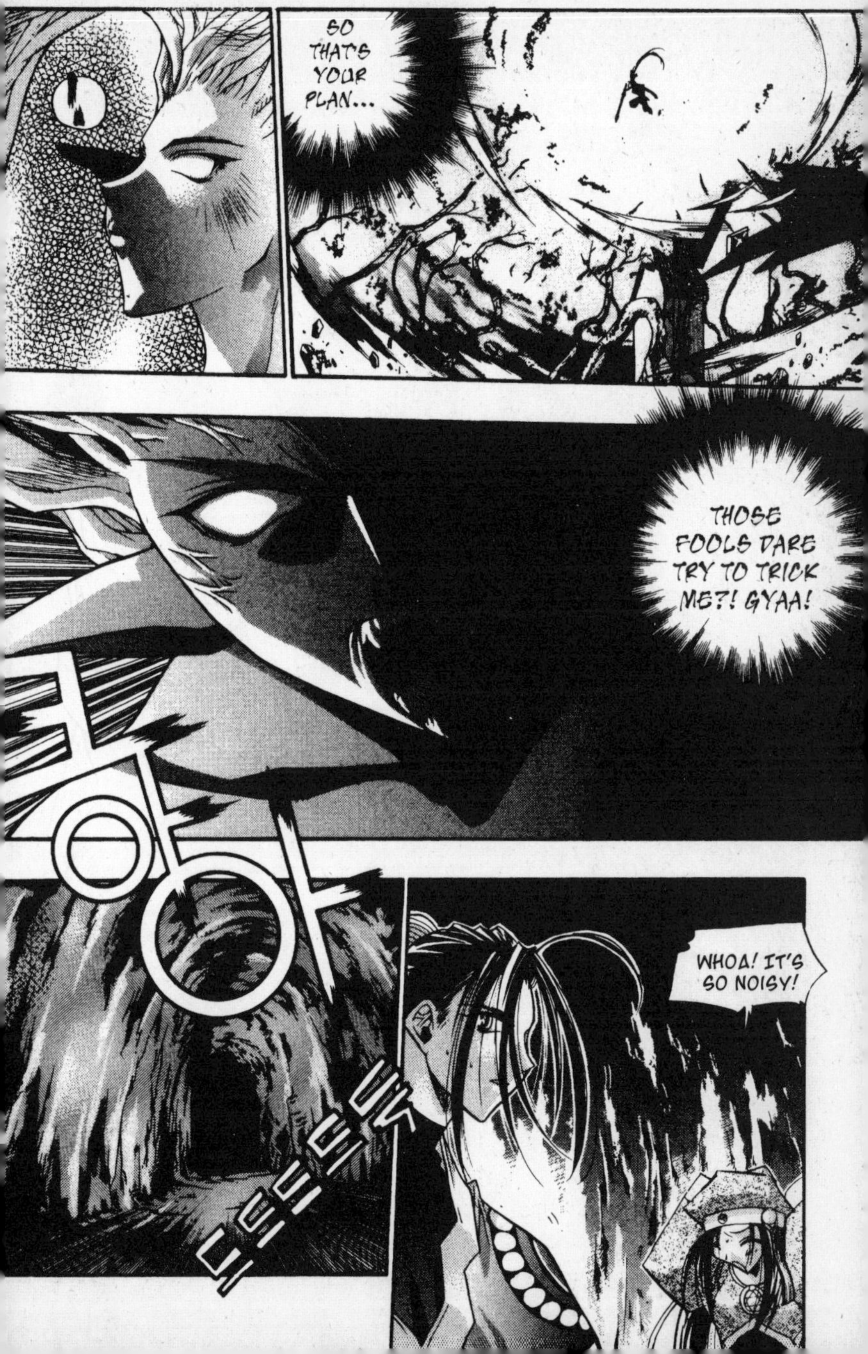
SO THAT'S YOUR PLAN...
THOSE FOOLS DARE TRY TO TRICK ME?! GYAA!
WHOA! IT'S SO NOISY!

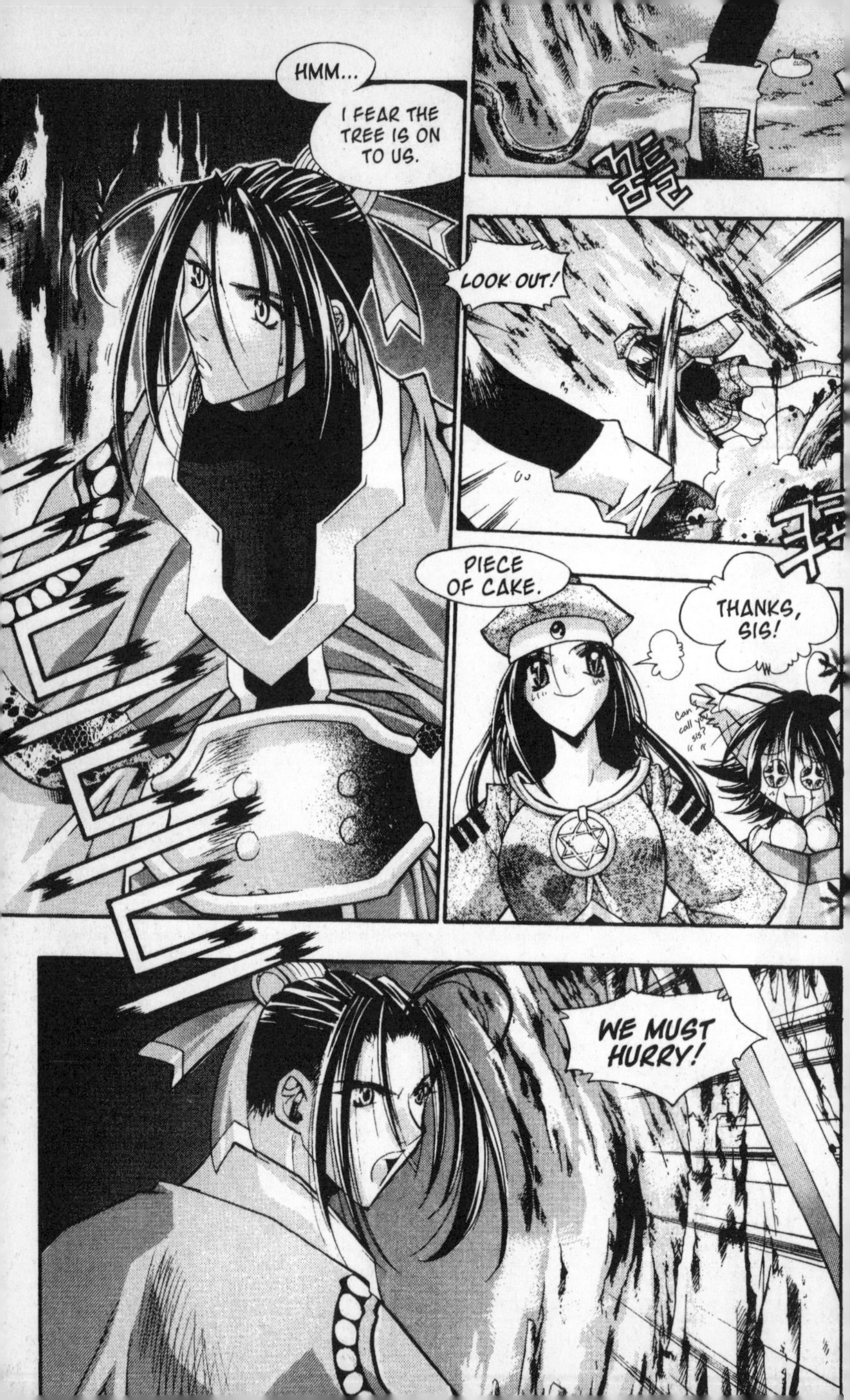
HMM...
I FEAR THE TREE IS ON TO US.
LOOK OUT!
PIECE OF CAKE.
THANKS, SIS!
Can I call you sis?
WE MUST HURRY!

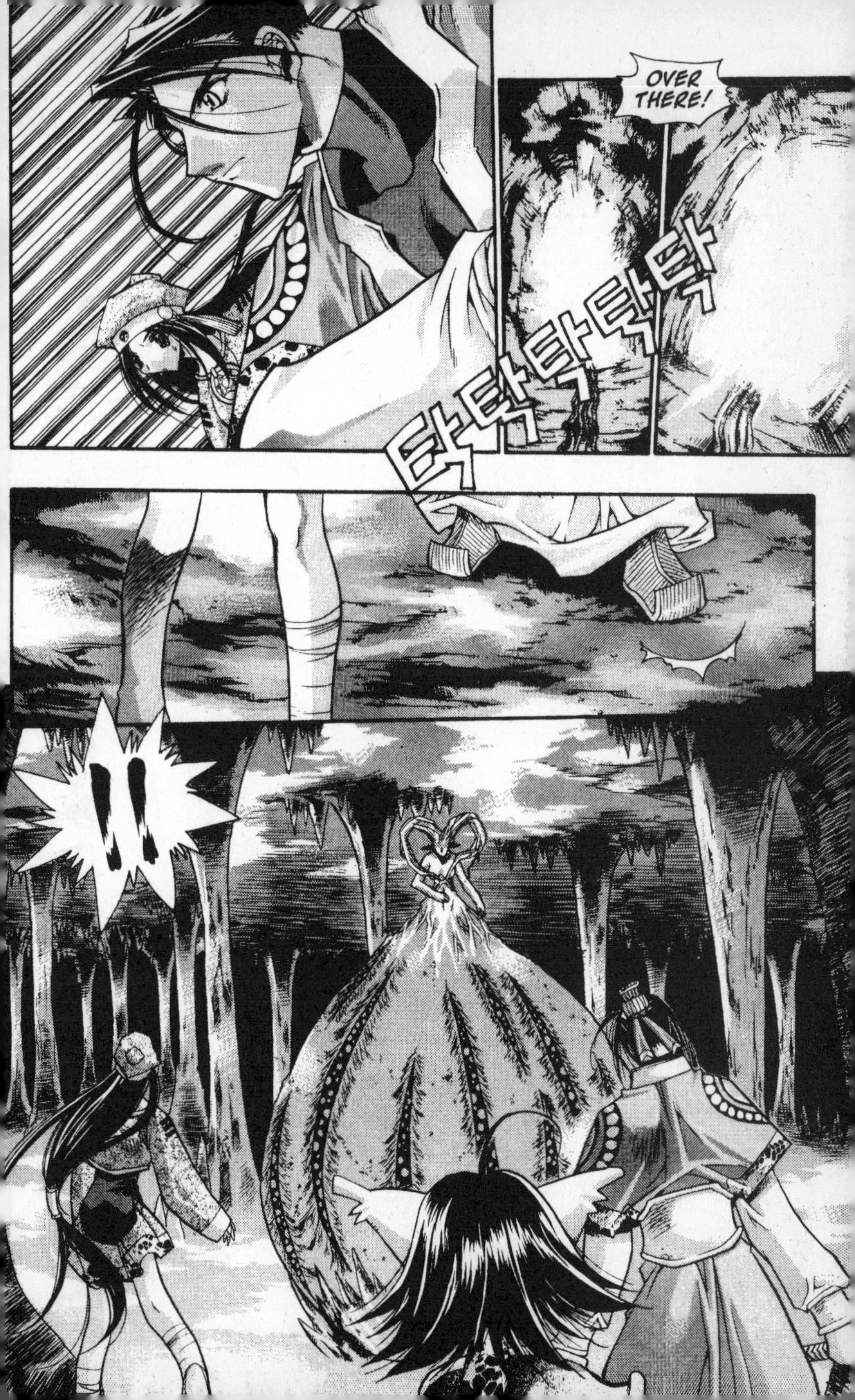
OVER THERE!
탁탁탁탁탁
!!

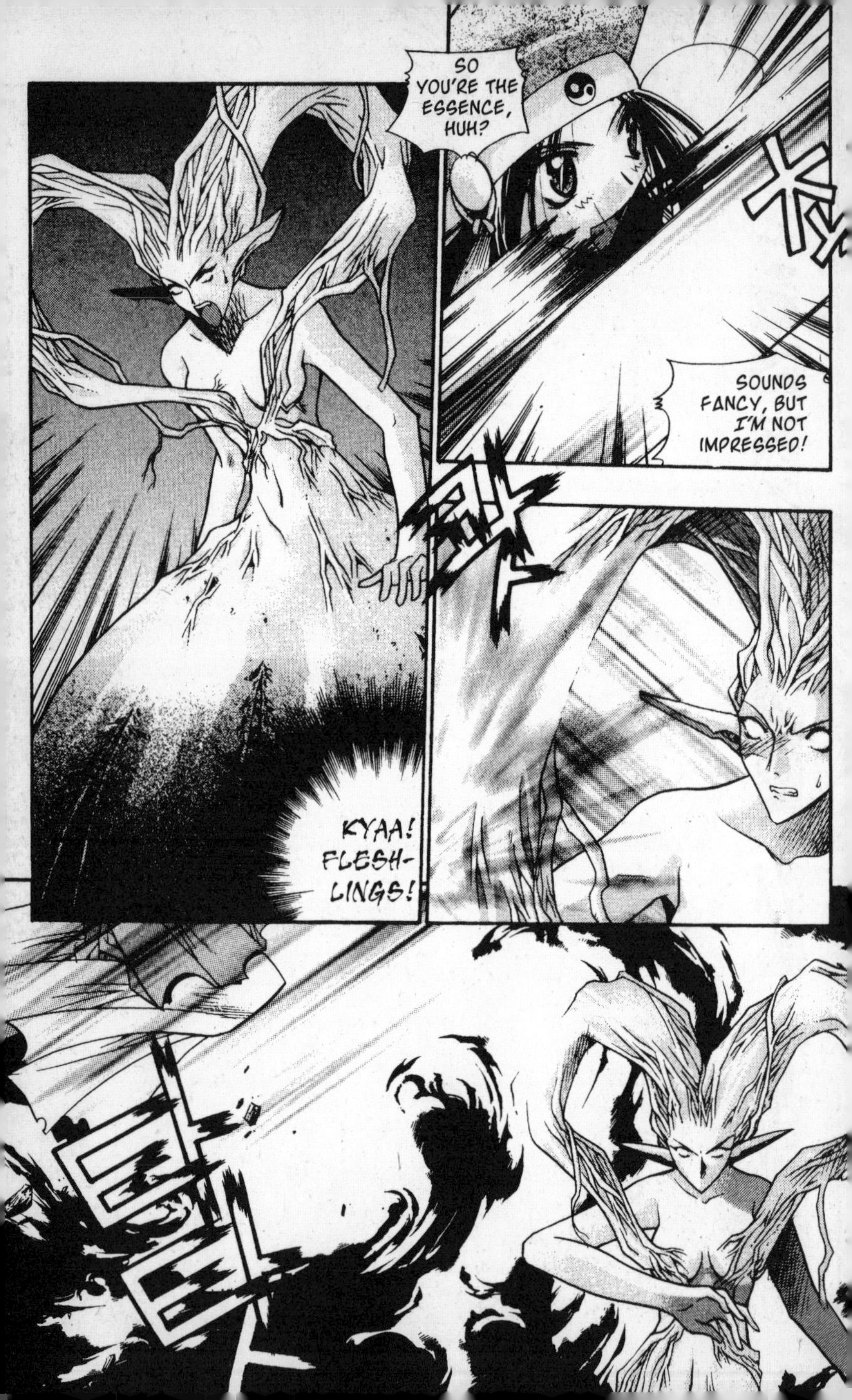
KYAA! FLESH-LINGS!
SO YOU'RE THE ESSENCE, HUH?
SOUNDS FANCY, BUT I'M NOT IMPRESSED!

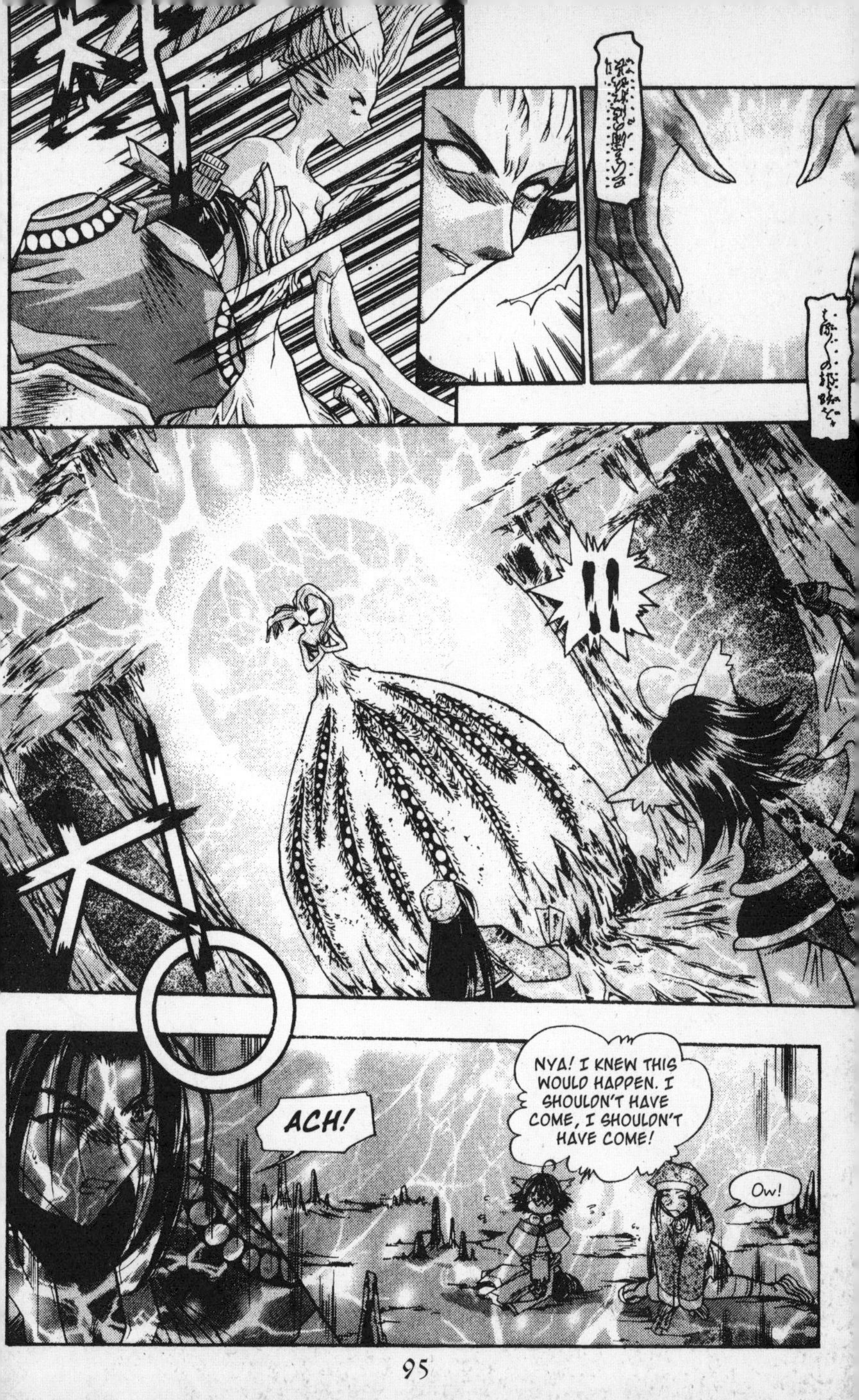
!!
ACH!
NYA! I KNEW THIS WOULD HAPPEN. I SHOULDN'T HAVE COME, I SHOULDN'T HAVE COME!
Ow!

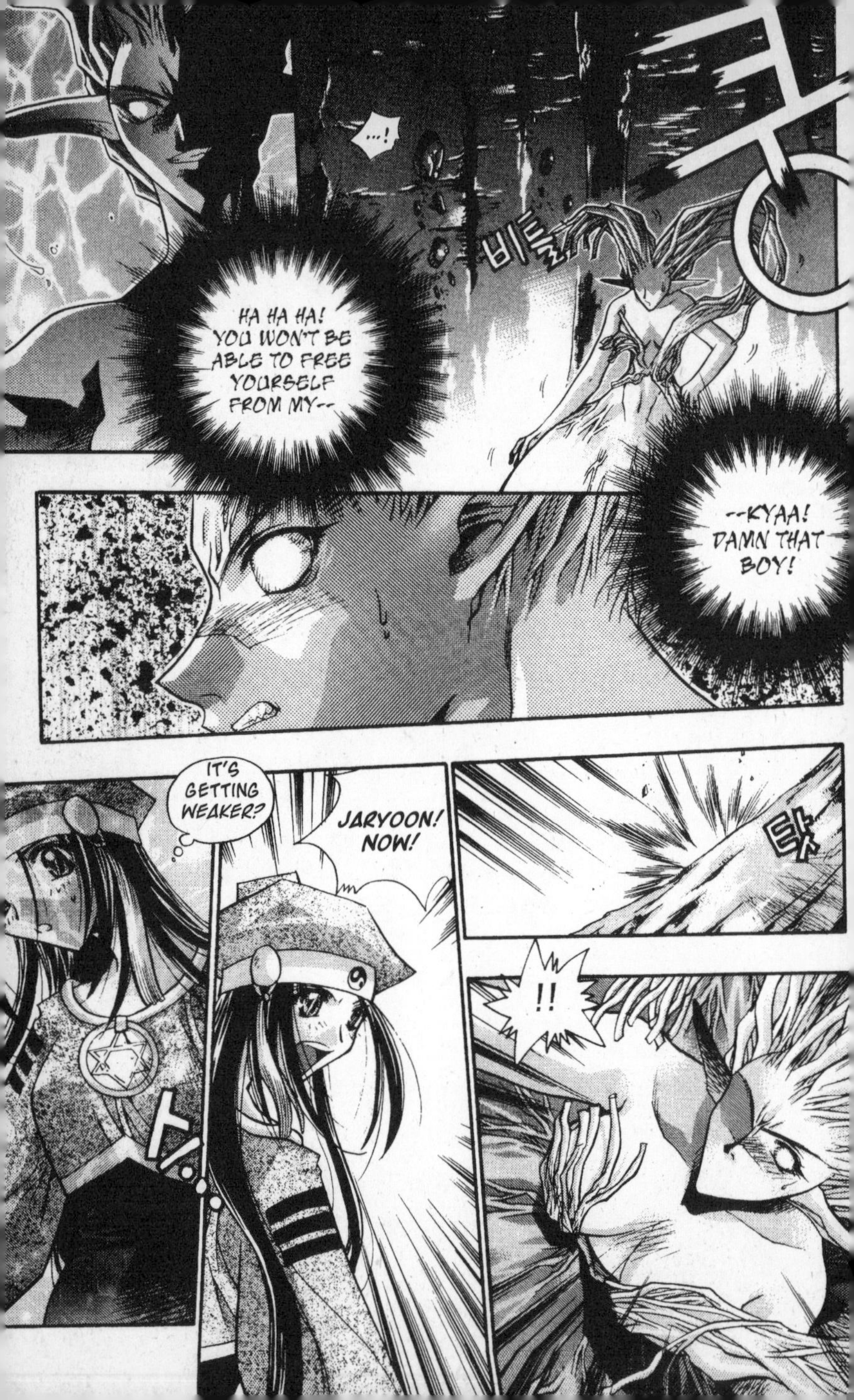
...!
HA HA HA! YOU WON'T BE ABLE TO FREE YOURSELF FROM MY--
--KYAA! DAMN THAT BOY!
IT'S GETTING WEAKER?
JARYOON! NOW!
탁
!!

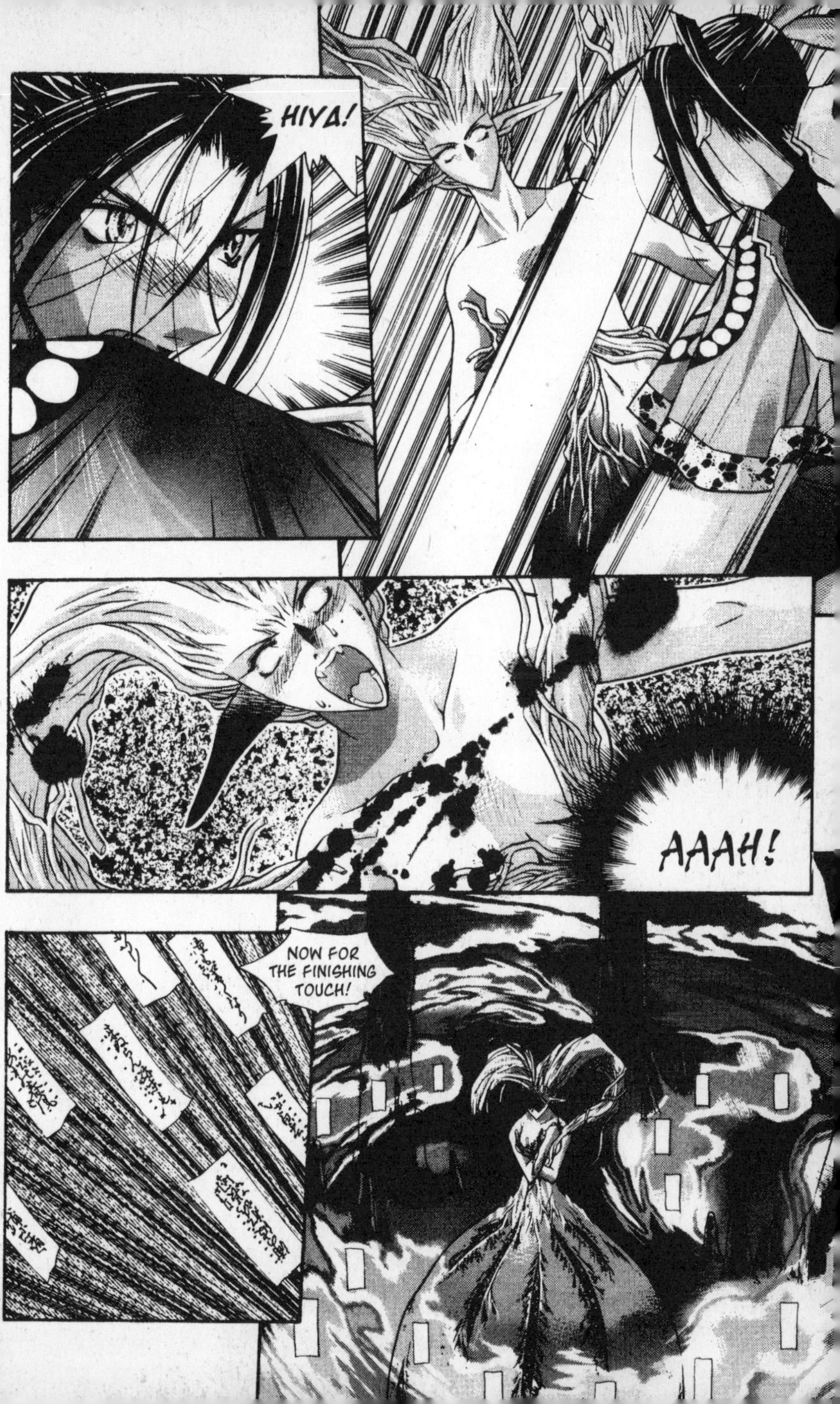
HIYA!
AAAH!
NOW FOR THE FINISHING TOUCH!

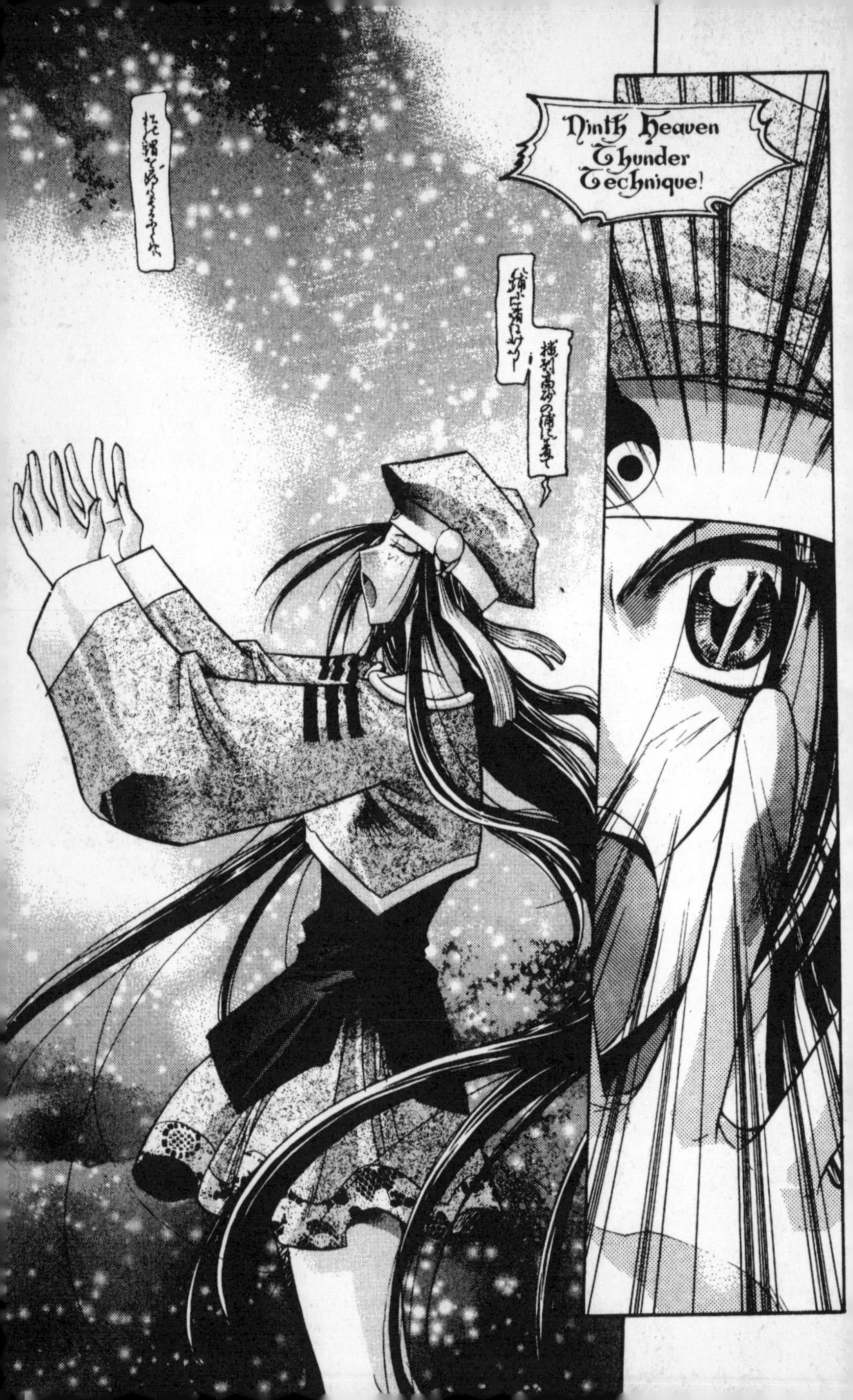
Ninth Heaven Thunder Technique!

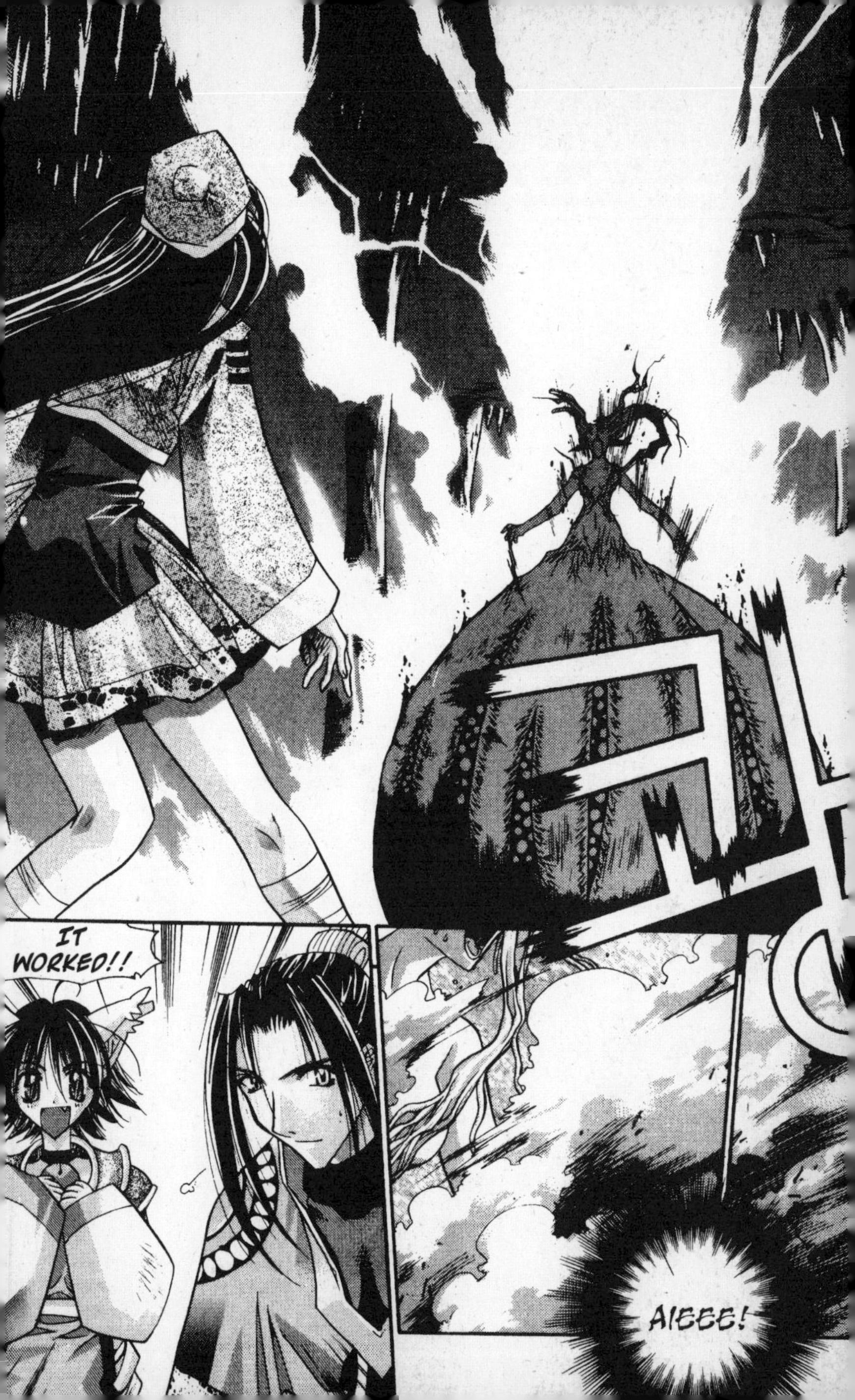
IT WORKED!!
AIEEE!

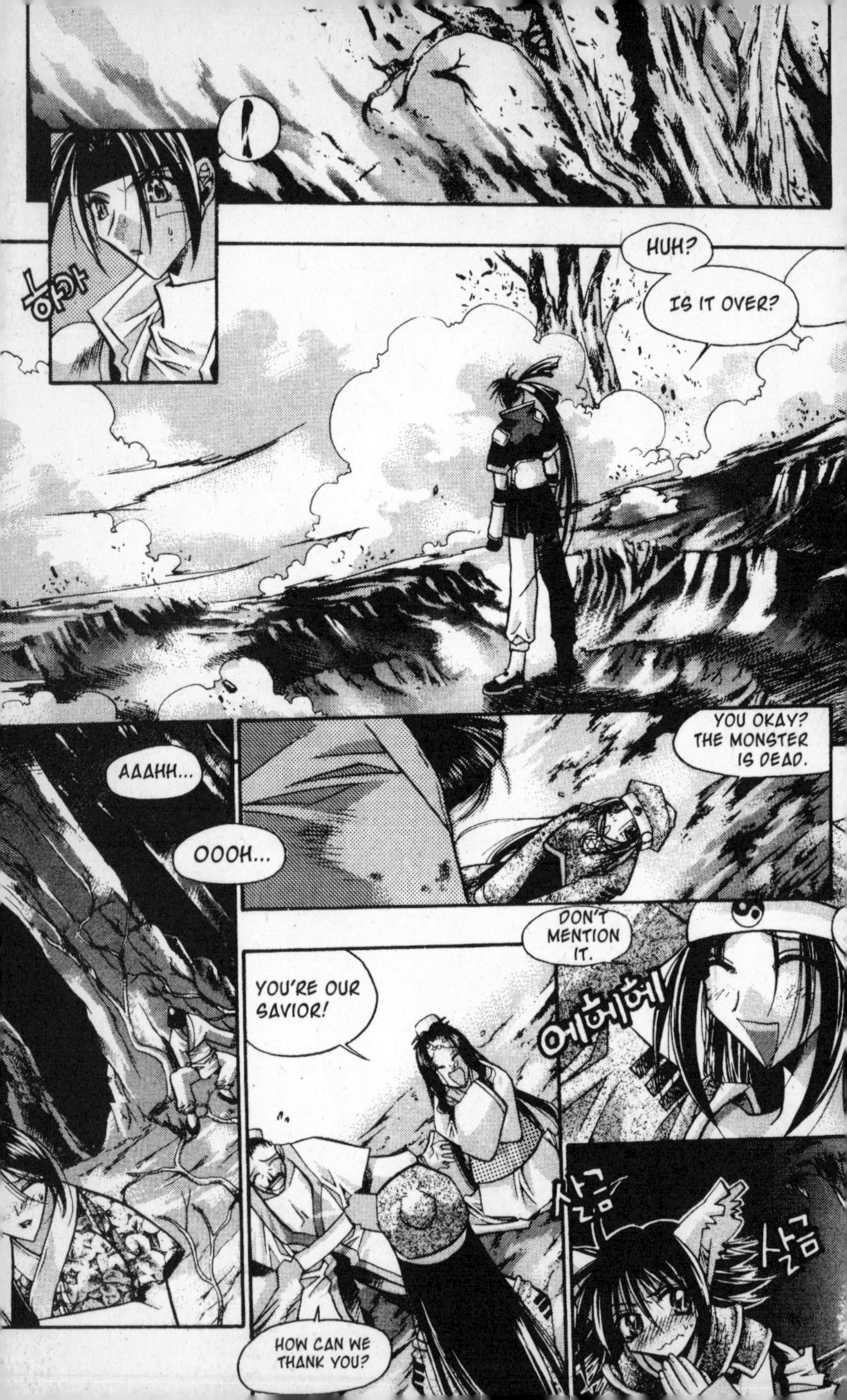
!
HUH?
IS IT OVER?
AAAHH...
OOOH...
YOU OKAY? THE MONSTER IS DEAD.
YOU'RE OUR SAVIOR!
DON'T MENTION IT.
에헤헤
HOW CAN WE THANK YOU?
살금
살금

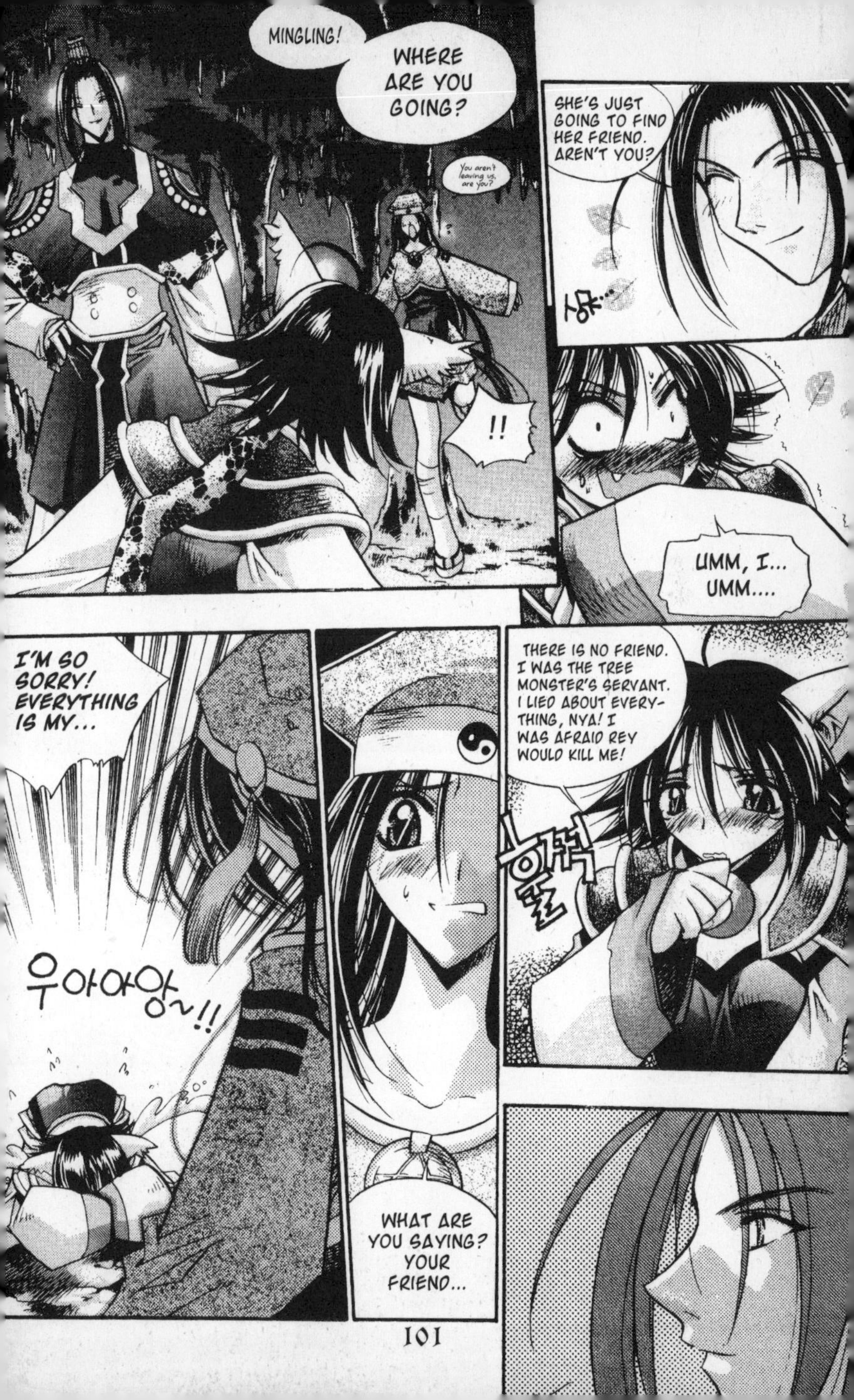
MINGLING!
WHERE ARE YOU GOING?
You aren't leaving us, are you?
!!
SHE'S JUST GOING TO FIND HER FRIEND. AREN'T YOU?
UMM, I... UMM....
I'M SO SORRY! EVERYTHING IS MY...
우아아앙~!!
WHAT ARE YOU SAYING? YOUR FRIEND...
THERE IS NO FRIEND. I WAS THE TREE MONSTER'S SERVANT. I LIED ABOUT EVERYTHING, NYA! I WAS AFRAID REY WOULD KILL ME!

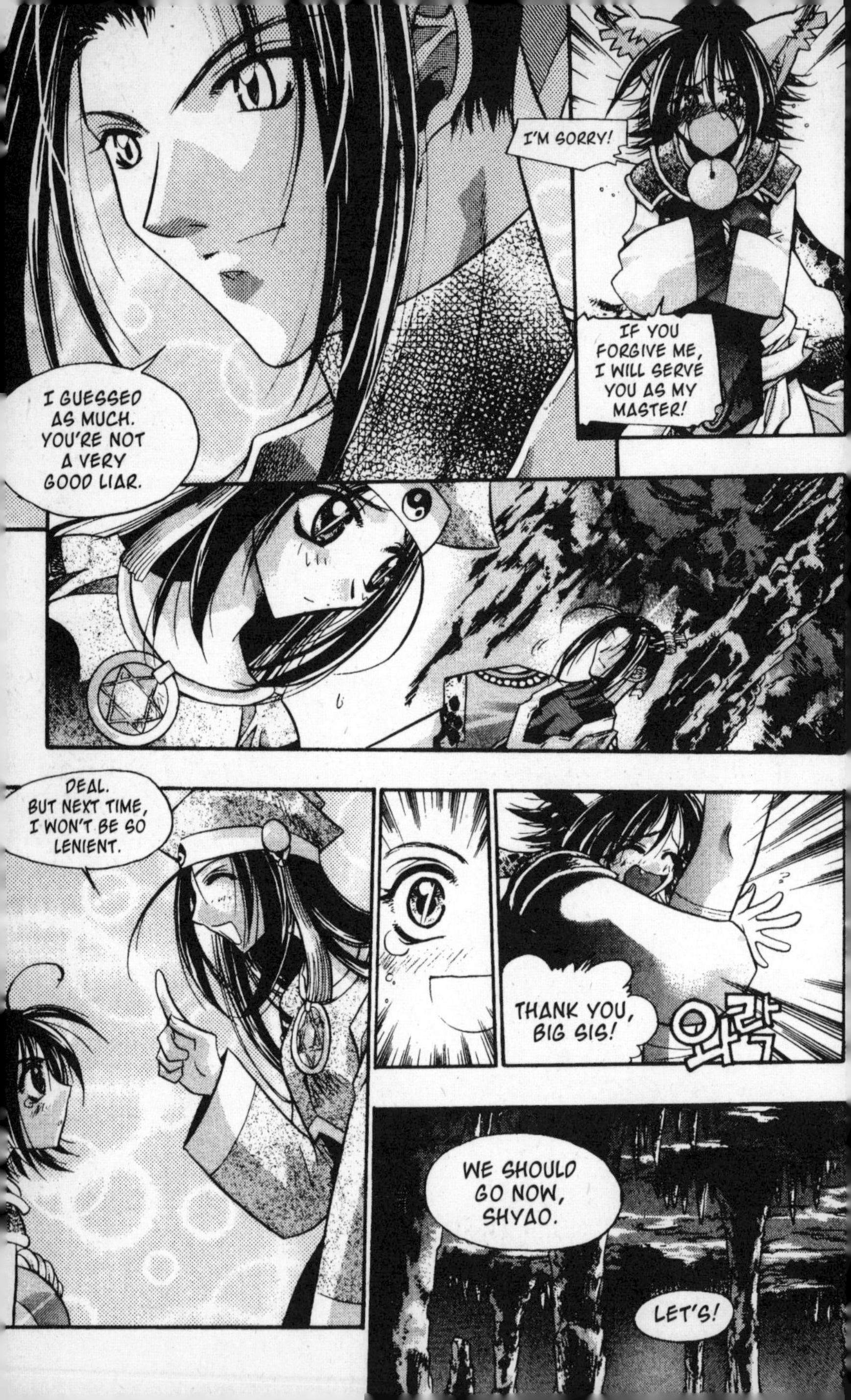
I GUESSED AS MUCH. YOU'RE NOT A VERY GOOD LIAR.
I'M SORRY!
IF YOU FORGIVE ME, I WILL SERVE YOU AS MY MASTER!
DEAL. BUT NEXT TIME, I WON'T BE SO LENIENT.
THANK YOU, BIG SIS!
와락
WE SHOULD GO NOW, SHYAO.
LET'S!

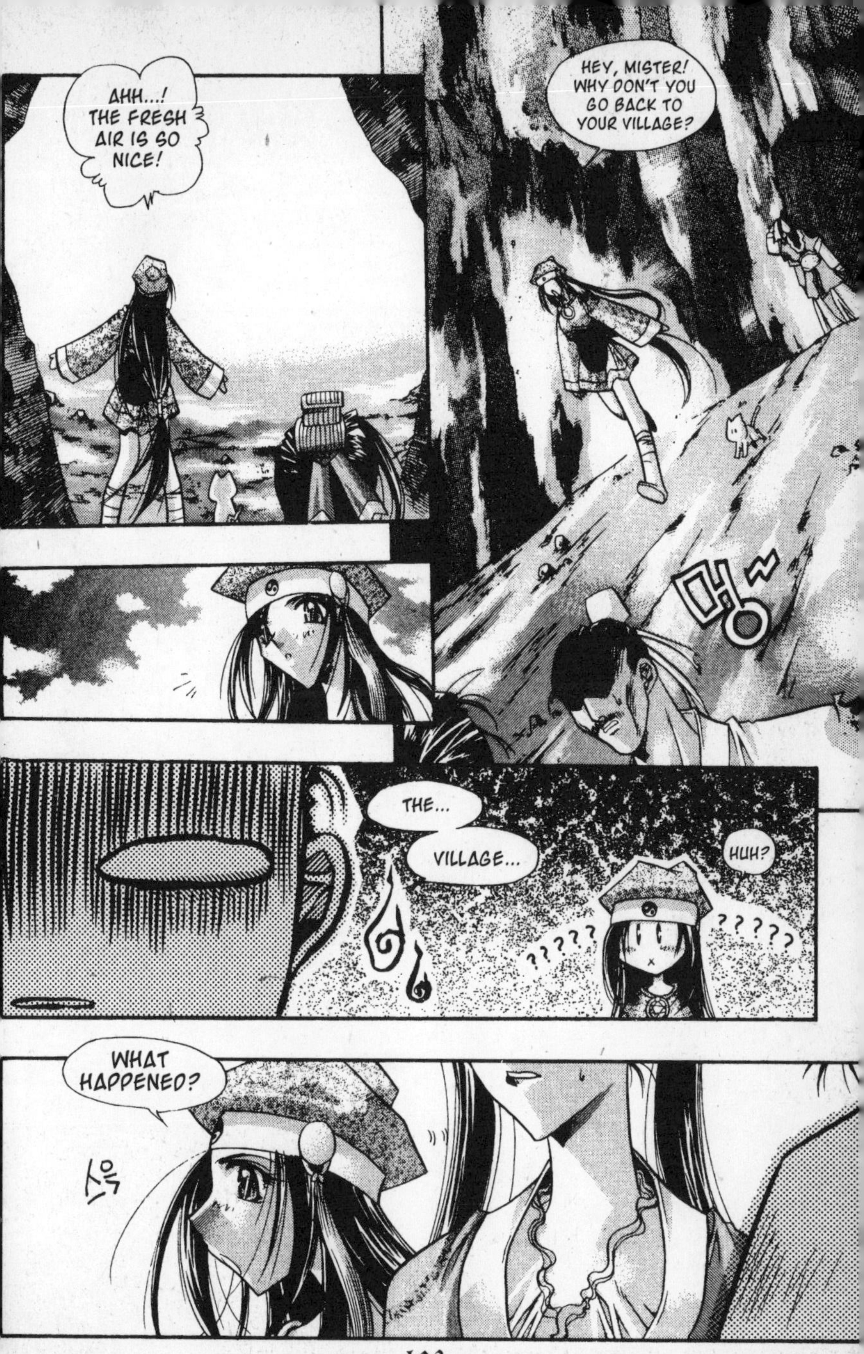
AHH...! THE FRESH AIR IS SO NICE!
HEY, MISTER! WHY DON'T YOU GO BACK TO YOUR VILLAGE?
THE...
VILLAGE...
HUH?
WHAT HAPPENED?

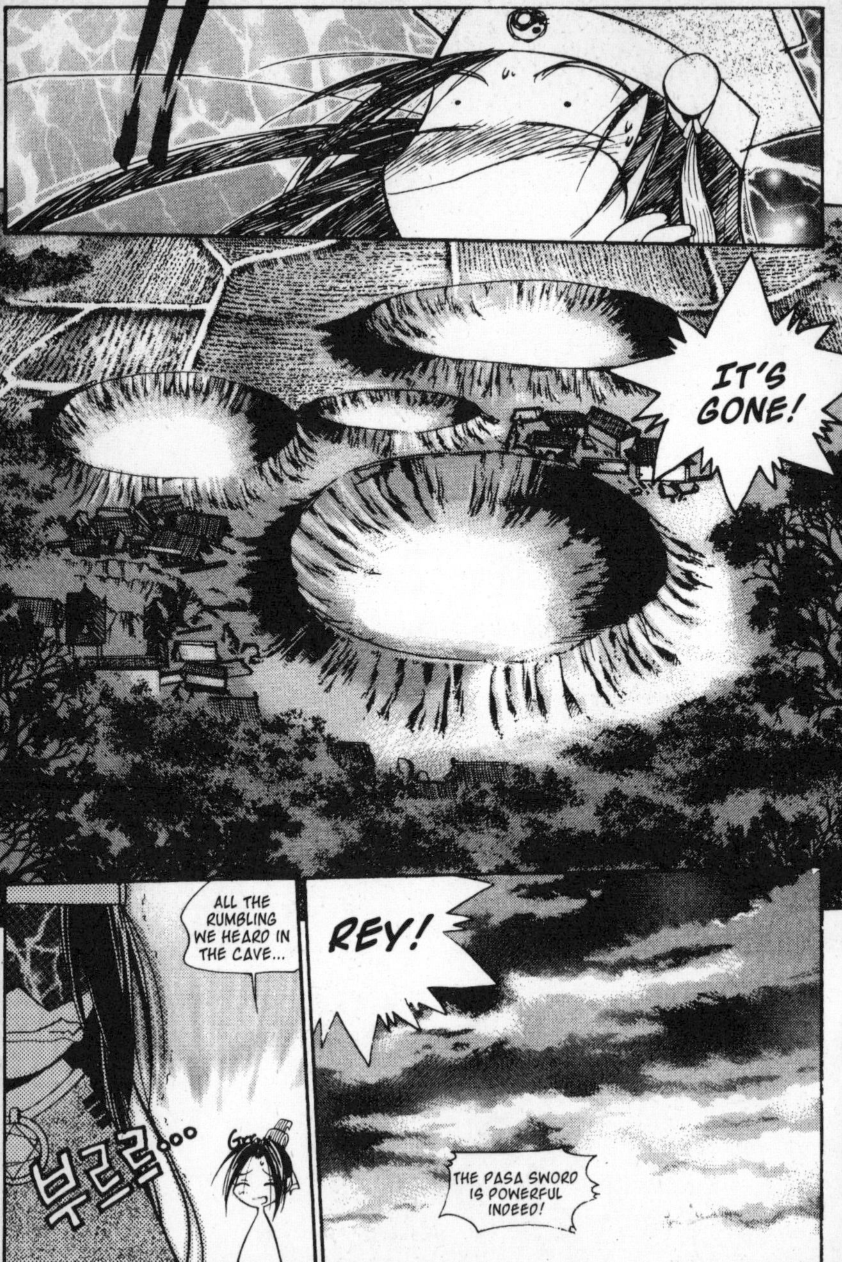
IT'S GONE!
ALL THE RUMBLING WE HEARD IN THE CAVE...
부르르...
REY!
THE PASA SWORD IS POWERFUL INDEED!

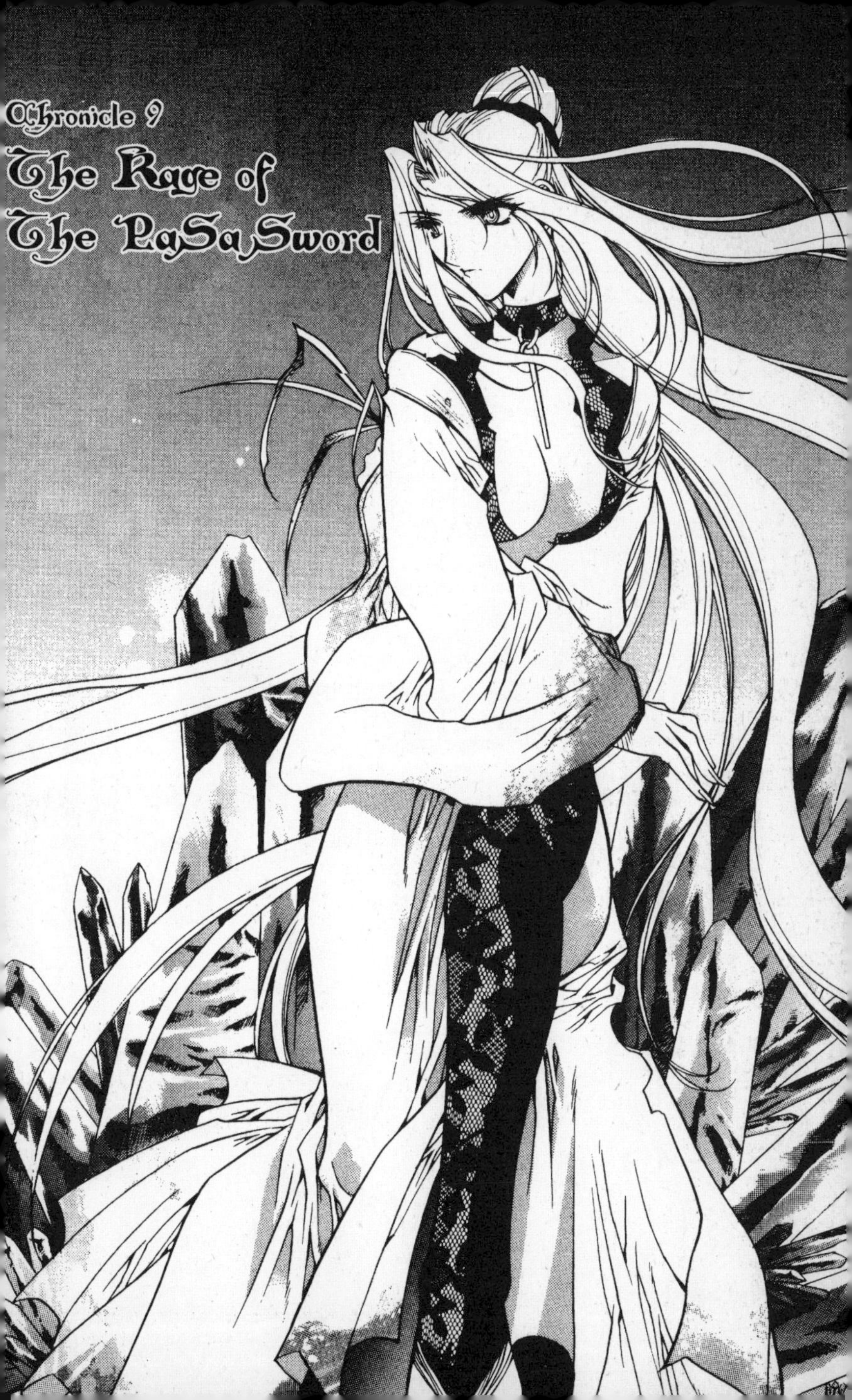
Chronicle 9
The Rage of
The PaSa Sword

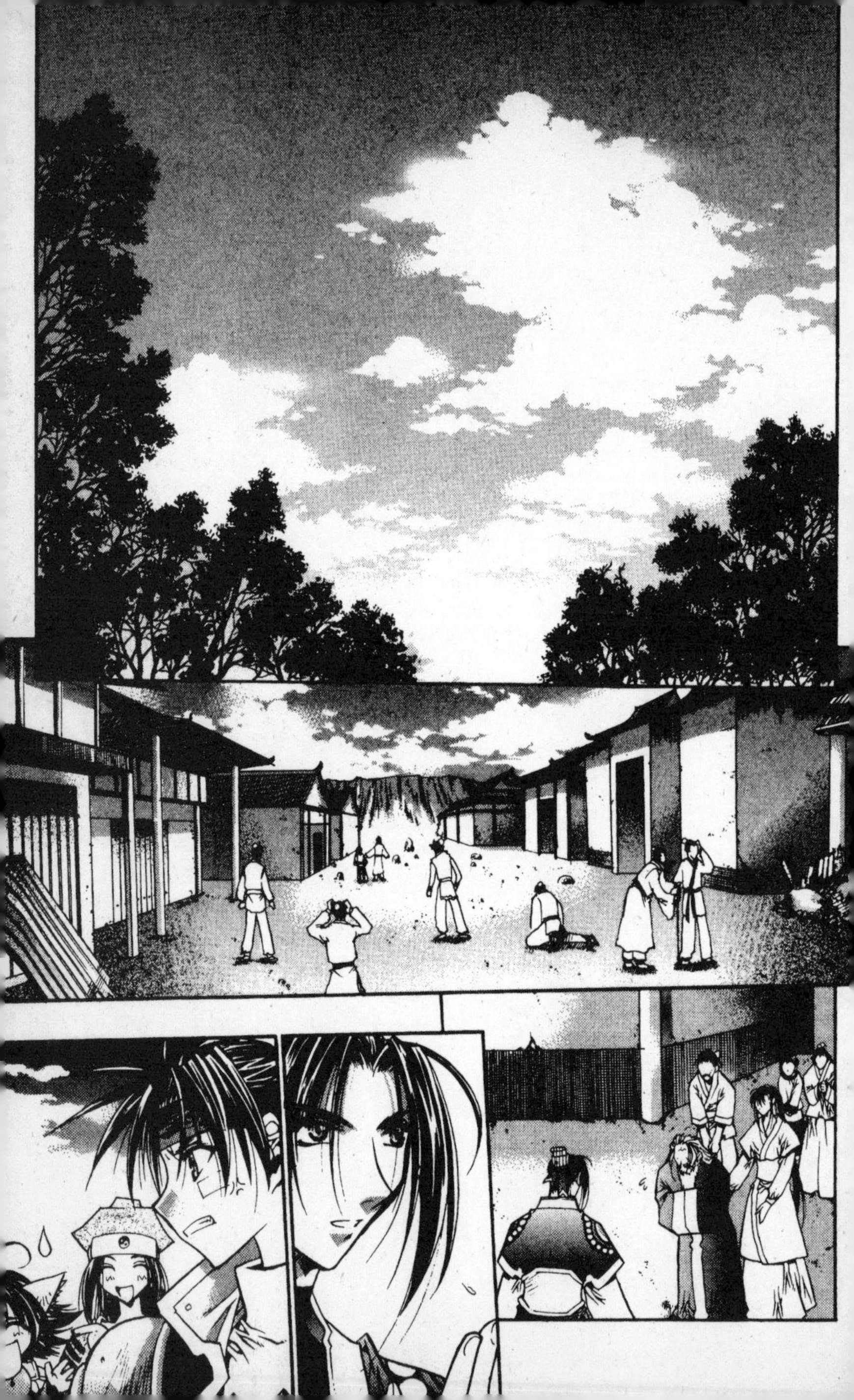

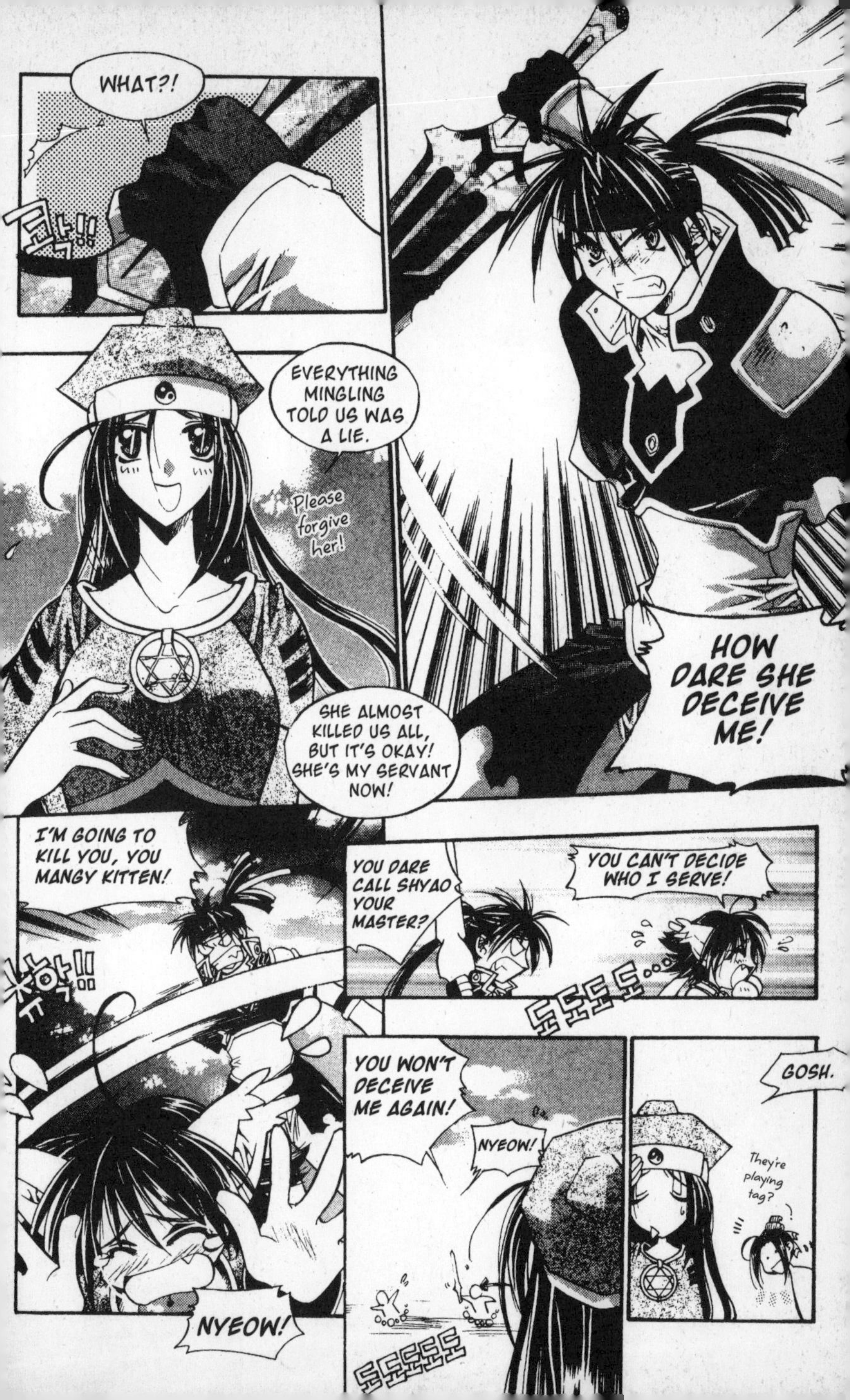
WHAT?!
EVERYTHING MINGLING TOLD US WAS A LIE.
Please forgive her!
SHE ALMOST KILLED US ALL, BUT IT'S OKAY! SHE'S MY SERVANT NOW!
HOW DARE SHE DECEIVE ME!
I'M GOING TO KILL YOU, YOU MANGY KITTEN!
NYEOW!
YOU DARE CALL SHYAO YOUR MASTER?
YOU CAN'T DECIDE WHO I SERVE!
YOU WON'T DECEIVE ME AGAIN!
NYEOW!
GOSH.
They're playing tag?

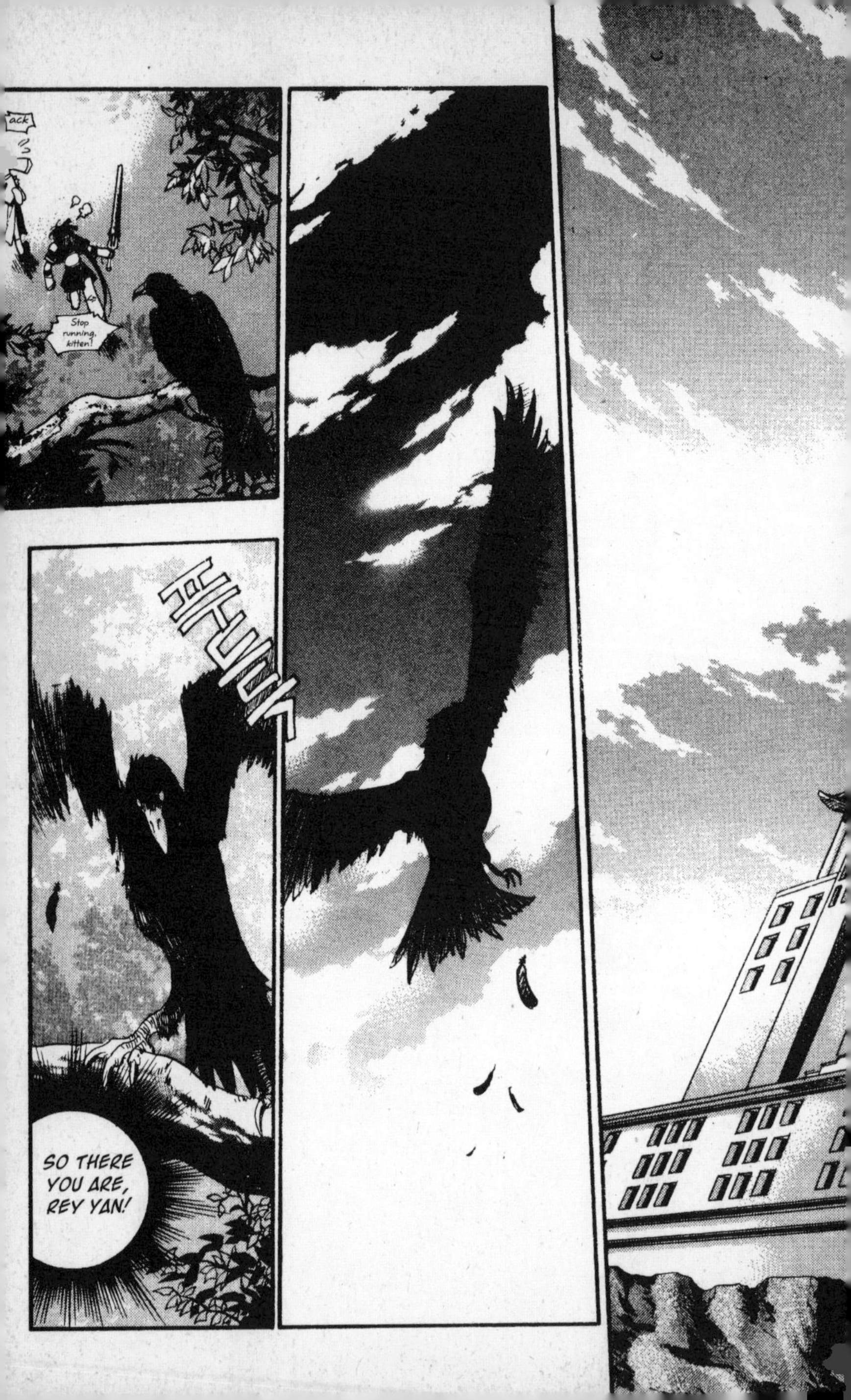
ack
Stop running, kitten!
푸드덕
SO THERE YOU ARE, REY YAN!

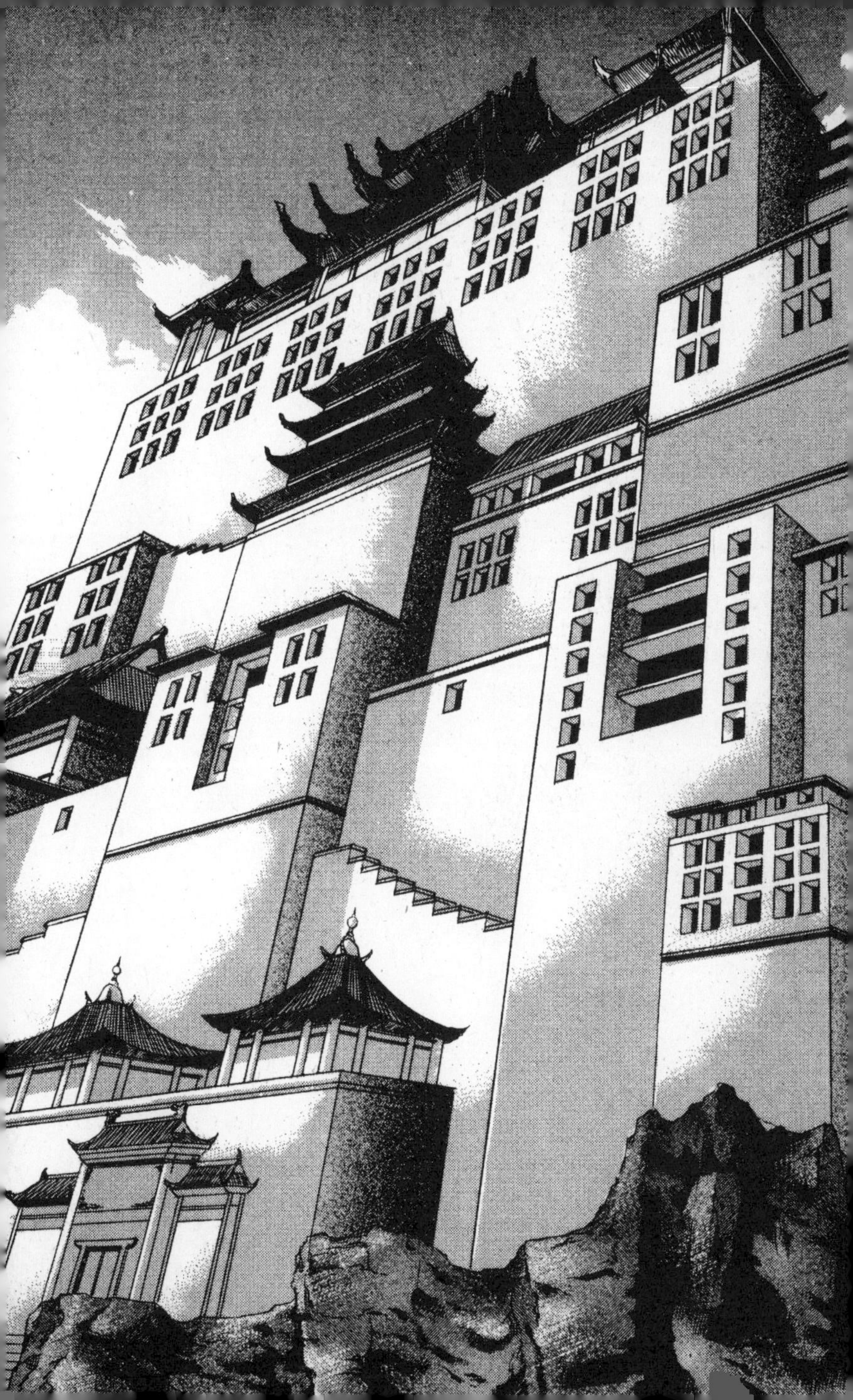

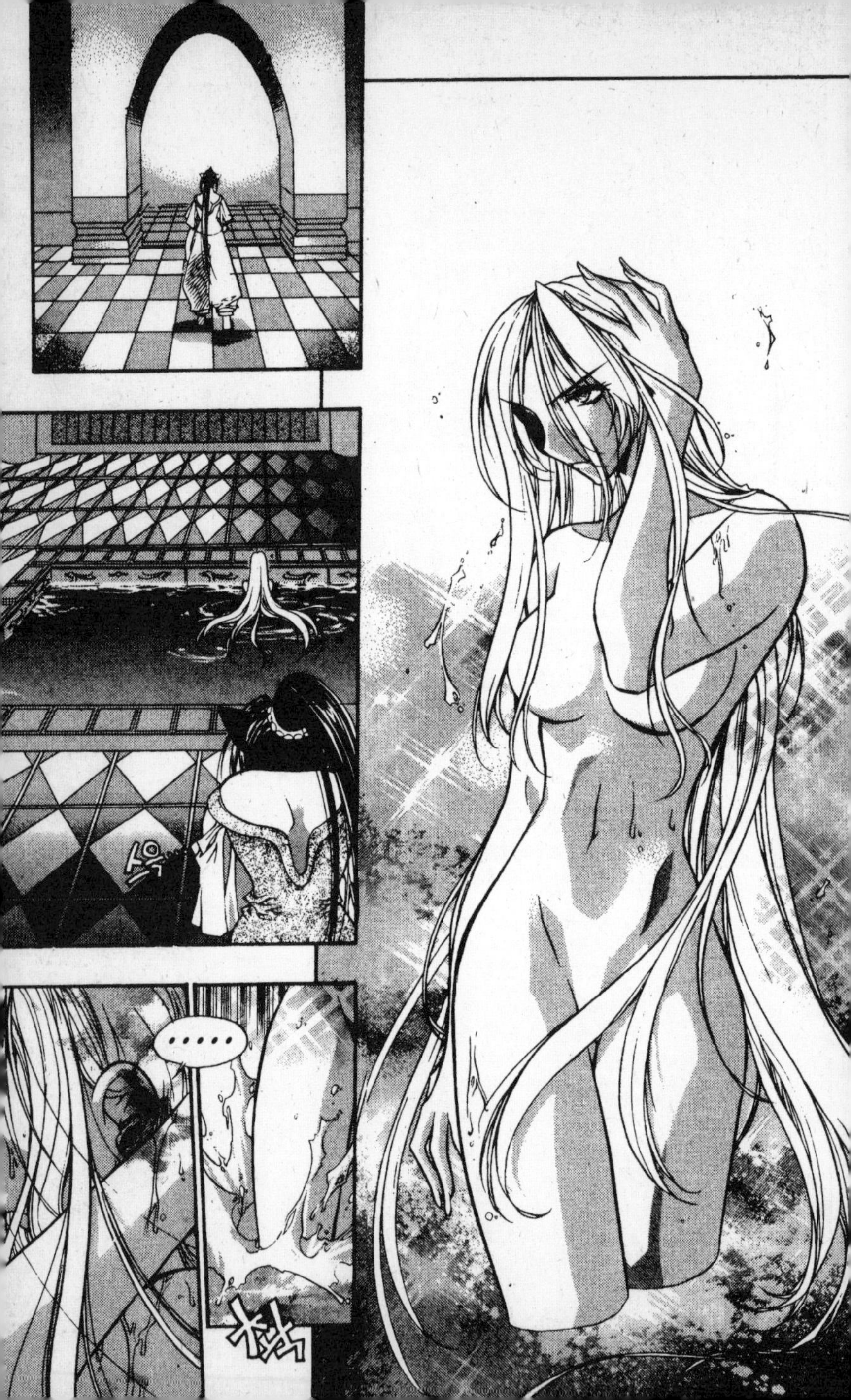
......

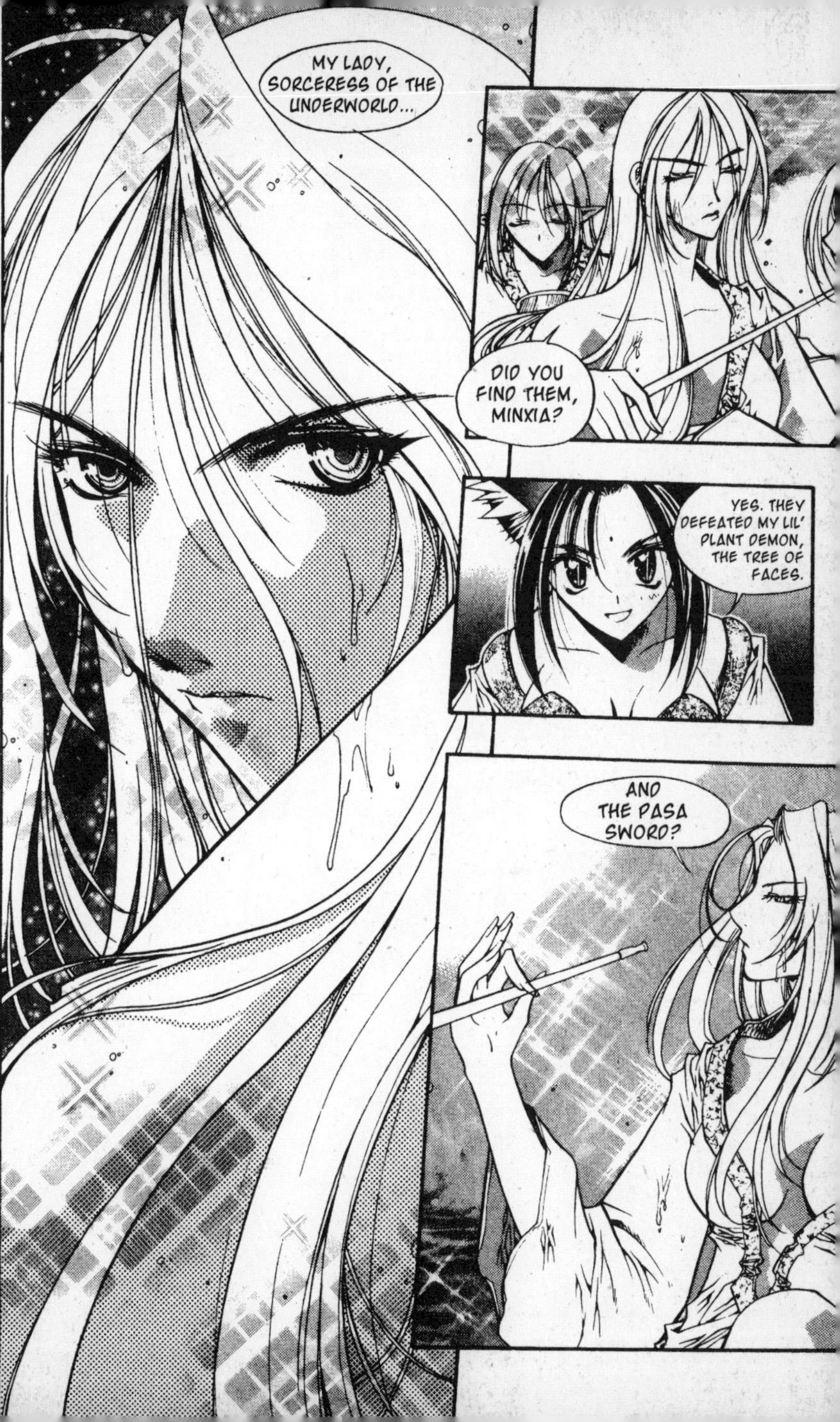
MY LADY, SORCERESS OF THE UNDERWORLD...
DID YOU FIND THEM, MINXIA?
YES. THEY DEFEATED MY LIL' PLANT DEMON, THE TREE OF FACES.
AND THE PASA SWORD?

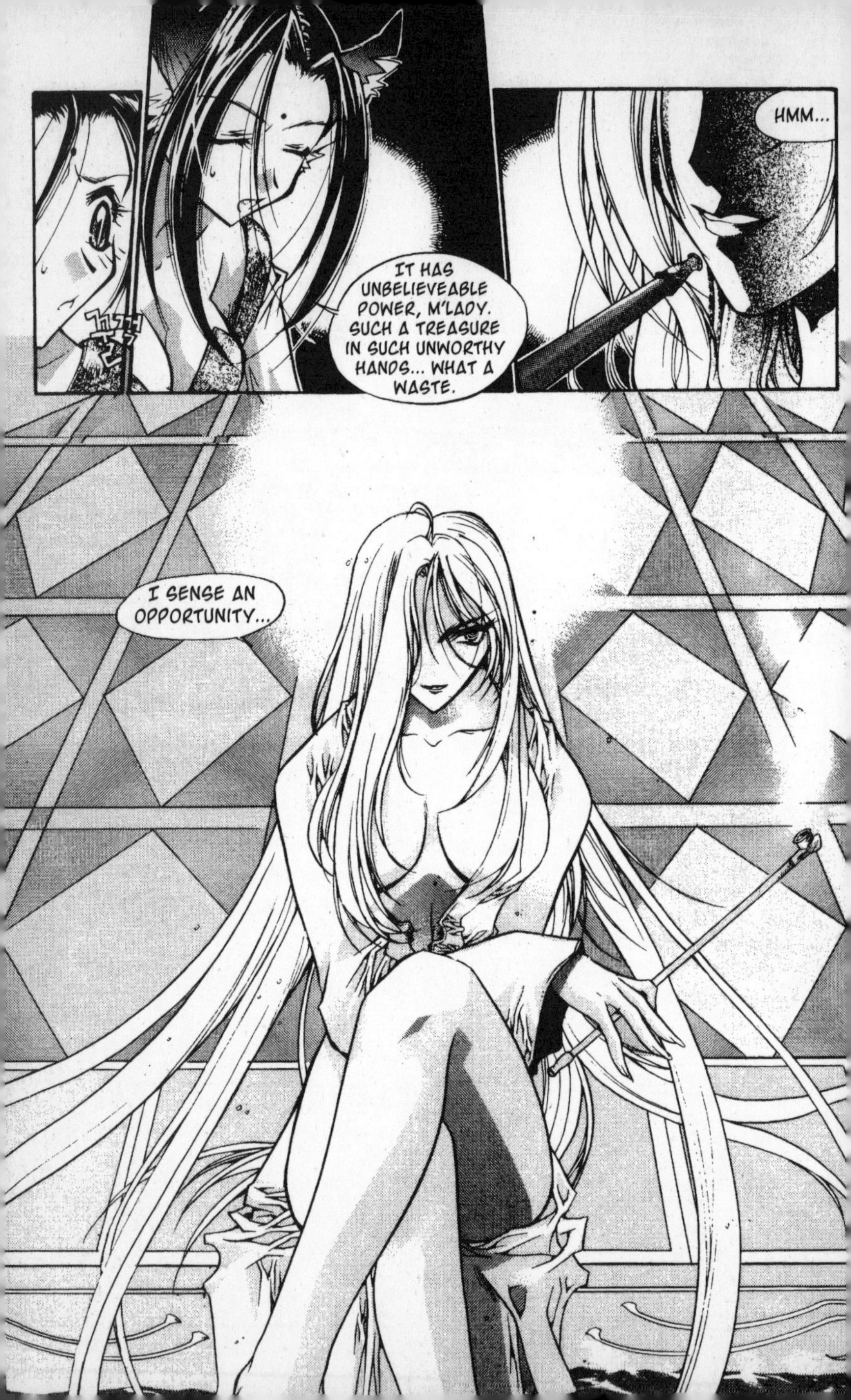
IT HAS UNBELIEVEABLE POWER, M'LADY. SUCH A TREASURE IN SUCH UNWORTHY HANDS... WHAT A WASTE.
HMM...
I SENSE AN OPPORTUNITY...

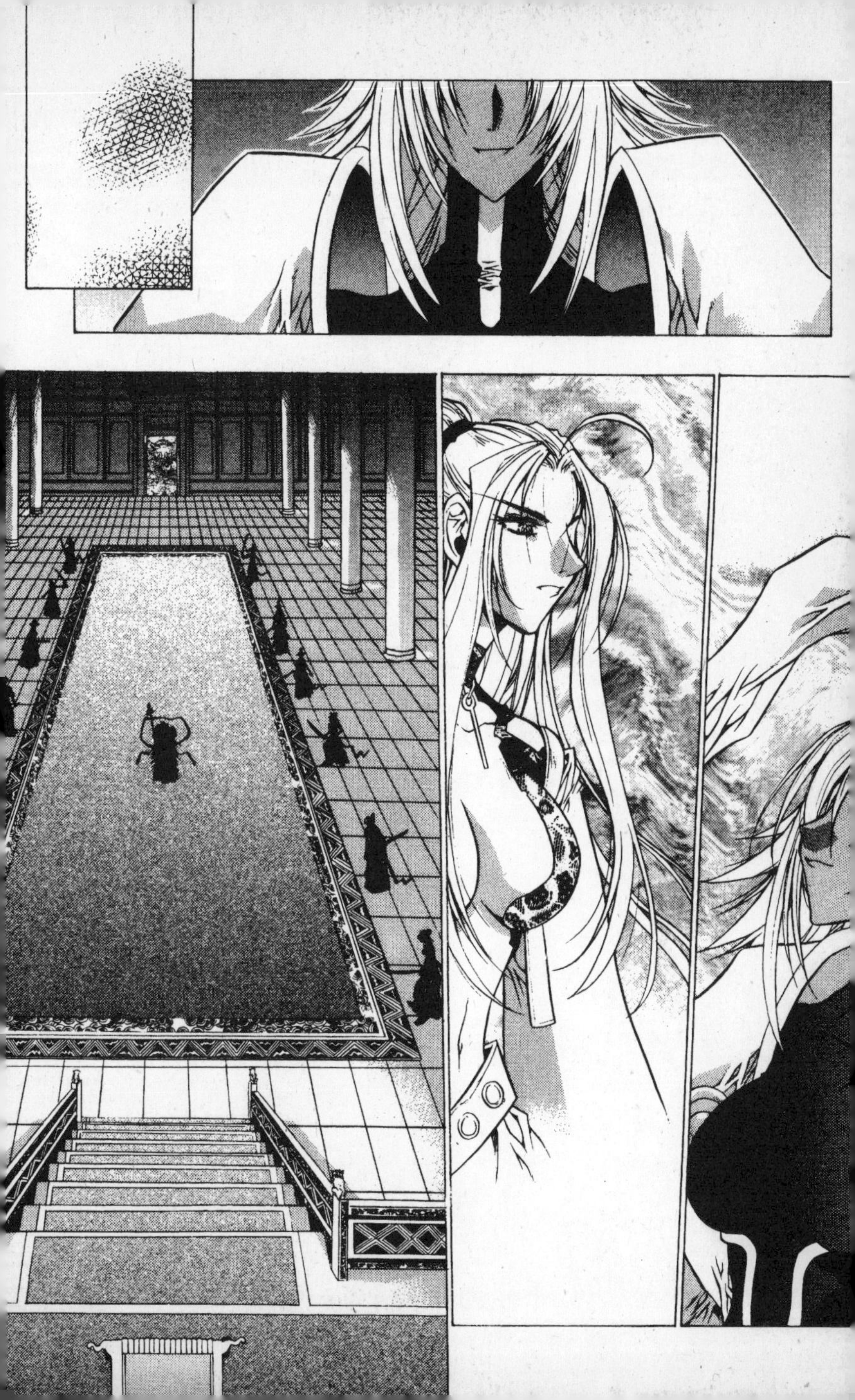

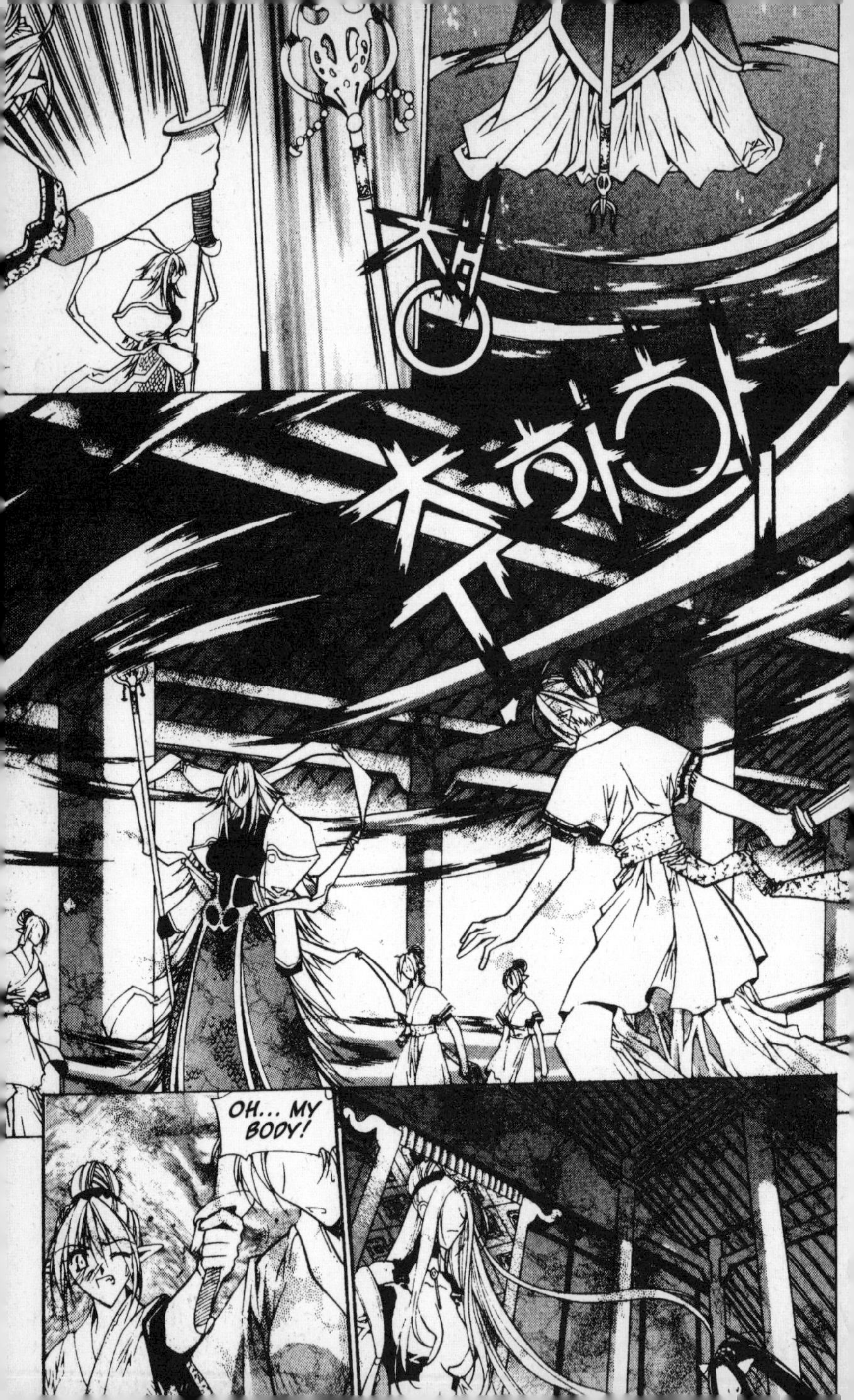
OH... MY BODY!

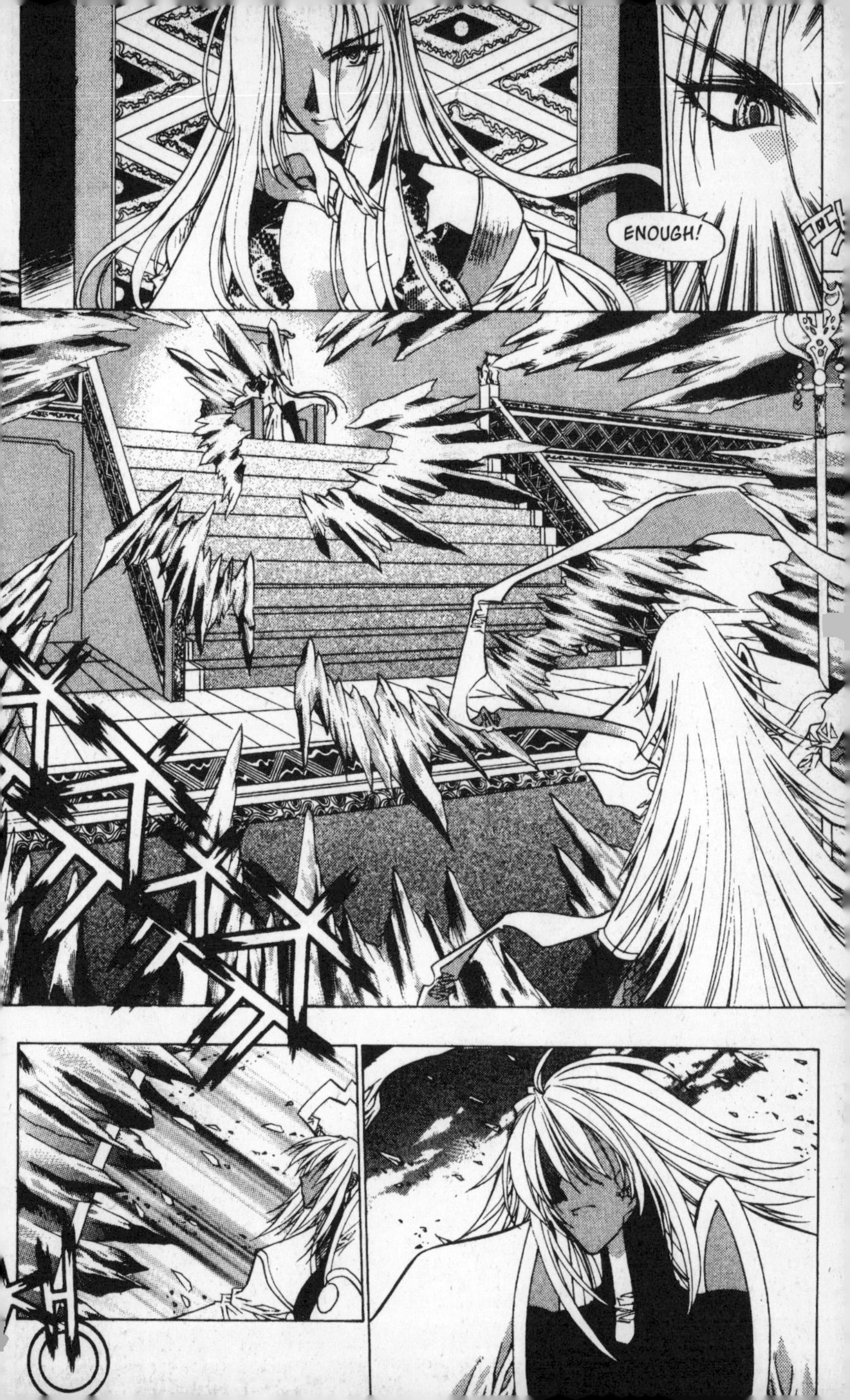
ENOUGH!

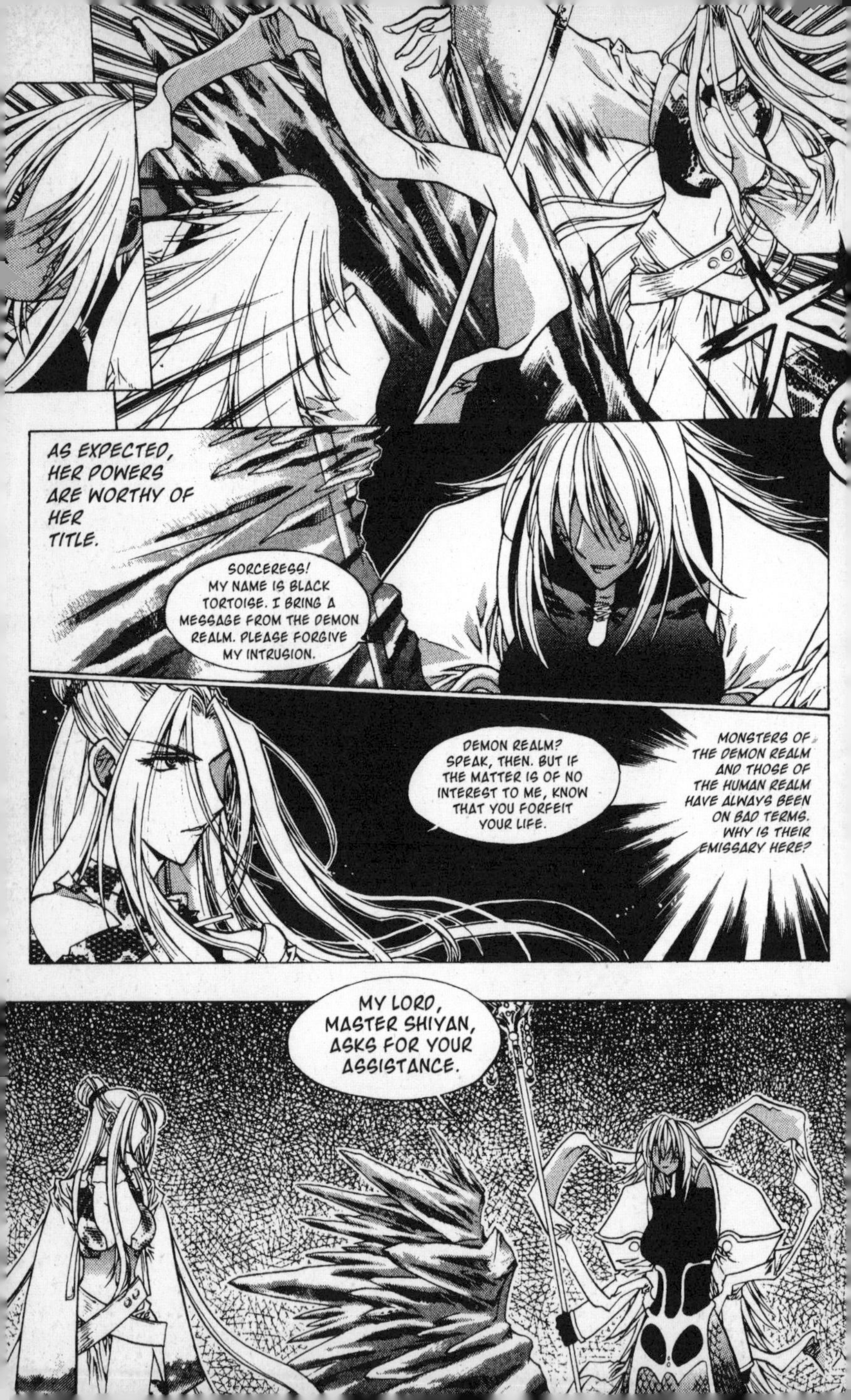
AS EXPECTED, HER POWERS ARE WORTHY OF HER TITLE.
SORCERESS! MY NAME IS BLACK TORTOISE. I BRING A MESSAGE FROM THE DEMON REALM. PLEASE FORGIVE MY INTRUSION.
DEMON REALM? SPEAK, THEN. BUT IF THE MATTER IS OF NO INTEREST TO ME, KNOW THAT YOU FORFEIT YOUR LIFE.
MONSTERS OF THE DEMON REALM AND THOSE OF THE HUMAN REALM HAVE ALWAYS BEEN ON BAD TERMS. WHY IS THEIR EMISSARY HERE?
MY LORD, MASTER SHIYAN, ASKS FOR YOUR ASSISTANCE.

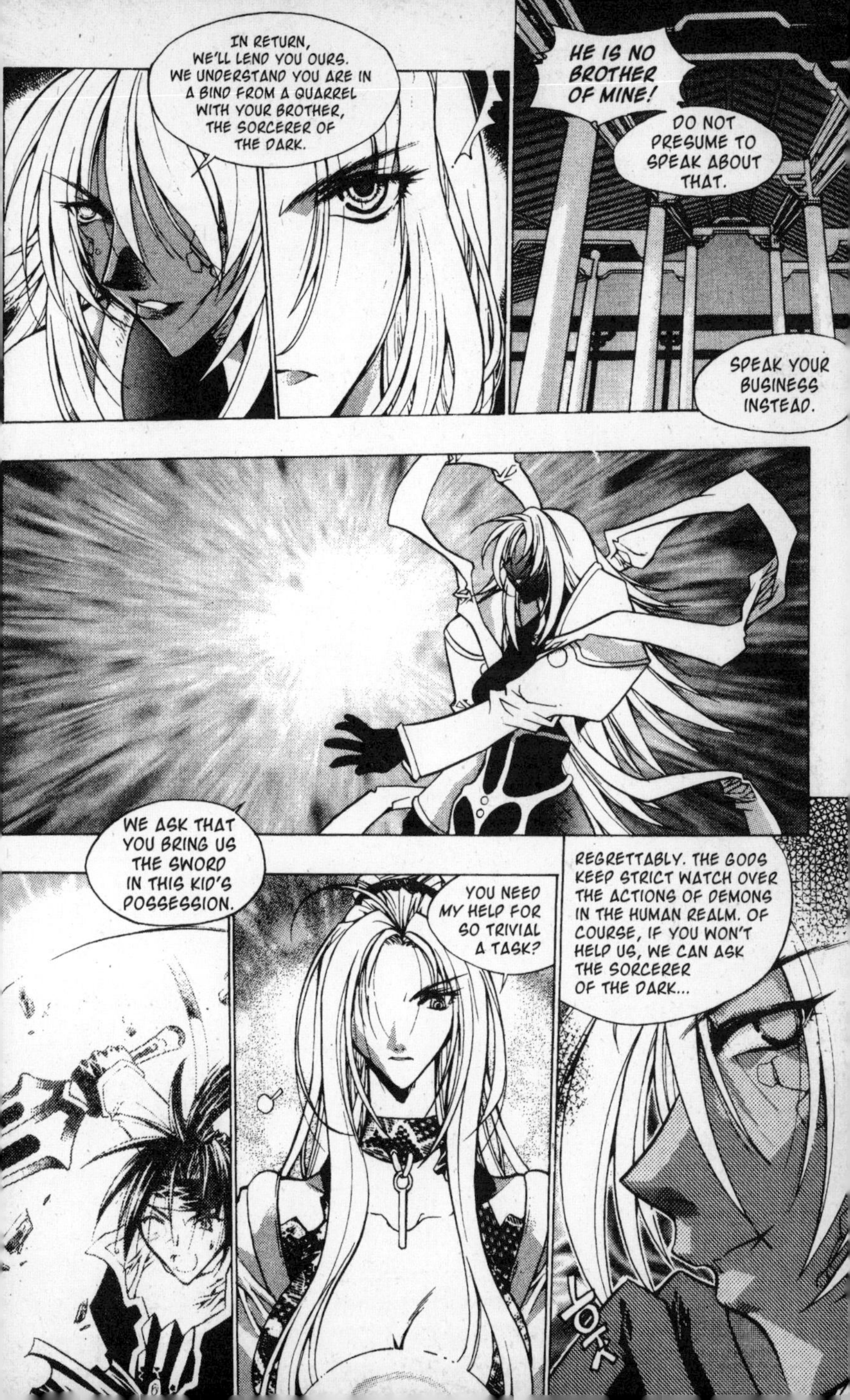
IN RETURN, WE'LL LEND YOU OURS. WE UNDERSTAND YOU ARE IN A BIND FROM A QUARREL WITH YOUR BROTHER, THE SORCERER OF THE DARK.
HE IS NO BROTHER OF MINE!
DO NOT PRESUME TO SPEAK ABOUT THAT.
SPEAK YOUR BUSINESS INSTEAD.
WE ASK THAT YOU BRING US THE SWORD IN THIS KID'S POSSESSION.
YOU NEED MY HELP FOR SO TRIVIAL A TASK?
REGRETTABLY. THE GODS KEEP STRICT WATCH OVER THE ACTIONS OF DEMONS IN THE HUMAN REALM. OF COURSE, IF YOU WON'T HELP US, WE CAN ASK THE SORCERER OF THE DARK...

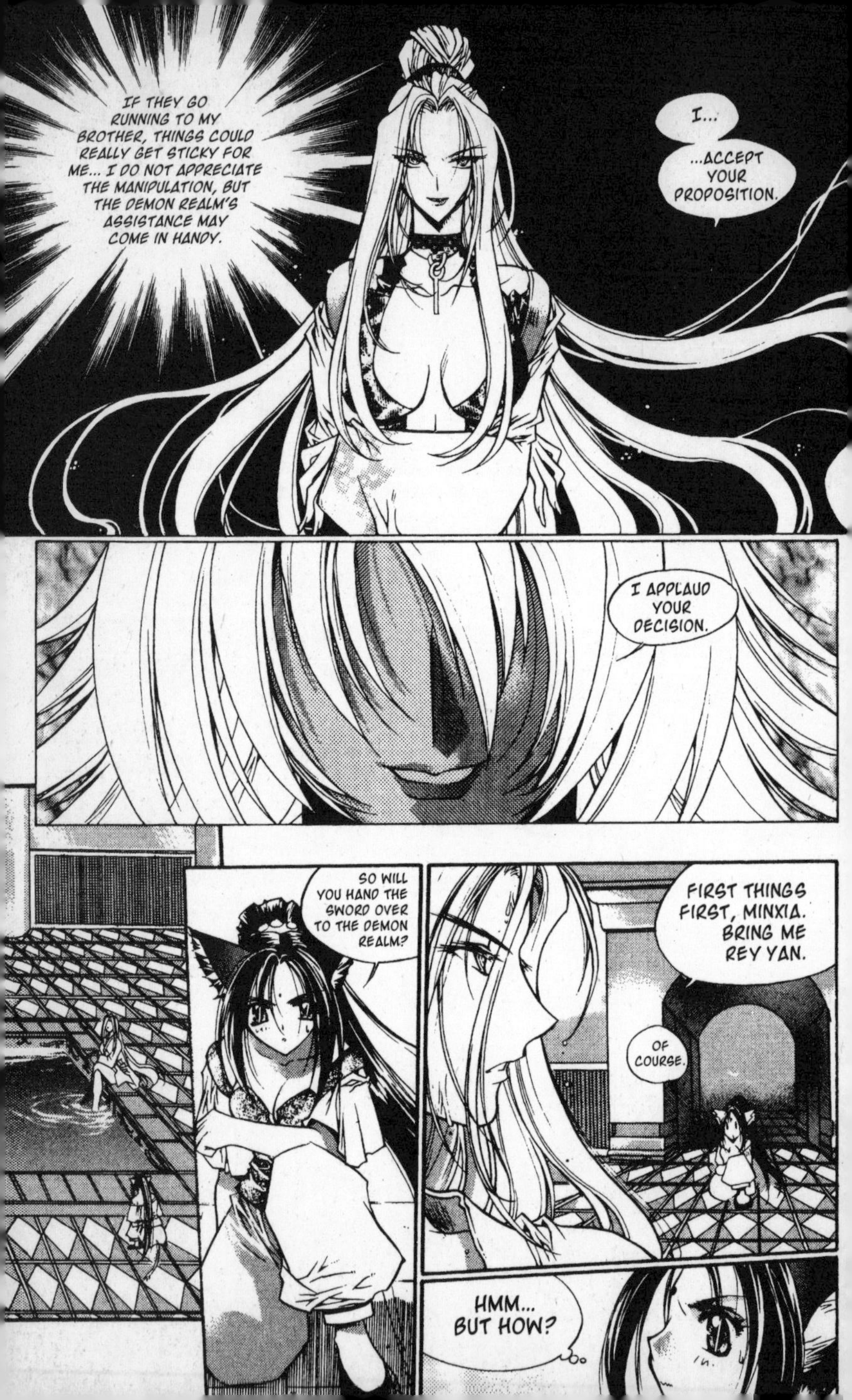
IF THEY GO RUNNING TO MY BROTHER, THINGS COULD REALLY GET STICKY FOR ME... I DO NOT APPRECIATE THE MANIPULATION, BUT THE DEMON REALM'S ASSISTANCE MAY COME IN HANDY.
I...
...ACCEPT YOUR PROPOSITION.
I APPLAUD YOUR DECISION.
SO WILL YOU HAND THE SWORD OVER TO THE DEMON REALM?
FIRST THINGS FIRST, MINXIA. BRING ME REY YAN.
OF COURSE.
HMM... BUT HOW?

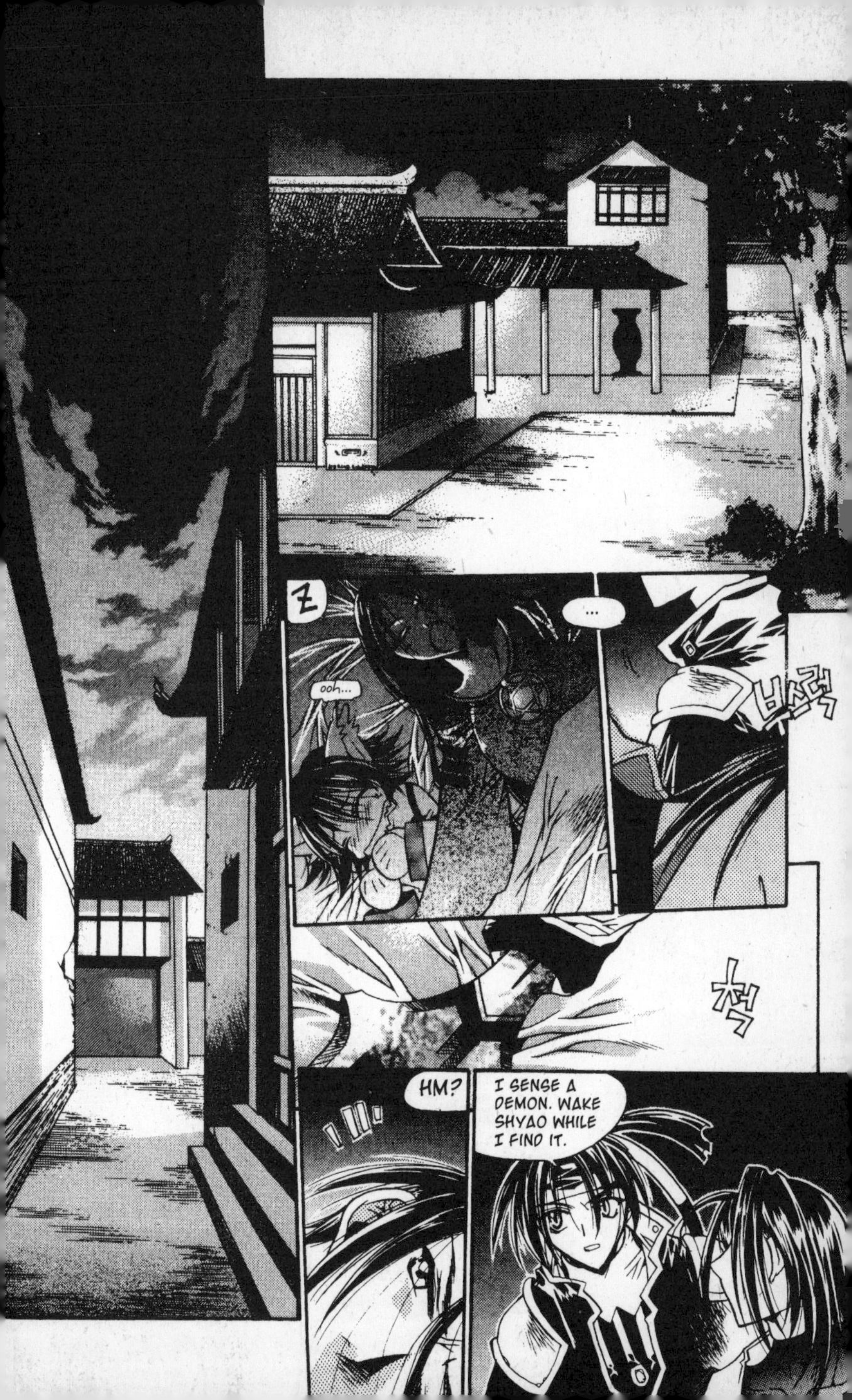
Z
ooh...
...
부스럭
척
HM?
I SENSE A DEMON. WAKE SHYAO WHILE I FIND IT.

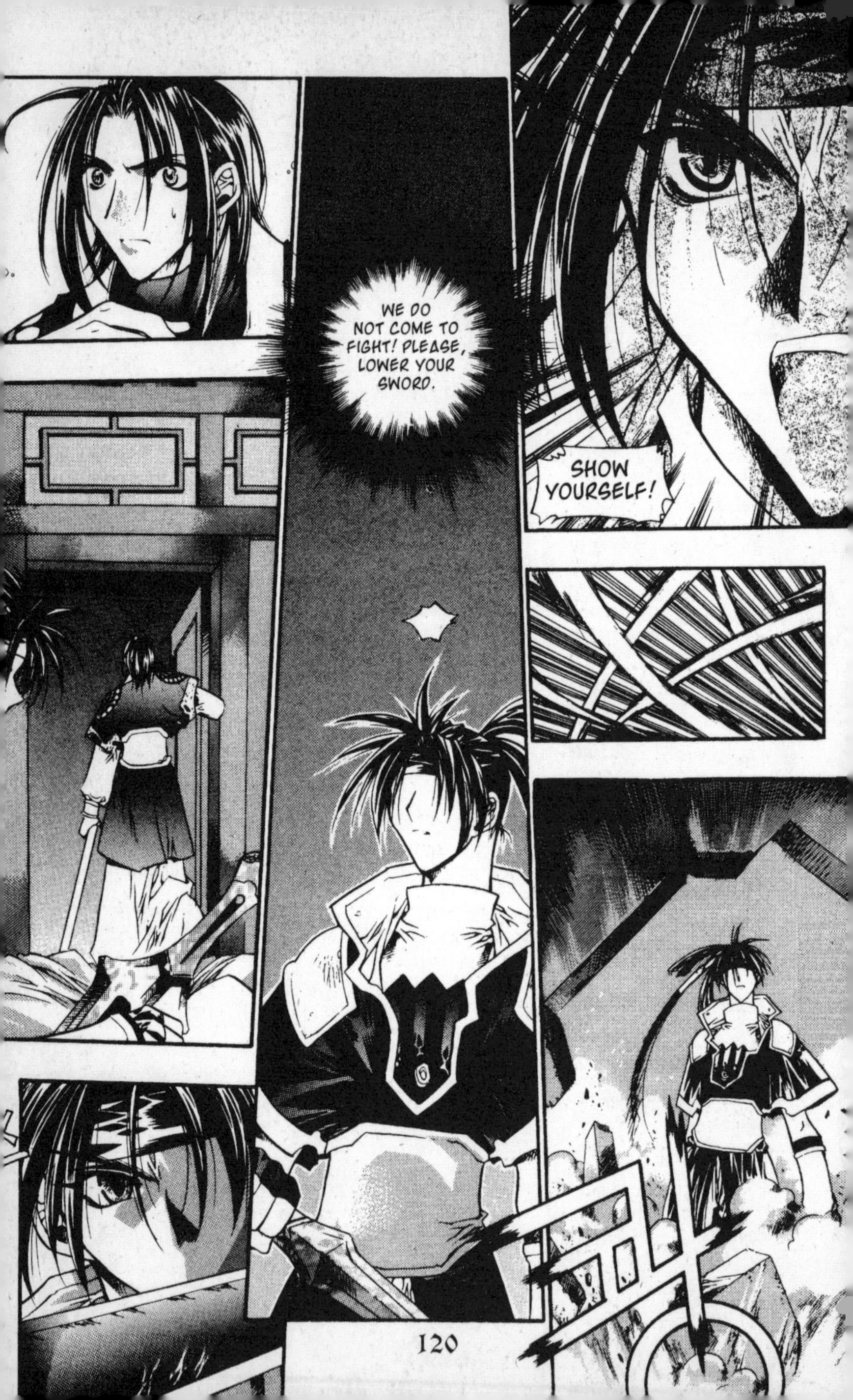
WE DO NOT COME TO FIGHT! PLEASE, LOWER YOUR SWORD.
SHOW YOURSELF!

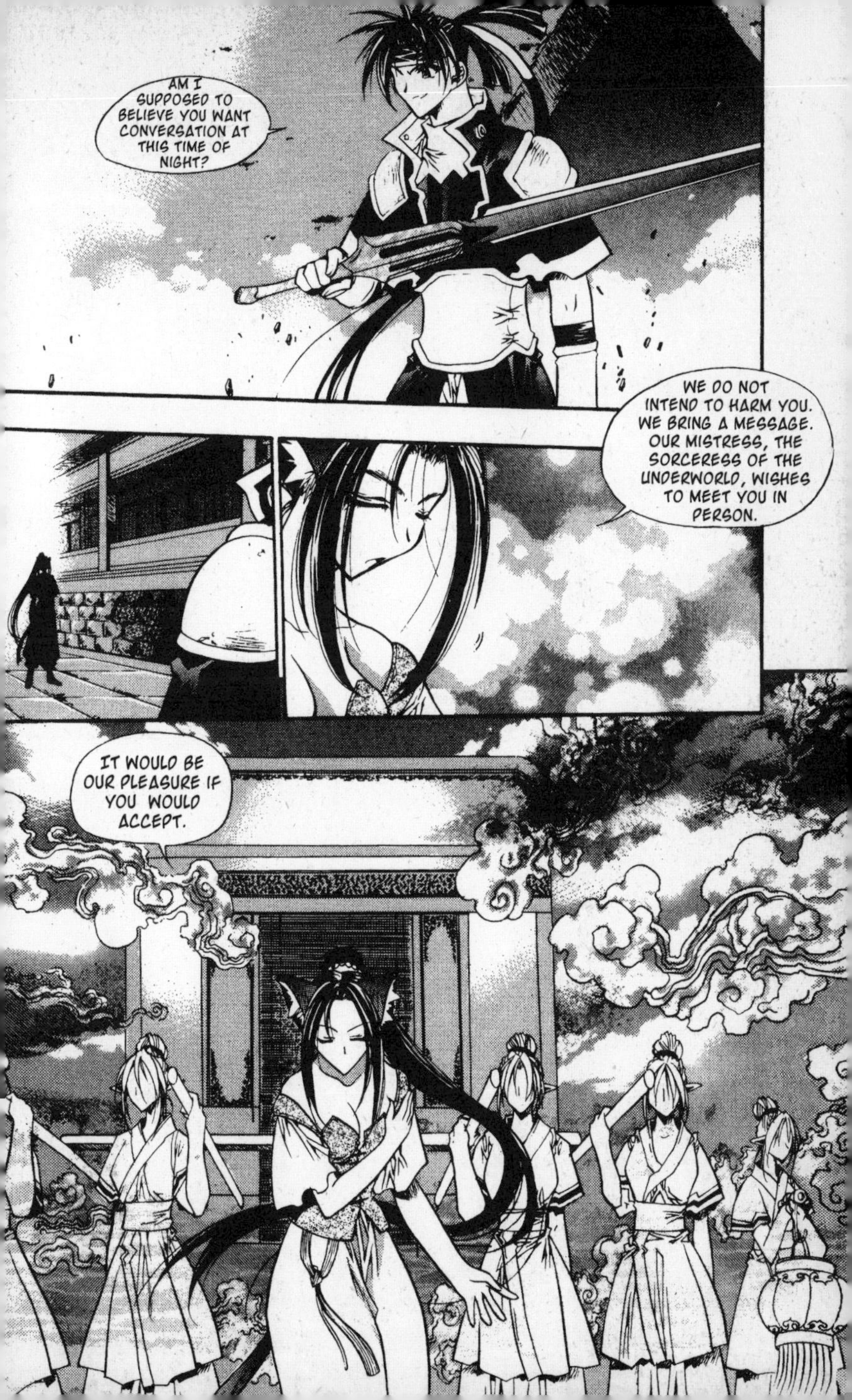
AM I SUPPOSED TO BELIEVE YOU WANT CONVERSATION AT THIS TIME OF NIGHT?
WE DO NOT INTEND TO HARM YOU. WE BRING A MESSAGE. OUR MISTRESS, THE SORCERESS OF THE UNDERWORLD, WISHES TO MEET YOU IN PERSON.
IT WOULD BE OUR PLEASURE IF YOU WOULD ACCEPT.

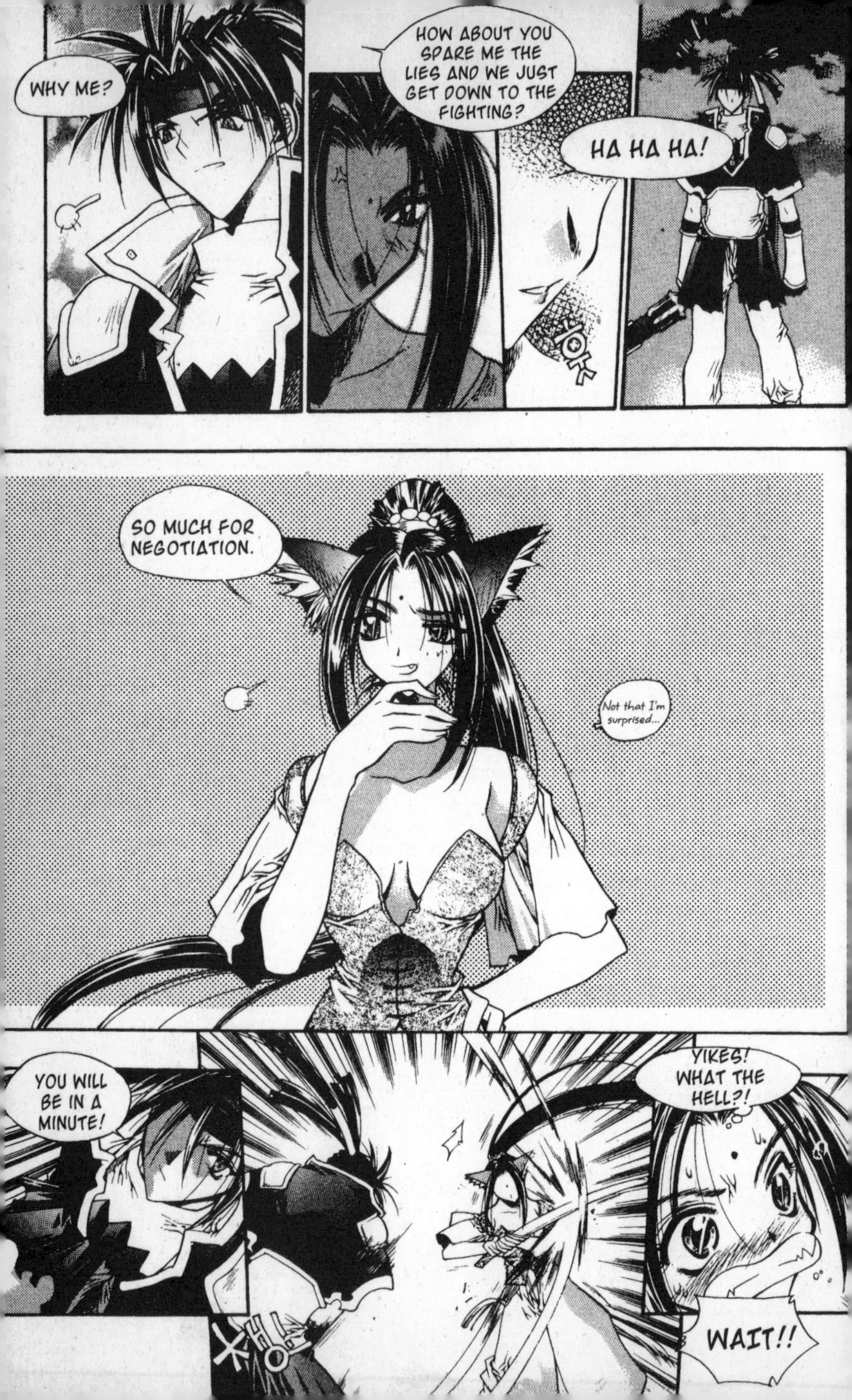
WHY ME?
HOW ABOUT YOU SPARE ME THE LIES AND WE JUST GET DOWN TO THE FIGHTING?
HA HA HA!
SO MUCH FOR NEGOTIATION.
Not that I'm surprised...
YOU WILL BE IN A MINUTE!
YIKES! WHAT THE HELL?!
WAIT!!

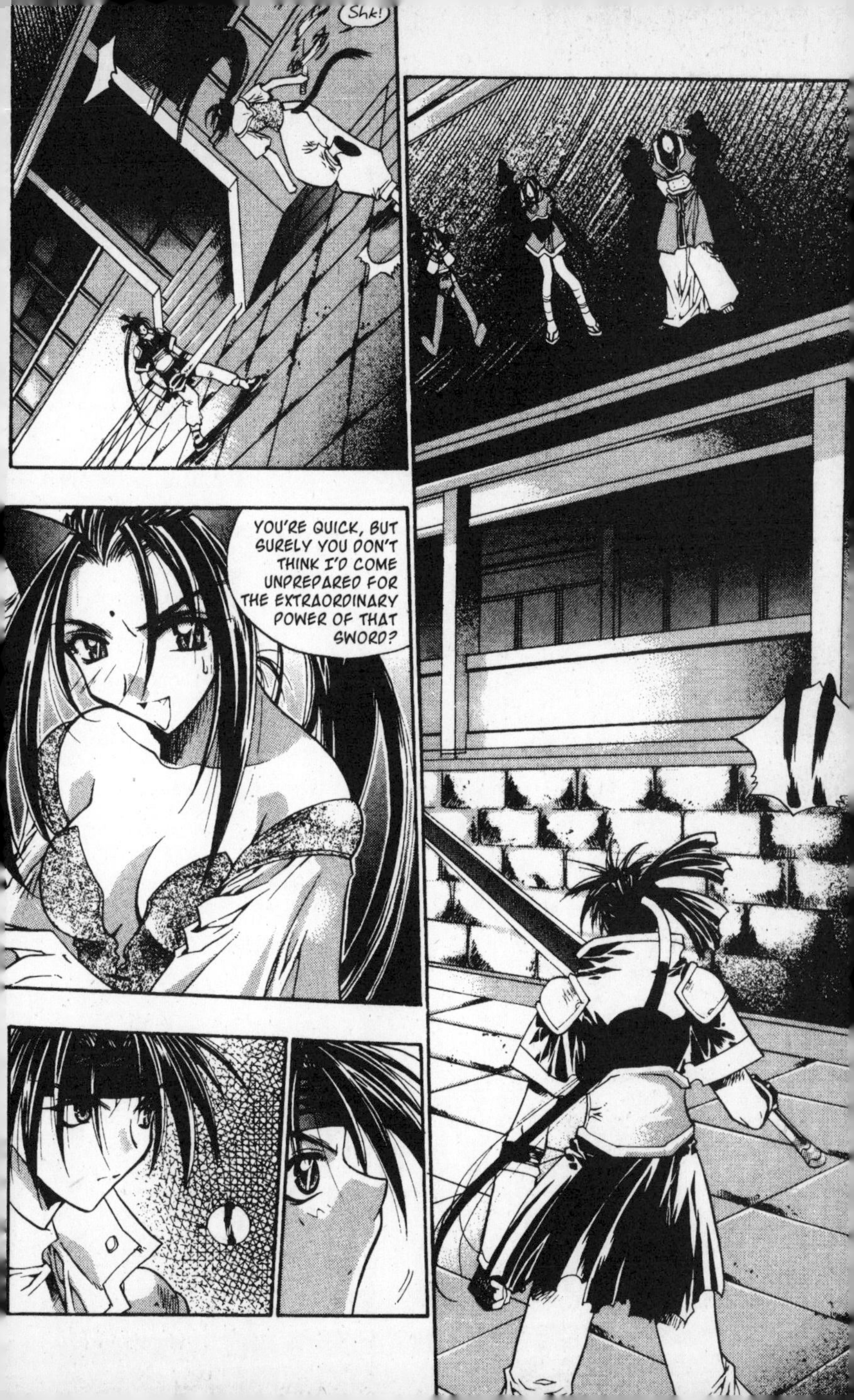
Shk!
YOU'RE QUICK, BUT SURELY YOU DON'T THINK I'D COME UNPREPARED FOR THE EXTRAORDINARY POWER OF THAT SWORD?

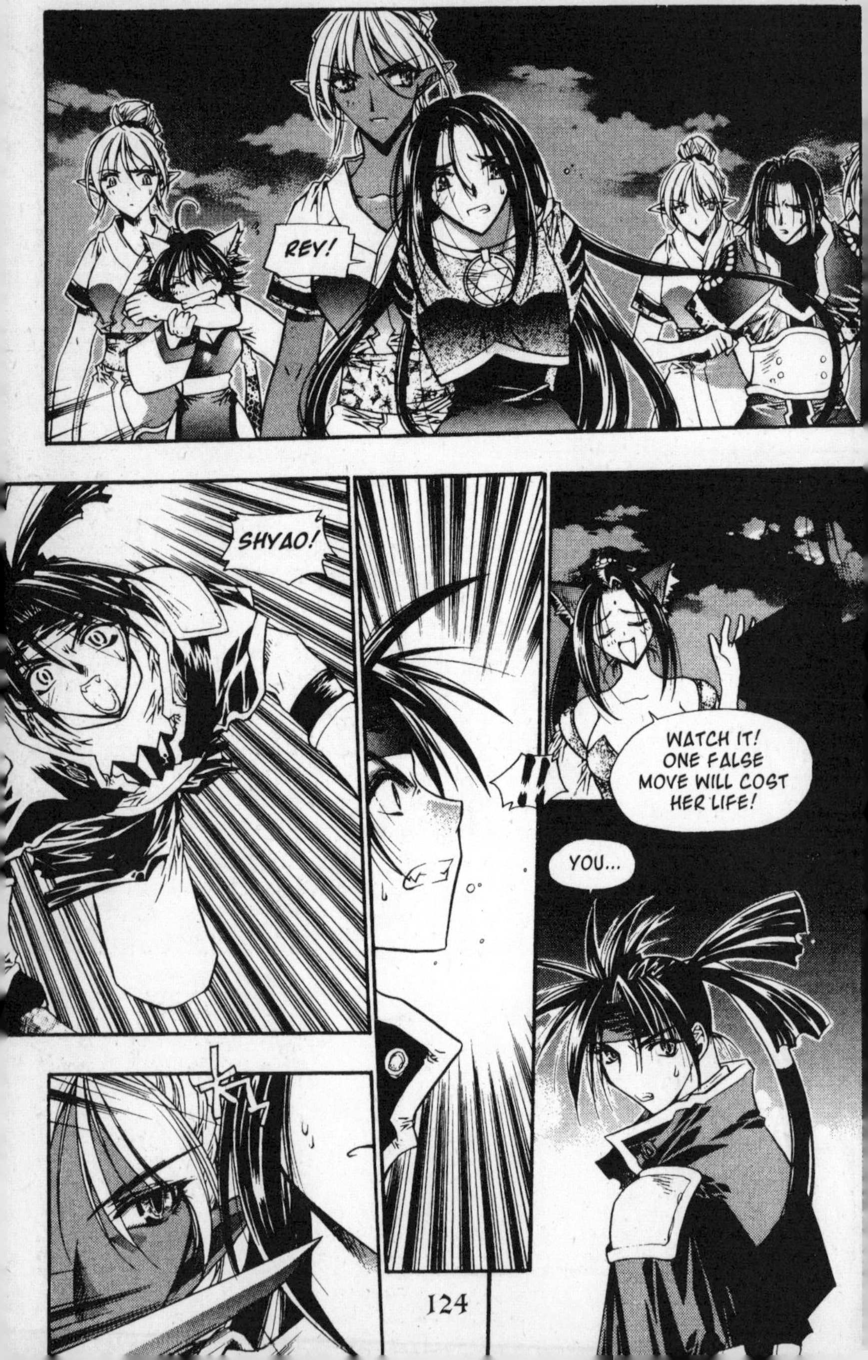
REY!
SHYAO!
WATCH IT! ONE FALSE MOVE WILL COST HER LIFE!
YOU...

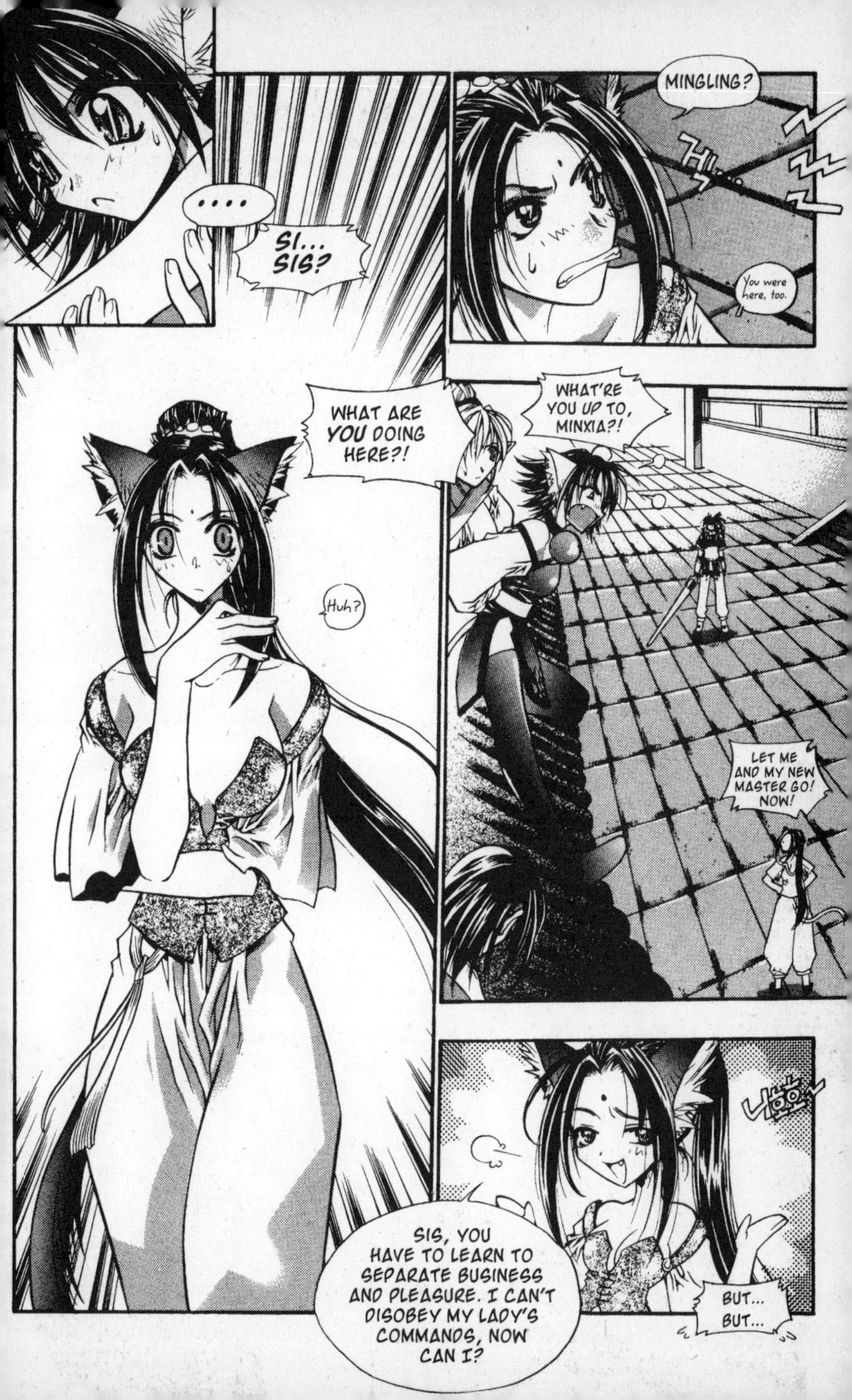

....
SI... SIS?
MINGLING?
You were here, too.
WHAT ARE YOU DOING HERE?!
Huh?
WHAT'RE YOU UP TO, MINXIA?!
LET ME AND MY NEW MASTER GO! NOW!
SIS, YOU HAVE TO LEARN TO SEPARATE BUSINESS AND PLEASURE. I CAN'T DISOBEY MY LADY'S COMMANDS, NOW CAN I?
BUT... BUT...

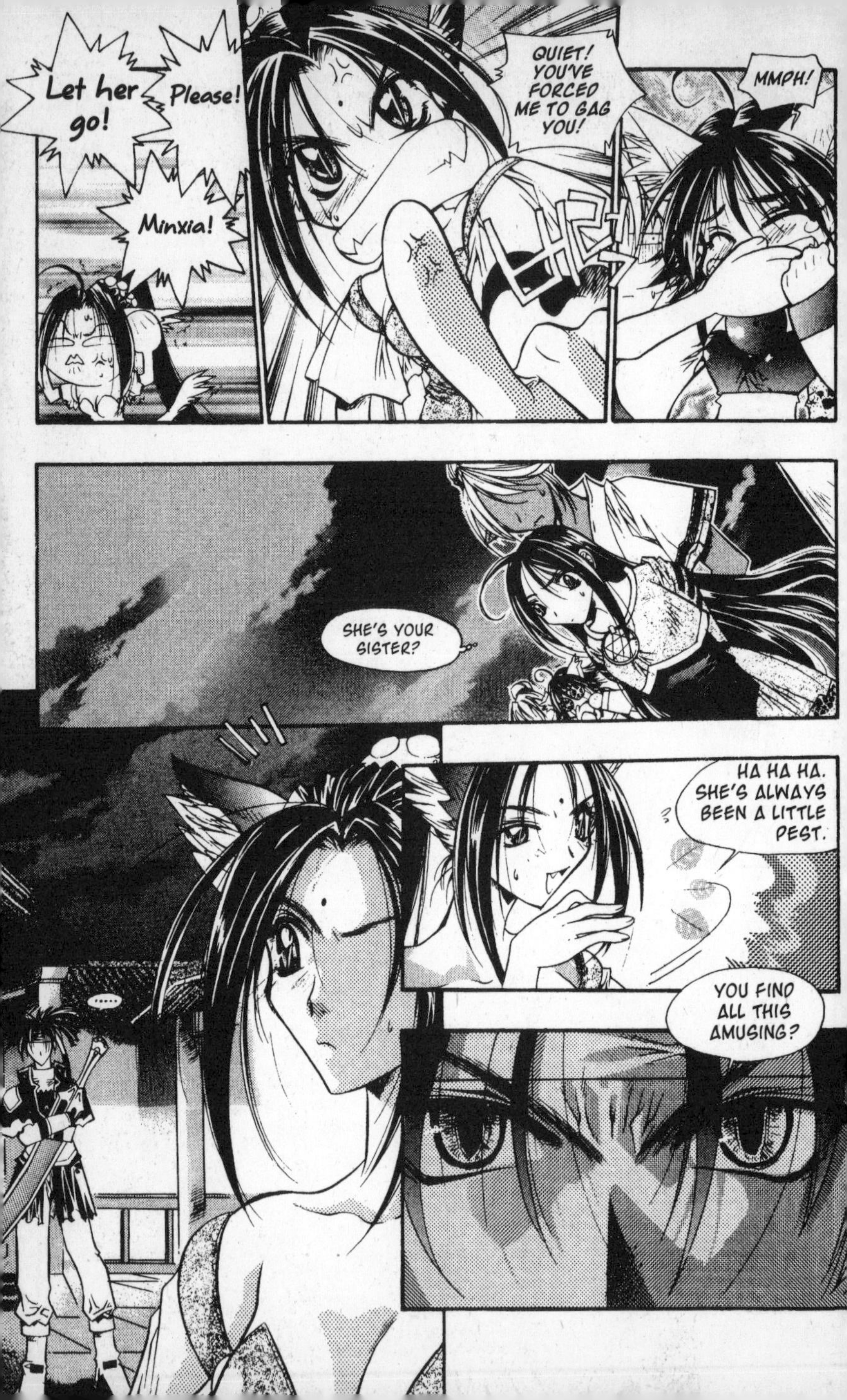
Let her go!
Please!
Minxia!
QUIET! YOU'VE FORCED ME TO GAG YOU!
MMPH!
SHE'S YOUR SISTER?
......
HA HA HA. SHE'S ALWAYS BEEN A LITTLE PEST.
YOU FIND ALL THIS AMUSING?

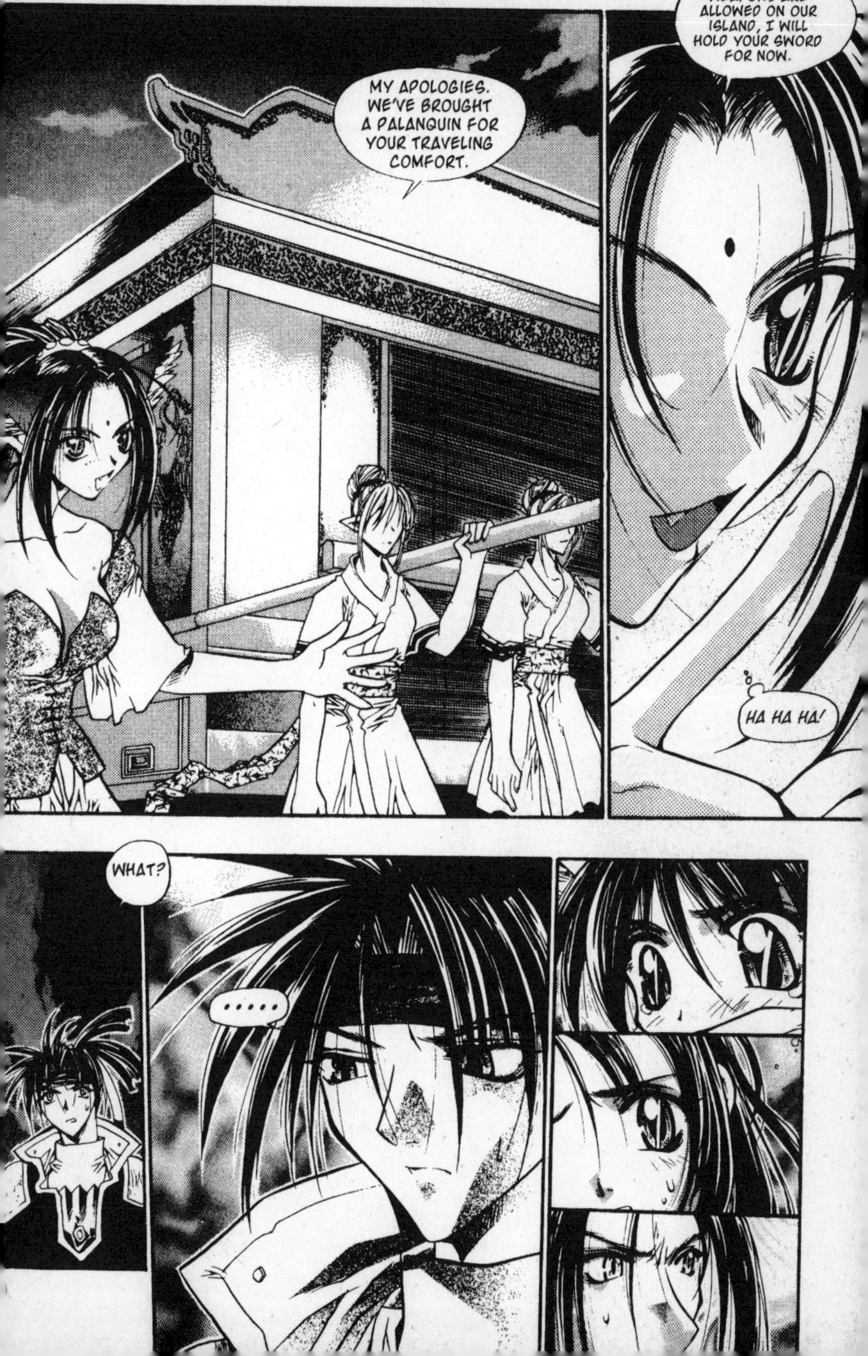
MY APOLOGIES. WE'VE BROUGHT A PALANQUIN FOR YOUR TRAVELING COMFORT.
BUT SINCE NO WEAPONS ARE ALLOWED ON OUR ISLAND, I WILL HOLD YOUR SWORD FOR NOW.
HA HA HA!
WHAT?
.....

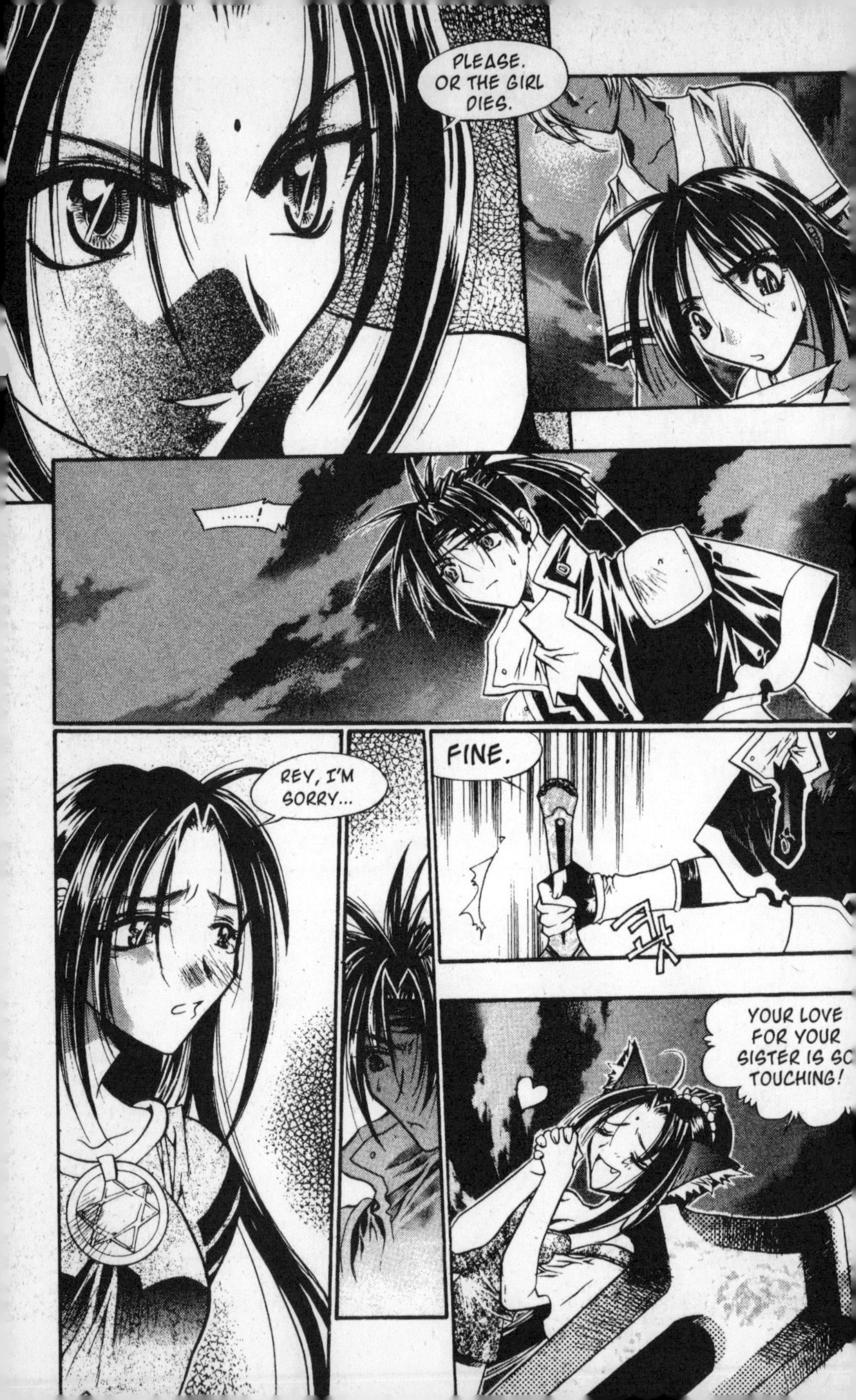
PLEASE. OR THE GIRL DIES.
......!
REY, I'M SORRY...
FINE.
YOUR LOVE FOR YOUR SISTER IS SO TOUCHING!

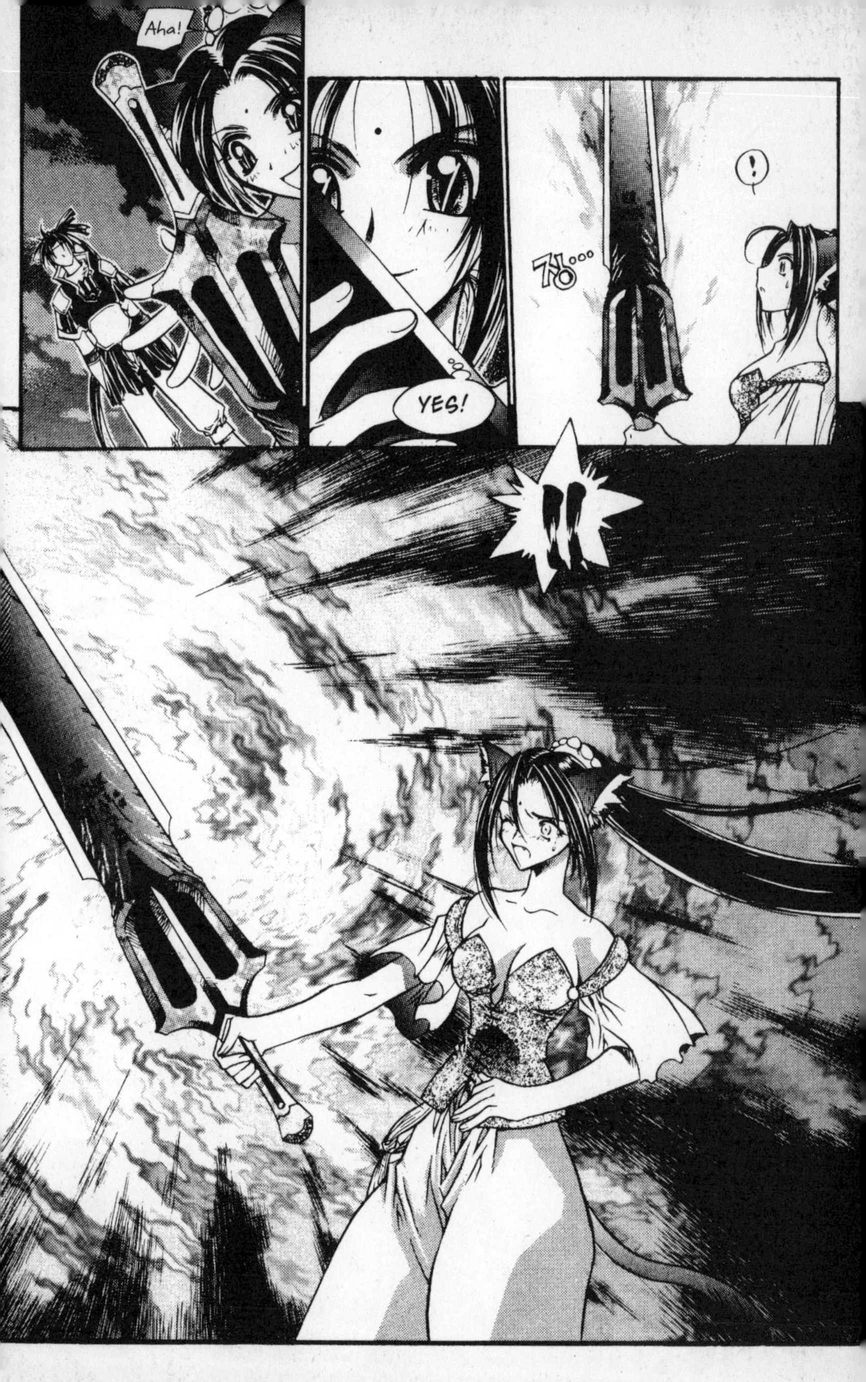

Aha!
YES!
!

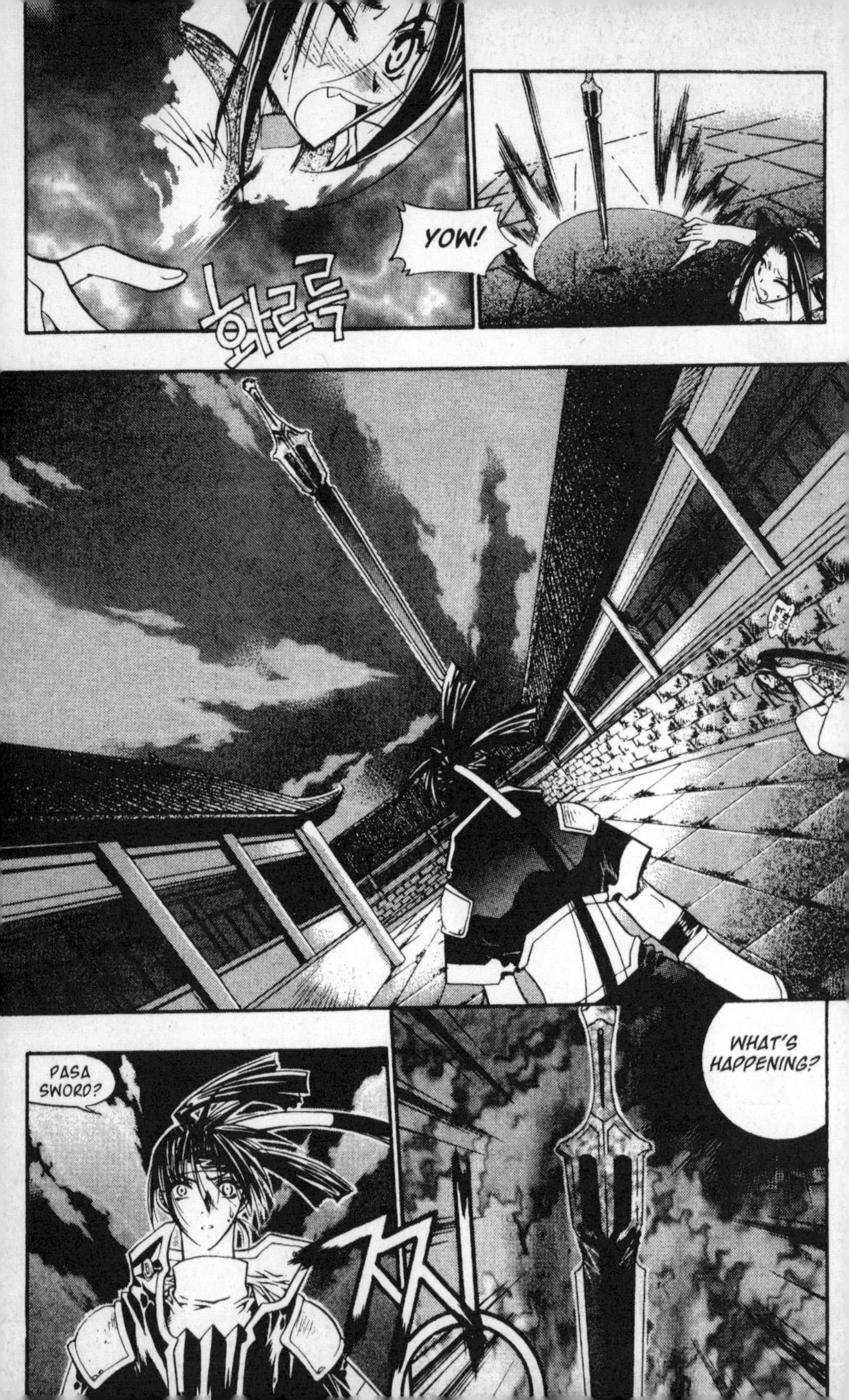

화르륵
YOW!
PASA SWORD?
WHAT'S HAPPENING?

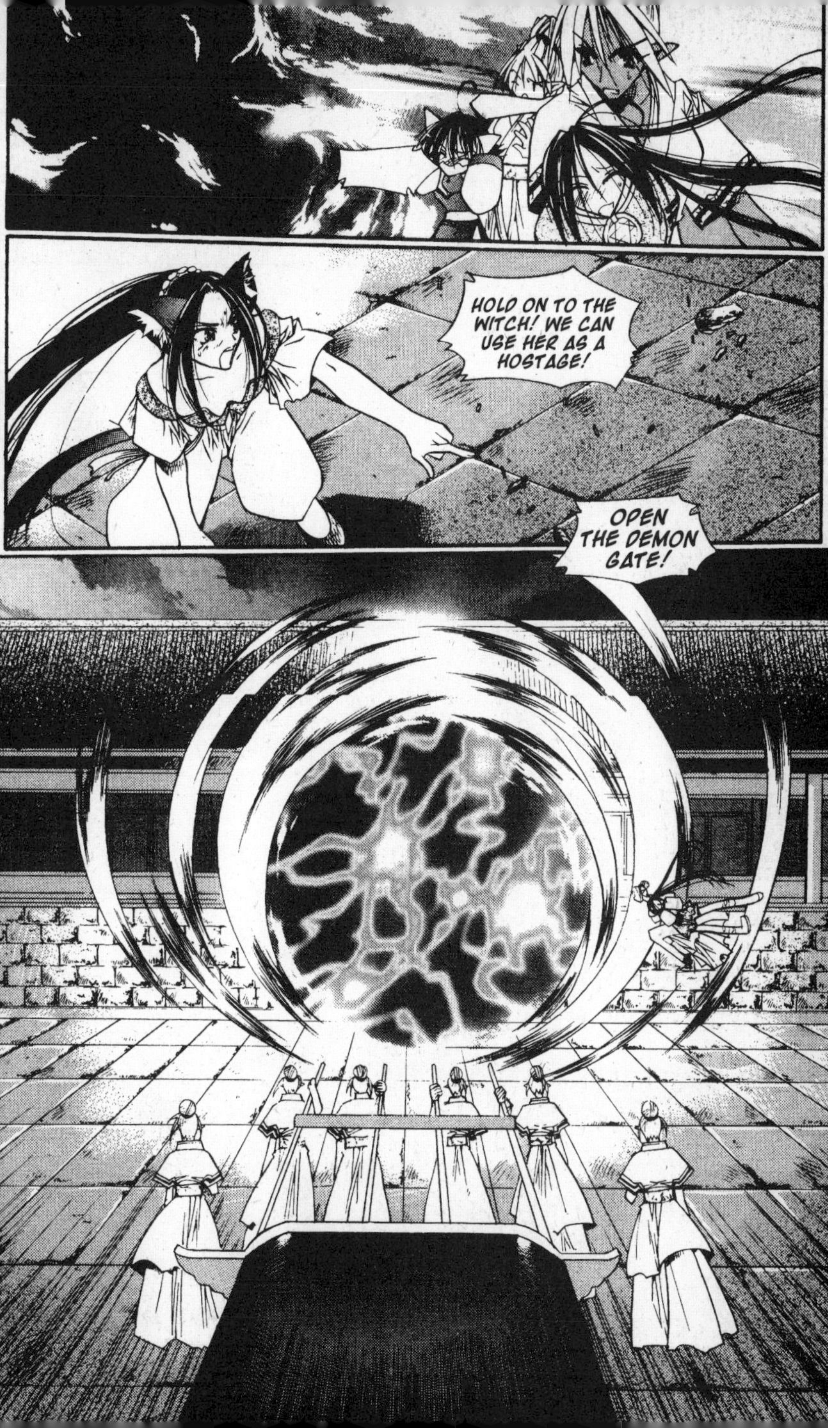
HOLD ON TO THE WITCH! WE CAN USE HER AS A HOSTAGE!
OPEN THE DEMON GATE!

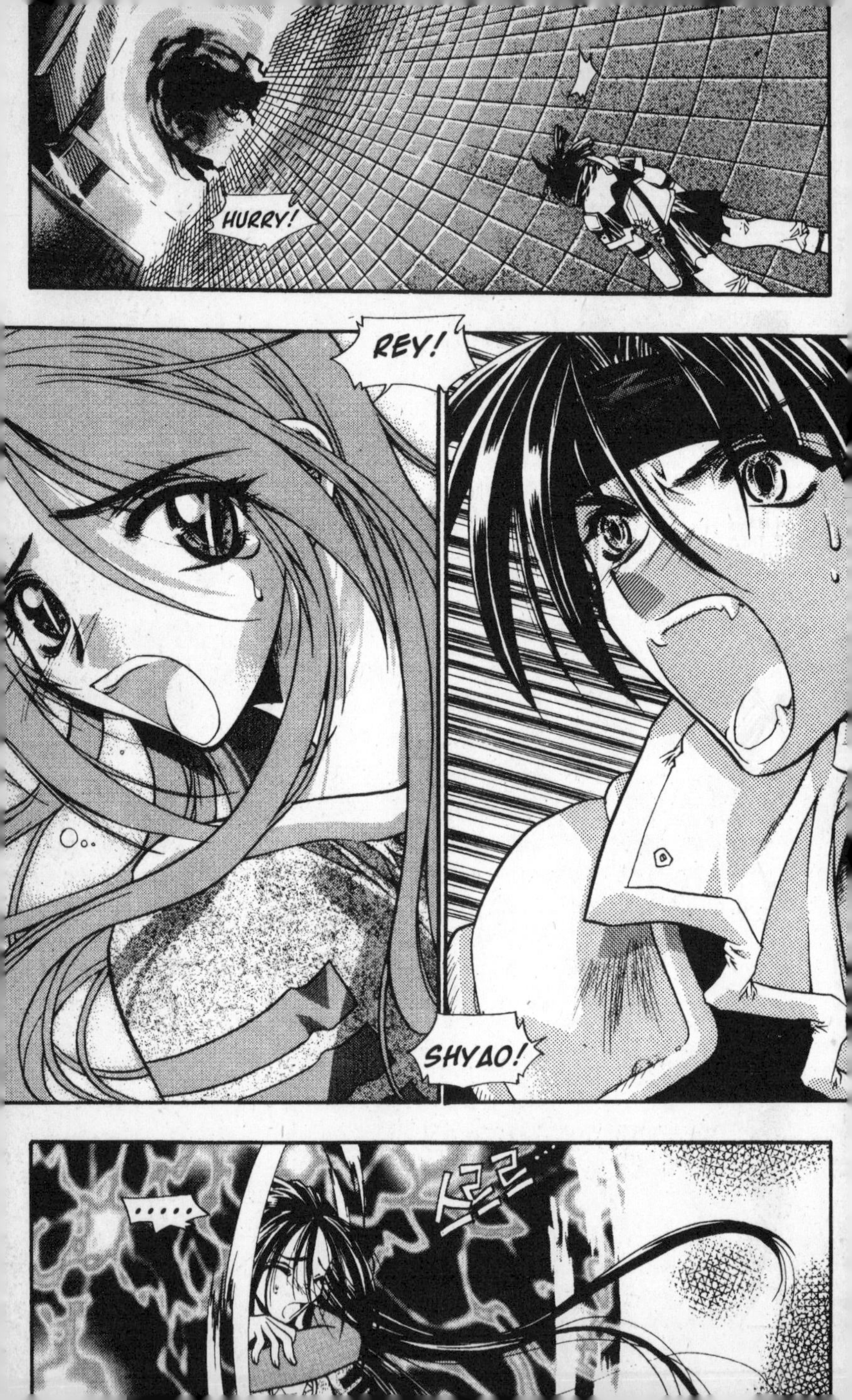
HURRY!
REY!
SHYAO!
......

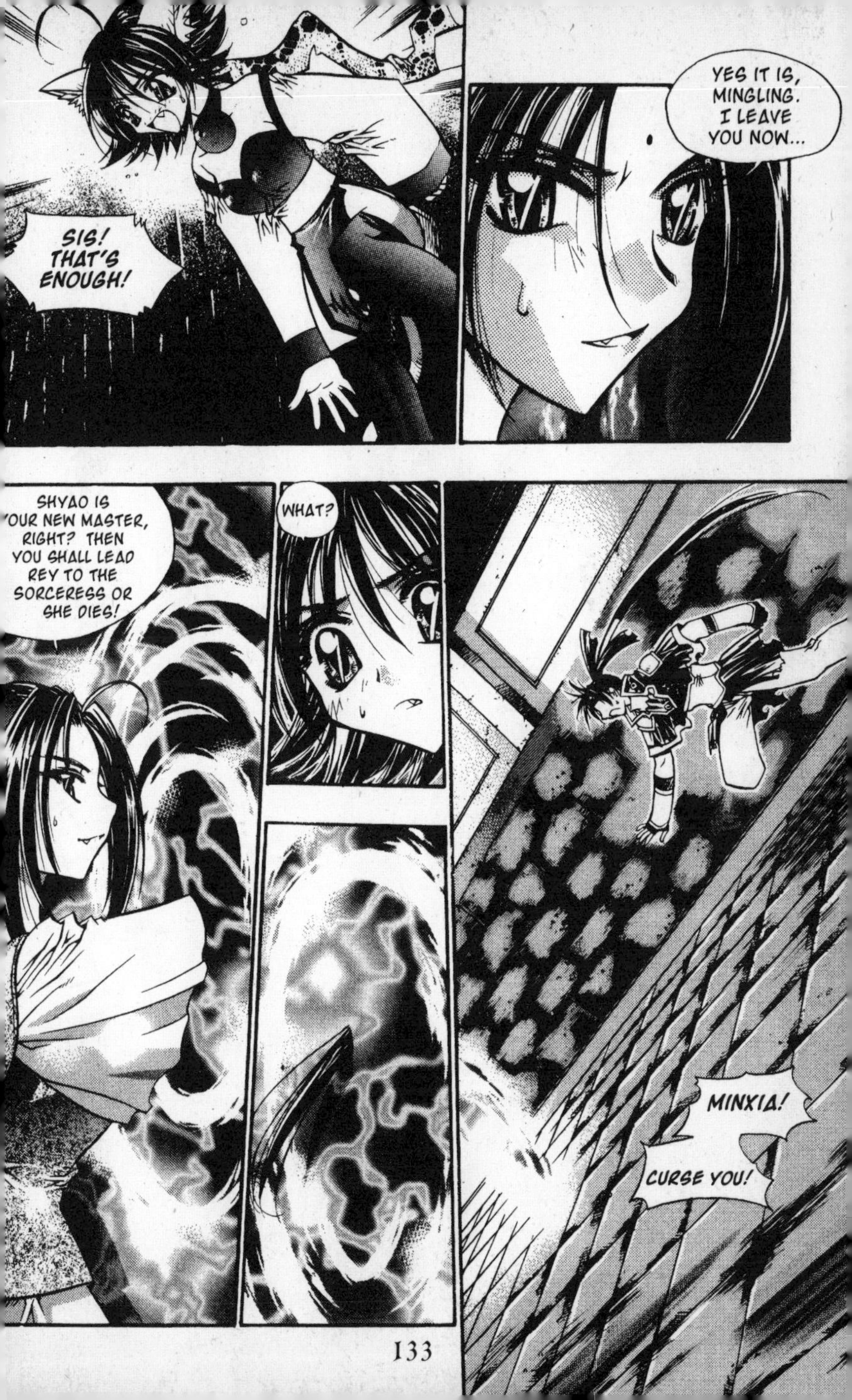
SIS! THAT'S ENOUGH!
YES IT IS, MINGLING. I LEAVE YOU NOW...
SHYAO IS OUR NEW MASTER, RIGHT? THEN YOU SHALL LEAD REY TO THE SORCERESS OR SHE DIES!
WHAT?
MINXIA!
CURSE YOU!

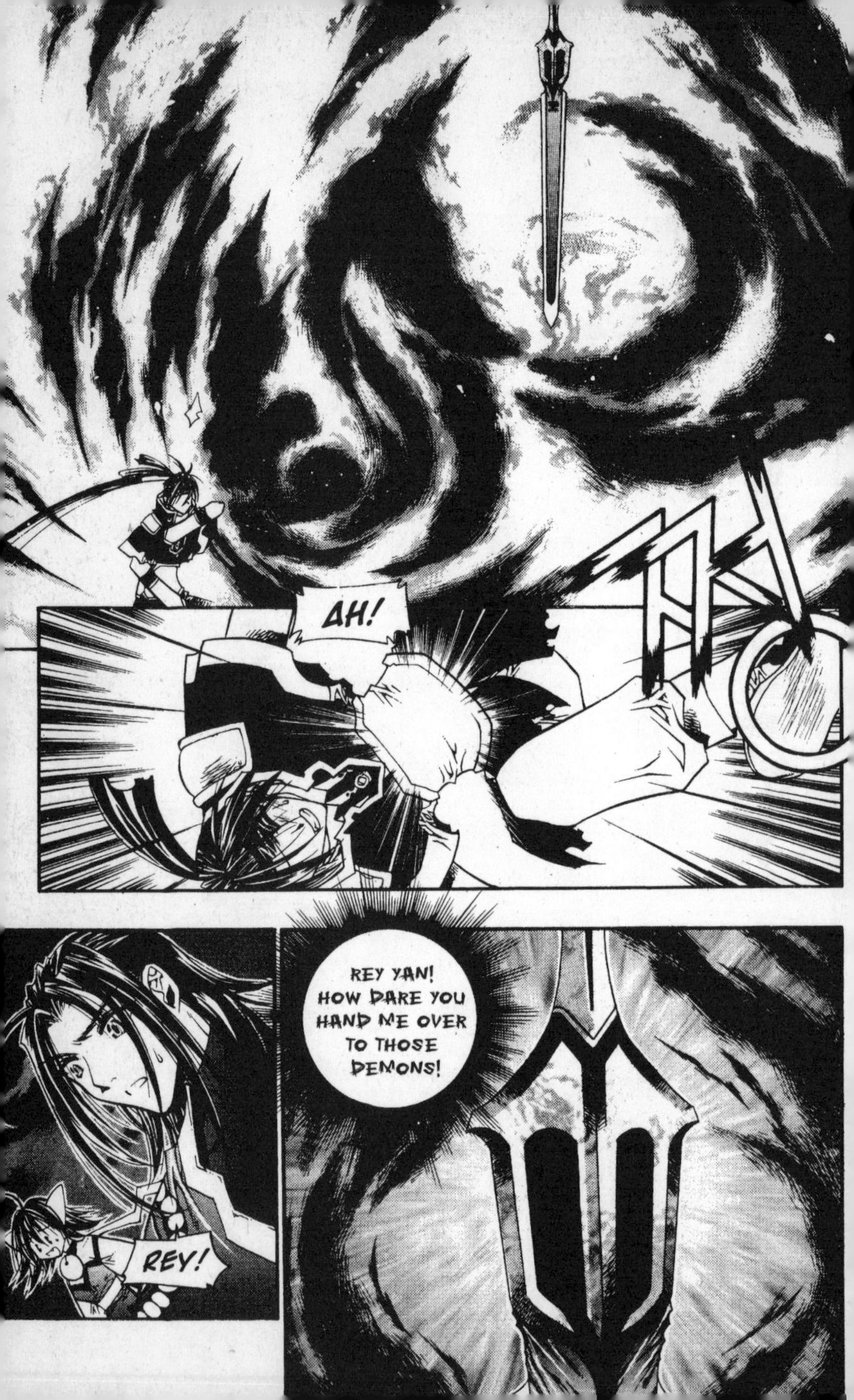
AH!
REY YAN! HOW DARE YOU HAND ME OVER TO THOSE DEMONS!
REY!

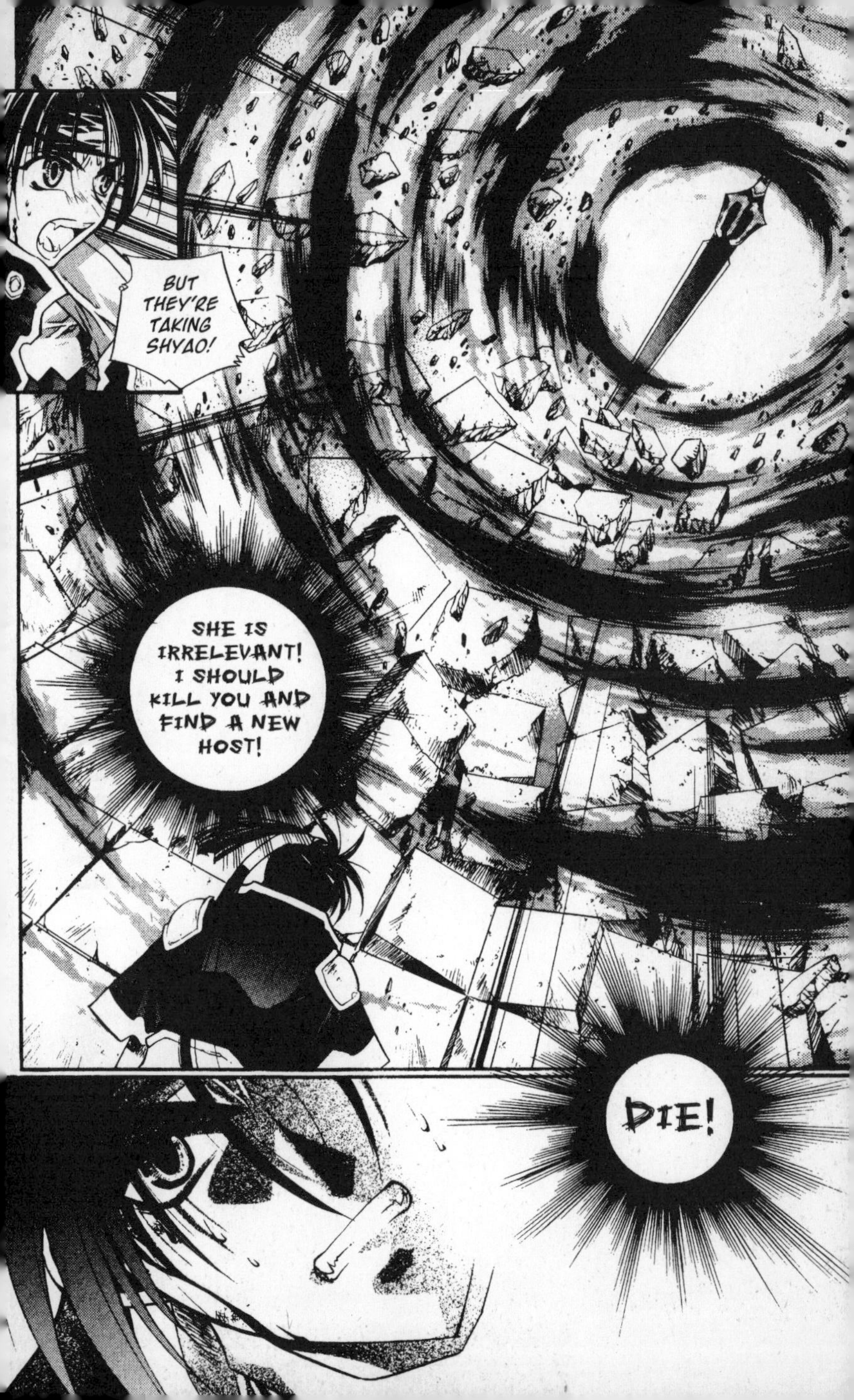
BUT THEY'RE TAKING SHYAO!
SHE IS IRRELEVANT! I SHOULD KILL YOU AND FIND A NEW HOST!
DIE!

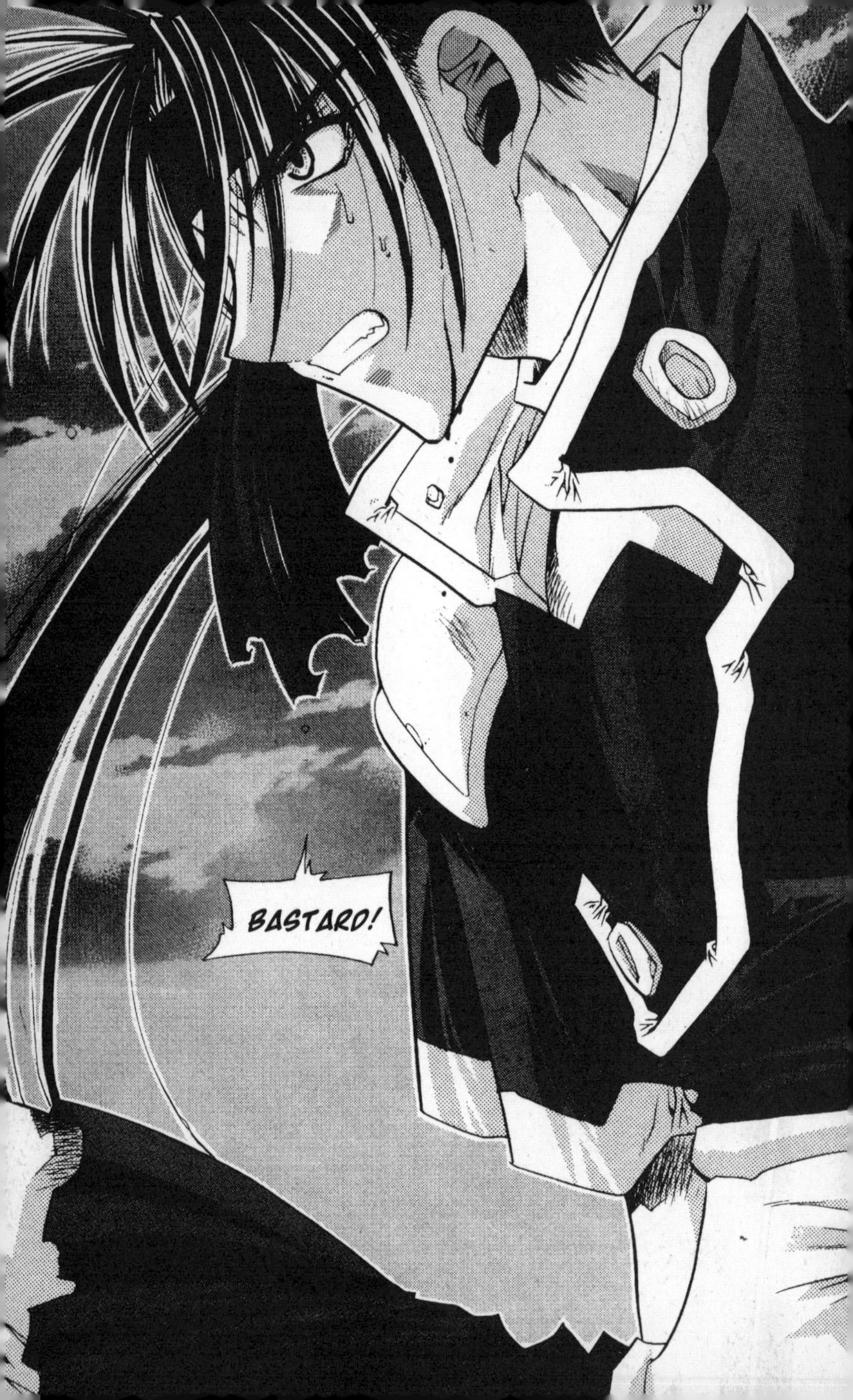
BASTARD!

Chronicle 10
Rey's Resolution

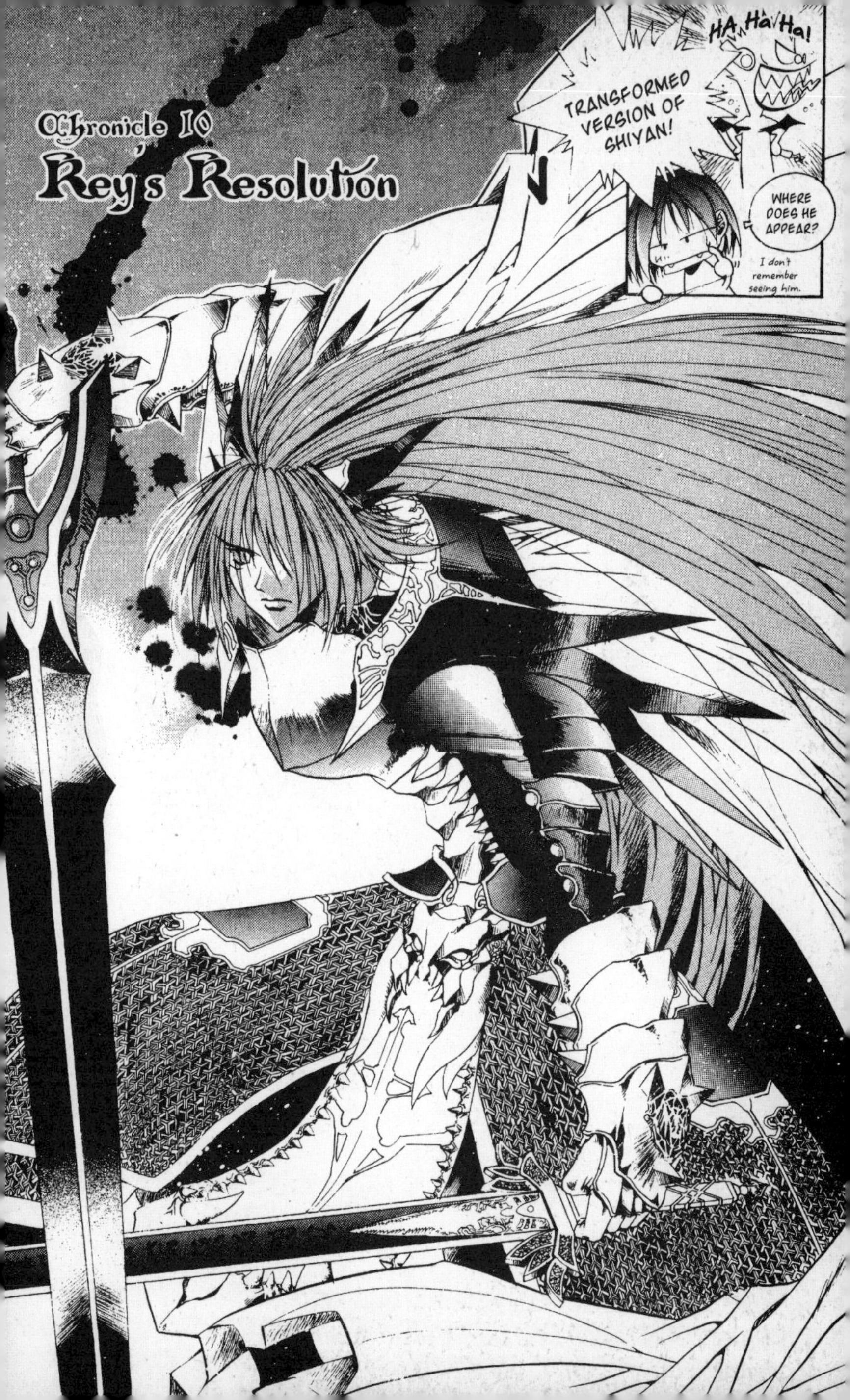
HA HA HA!
TRANSFORMED VERSION OF SHIYAN!
WHERE DOES HE APPEAR?
I don't remember seeing him.

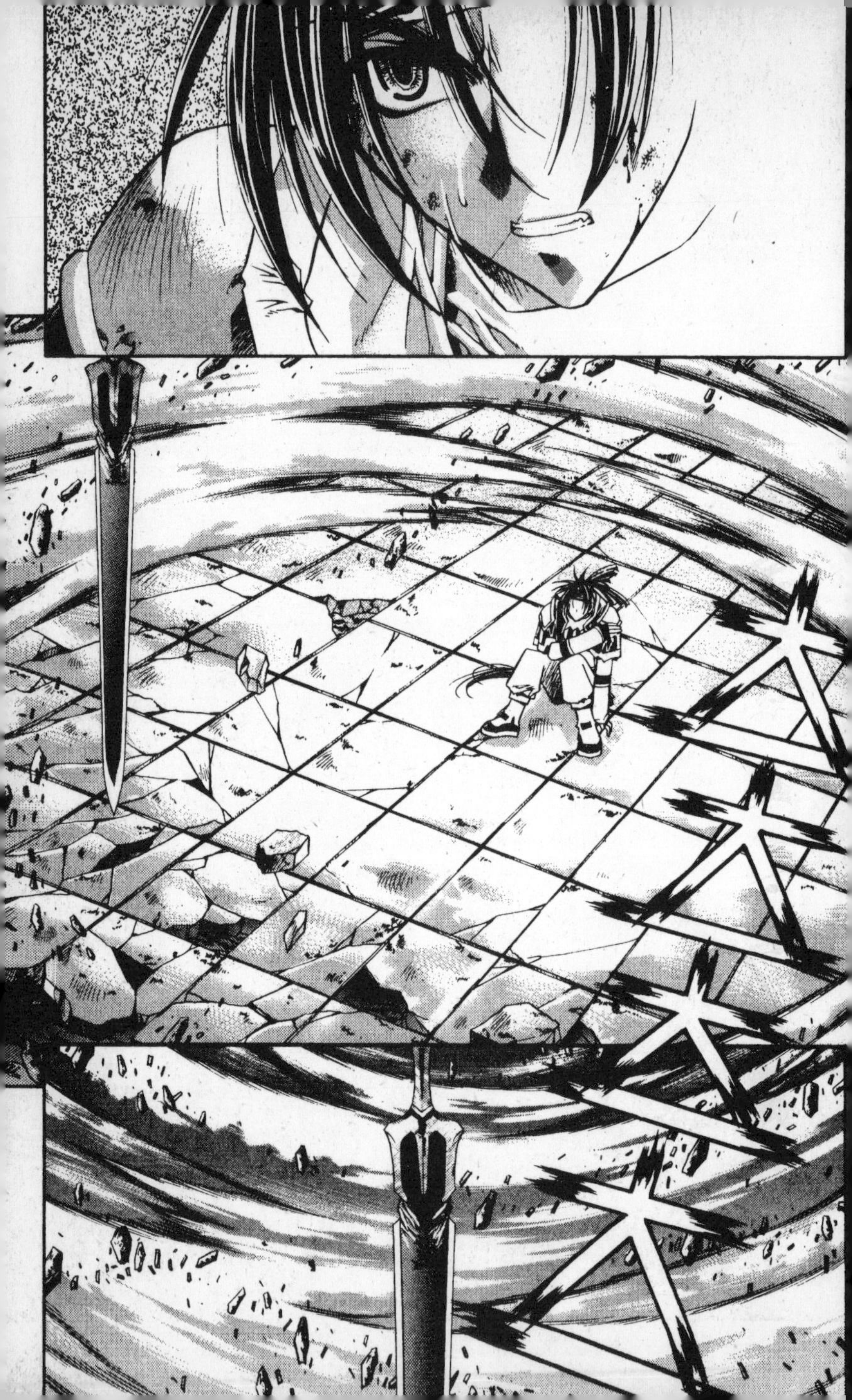

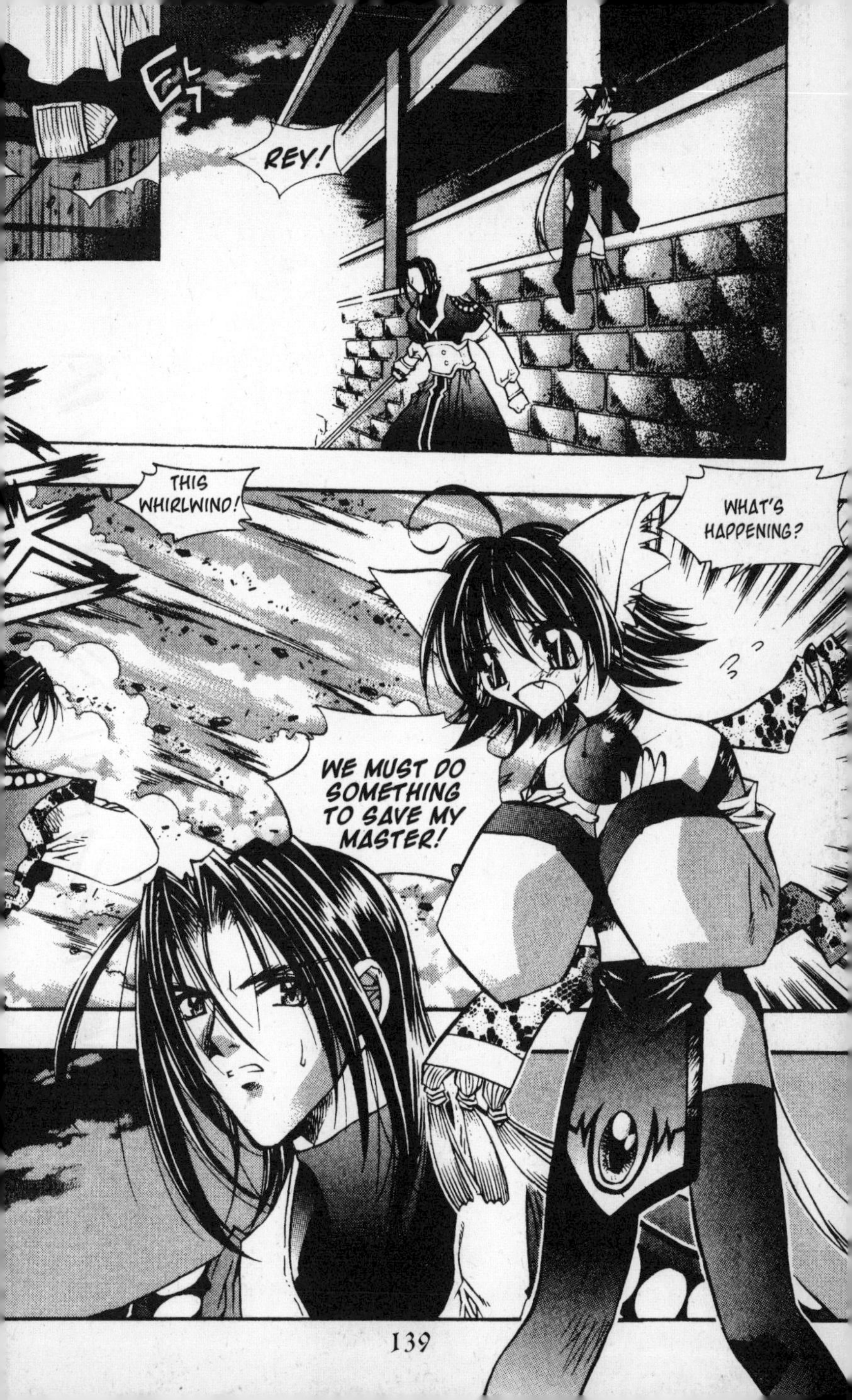
REY!
WHAT'S HAPPENING?
THIS WHIRLWIND!
WE MUST DO SOMETHING TO SAVE MY MASTER!

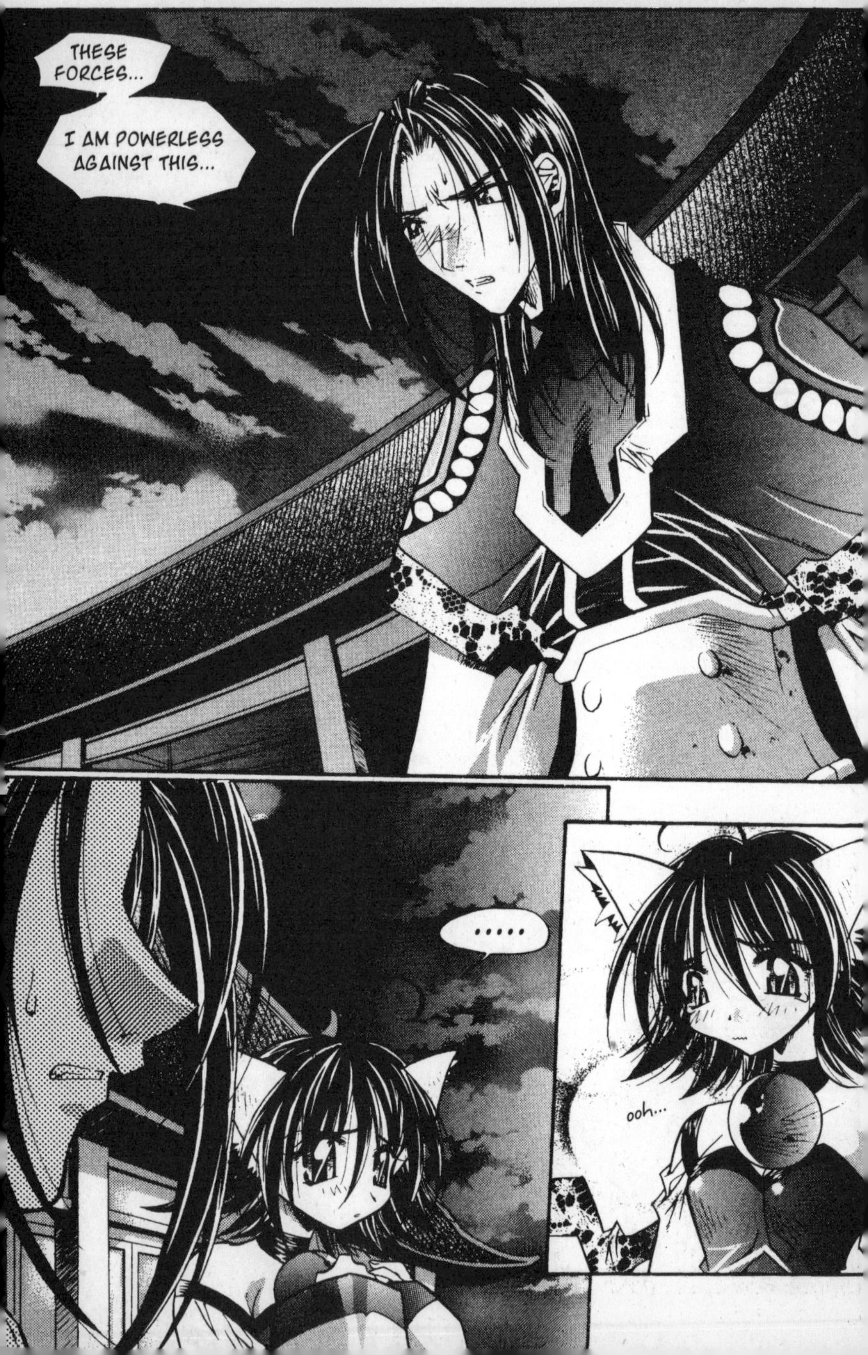
THESE FORCES...
I AM POWERLESS AGAINST THIS...
.....
ooh...

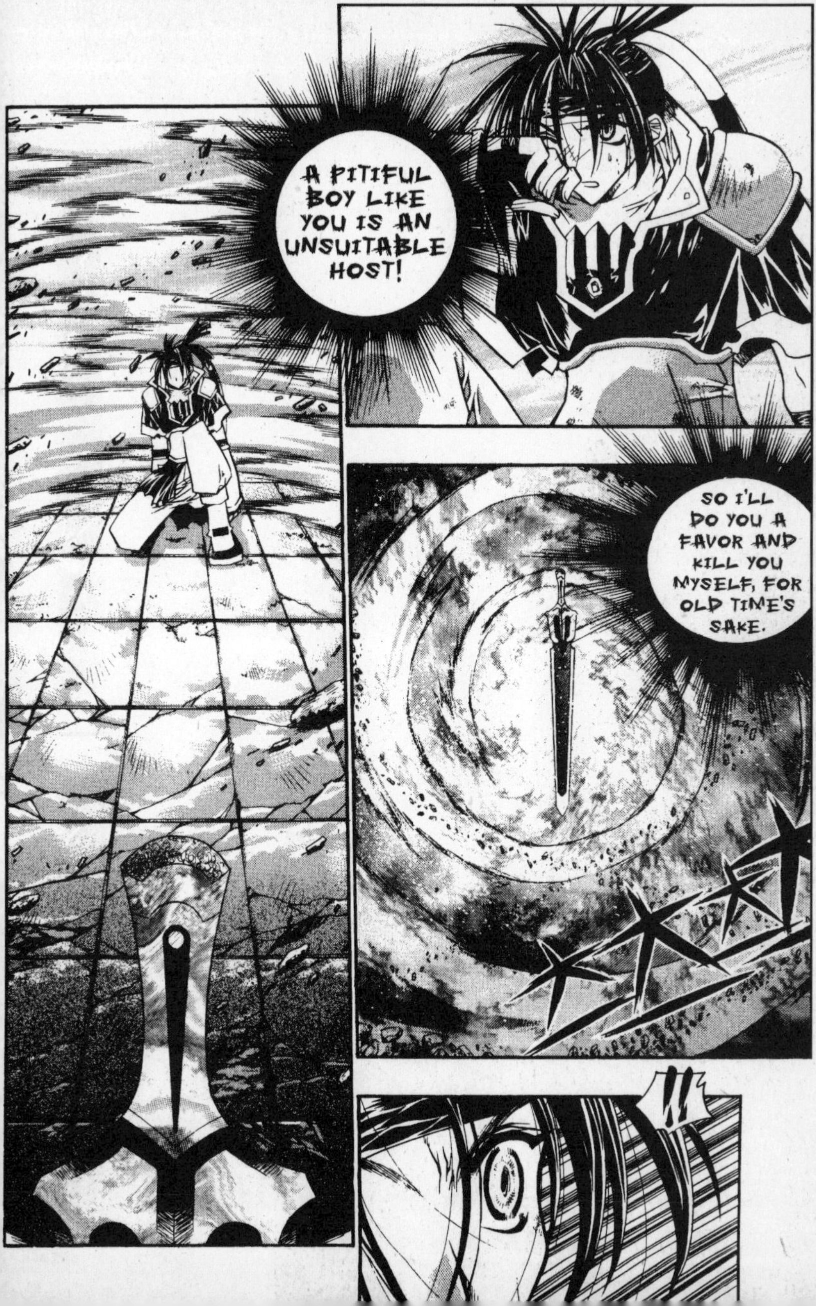
A PITIFUL BOY LIKE YOU IS AN UNSUITABLE HOST!
SO I'LL DO YOU A FAVOR AND KILL YOU MYSELF, FOR OLD TIME'S SAKE.
!!

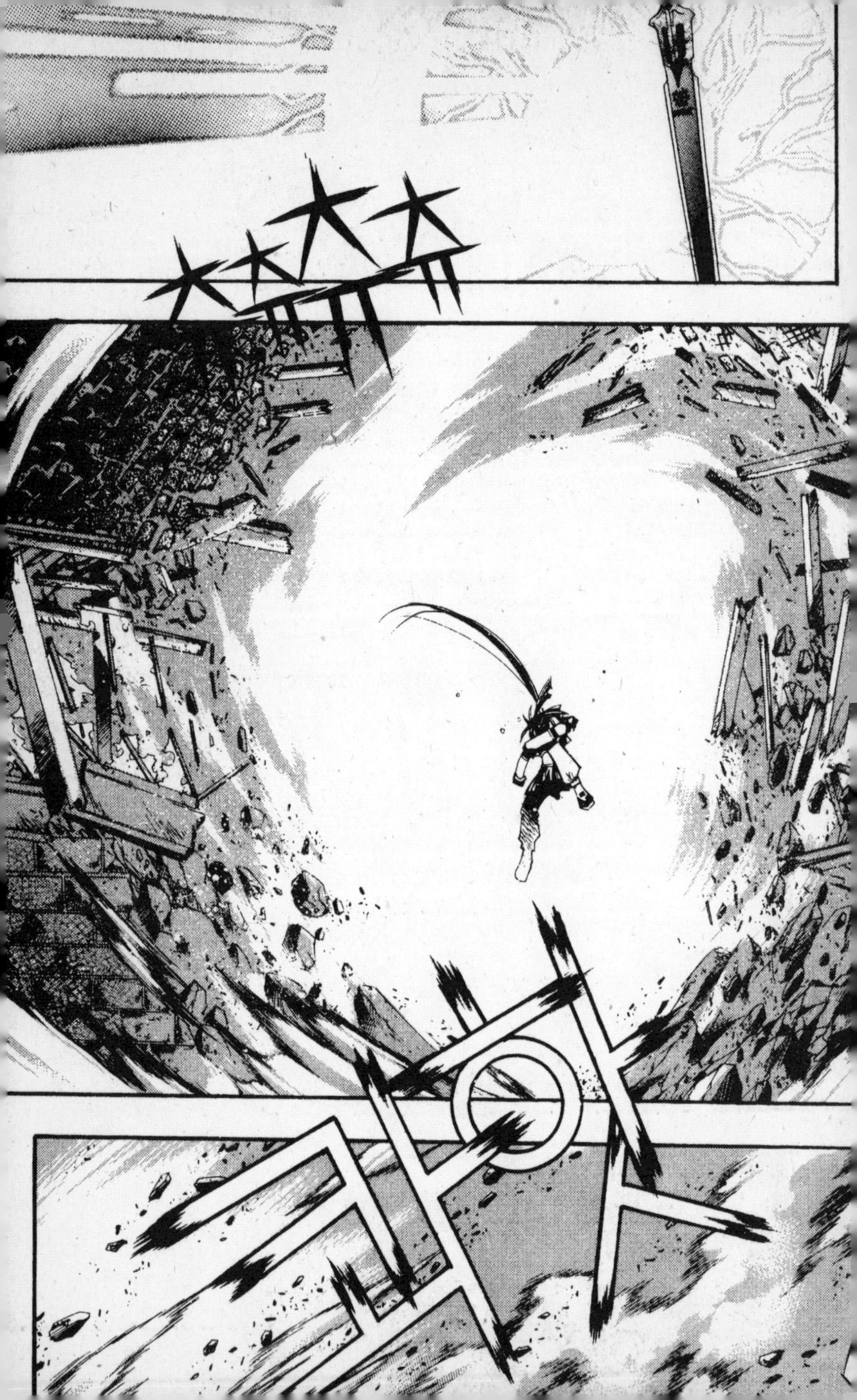

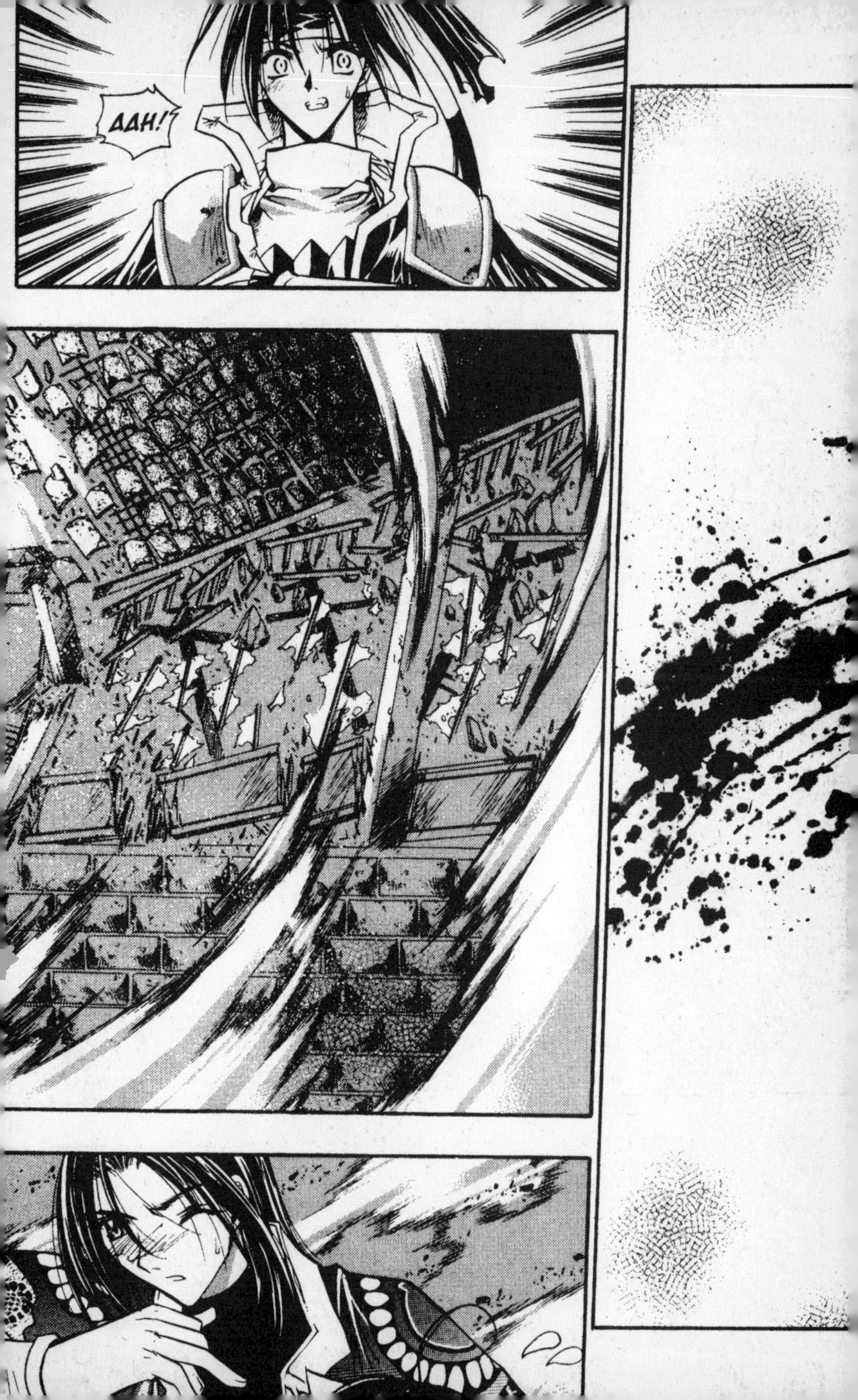
AAH!

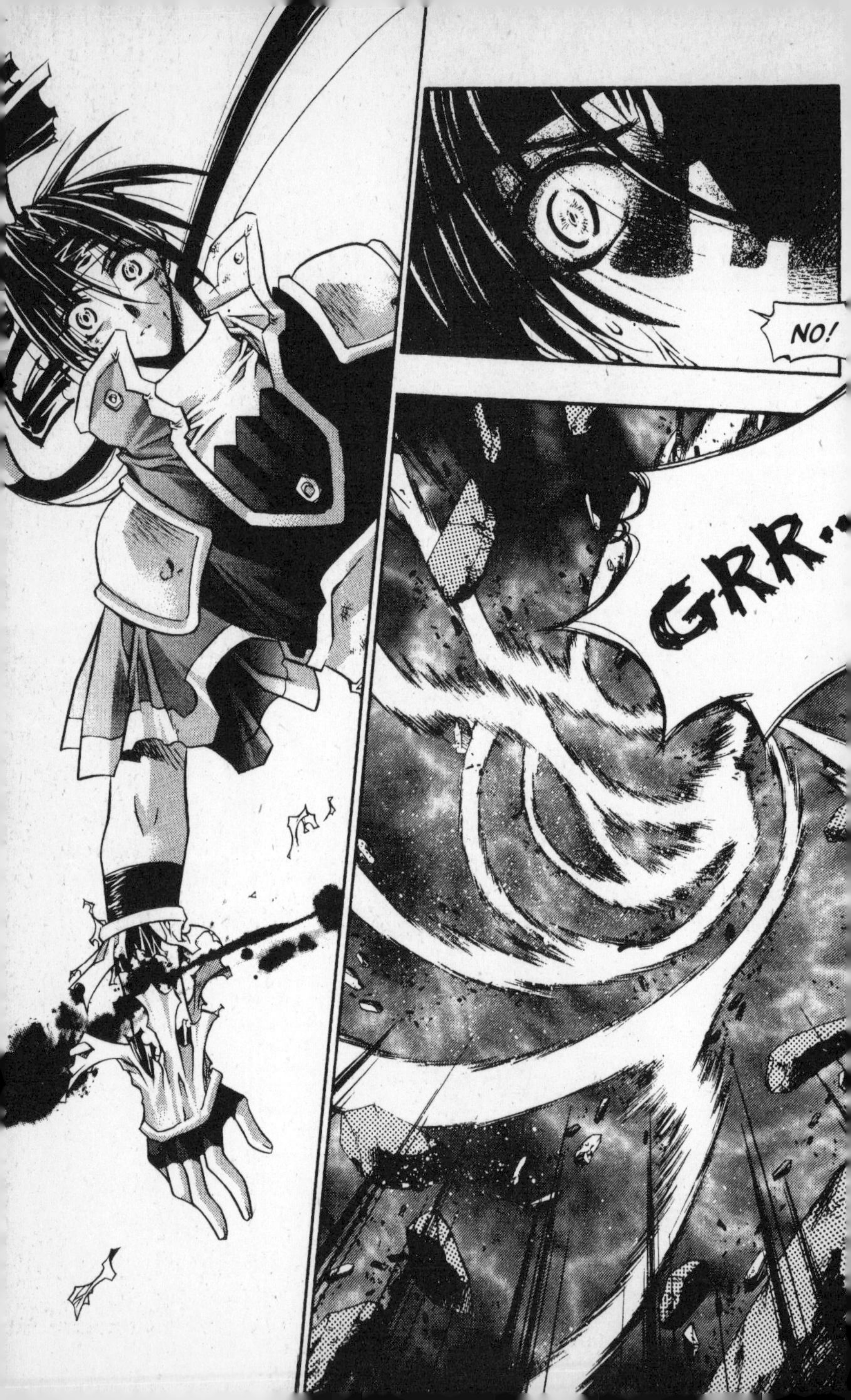
NO!
GRR...

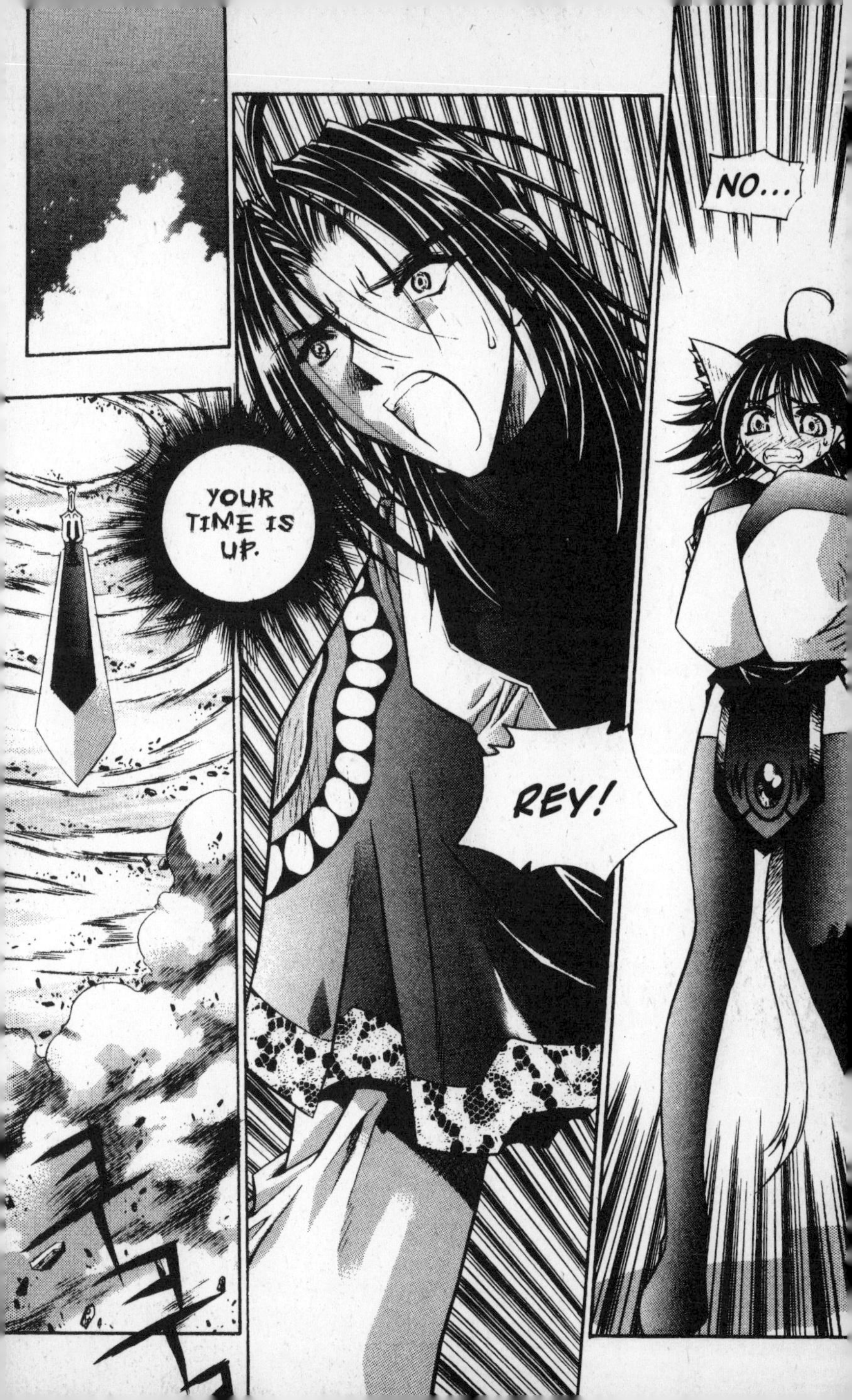
YOUR TIME IS UP.
REY!
NO...

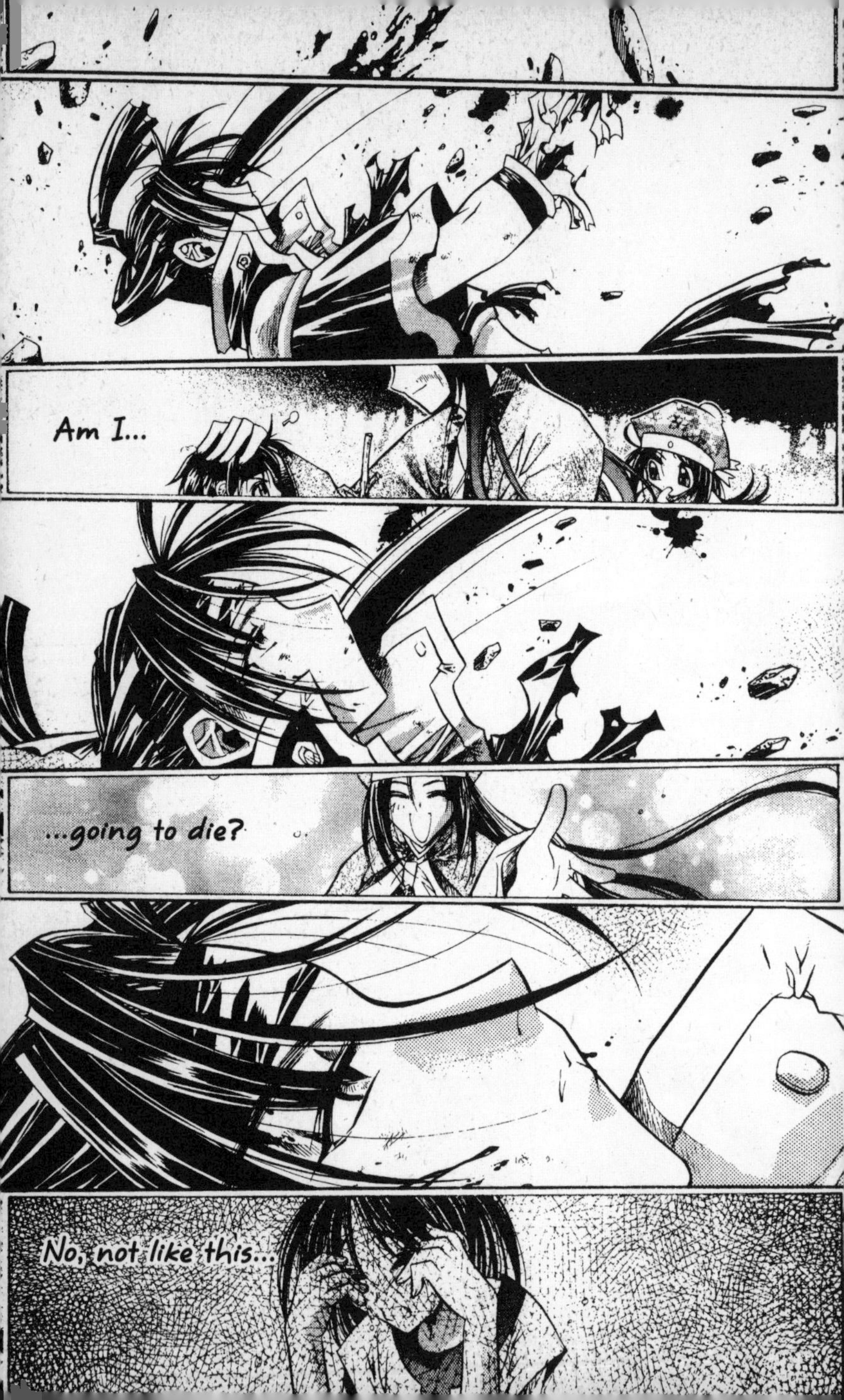
Am I...
...going to die?
No, not like this...

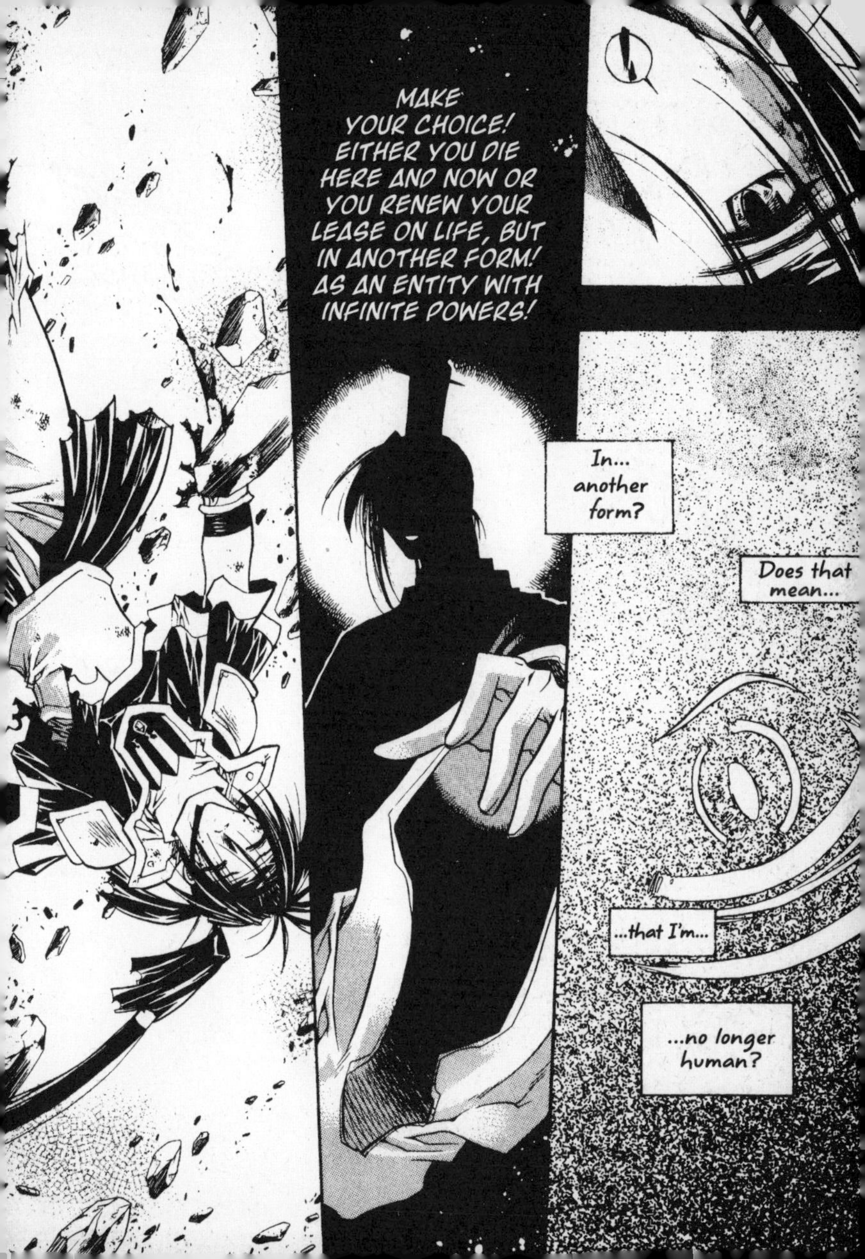
MAKE YOUR CHOICE! EITHER YOU DIE HERE AND NOW OR YOU RENEW YOUR LEASE ON LIFE, BUT IN ANOTHER FORM! AS AN ENTITY WITH INFINITE POWERS!
In... another form?
Does that mean...
...that I'm...
...no longer human?

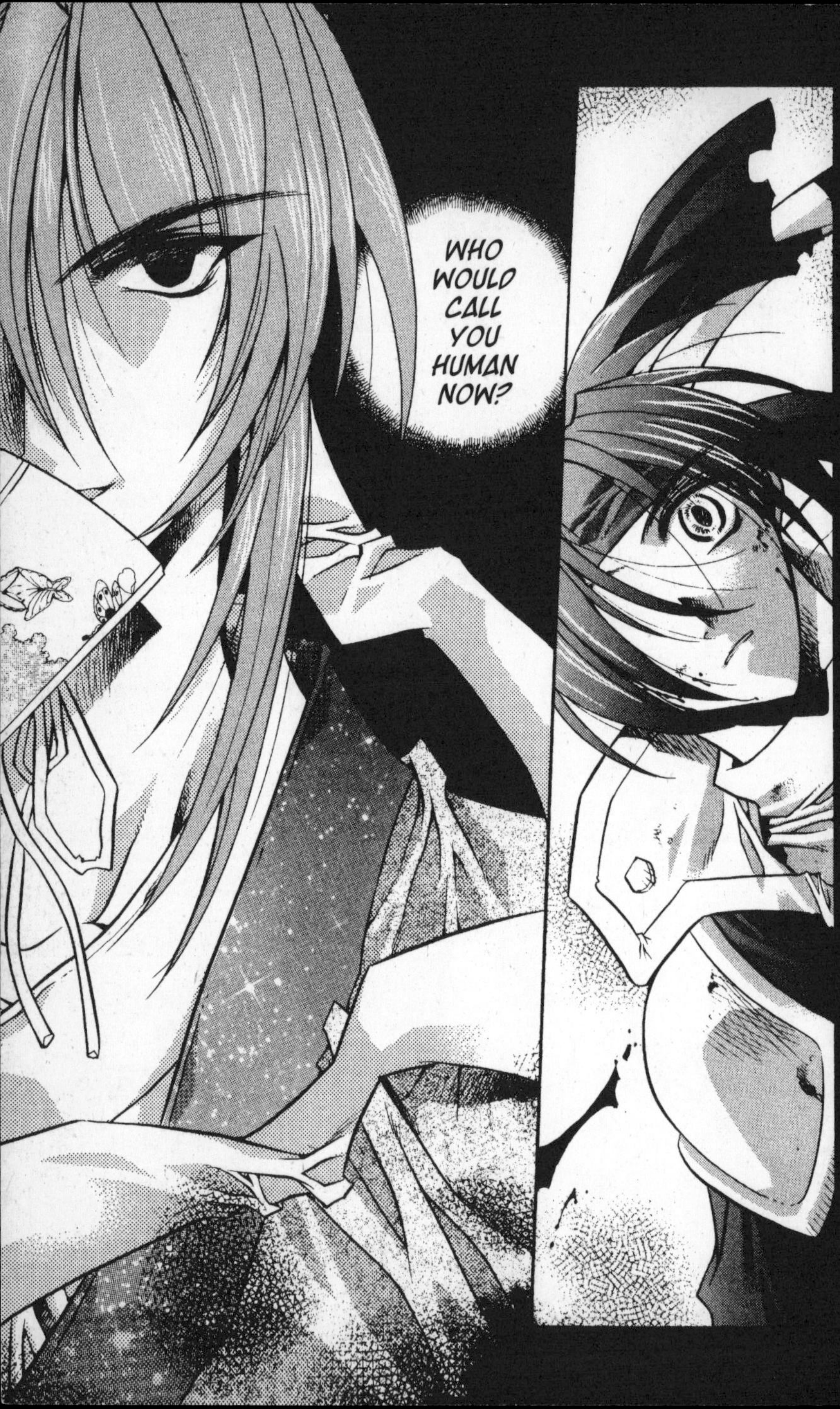
WHO WOULD CALL YOU HUMAN NOW?

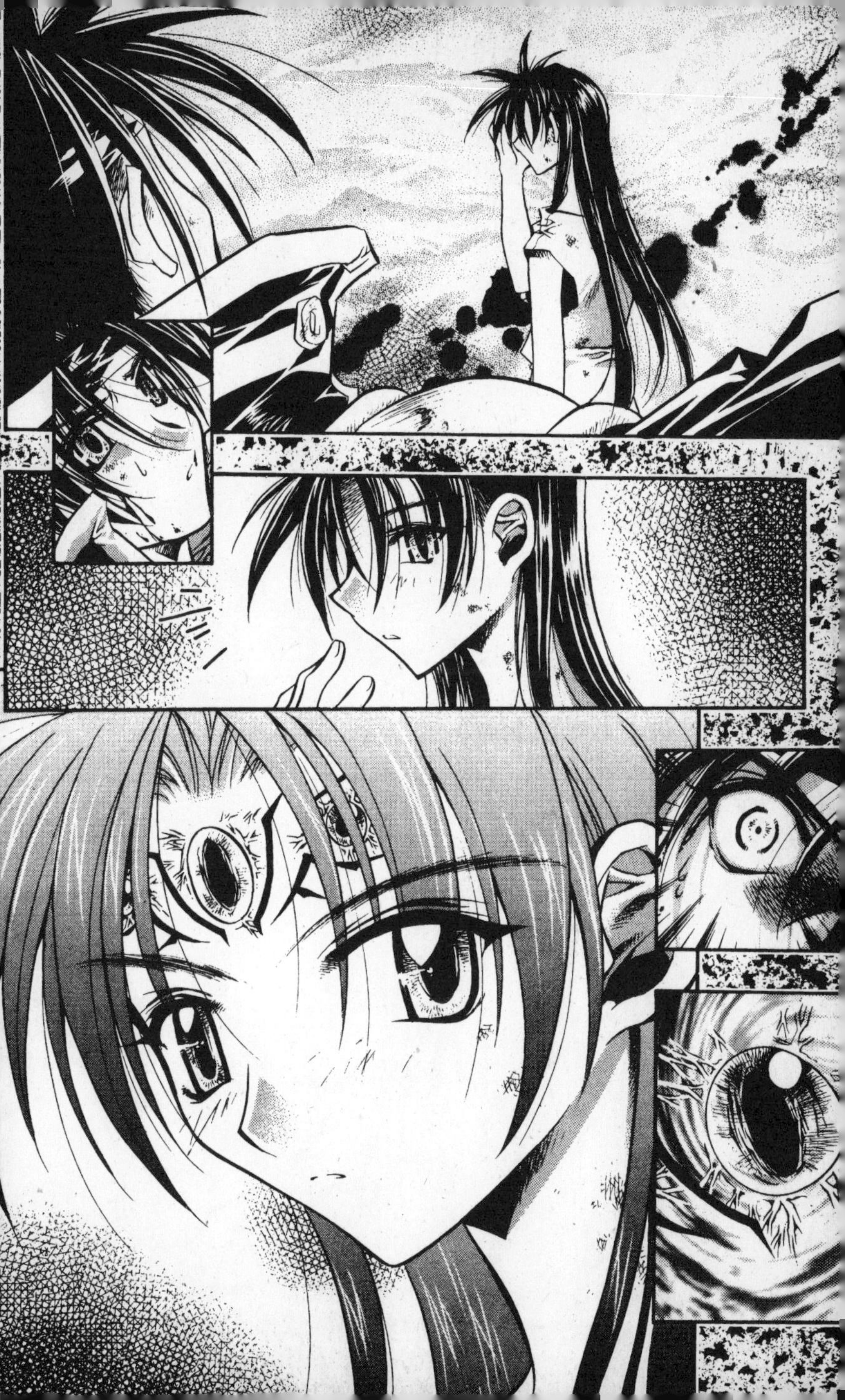

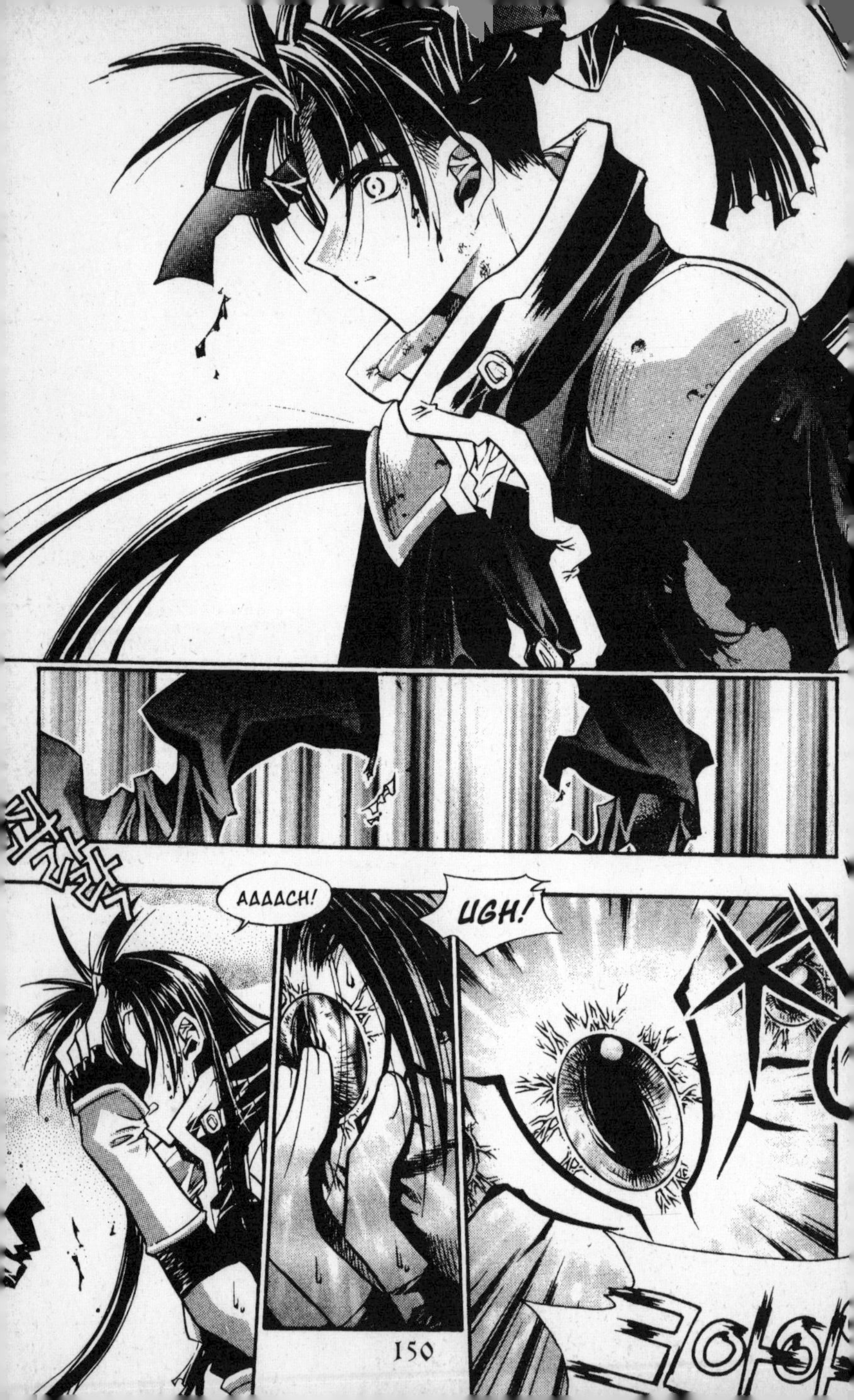
AAAACH!
UGH!

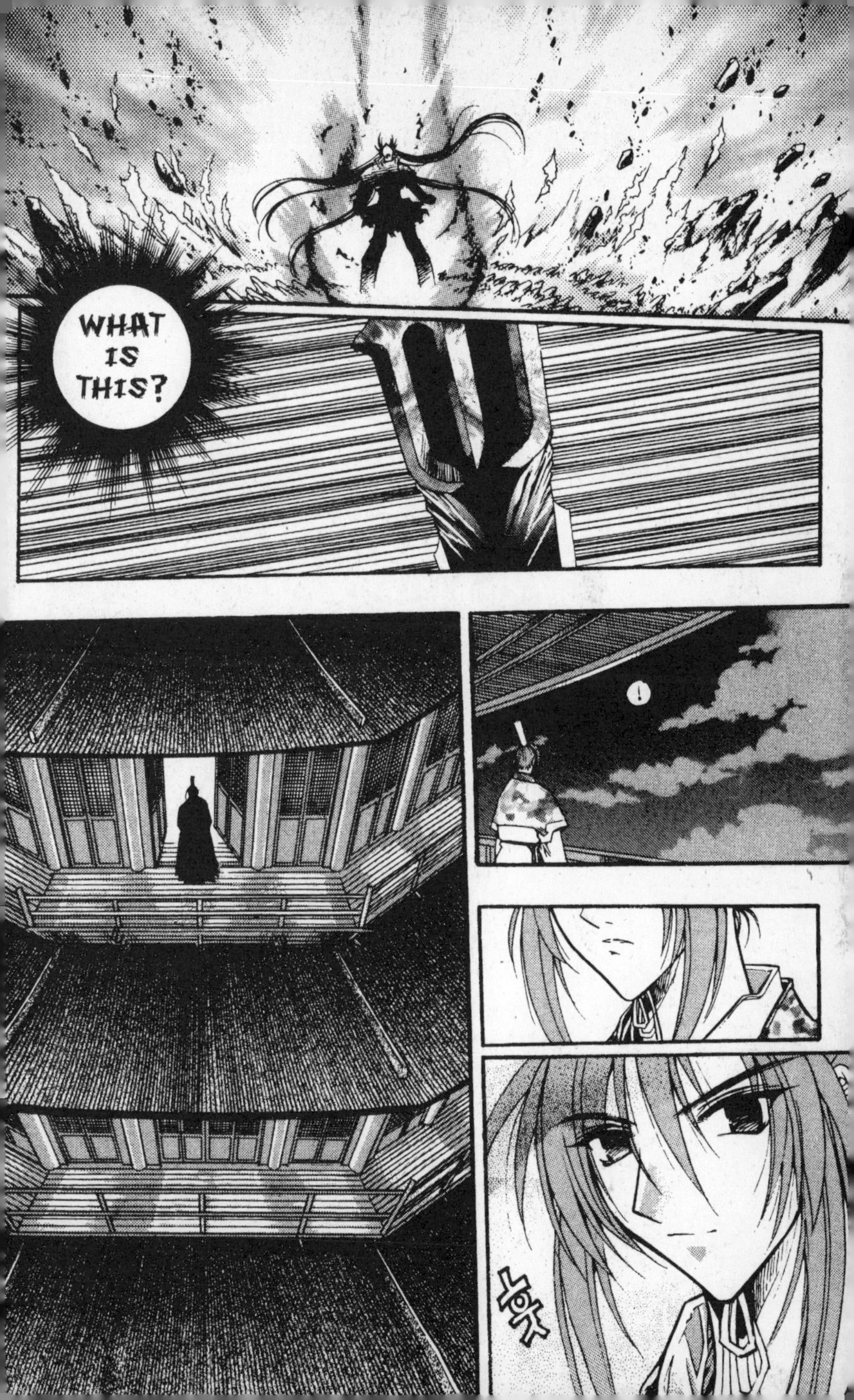
WHAT IS THIS?
!
YOK

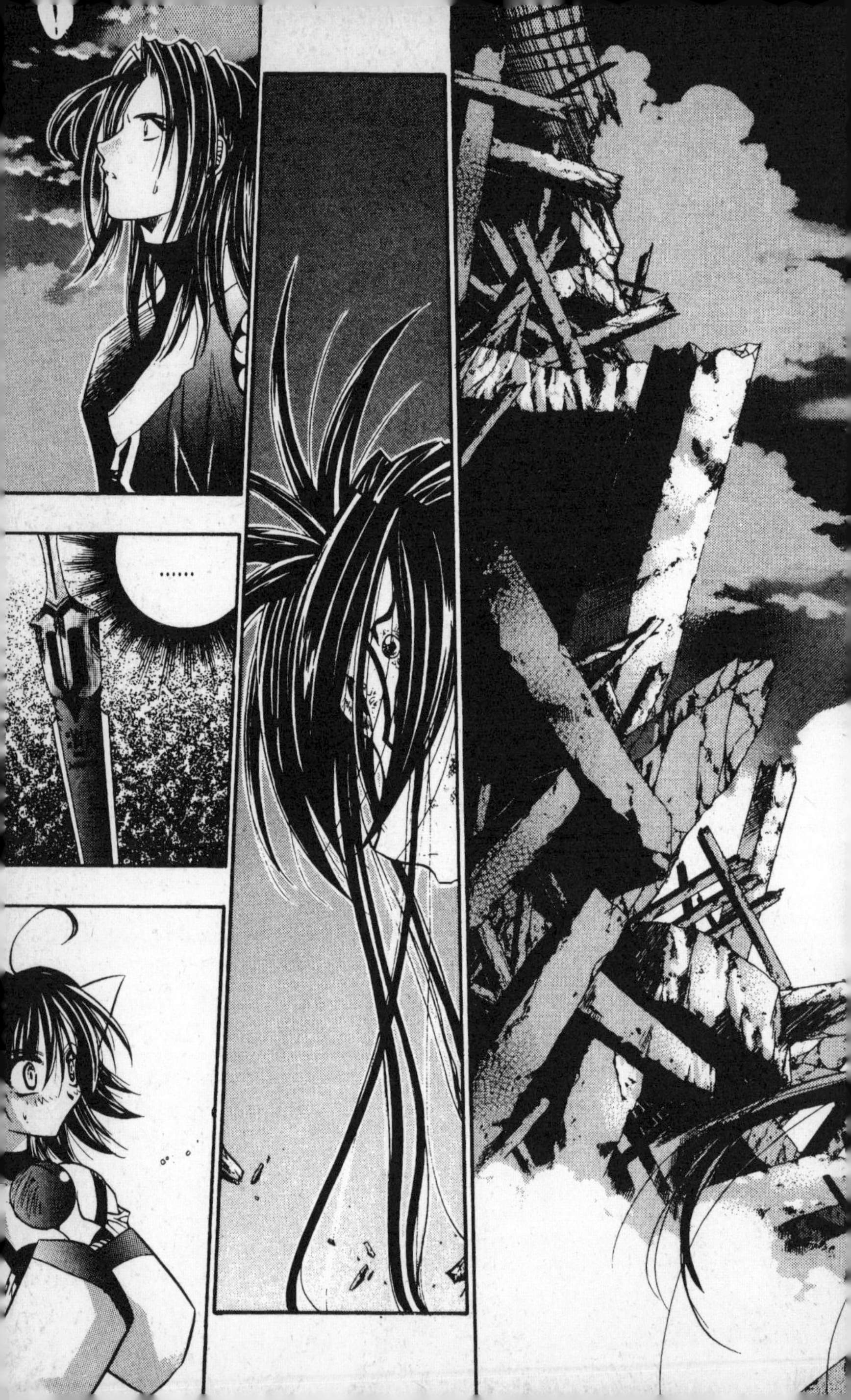
!
......

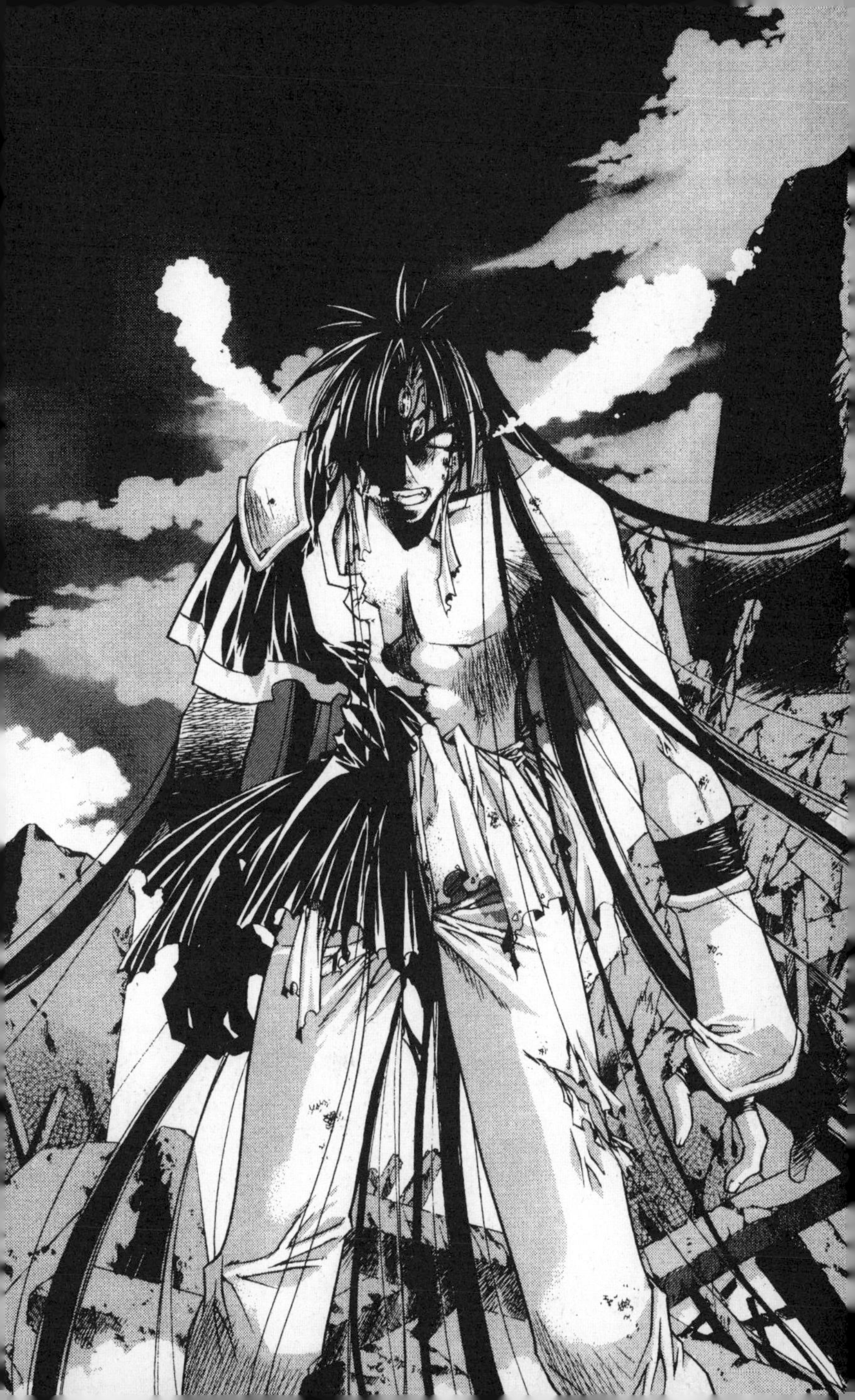

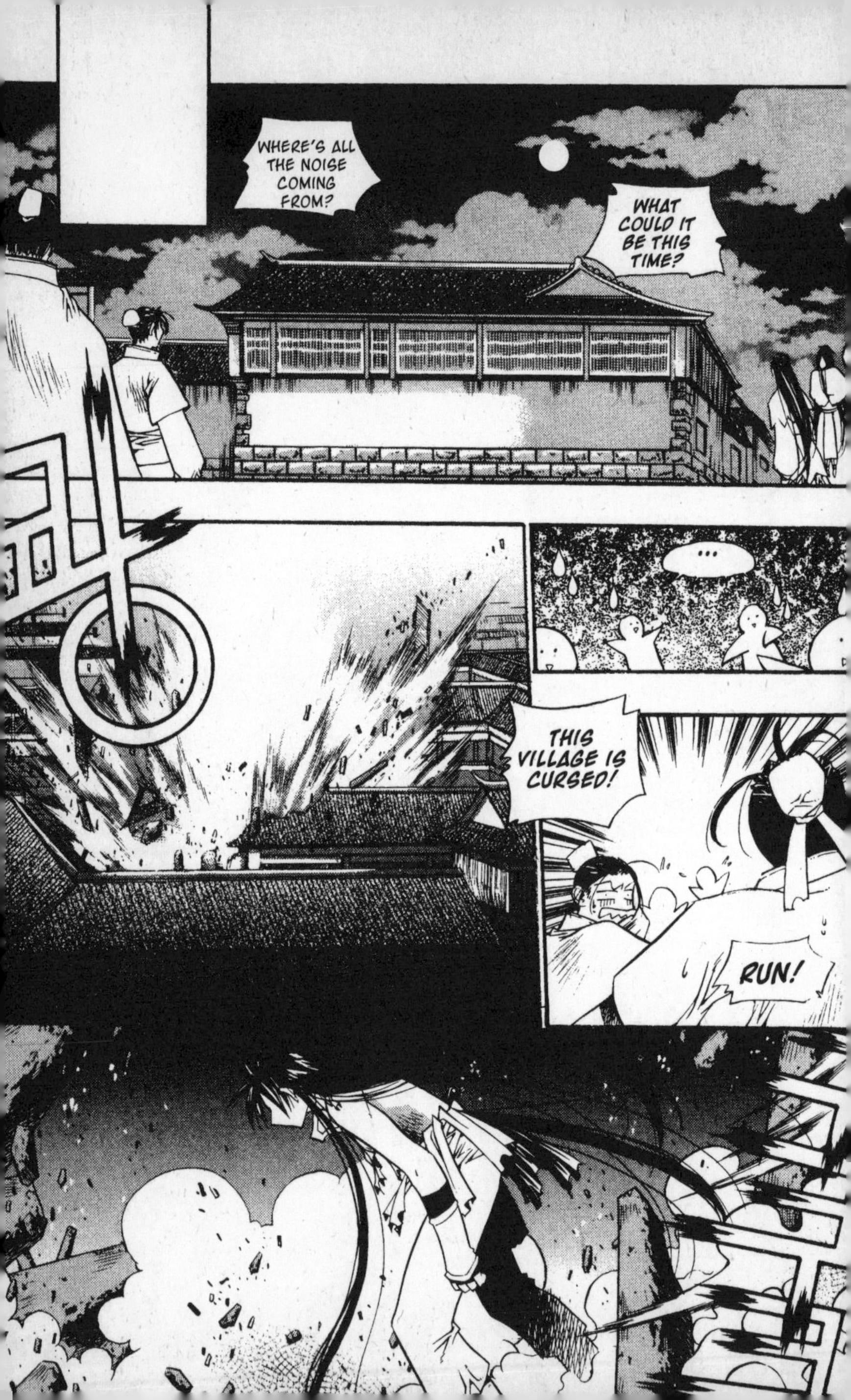
WHERE'S ALL THE NOISE COMING FROM?
WHAT COULD IT BE THIS TIME?
...
THIS VILLAGE IS CURSED!
RUN!

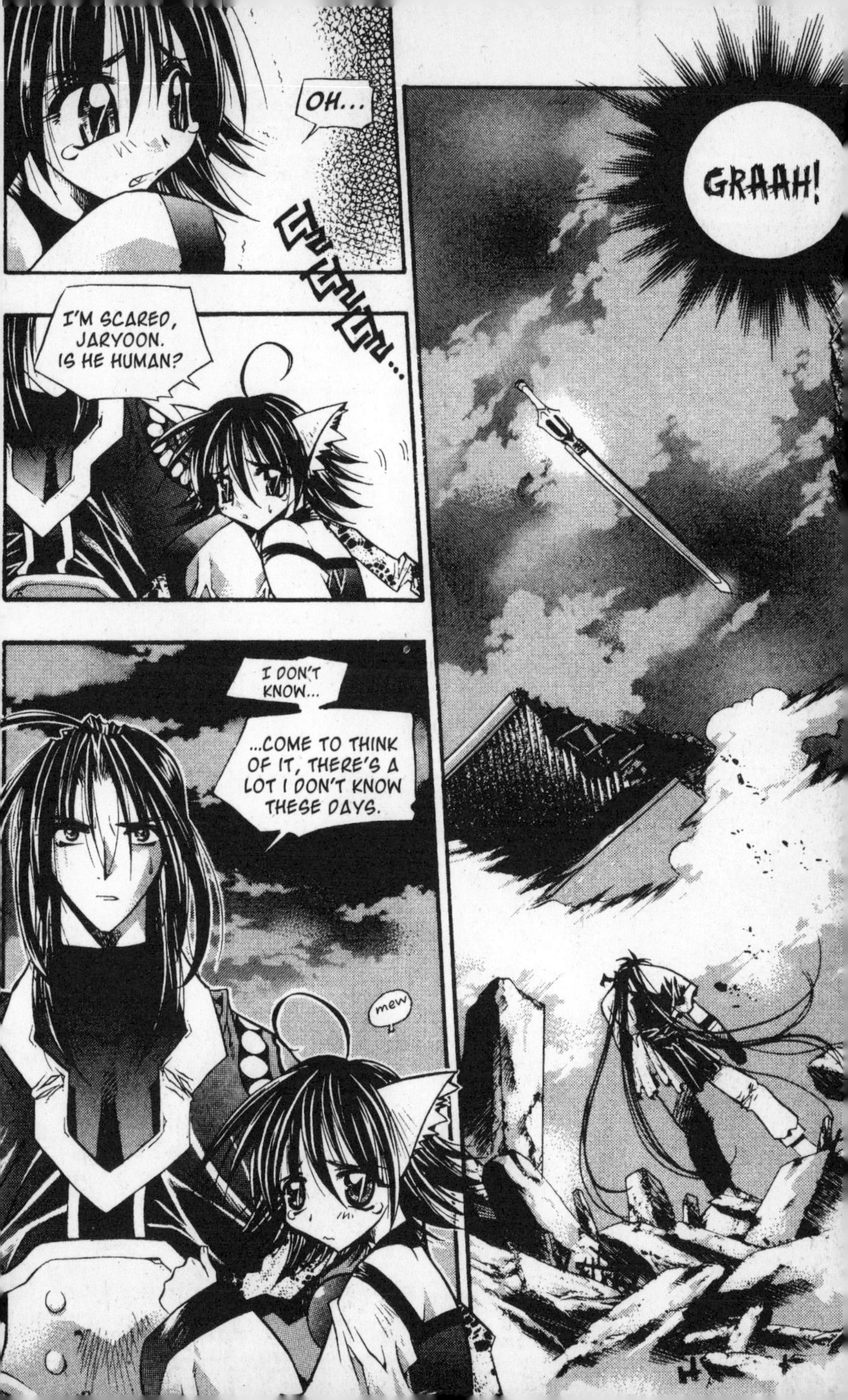
OH...
I'M SCARED, JARYOON. IS HE HUMAN?
I DON'T KNOW...
...COME TO THINK OF IT, THERE'S A LOT I DON'T KNOW THESE DAYS.
mew
GRAAH!

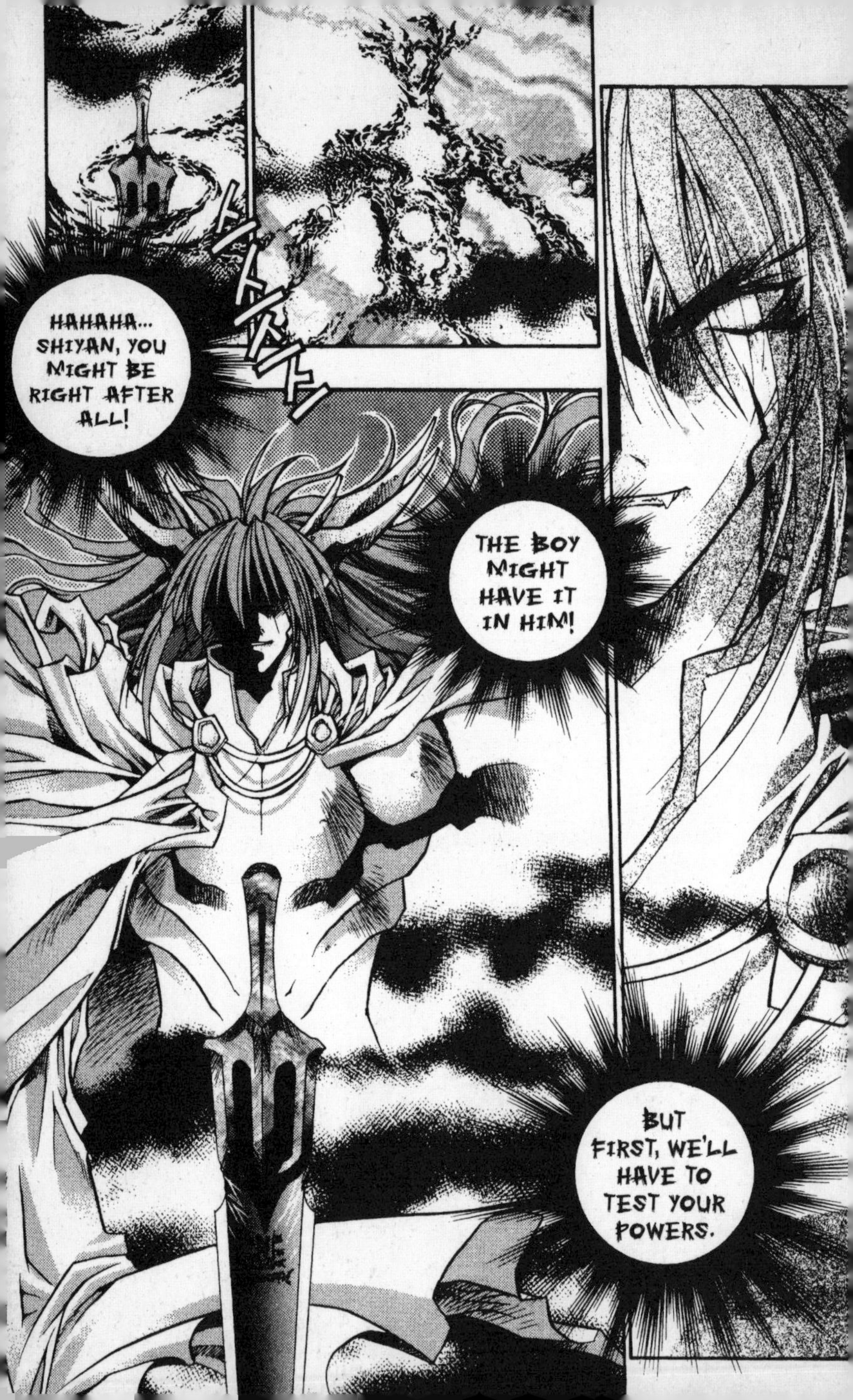
HAHAHA... SHIYAN, YOU MIGHT BE RIGHT AFTER ALL!
THE BOY MIGHT HAVE IT IN HIM!
BUT FIRST, WE'LL HAVE TO TEST YOUR POWERS.

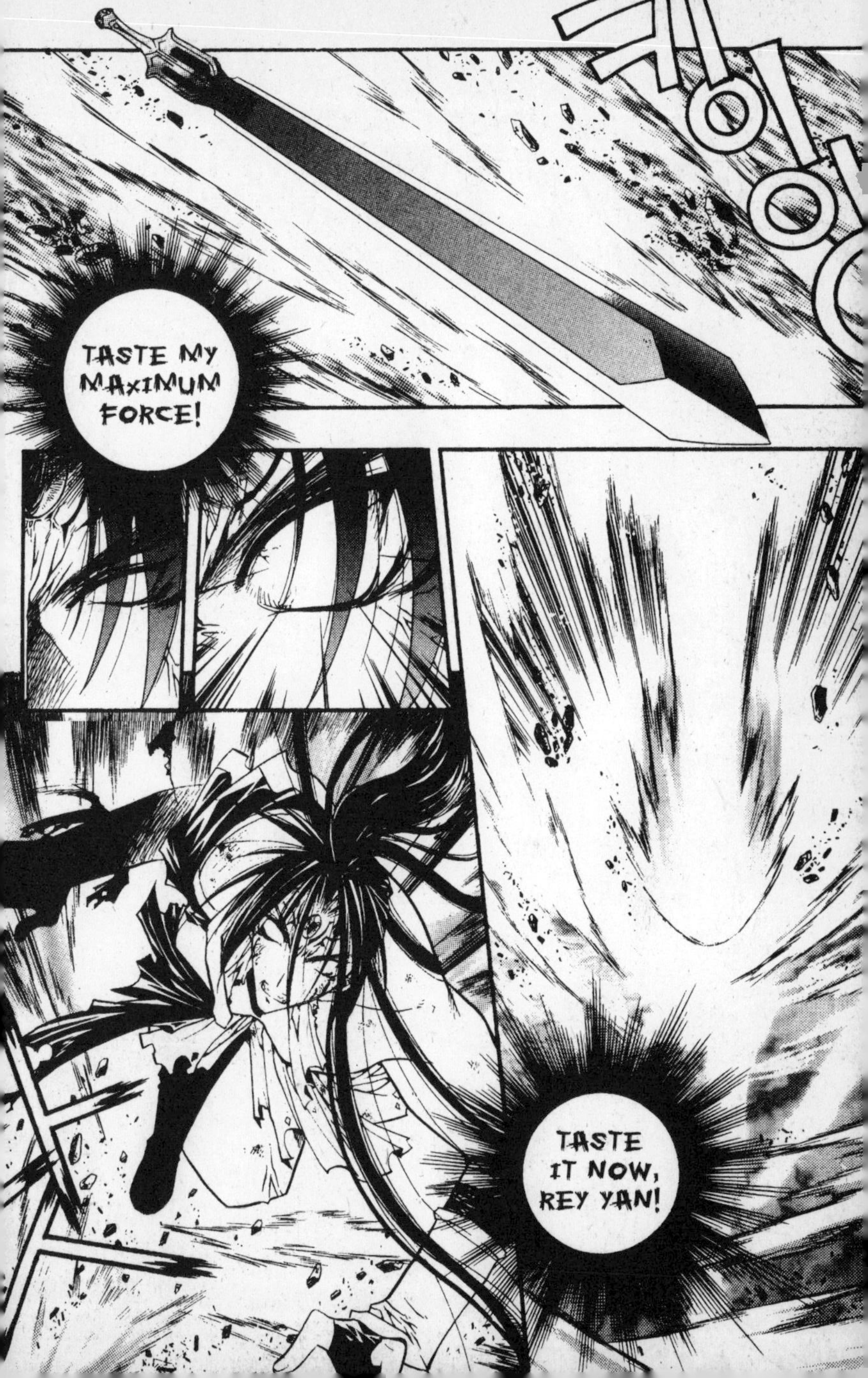
TASTE MY MAXIMUM FORCE!
TASTE IT NOW, REY YAN!

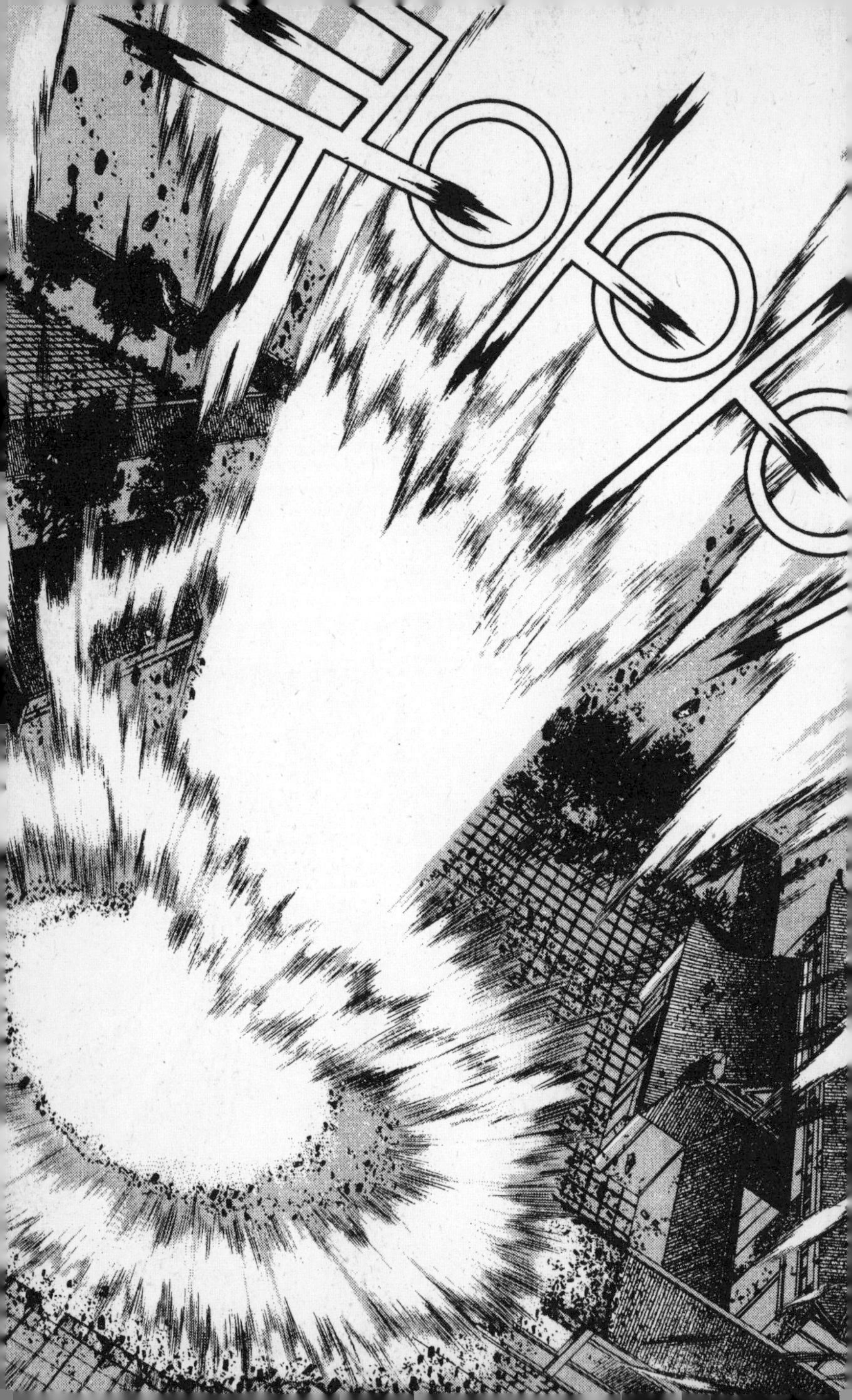

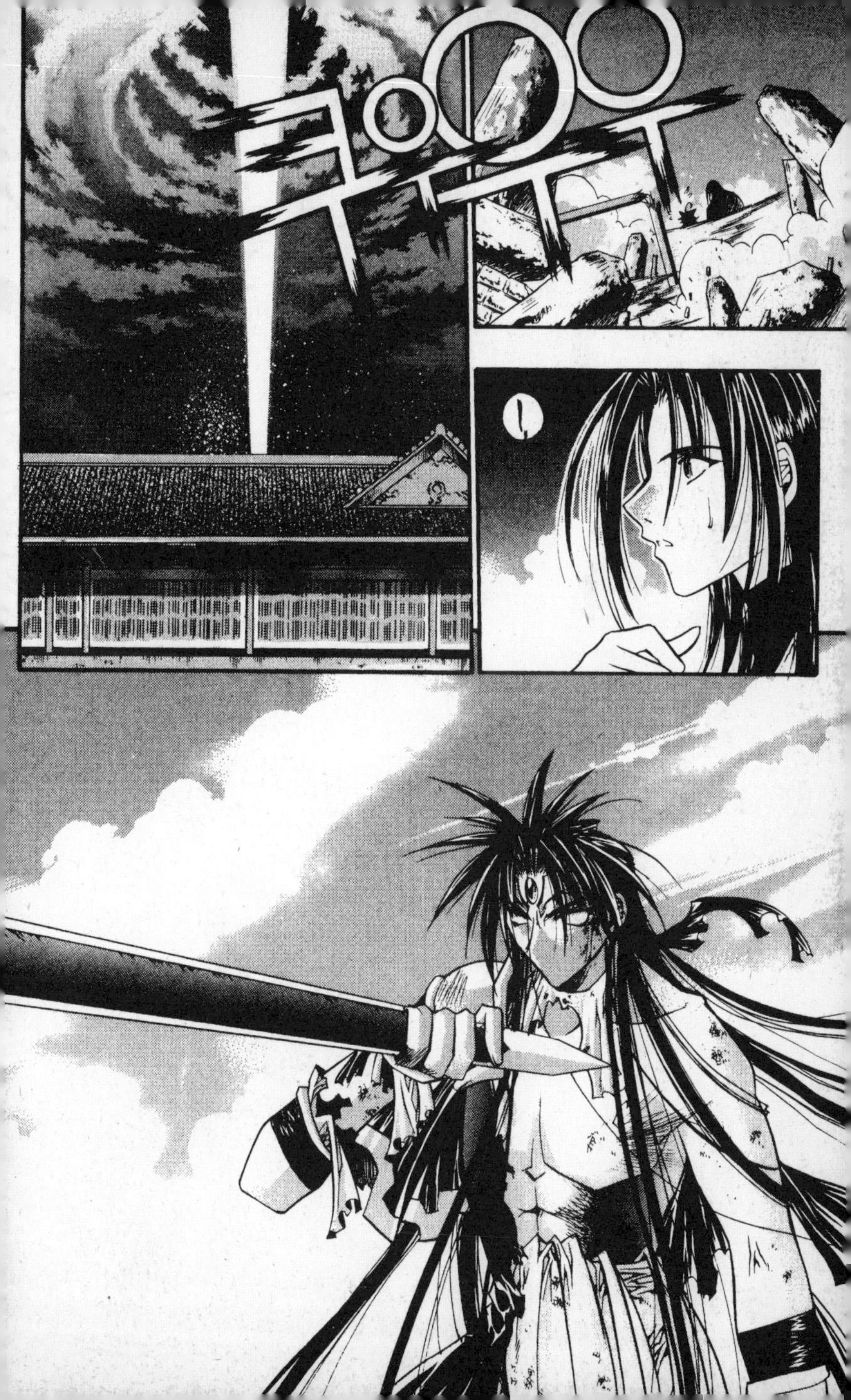
!

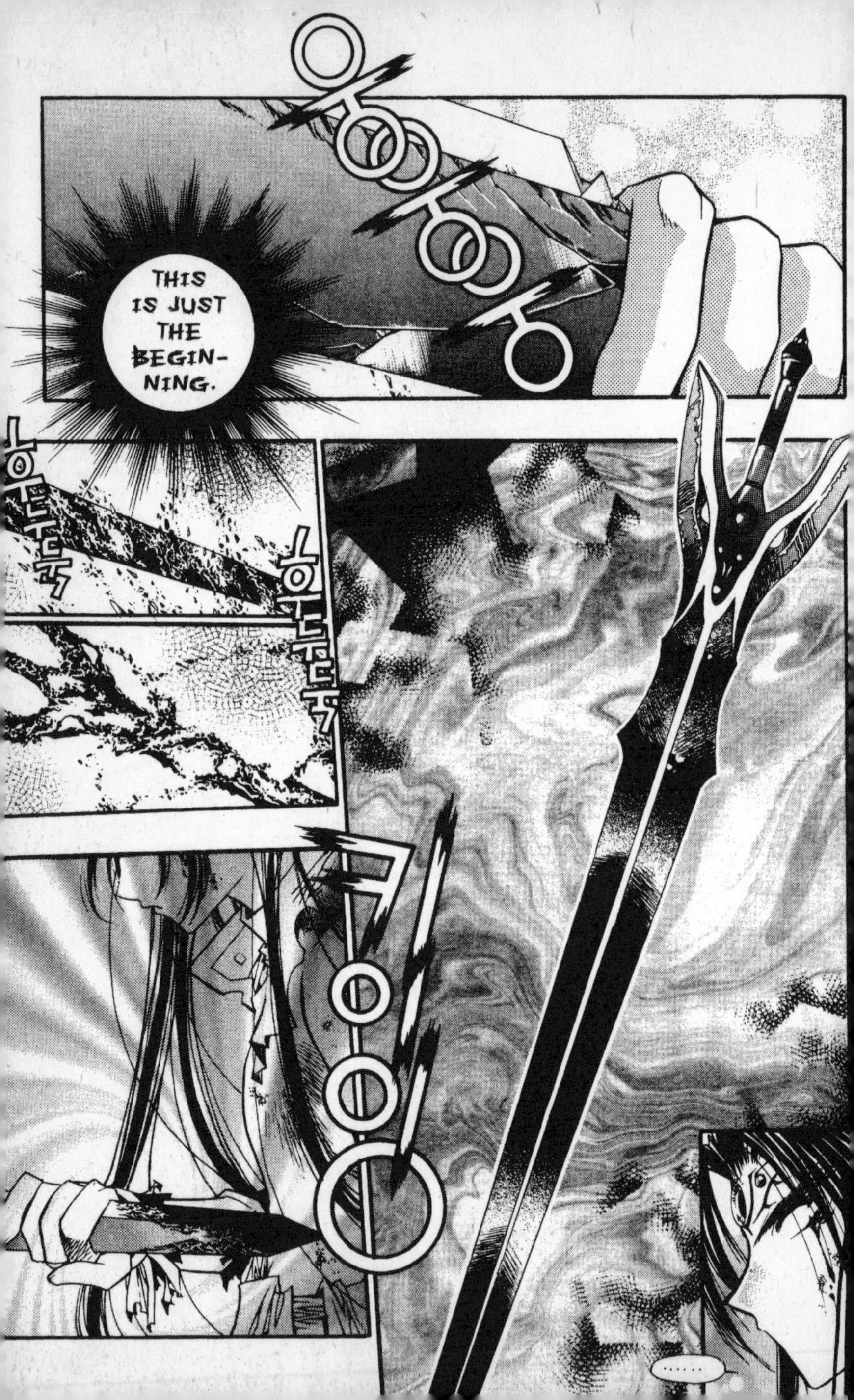
THIS IS JUST THE BEGIN- NING.
......

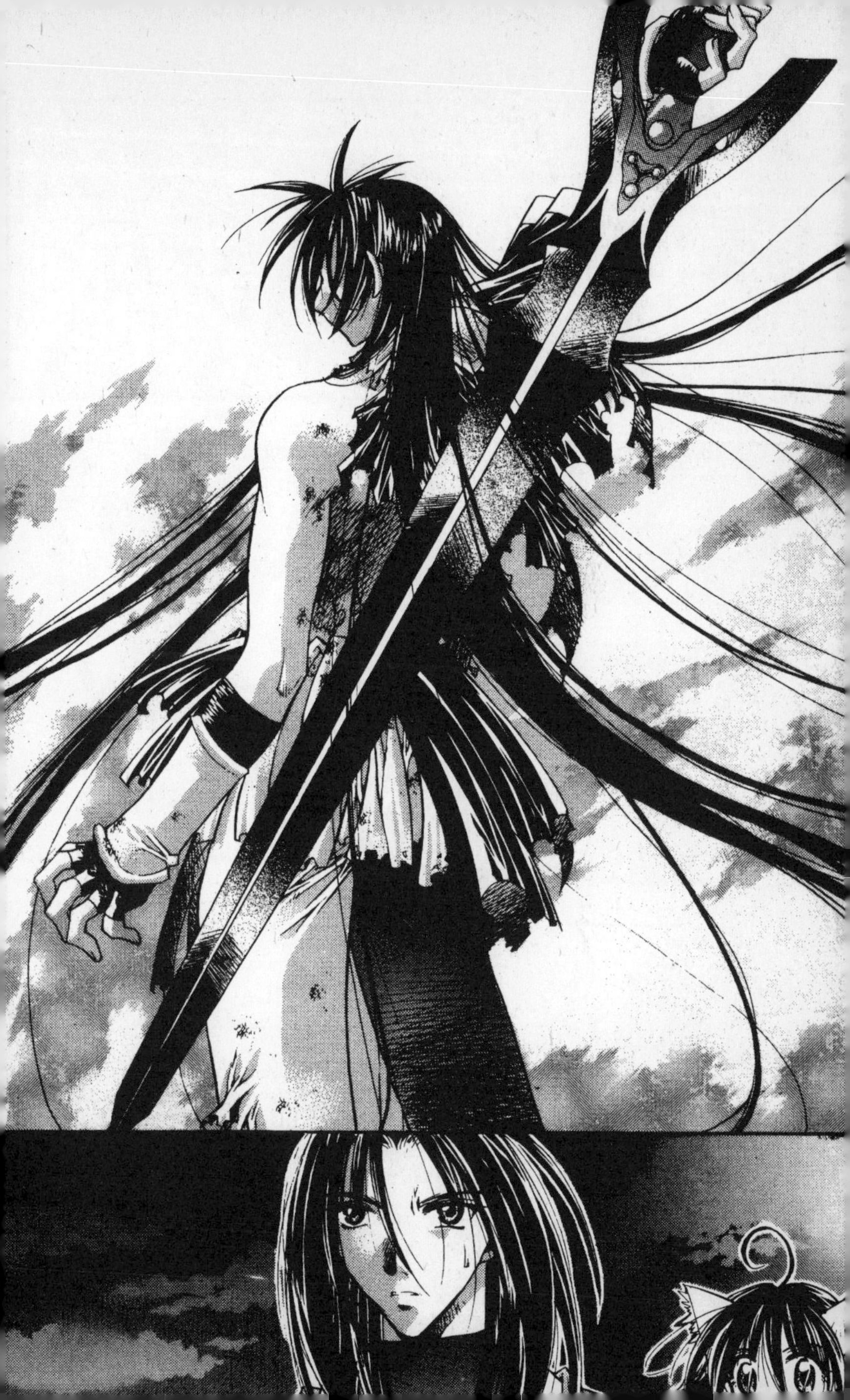

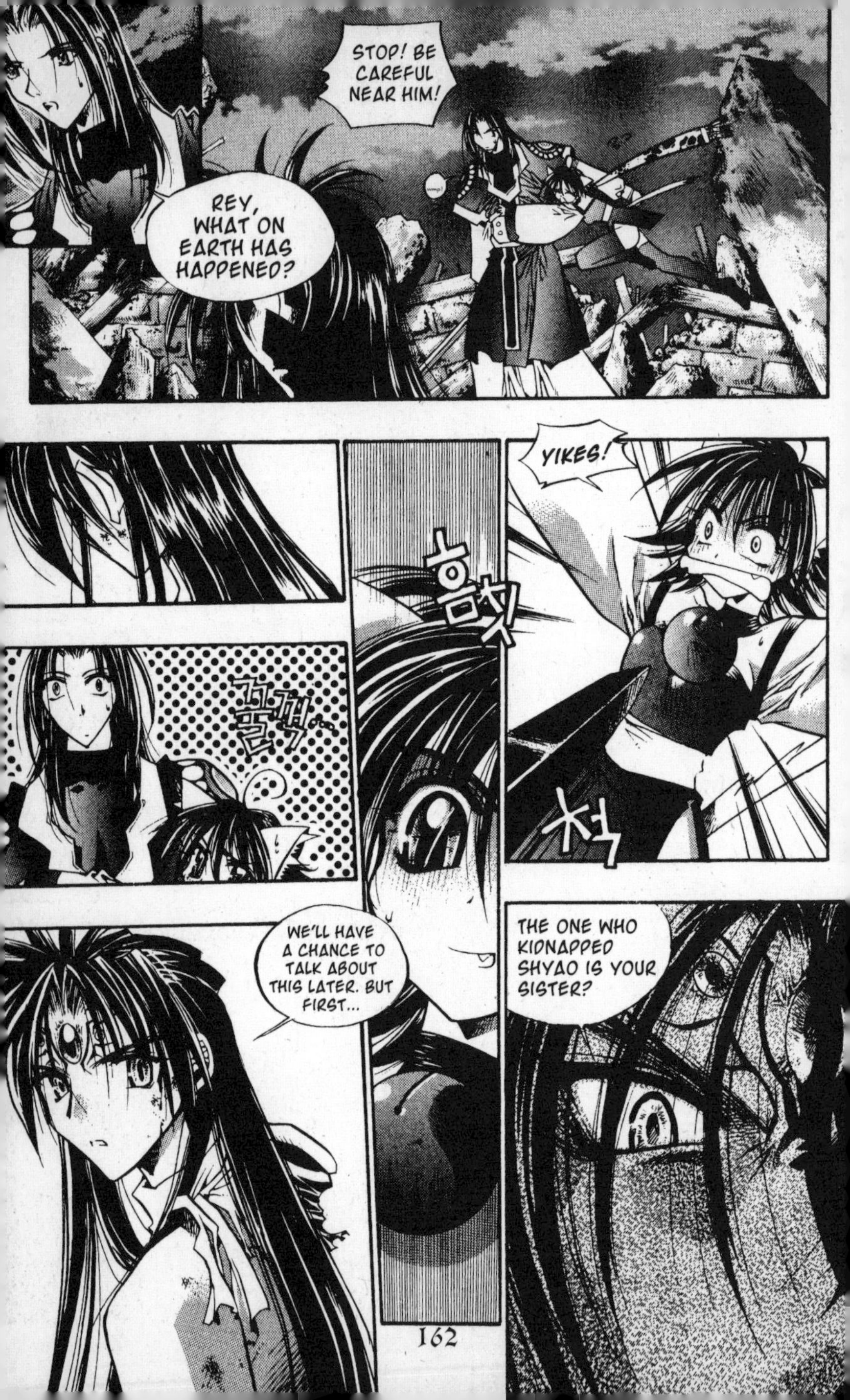
STOP! BE CAREFUL NEAR HIM!
REY, WHAT ON EARTH HAS HAPPENED?
흠칫
YIKES!
척
WE'LL HAVE A CHANCE TO TALK ABOUT THIS LATER. BUT FIRST...
THE ONE WHO KIDNAPPED SHYAO IS YOUR SISTER?

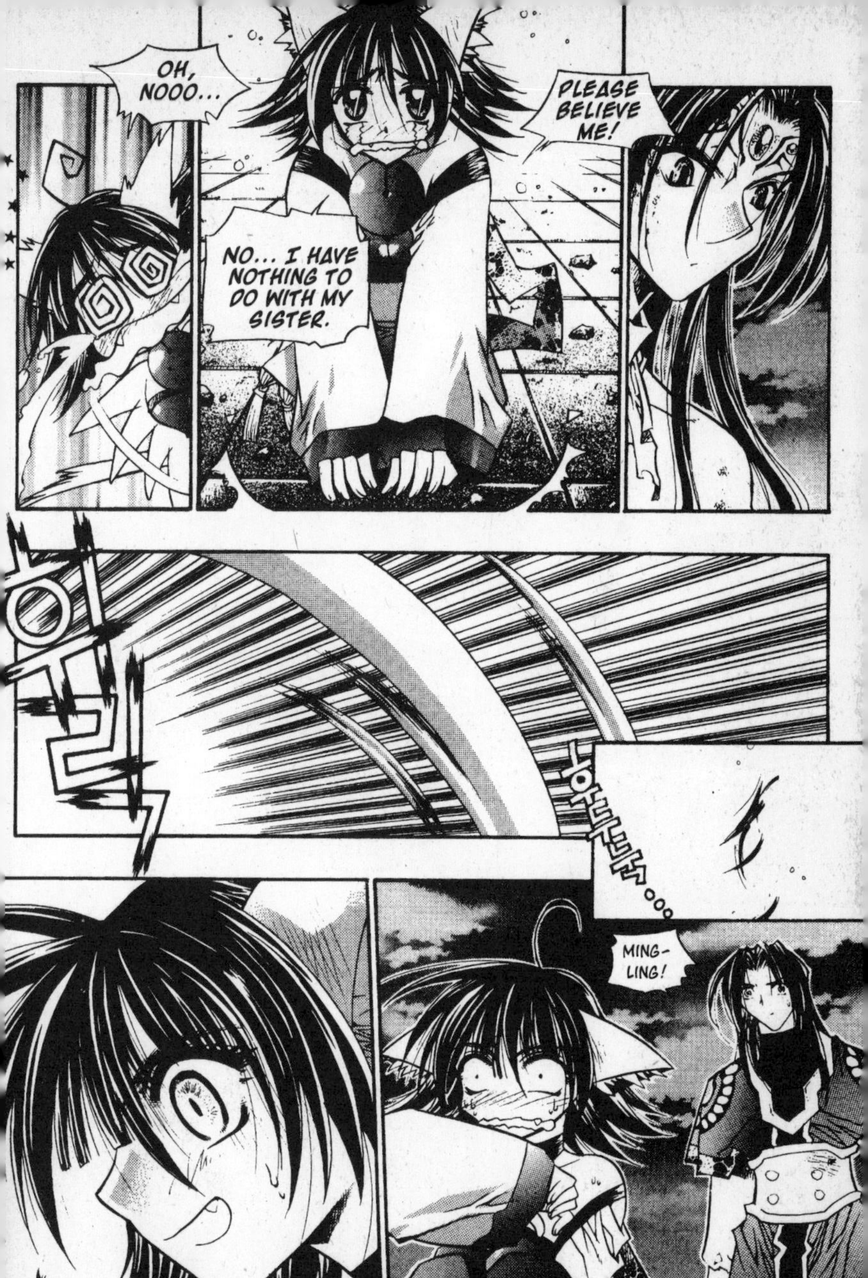
OH, NOOO...
NO... I HAVE NOTHING TO DO WITH MY SISTER.
PLEASE BELIEVE ME!
MING-LING!

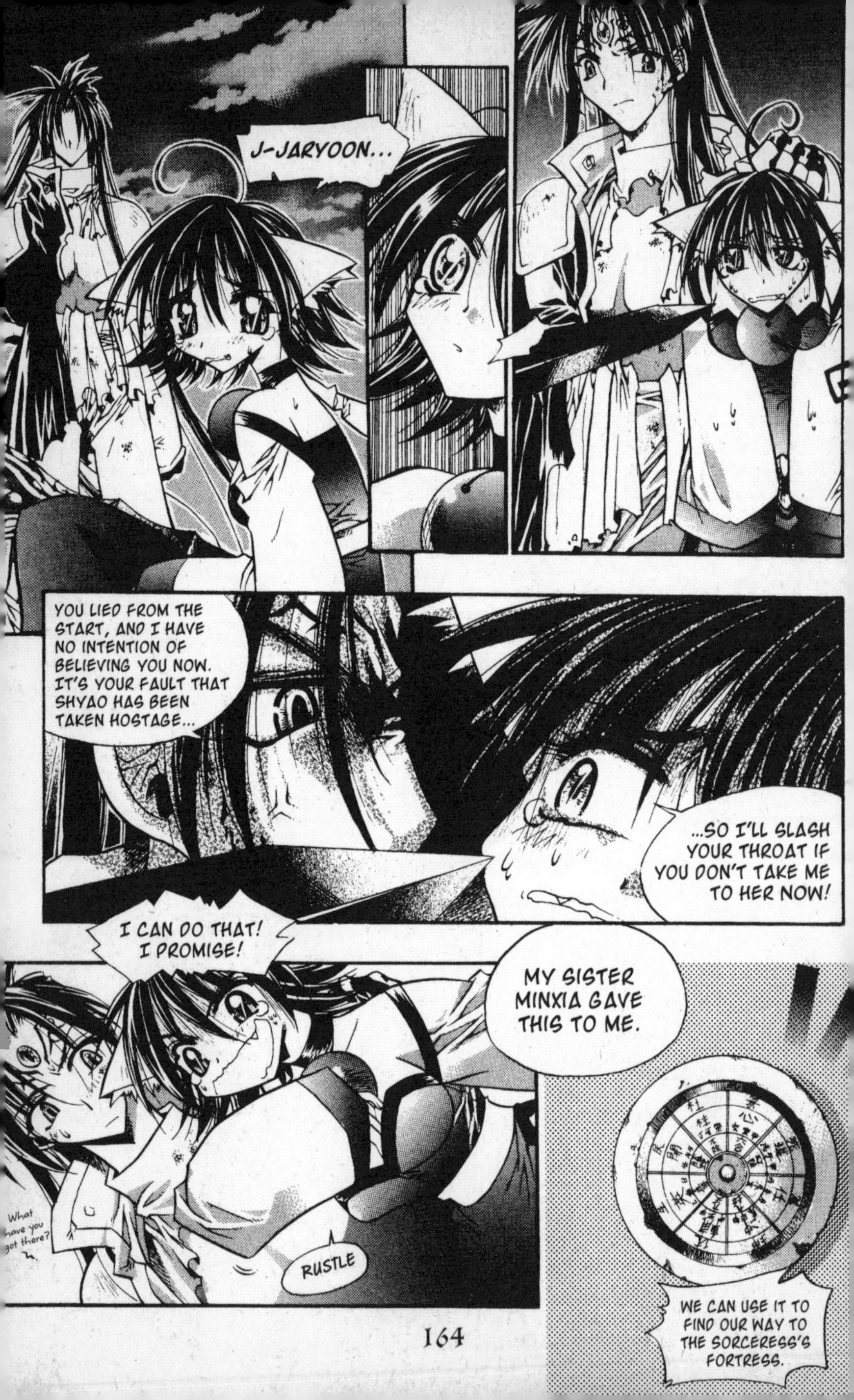
J-JARYOON...
YOU LIED FROM THE START, AND I HAVE NO INTENTION OF BELIEVING YOU NOW. IT'S YOUR FAULT THAT SHYAO HAS BEEN TAKEN HOSTAGE...
...SO I'LL SLASH YOUR THROAT IF YOU DON'T TAKE ME TO HER NOW!
I CAN DO THAT! I PROMISE!
What have you got there?
RUSTLE
MY SISTER MINXIA GAVE THIS TO ME.
WE CAN USE IT TO FIND OUR WAY TO THE SORCERESS'S FORTRESS.

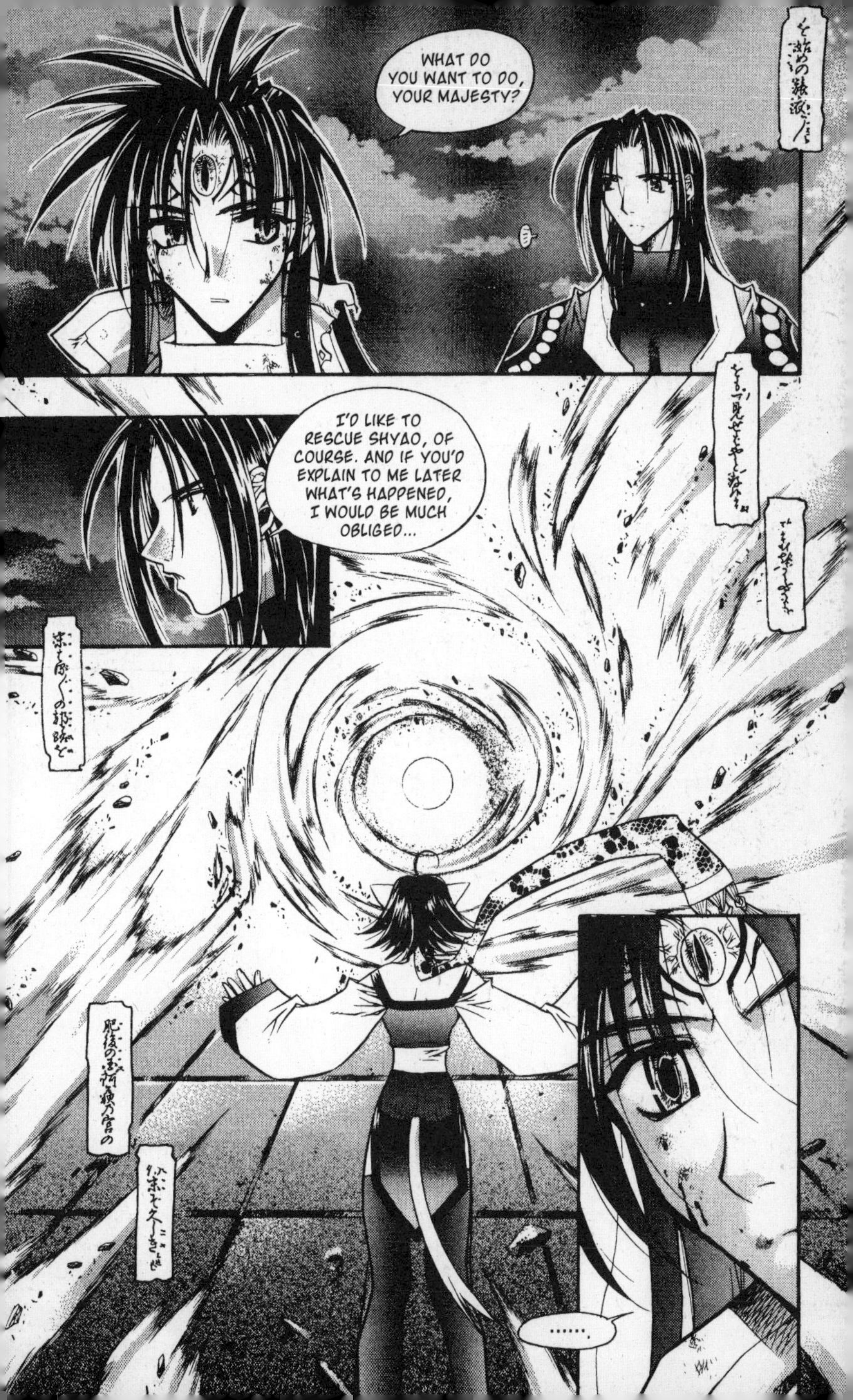
WHAT DO YOU WANT TO DO, YOUR MAJESTY?
I'D LIKE TO RESCUE SHYAO, OF COURSE. AND IF YOU'D EXPLAIN TO ME LATER WHAT'S HAPPENED, I WOULD BE MUCH OBLIGED...
....

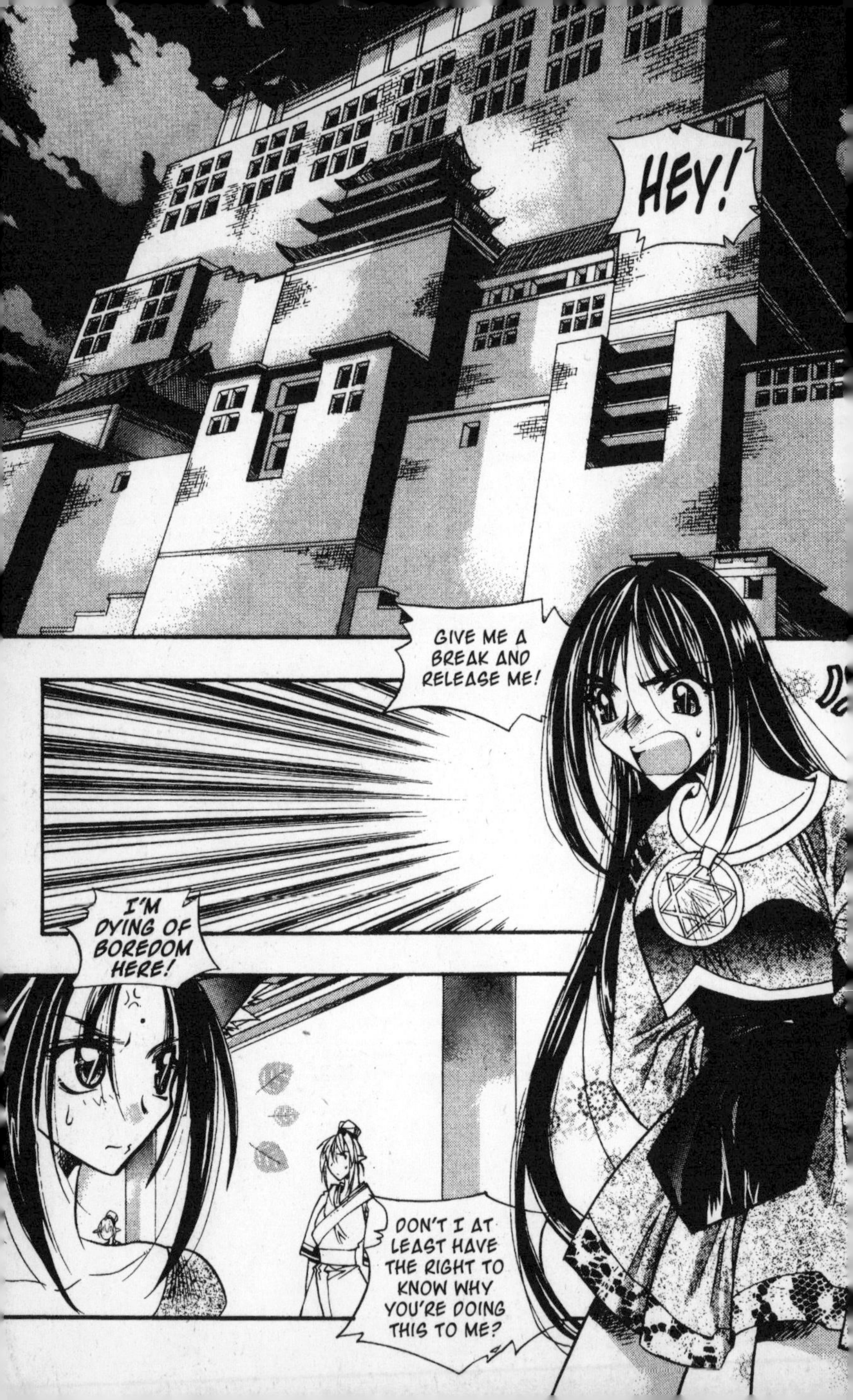
HEY!
GIVE ME A BREAK AND RELEASE ME!
I'M DYING OF BOREDOM HERE!
DON'T I AT LEAST HAVE THE RIGHT TO KNOW WHY YOU'RE DOING THIS TO ME?

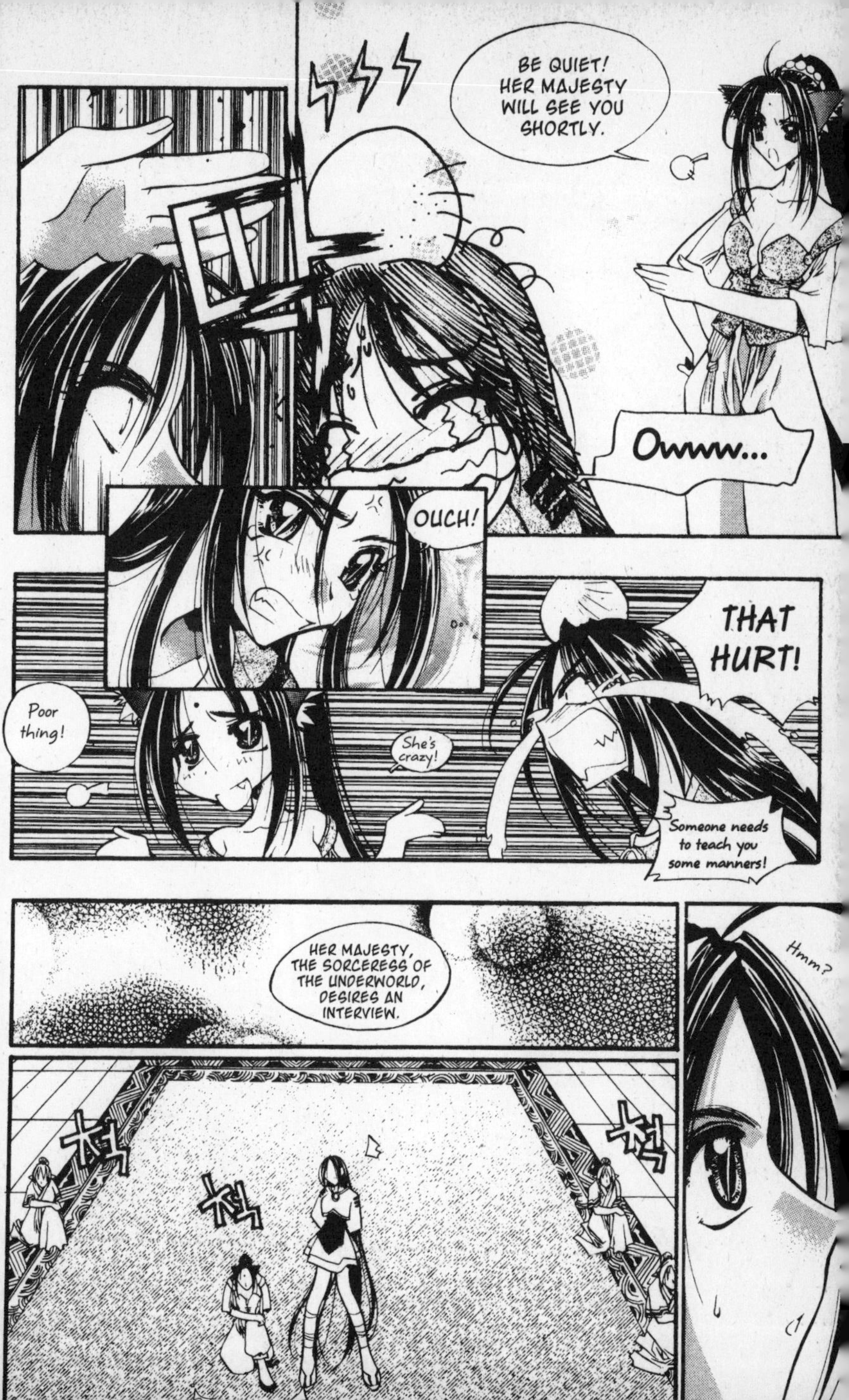
BE QUIET! HER MAJESTY WILL SEE YOU SHORTLY.
Owww...
OUCH!
Poor thing!
She's crazy!
THAT HURT!
Someone needs to teach you some manners!
HER MAJESTY, THE SORCERESS OF THE UNDERWORLD, DESIRES AN INTERVIEW.
Hmm?

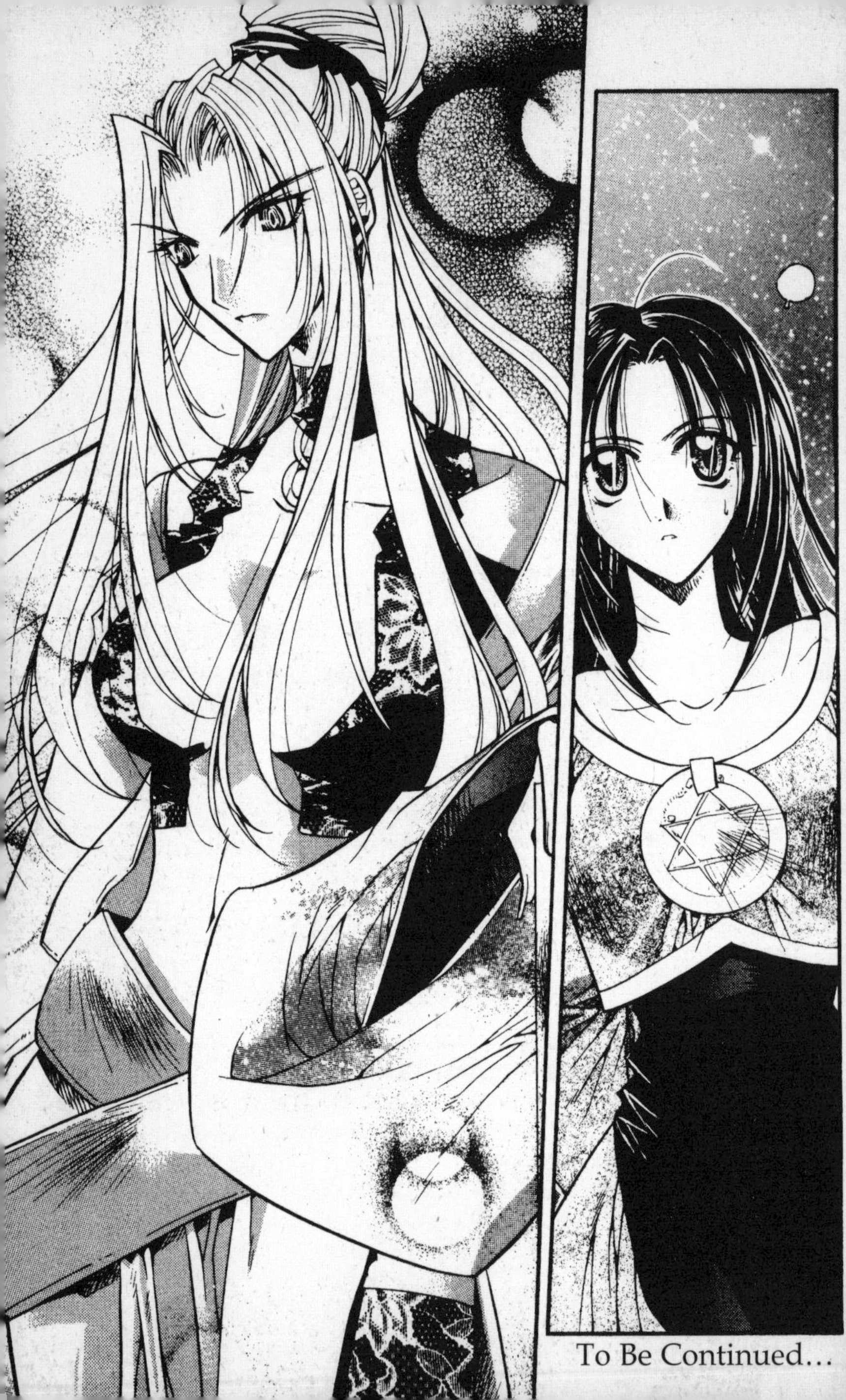

To Be Continued…

CHRONICLES OF THE CURSED SWORD

Rey, Jaryoon and Mingling have made it at last to the capital city Zhou, but not all is as they expected. The seeds of corruption have spread to the most unexpected places and no one can be trusted— not even the emperor. But before the kingdom can be set straight, there's the matter of Shyao's kidnapping to resolve. Who is the sorceress that kidnapped her, and what is her agenda? Find out in the next volume of Chronicles of the Cursed Sword!

AUTHOR: YEO BEOP-RYONG
ILLUSTRATOR: PARK HUI-JIN

③

Faeries' Landing

Story and Art by
YOU HYUN

Coming in January 2004 from TOKYOPOP®

Welcome to Faeries' Landing, a place where the real world and the
Faerie realm collide. 16-year-old Ryang, like most people, doesn't
realize that supernatural beings descend to his town at night, but when
he stumbles upon the Faerie Bath, he ends up becoming the guardian of
a grounded faerie. Having an otherworldly babe hanging on you 24-7
doesn't sound so bad at first, but when Fanta reads Ryang's fortune, he
finds out that it is his destiny to encounter 108 doomed relationships.
It's too much of a good thing when this girl-shy loser finds himself
surrounded by dozens lovely ladies both mortal and ethereal.

For more information on this and other series, visit www.
TOKYOPOP.com

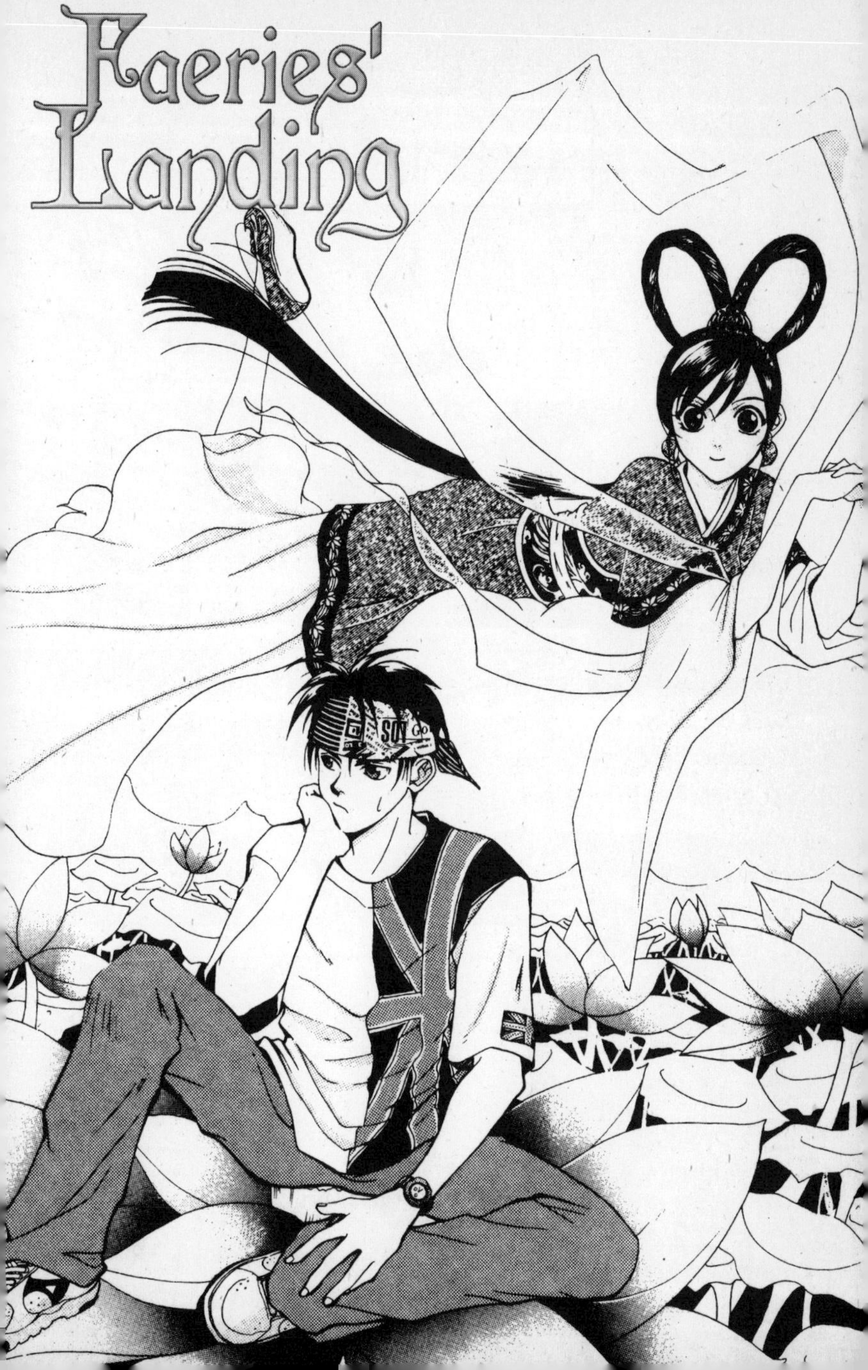
Faeries' Landing

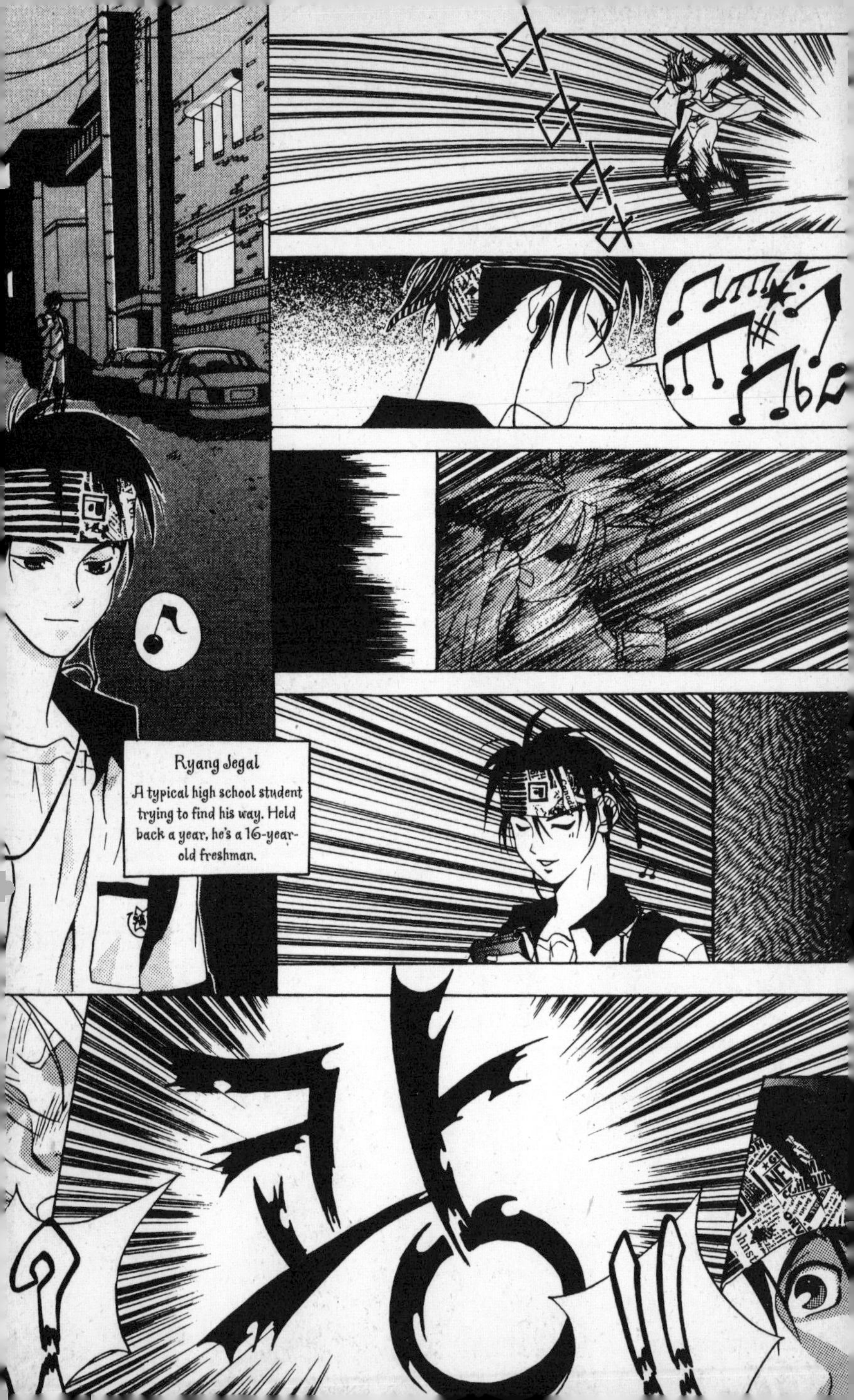
Ryang Jegal
A typical high school student trying to find his way. Held back a year, he's a 16-year-old freshman.

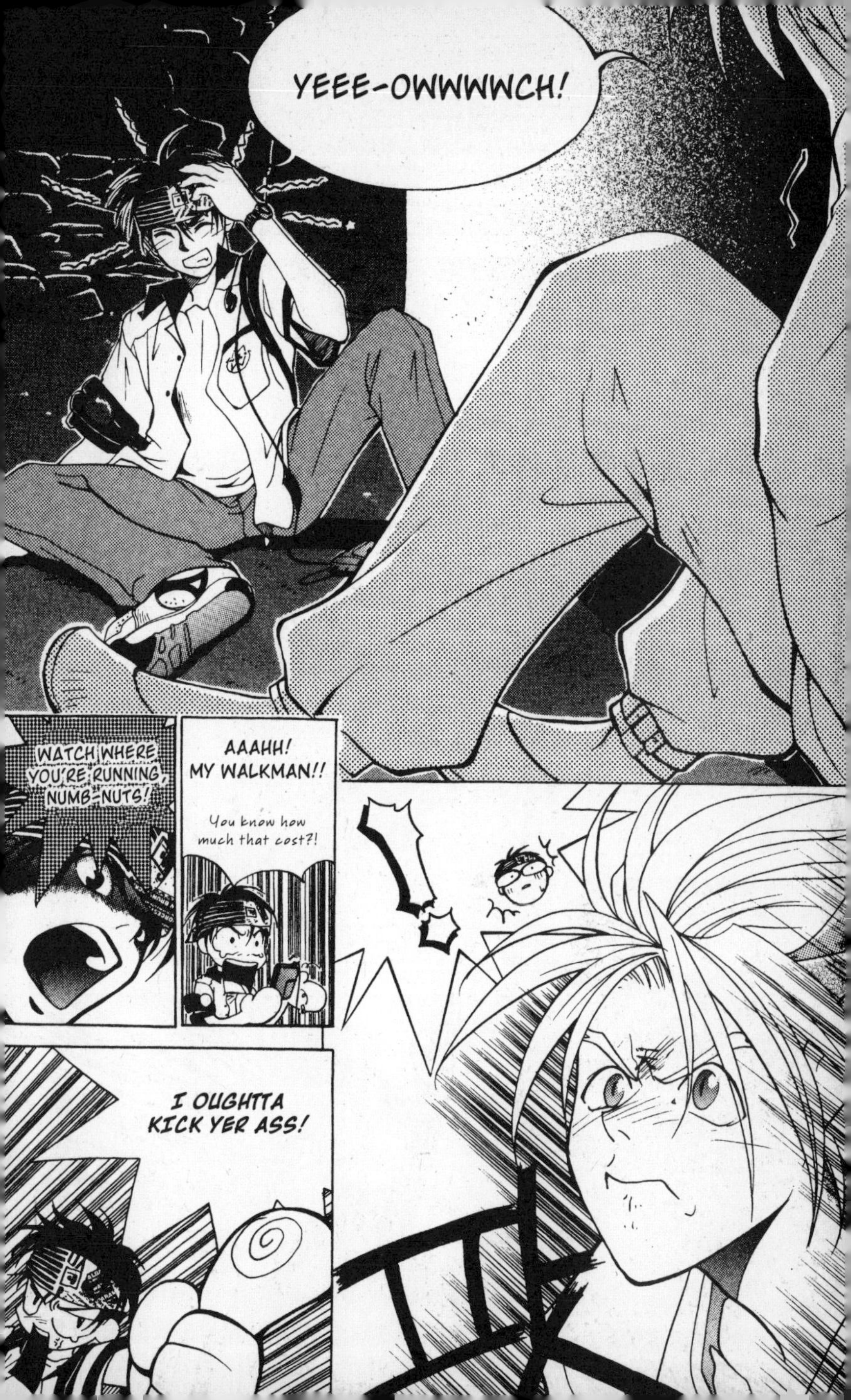
YEEE-OWWWWCH!
WATCH WHERE YOU'RE RUNNING, NUMB-NUTS!
AAAHH! MY WALKMAN!!
You know how much that cost?!
I OUGHTTA KICK YER ASS!

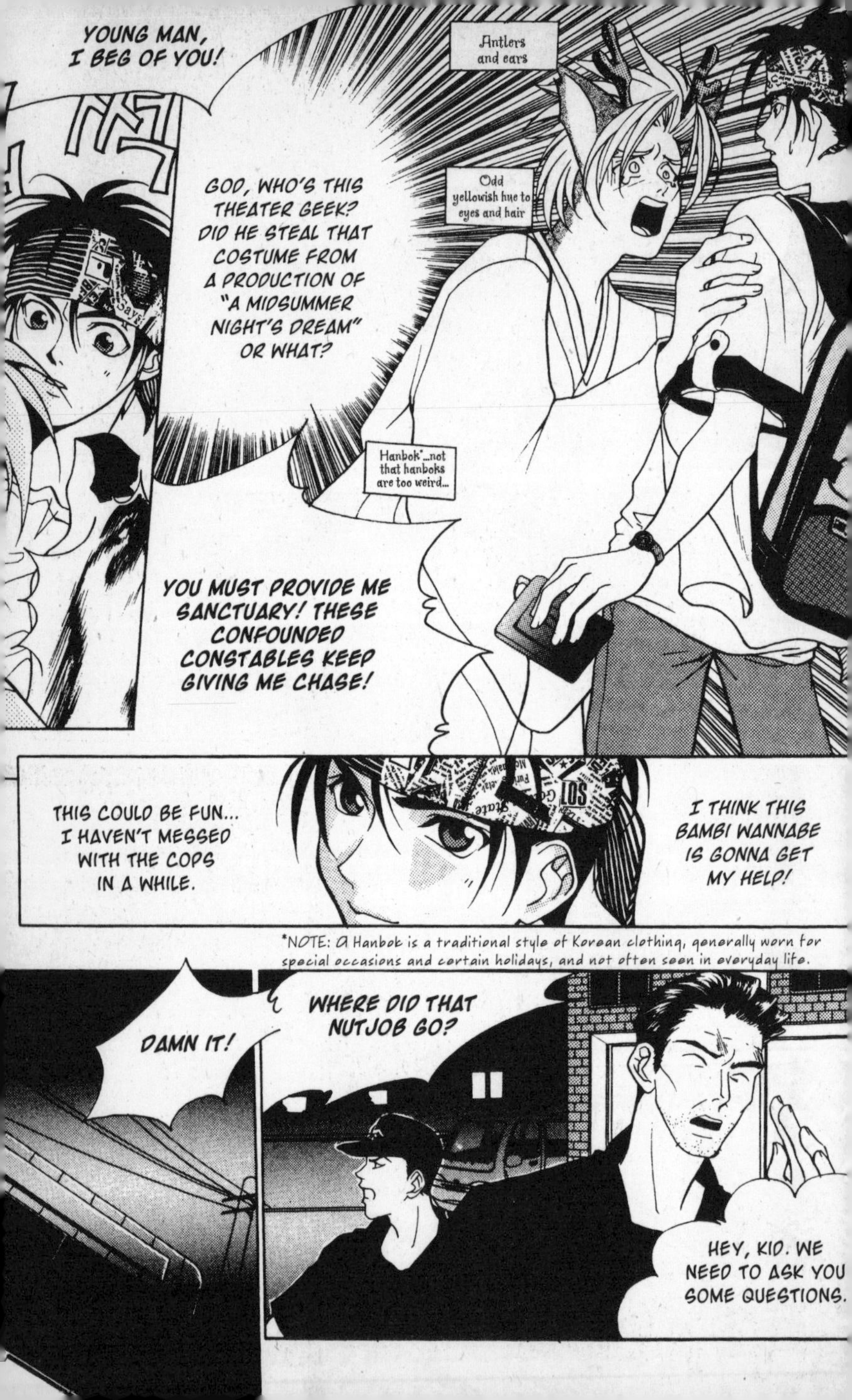
YOUNG MAN, I BEG OF YOU!
Antlers and ears
GOD, WHO'S THIS THEATER GEEK? DID HE STEAL THAT COSTUME FROM A PRODUCTION OF "A MIDSUMMER NIGHT'S DREAM" OR WHAT?
Odd yellowish hue to eyes and hair
Hanbok*...not that hanboks are too weird...
YOU MUST PROVIDE ME SANCTUARY! THESE CONFOUNDED CONSTABLES KEEP GIVING ME CHASE!
THIS COULD BE FUN... I HAVEN'T MESSED WITH THE COPS IN A WHILE.
I THINK THIS BAMBI WANNABE IS GONNA GET MY HELP!
DAMN IT!
WHERE DID THAT NUTJOB GO?
HEY, KID. WE NEED TO ASK YOU SOME QUESTIONS.

*NOTE: A Hanbok is a traditional style of Korean clothing, generally worn for special occasions and certain holidays, and not often seen in everyday life.

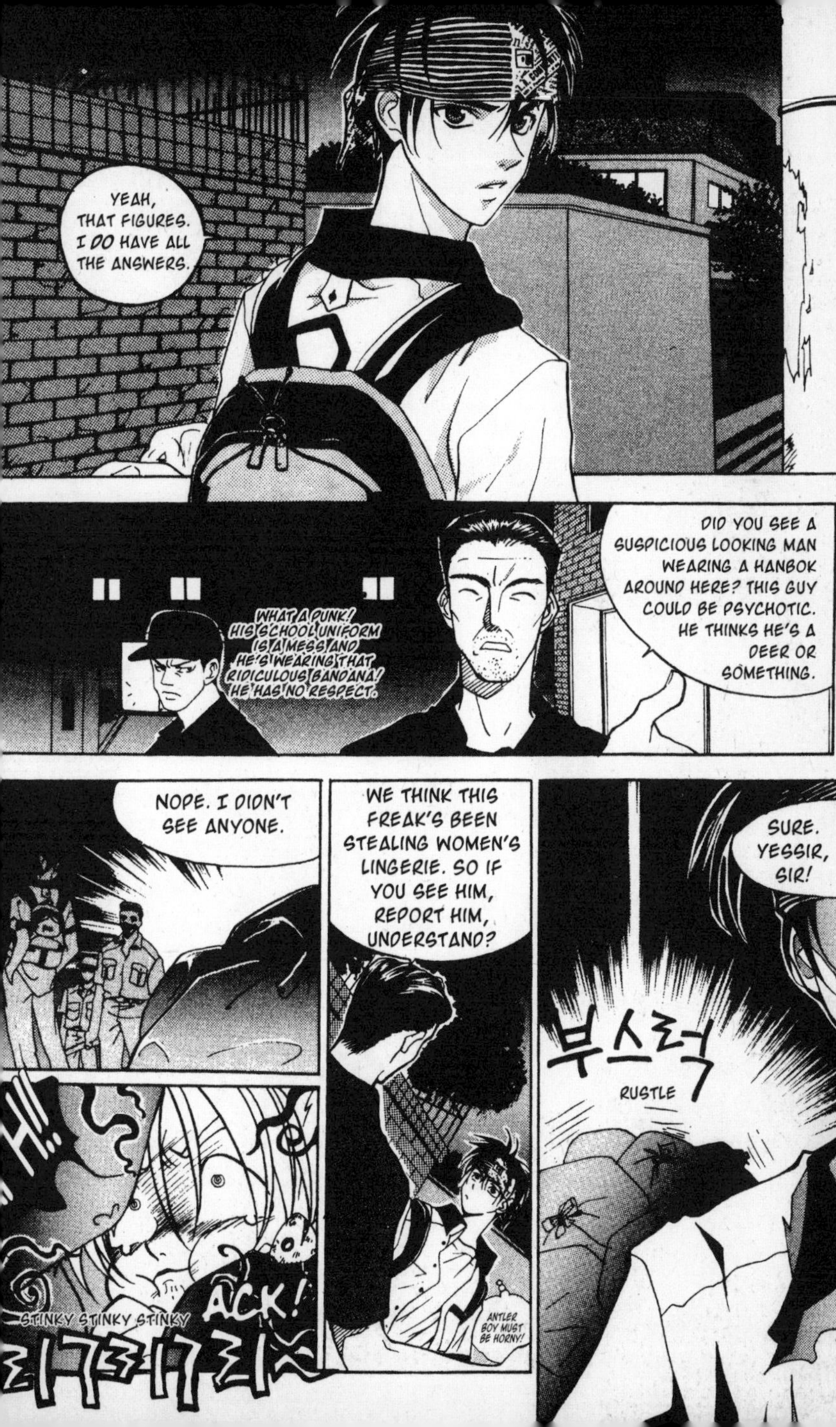
YEAH, THAT FIGURES. I DO HAVE ALL THE ANSWERS.
WHAT A PUNK! HIS SCHOOL UNIFORM IS A MESS AND HE'S WEARING THAT RIDICULOUS BANDANA! HE HAS NO RESPECT.
DID YOU SEE A SUSPICIOUS LOOKING MAN WEARING A HANBOK AROUND HERE? THIS GUY COULD BE PSYCHOTIC. HE THINKS HE'S A DEER OR SOMETHING.
NOPE. I DIDN'T SEE ANYONE.
STINKY STINKY STINKY
ACK!
WE THINK THIS FREAK'S BEEN STEALING WOMEN'S LINGERIE. SO IF YOU SEE HIM, REPORT HIM, UNDERSTAND?
ANTLER BOY MUST BE HORNY!
SURE. YESSIR, SIR!
부스럭
RUSTLE

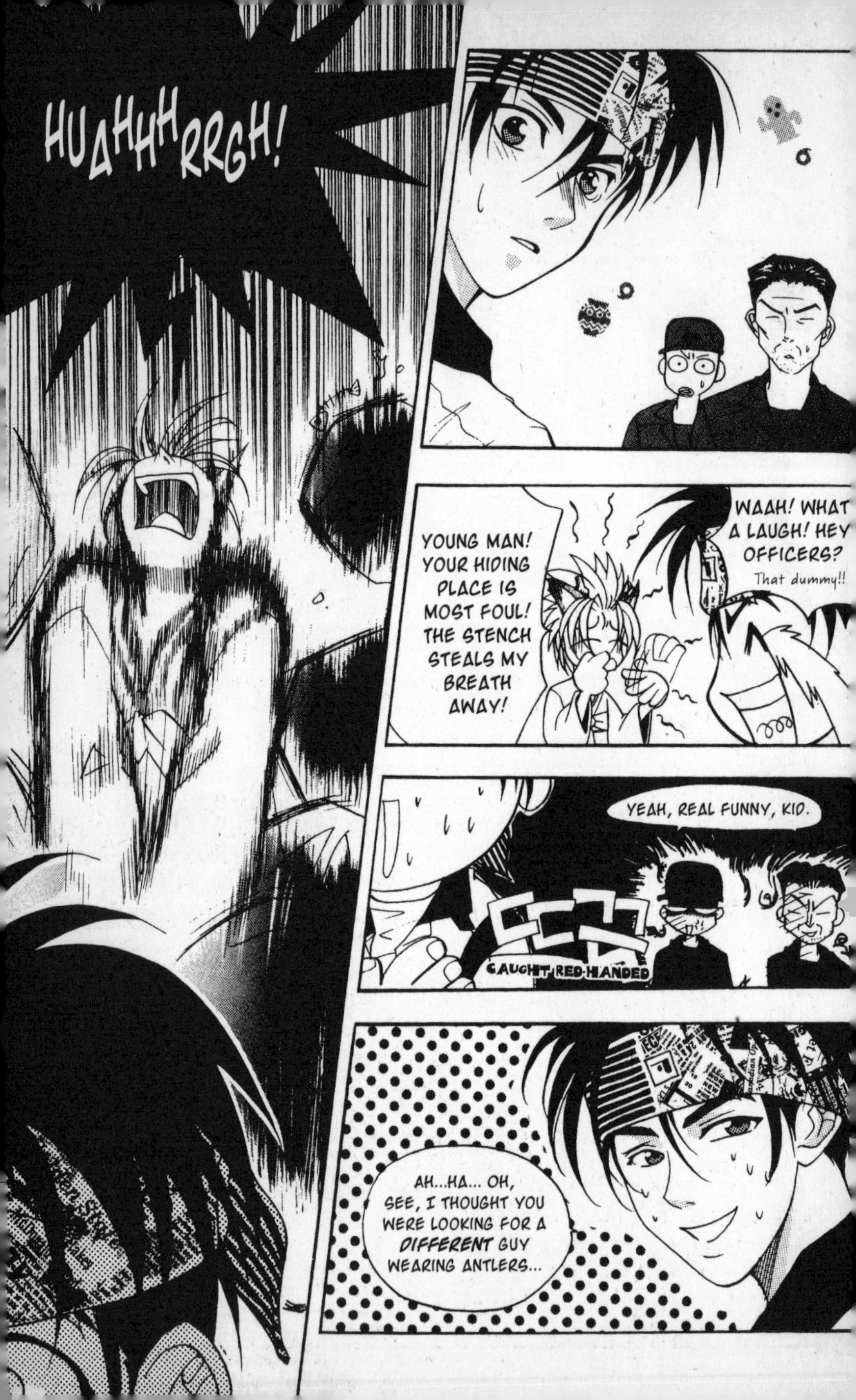
HUAHHHRRGH!
YOUNG MAN! YOUR HIDING PLACE IS MOST FOUL! THE STENCH STEALS MY BREATH AWAY!
WAAH! WHAT A LAUGH! HEY OFFICERS?
That dummy!!
YEAH, REAL FUNNY, KID.
CAUGHT RED-HANDED
AH...HA... OH, SEE, I THOUGHT YOU WERE LOOKING FOR A *DIFFERENT* GUY WEARING ANTLERS...

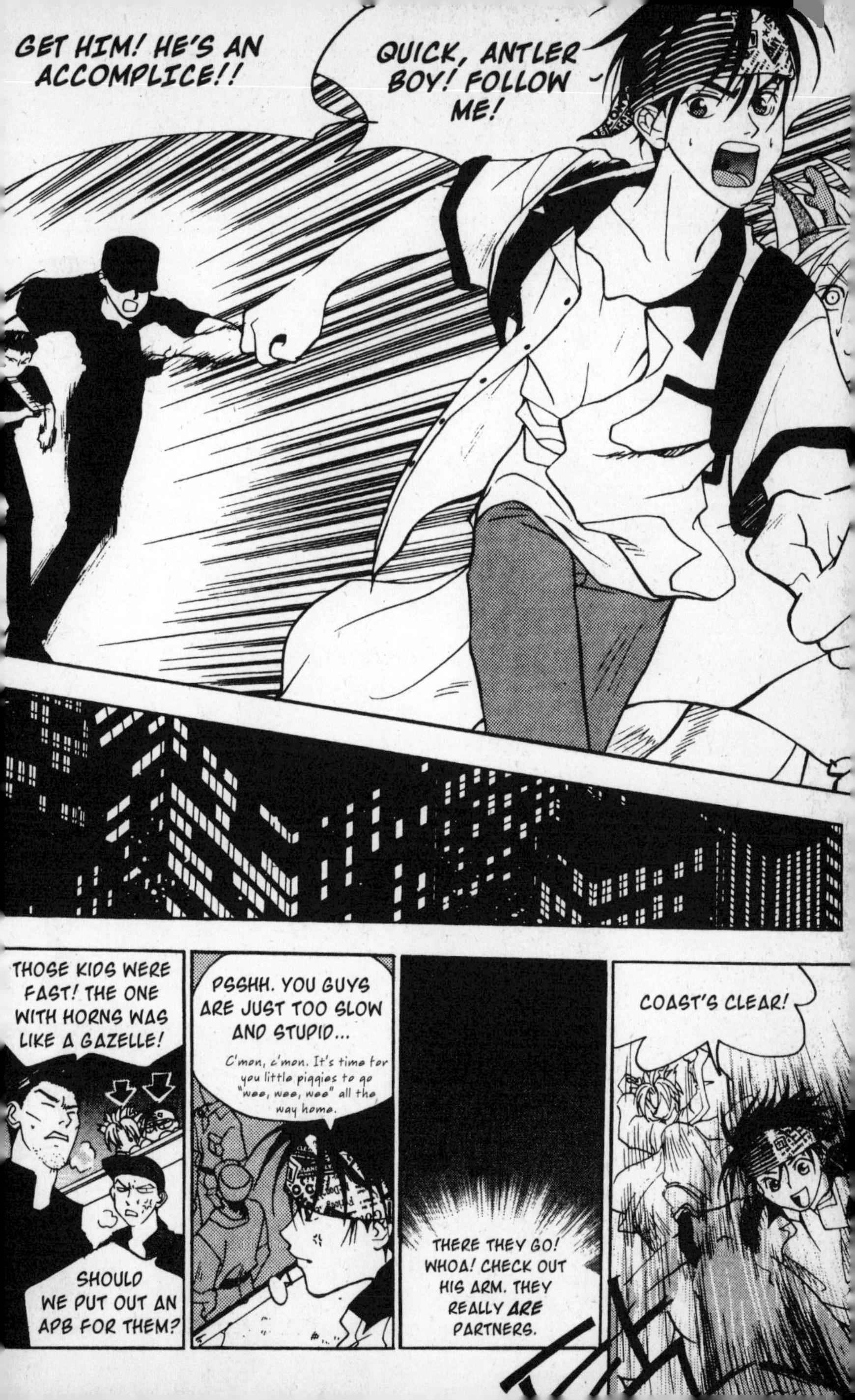
GET HIM! HE'S AN ACCOMPLICE!!
QUICK, ANTLER BOY! FOLLOW ME!
THOSE KIDS WERE FAST! THE ONE WITH HORNS WAS LIKE A GAZELLE!
SHOULD WE PUT OUT AN APB FOR THEM?
PSSHH. YOU GUYS ARE JUST TOO SLOW AND STUPID...
C'mon, c'mon. It's time for you little piggies to go "wee, wee, wee" all the way home.
THERE THEY GO! WHOA! CHECK OUT HIS ARM. THEY REALLY ARE PARTNERS.
COAST'S CLEAR!

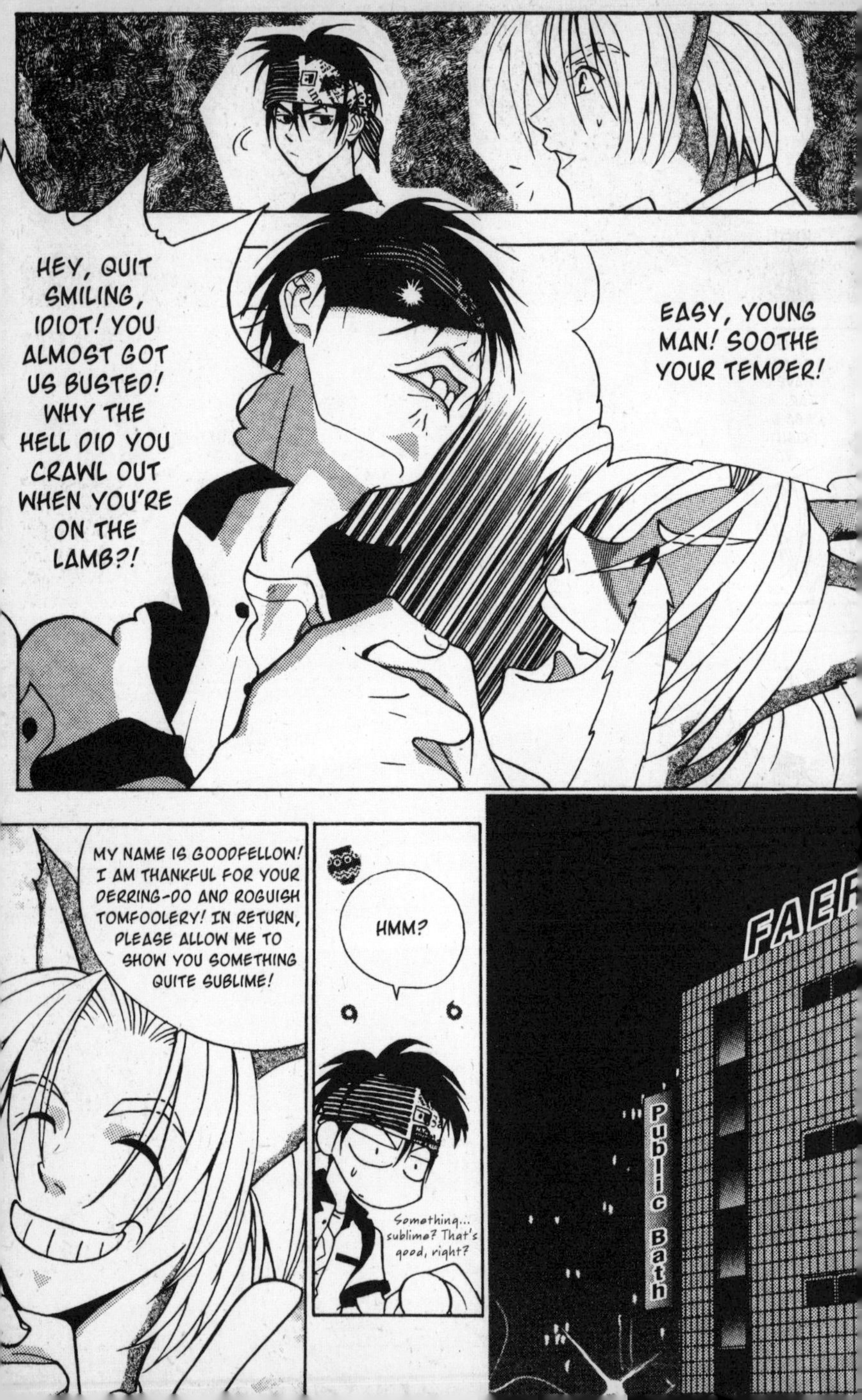
HEY, QUIT SMILING, IDIOT! YOU ALMOST GOT US BUSTED! WHY THE HELL DID YOU CRAWL OUT WHEN YOU'RE ON THE LAMB?!
EASY, YOUNG MAN! SOOTHE YOUR TEMPER!
MY NAME IS GOODFELLOW! I AM THANKFUL FOR YOUR DERRING-DO AND ROGUISH TOMFOOLERY! IN RETURN, PLEASE ALLOW ME TO SHOW YOU SOMETHING QUITE SUBLIME!
HMM?
Something... sublime? That's good, right?
FAER
Public Bath

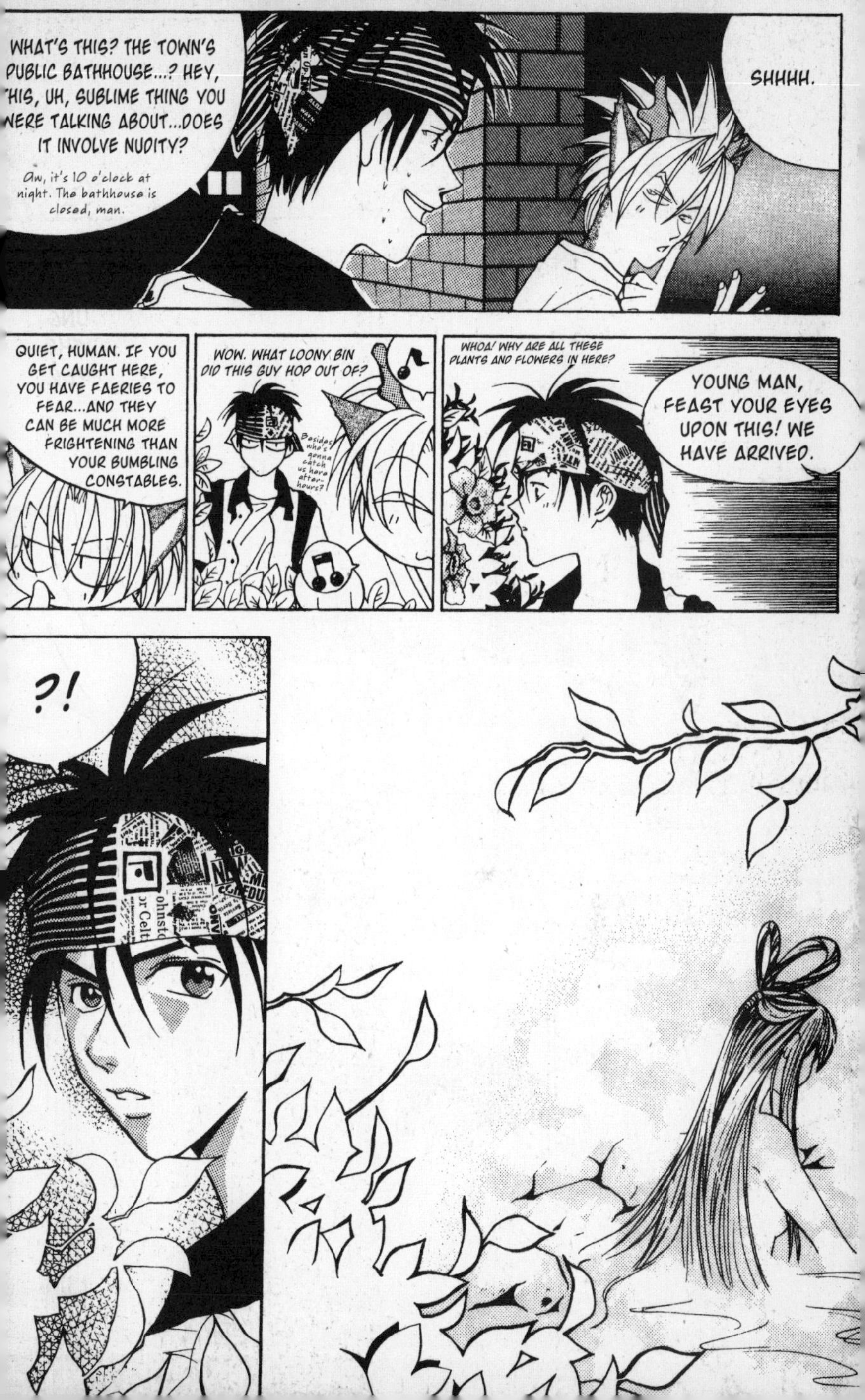
WHAT'S THIS? THE TOWN'S PUBLIC BATHHOUSE...? HEY, THIS, UH, SUBLIME THING YOU WERE TALKING ABOUT...DOES IT INVOLVE NUDITY?
Aw, it's 10 o'clock at night. The bathhouse is closed, man.
SHHHH.
QUIET, HUMAN. IF YOU GET CAUGHT HERE, YOU HAVE FAERIES TO FEAR...AND THEY CAN BE MUCH MORE FRIGHTENING THAN YOUR BUMBLING CONSTABLES.
WOW. WHAT LOONY BIN DID THIS GUY HOP OUT OF?
Besides, who's gonna catch us here after-hours?
WHOA! WHY ARE ALL THESE PLANTS AND FLOWERS IN HERE?
YOUNG MAN, FEAST YOUR EYES UPON THIS! WE HAVE ARRIVED.
?!

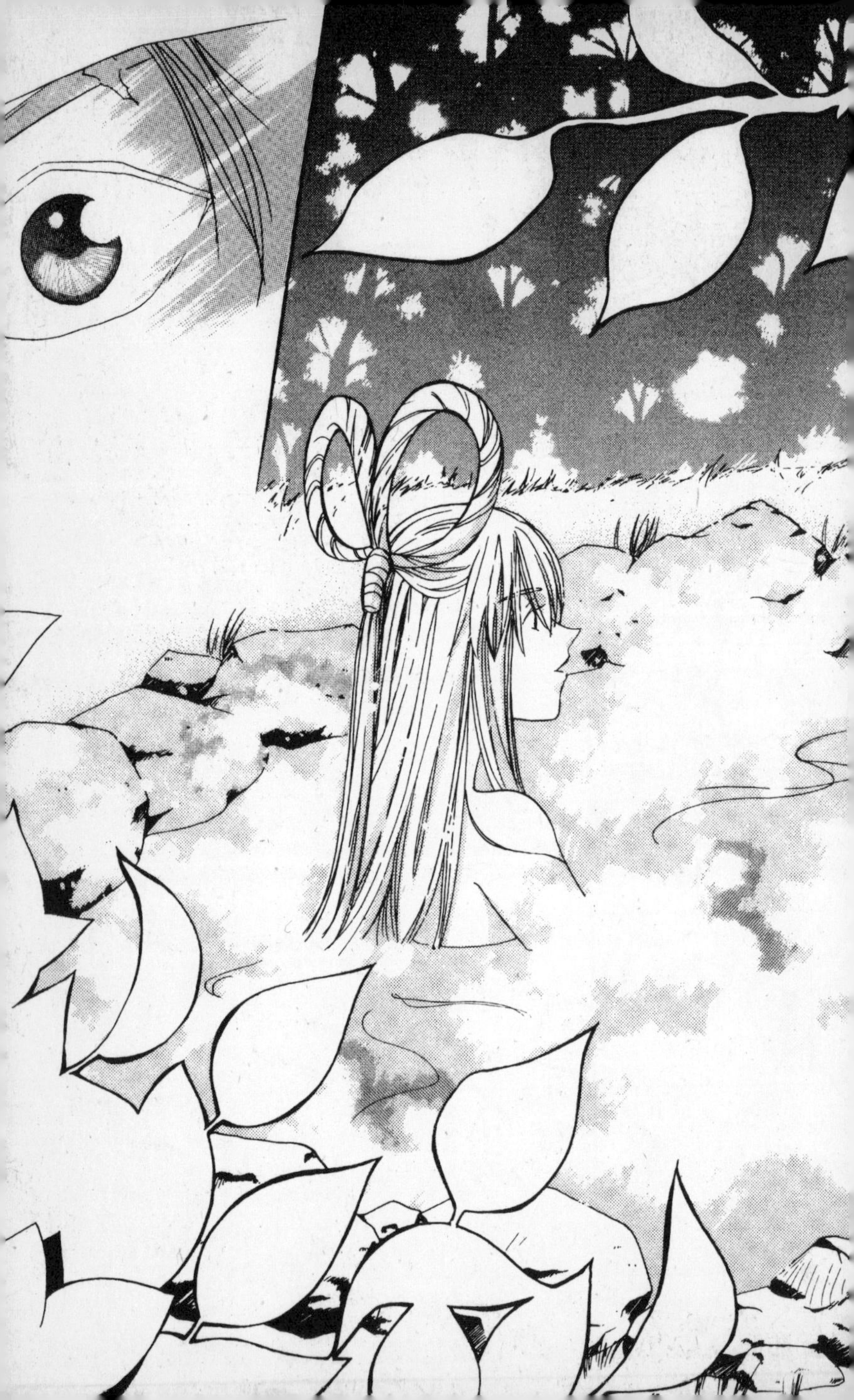

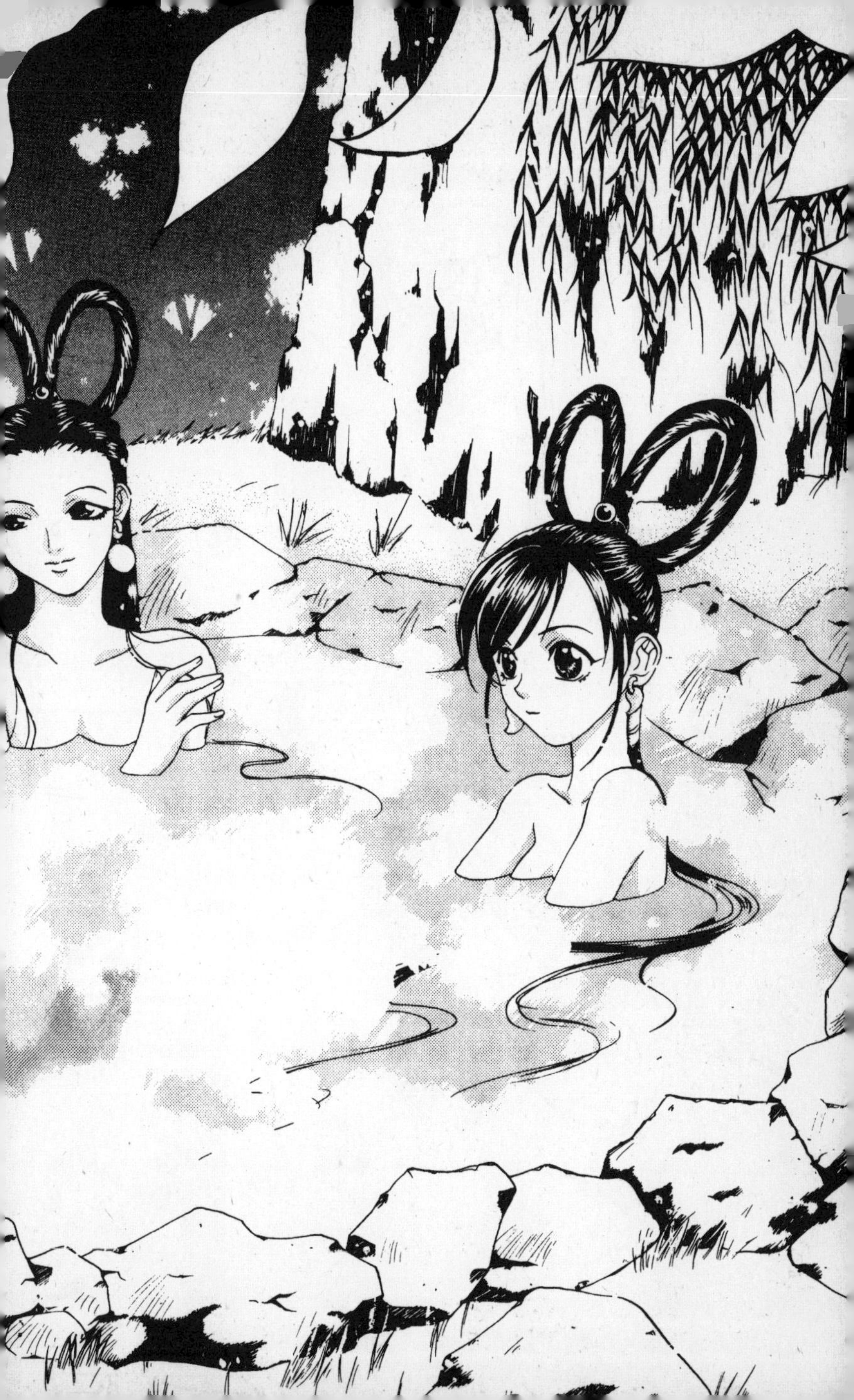

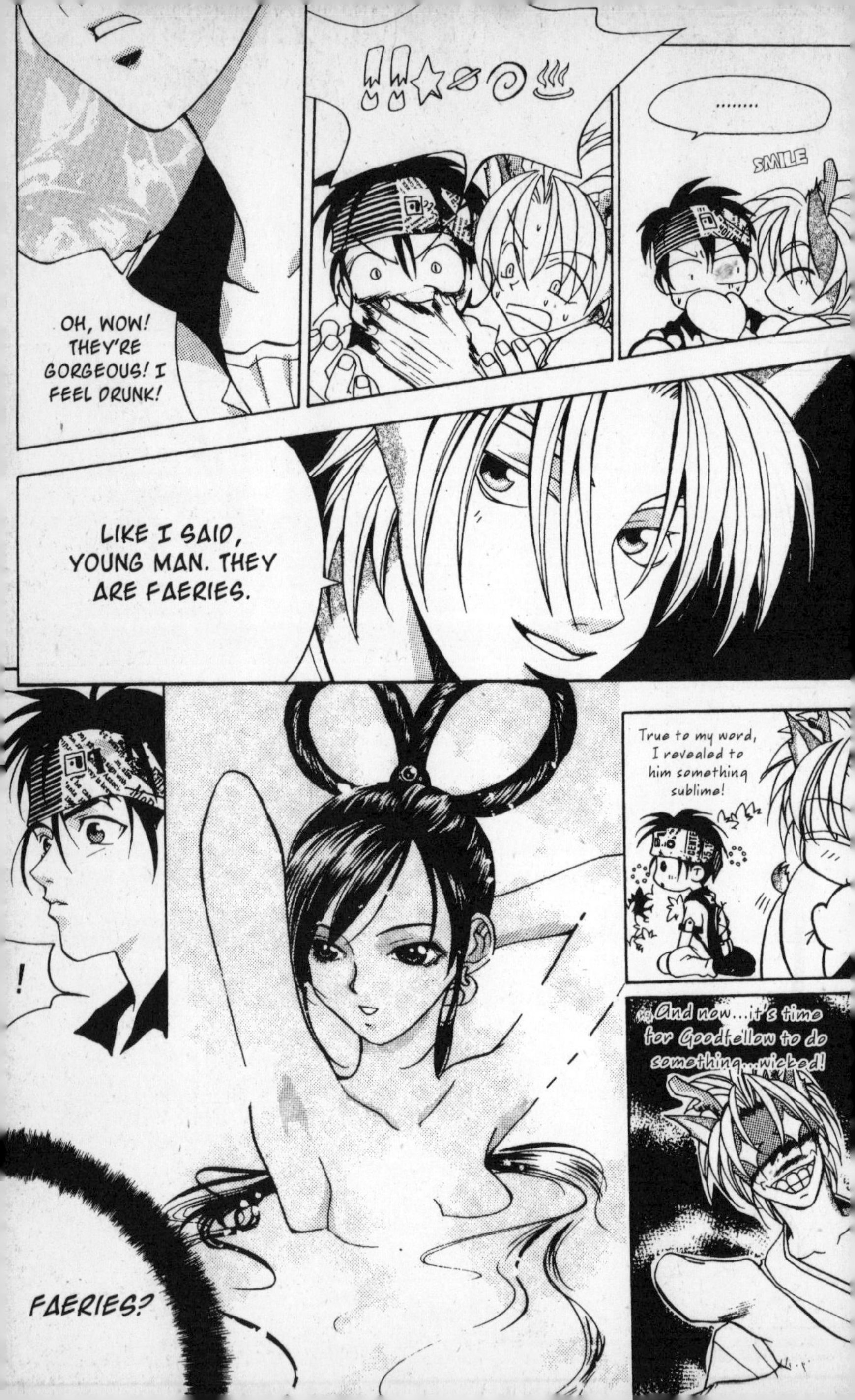

OH, WOW! THEY'RE GORGEOUS! I FEEL DRUNK!
!!☆
....
SMILE
LIKE I SAID, YOUNG MAN. THEY ARE FAERIES.
!
FAERIES?
True to my word, I revealed to him something sublime!
And now...it's time for Goodfellow to do something...wicked!

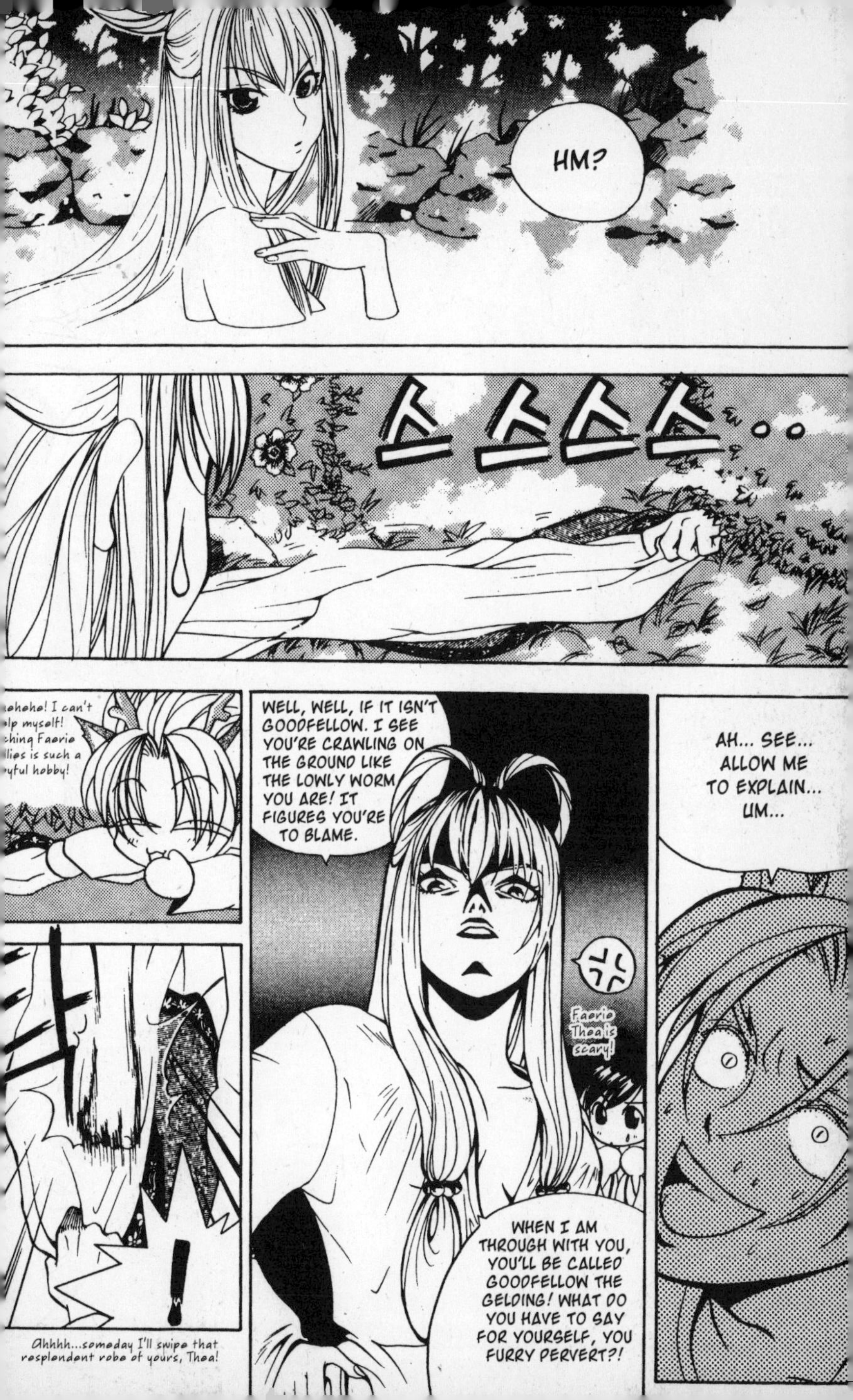
HM?
스스스스...
ohoho! I can't lp myself! ching Faerie llies is such a yful hobby!
Ahhhh...someday I'll swipe that resplendent robe of yours, Thea!
WELL, WELL, IF IT ISN'T GOODFELLOW. I SEE YOU'RE CRAWLING ON THE GROUND LIKE THE LOWLY WORM YOU ARE! IT FIGURES YOU'RE TO BLAME.
Faerie Thea is scary!
WHEN I AM THROUGH WITH YOU, YOU'LL BE CALLED GOODFELLOW THE GELDING! WHAT DO YOU HAVE TO SAY FOR YOURSELF, YOU FURRY PERVERT?!
AH... SEE... ALLOW ME TO EXPLAIN... UM...

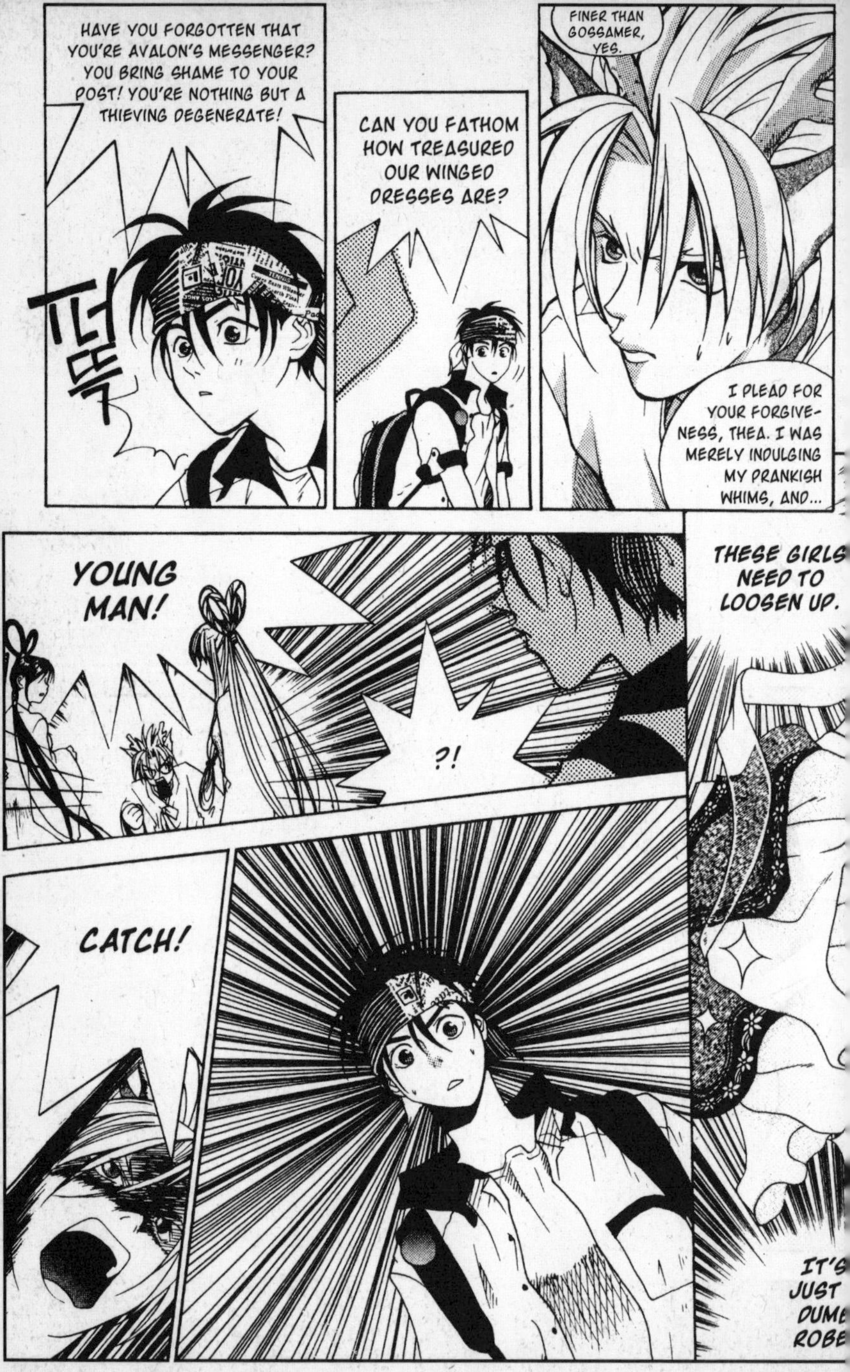

HAVE YOU FORGOTTEN THAT YOU'RE AVALON'S MESSENGER? YOU BRING SHAME TO YOUR POST! YOU'RE NOTHING BUT A THIEVING DEGENERATE!
CAN YOU FATHOM HOW TREASURED OUR WINGED DRESSES ARE?
FINER THAN GOSSAMER, YES.
I PLEAD FOR YOUR FORGIVENESS, THEA. I WAS MERELY INDULGING MY PRANKISH WHIMS, AND...
YOUNG MAN!
?!
CATCH!
THESE GIRLS NEED TO LOOSEN UP.
IT'S JUST DUMB ROBE

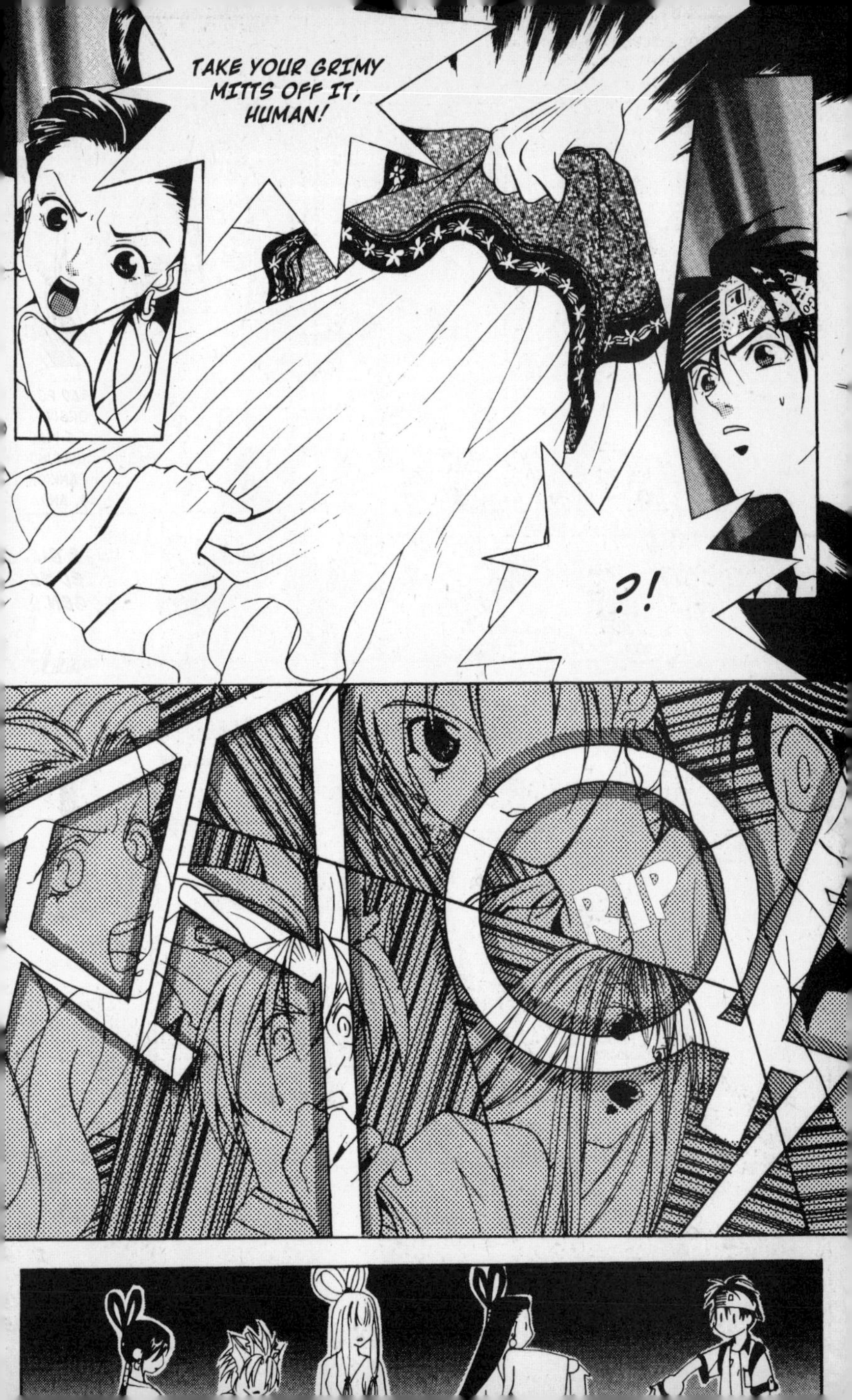
TAKE YOUR GRIMY MITTS OFF IT, HUMAN!
?!
RIP

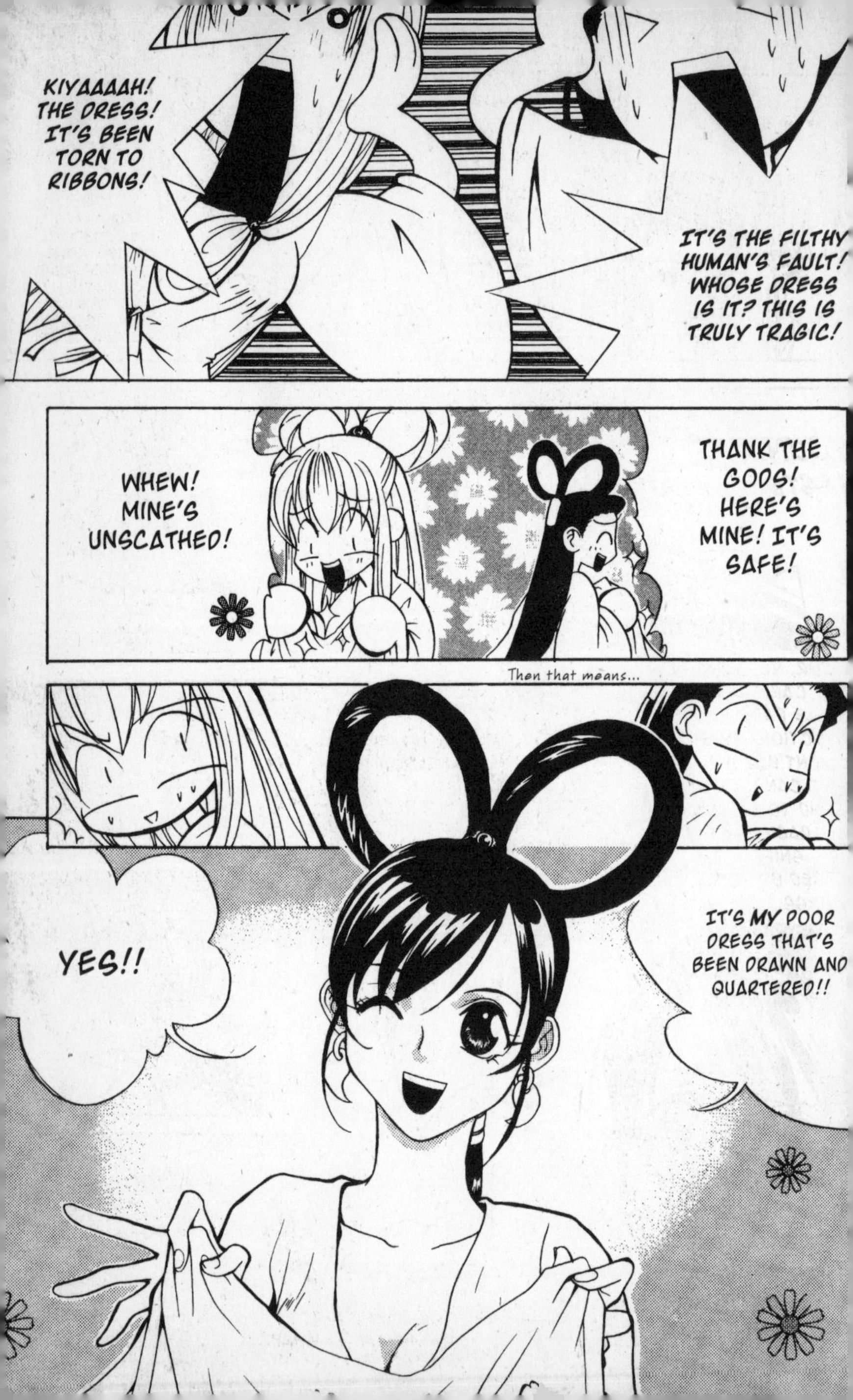
KIYAAAAH! THE DRESS! IT'S BEEN TORN TO RIBBONS!
IT'S THE FILTHY HUMAN'S FAULT! WHOSE DRESS IS IT? THIS IS TRULY TRAGIC!
WHEW! MINE'S UNSCATHED!
THANK THE GODS! HERE'S MINE! IT'S SAFE!
Then that means...
YES!!
IT'S MY POOR DRESS THAT'S BEEN DRAWN AND QUARTERED!!

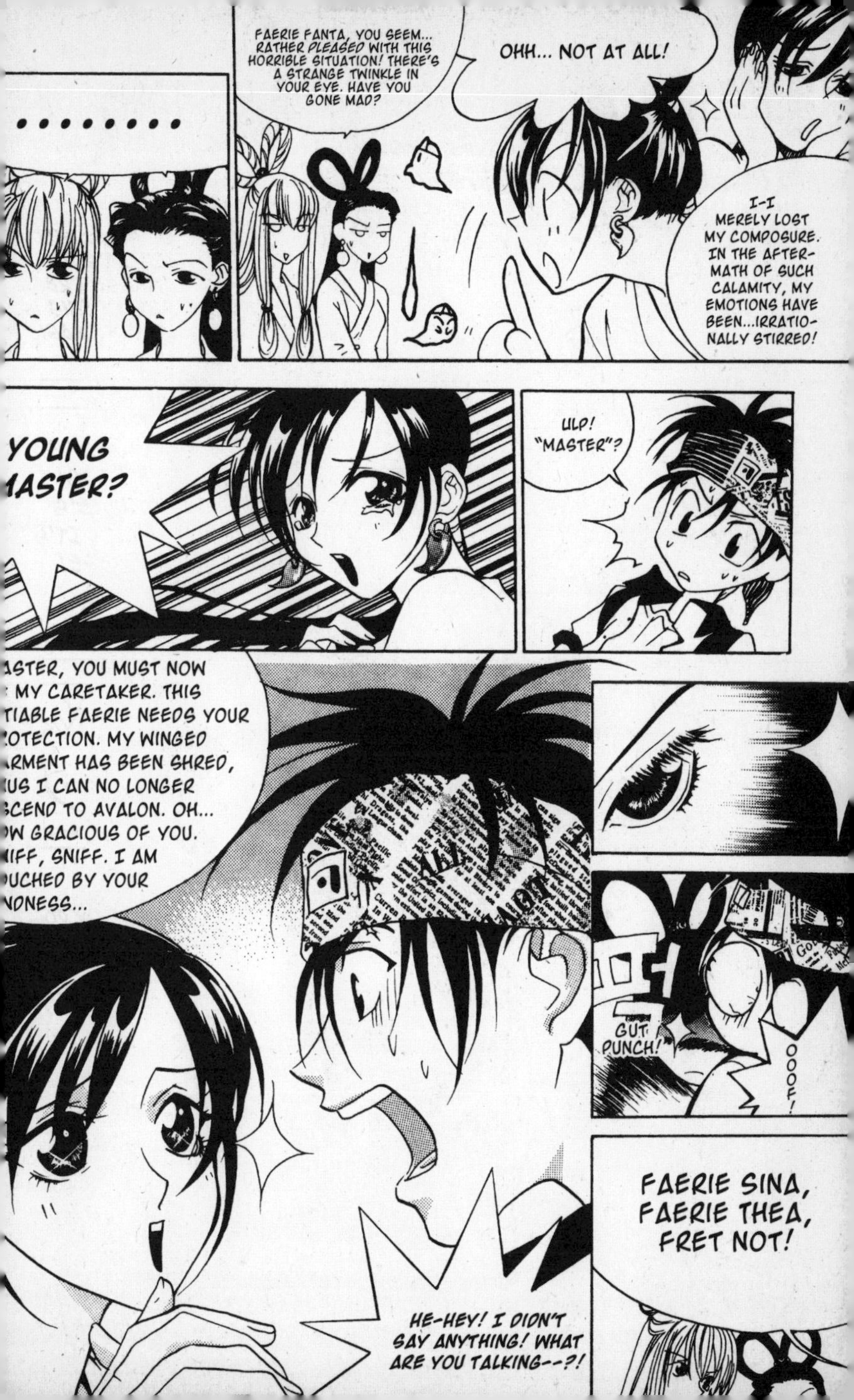
....
FAERIE FANTA, YOU SEEM... RATHER PLEASED WITH THIS HORRIBLE SITUATION! THERE'S A STRANGE TWINKLE IN YOUR EYE. HAVE YOU GONE MAD?
OHH... NOT AT ALL!
I-I MERELY LOST MY COMPOSURE. IN THE AFTER-MATH OF SUCH CALAMITY, MY EMOTIONS HAVE BEEN...IRRATIO-NALLY STIRRED!
YOUNG ASTER?
ULP! "MASTER"?
ASTER, YOU MUST NOW MY CARETAKER. THIS TIABLE FAERIE NEEDS YOUR OTECTION. MY WINGED RMENT HAS BEEN SHRED, US I CAN NO LONGER SCEND TO AVALON. OH... W GRACIOUS OF YOU. IFF, SNIFF. I AM UCHED BY YOUR NDNESS...
GUT PUNCH!
OOOF!
HE-HEY! I DIDN'T SAY ANYTHING! WHAT ARE YOU TALKING--?!
FAERIE SINA, FAERIE THEA, FRET NOT!

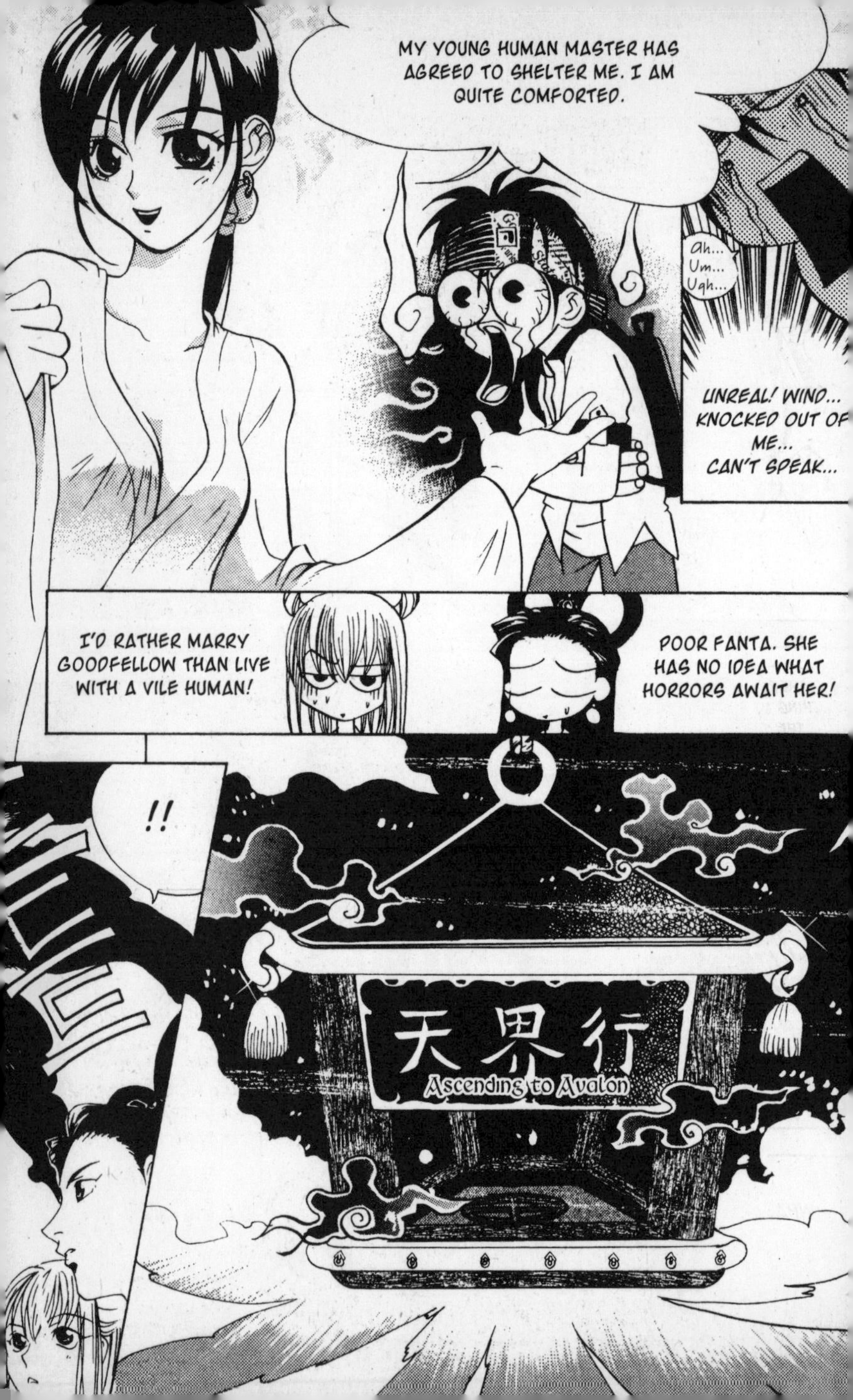
MY YOUNG HUMAN MASTER HAS AGREED TO SHELTER ME. I AM QUITE COMFORTED.
Ah... Um... Ugh...
UNREAL! WIND... KNOCKED OUT OF ME... CAN'T SPEAK...
I'D RATHER MARRY GOODFELLOW THAN LIVE WITH A VILE HUMAN!
POOR FANTA. SHE HAS NO IDEA WHAT HORRORS AWAIT HER!
!!
天界行
Ascending to Avalon

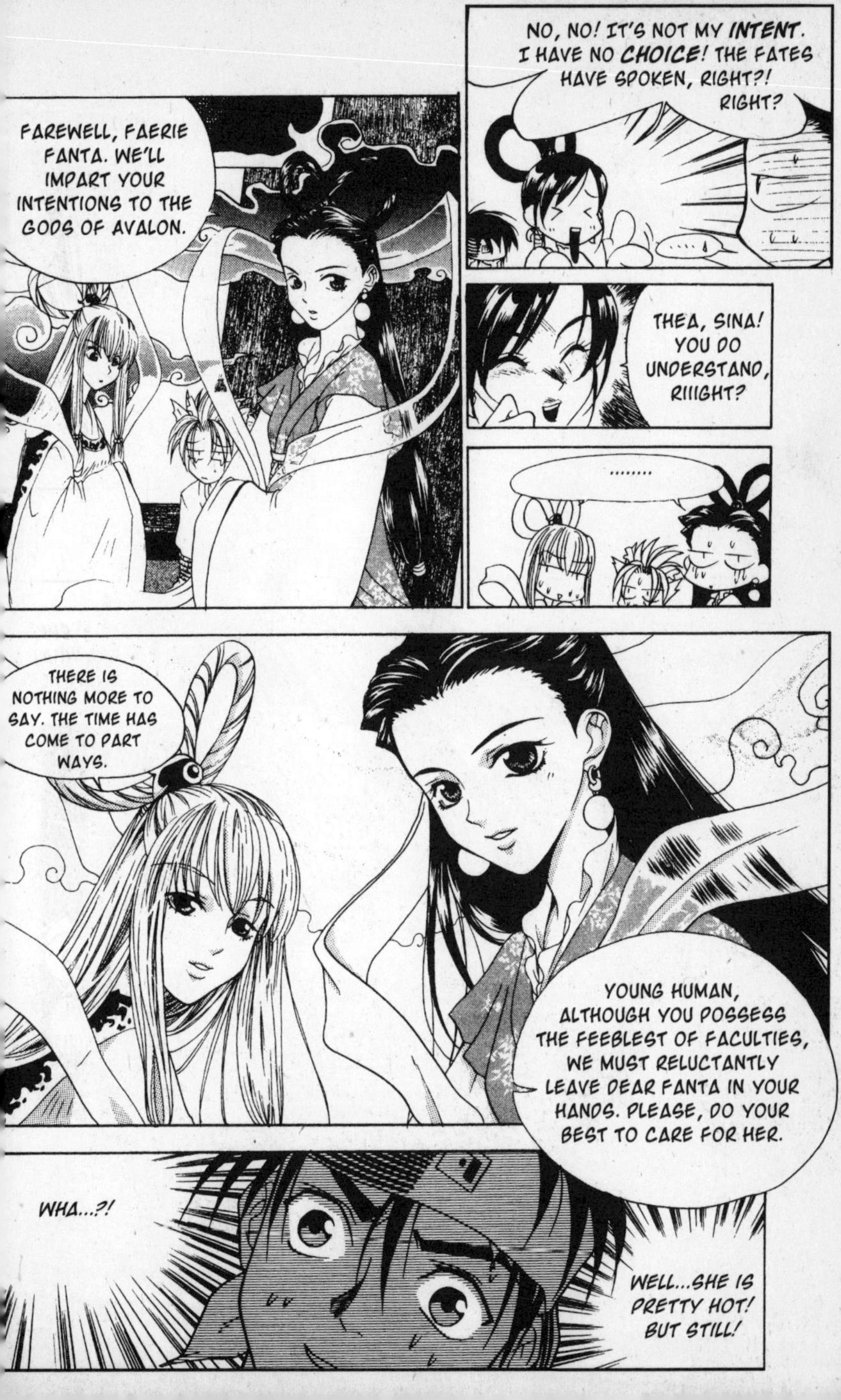
FAREWELL, FAERIE FANTA. WE'LL IMPART YOUR INTENTIONS TO THE GODS OF AVALON.
NO, NO! IT'S NOT MY INTENT. I HAVE NO CHOICE! THE FATES HAVE SPOKEN, RIGHT?! RIGHT?
.....
THEA, SINA! YOU DO UNDERSTAND, RIIIGHT?
....
THERE IS NOTHING MORE TO SAY. THE TIME HAS COME TO PART WAYS.
YOUNG HUMAN, ALTHOUGH YOU POSSESS THE FEEBLEST OF FACULTIES, WE MUST RELUCTANTLY LEAVE DEAR FANTA IN YOUR HANDS. PLEASE, DO YOUR BEST TO CARE FOR HER.
WHA...?!
WELL...SHE IS PRETTY HOT! BUT STILL!

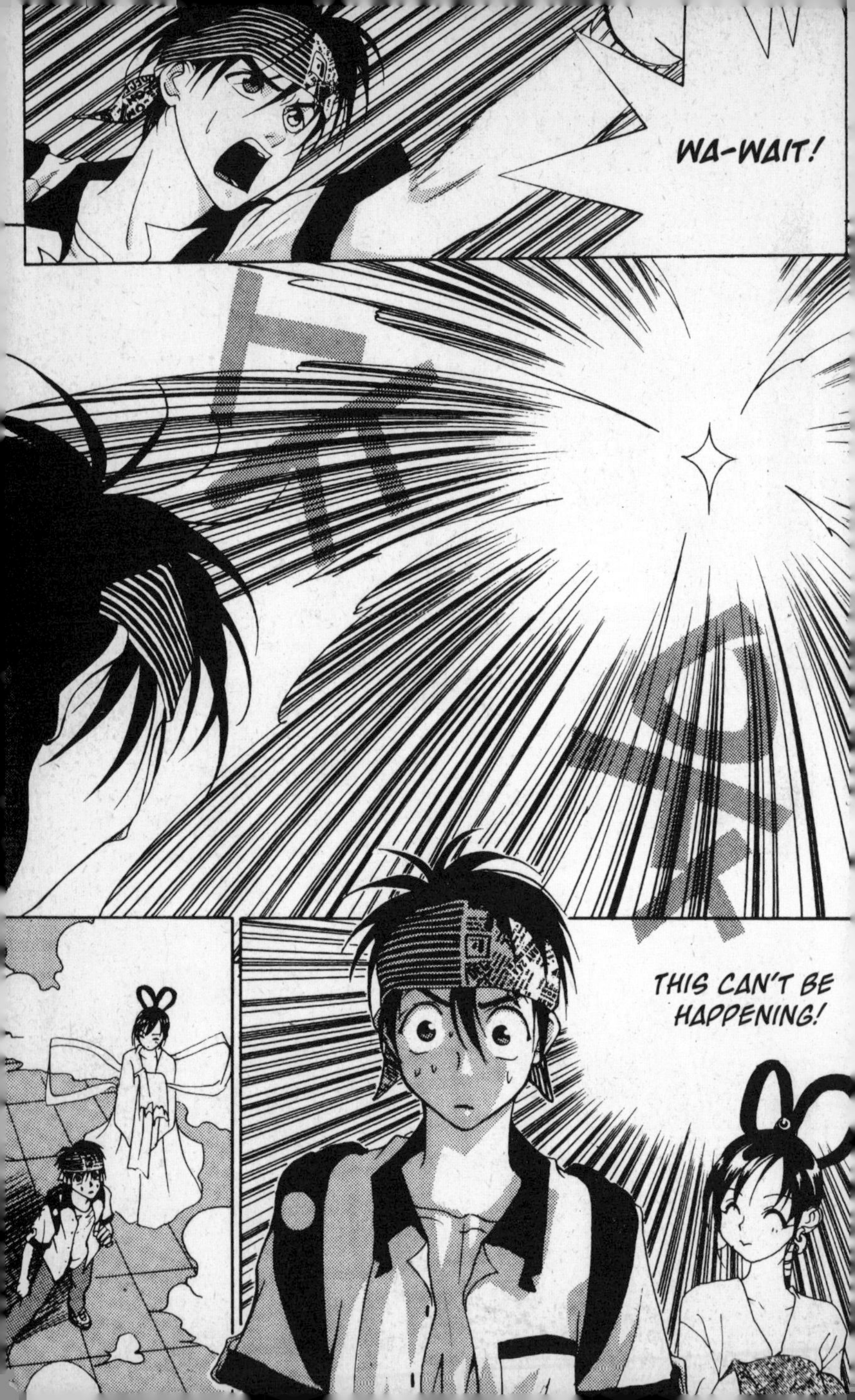
WA-WAIT!
THIS CAN'T BE HAPPENING!